MW01482354

FROM PEASANTS TO LABOURERS

McGILL-QUEEN'S STUDIES IN ETHNIC HISTORY
SERIES ONE: DONALD HARMAN AKENSON, EDITOR

MCGILL-QUEEN'S STUDIES IN ETHNIC HISTORY
SERIES TWO: JOHN ZUCCHI, EDITOR

From Peasants
to Labourers

*Ukrainian and Belarusan Immigration
from the Russian Empire to Canada*

VADIM KUKUSHKIN

McGill-Queen's University Press
Montreal & Kingston · London · Ithaca

Legal deposit third quarter 2007
Bibliothèque nationale du Québec

Printed in Canada on acid-free paper that is 100% ancient forest free
(100% post-consumer recycled), processed chlorine free

This book has been published with the help of a grant from the
Canadian Federation for the Humanities and Social Sciences, through
the Aid to Scholarly Publications Programme, using funds provided
by the Social Sciences and Humanities Research Council of Canada.

McGill-Queen's University Press acknowledges the support of the
Canada Council for the Arts for our publishing program. We also
acknowledge the financial support of the Government of Canada through
the Book Publishing Industry Development Program (BPIDP) for our
publishing activities.

Library and Archives Canada Cataloguing in Publication

Kukushkin, Vadim, 1969–
    From peasants to labourers: Ukrainian and Belarusan immigration from
    the Russian Empire to Canada / Vadim Kukushkin.

    Includes bibliographical references and index.
    ISBN 978-0-7735-3267-0

    1. Russia, Western – Emigration and immigration – Economic aspects –
    History – 20th century. 2. Canada – Emigration and immigration –
    Economic aspects – History – 20th century. 3. Belarusians – Canada –
    History – 20th century. 4. Ukrainians – Canada – History – 20th century.
    I. Title.

    FC104.K88 2007   304.8'710477   C2007-902645-1

This book was typeset by Interscript in 10/13 Sabon.

Contents

Tables, Figures, and Maps

FIGURES

MAPS

Abbreviations

AC	Archives of the Archdiocese of Canada, Orthodox Church in America
AO	Archives of Ontario
ARCA	Alaskan Russian Church Archives, Library of Congress
CBA	Canadian Baptist Archives
GARF	Gosudarstvennyi arkhiv Rossiiskoi Federatsii (State Archives of the Russian Federation)
LAC	Library and Archives Canada
Li-Ra-Ma	Likacheff-Ragosine-Mathers Collection
RGIA	Rossiiskii gosudarstvennyi istoricheskii arkhiv (Russian State Historical Archives)
SSPP	Archives of the Saint Peter and Saint Paul Orthodox Church, Montreal
UCA	United Church Archives

Acknowledgments

This book would not have seen the light of day without the assistance of many people who generously gave me their time and knowledge. Marilyn Barber, who supervised my doctoral dissertation, brought her good humour, patience, and expertise in the field of Canadian immigration and social history to steer me through four years of research, restoring my enthusiasm in the project every time it began to wane. Larry Black, former director of Carleton University's Centre for Research on Canadian-Russian Relations, was the first to introduce me to the treasure-box of the Likacheff-Ragosine-Mathers Collection and endured my numerous raids on the Centre's archival holdings. Frances Swyripa read most of this work in its manuscript form and encouraged me to proceed with publication. Carter Elwood, Bruce Elliott, Mark Stolarik, Jars Balan, Andrij Makuch, and Heather Coleman offered advice and friendly support when I most needed them.

I am greatly indebted to the staff at Library and Archives Canada, especially to Myron Momryk, who positively seemed to know every Canadian archival file related to Slavic immigrants. My sincere thanks also go to archivists and librarians at the Canadian Baptist Archives, United Church Archives, Thomas Fisher Rare Book Library at the University of Toronto, Russian State Historical Archives, State Archives of the Russian Federation, Russian State Library (Moscow), Russian National Library (St Petersburg), and the National Library of Belarus. Callista Kelly and her colleagues at Carleton University's Interlibrary Loan Department patiently and expeditiously dealt with my countless requests of esoteric Slavic-language sources. His Grace Archbishop Seraphim (Storheim), the late Sister Dorothea (Miroshnichenko), Rev. Alexander Janowski, and Rev. Miroslaw Woitiuk kindly allowed me to peruse the records of the Russian Orthodox Church in their custody. Yuri Akimov and Nadezhda Vasilieva helped me obtain rare materials from St Petersburg. Dariusz Ciach and Brian Ally did a splendid job of preparing the maps.

The staff at McGill-Queen's University Press did their best to make the publishing process as smooth as possible. John Zucchi, general editor of the Studies in Ethnic History series, gave the manuscript two thumbs up, entrusting it to Jonathan Crago and Joan McGilvray, who never failed to promptly answer my inquiries and to offer assistance. My copy editor Maia Stepenberg went through the manuscript with a fine tooth comb, helping me sharpen my writing and dispose of many awkward and indigestible phrases.

I would also like to thank the funding agencies and institutions whose support helped me at various stages of this project: Foreign Affairs and International Trade Canada, Carleton University, Ontario Graduate Scholarship Program, Immigration and Ethnic History Society, Open Society Institute, the University of Alberta, and the Social Sciences and Humanities Research Council of Canada.

A Note on Transliteration, Terminology, and Dates

Given that this study encompasses two calendar systems, several ethnic groups, and a number of languages, an explanation regarding the use of terminology, transliteration systems, and dates is in order. These choices are always difficult to make in studies dealing with Eastern European history due to the diverse character of population in the region and numerous boundary changes that have occurred during and since the period under review. It is hardly possible to devise a perfect template that would do equal justice to both historical and present-day criteria. My decisions regarding these issues were dictated by the considerations of consistency and the nature of the sources at hand, rather than by a preference for one or another political or national orientation.

Russia and Russian. Following a long tradition in Western historiography, I frequently use the word "Russia" as a shorter and more convenient substitute for the "Russian Empire" rather than as a term applying only to territories populated by ethnic Russians. Thus, the expression "emigrants from Russia" applies to any group of people that emigrated from the tsarist empire, regardless of their ethnicity. However, I have generally tried to avoid using expressions such as "Russian immigrants" or "Russian workers" in regard to people who were not ethnically Russian. Instead, I use the terms "Russian subjects" or "Russian-born immigrants," which are more historically accurate if somewhat awkward.

Belarus and Belarusan. Historically these terms have had several Latin-alphabet variants, including "Byelorussia," "Belorussia," "Bielorussia," and others (with the corresponding adjective forms). Following the spelling adopted in the *Encyclopedia of Canada's Peoples* and the *Harvard Encyclopedia of American Ethnic Groups*, I have chosen to use "Belarus" and the corresponding adjective "Belarusan."

Transliteration of Personal Names. Because of the similarity of Slavic surnames and the fluid state of ethnic identities in Eastern Europe, it is often difficult to establish the precise ethnic origin of an individual and apply the proper transliteration style, especially when his or her place of birth in the Russian Empire is not known. In all cases when a person's ethnicity could be determined with certainty based on the available information, I use the corresponding transliteration style (i.e., Ukrainian for Ukrainian names, Belarusan for Belarusan names). When no such information can be obtained, personal names found in Russian sources are transliterated into English according to the Library of Congress Russian transliteration style (e.g., Гаврилюк appears as Gavriliuk, not Havryliuk, and Гришкевич – as Grishkevich rather than Hryshkevich, Hryškievič or Gryszkiewicz). In some cases I use the established English-language form even if it is different from the Library of Congress system (e.g., Matthew Shatulsky).

Transliteration of Place Names. In the choice of English spelling for place names that originally appear in Cyrillic, I use a combination of the principal historical and present-day political boundaries. The names of administrative subdivisions within the Russian Empire (provinces and districts) with the exception of Volhynia follow the Library of Congress Russian transliteration style. The English spelling of towns and villages in Ukraine and Belarus is determined by the official language of the country in which the town or village is currently located (i.e., names of Ukrainian towns are rendered in English following the Ukrainian transliteration system, etc.).

Dates. The reader of this book is asked to bear with dates expressed alternately in two calendars and sometimes without an indication of the calendar used. Dates in all citations from Russian diplomatic correspondence and newspapers published in the Russian Empire are shown here according to the Julian calendar, which was officially used in Russia before 1917 and ran thirteen days behind the Gregorian calendar adopted in Western Europe and America. The only exceptions are cases when official Russian documents were addressed to Canadian agencies, in which case their authors used the Gregorian calendar. In references to Russian immigrant periodicals, I chose to cite the date of publication according to the Gregorian calendar. The greatest difficulty is determining the calendar used by immigrants in their personal correspondence, for there seems to be no clear pattern. Thus when a particular immigrant letter is cited, its date is simply copied from the original, without reference to the calendar used.

Russian immigrants arriving at Quebec, CA 1911
William James Topley/Library and Archives Canada/PA-010158

Interior view of a stationman's shack. Four Russians, occupants of the shack
Library and Archives Canada/C-056822

Baptist preacher John Kolesnikoff with immigrants
Canadian Baptist Archives

Russian-America Line Poster
Likacheff-Ragosine-Mathers Collection/Library and Archives Canada

ГАВАРЫСТВО АПЕКІ НАД ЭМІГРАНТАМІ

АДРЭС: ВАРШАВА, ЭРЫВАНСКАЯ ВУЛІЦА, № 2.
ВІЛЕНСКАЕ БЮРО: ВІЛЬНЯ, КАЗАНСКАЯ, № 3.

РАДЫ

ДЛЯ ЭМІГРАНТОУ, КАТОРЫЕ ЕДУЦЬ

У АМЭРЫКУ,

А ТАКЖЭ РАЗМОВЫ БЕЛАРУСКО-АНГЛІЦКІЕ

Павэдле Явэпа Околовіча.

ВІЛЬНЯ 1912.

КОШТАМ ТАВАРЫСТВА АПЕКІ НАД ЭМІГРАНТАМІ.

"Rady dlia emihrantou, katorye eduts' v Ameryku" –
the first Belarusan-English emigrant guide, 1912
National Library of Belarus

FROM PEASANTS TO LABOURERS

Introduction

My father, Tony Gretzky, had gone to Chicago from Russia before he came
to Canada. His family had been landowners in the old country, supporters
of the czar. When anyone asked my father whether he was Russian, he'd say,
"Nyet. Belarus."

Walter Gretzky, *On Family, Hockey and Healing*

Canadian immigration historiography has come a long way from the
times when mapping Canada's ethnic landscape and simply "getting
the facts right" were the primary tasks of those working in the field.
Since Donald Avery wrote his pioneering *"Dangerous Foreigners"* a
quarter century ago, historians have made substantial progress in
studying immigrant worker communities in twentieth-century Canada.[1]
Italian navvies in Montreal, Finnish domestics in Sudbury, and Jewish
garment workers in Toronto all claimed their place in Canadian history
as it moved away from the past focus on great statesmen, empire build-
ers, and valorous warriors towards a broader and more inclusive version of the nation's past.[2] Yet there are still gaps to be filled. Unlikely as
it may seem, we still know virtually nothing about Slavic labour immigrants who came to Canada prior to 1914 from the Russian Empire,
especially from territories east of Congress Poland. The deeply entrenched view of the Russian imperial state as an autocratic Leviathan
intent on keeping its borders air-tight for anyone except Jews, religious
sectarians, and other "undesirables" still continues to hold.[3] Historians
seem to take it for granted that if Russian, Ukrainian, and Belarusan
peasants in the tsarist empire moved anywhere at all, it was either for
seasonal work in the cities or to a homestead in Siberia.[4] Another commonly held stereotype views political and religious oppression as the
main reasons which prompted subjects of the tsar to emigrate, thus
downplaying the significance of economic motives. Because of the way
in which the history of immigration from Russia has been written, the

reader can be fully excused for thinking that Jews, Germans, Mennonites, and Doukhobors were the only inhabitants of the tsarist empire
ever to make their way to Canadian shores.[5]

In reality, a substantial proportion, if not the majority, of Russian-
subject immigrants to Canada between 1905 and 1914 were Ukrainian
and Belarusan peasants who voted with their feet against the socio-
economic conditions on the empire's western frontier. They came from
a large territory between the Dnieper River and Congress Poland,
which comprised the territory of today's Belarus and the eastern part of
Ukraine (also known as Dnieper Ukraine). Like Tony Gretzky, most
of them were "supporters of the czar" and had no political or religious
reasons to emigrate. Nearly all Ukrainians and Belarusans who left the
tsarist empire before 1914 were temporary labour migrants, attracted
by employment opportunities in the extractive and manufacturing
industries of the western hemisphere. This made Russian Ukrainians
different from their "Ruthenian" neighbours in the Austrian provinces
of Galicia and Bukovyna (western Ukraine), who entered Canada primarily as farmers, creating several bloc settlements on the Prairies.

For labour migrants from the tsarist empire, Canada was just one of
several main destinations. Belarusans, in fact, overwhelmingly went to
the United States, while many Ukrainians also migrated to Argentina
and Brazil. The coming of Ukrainian and Belarusan peasants to Canadian shores reflected the changing sources and character of transatlantic migration flows in the late nineteenth and early twentieth centuries.
Throughout the nineteenth century, the majority of Canada's immigrants were recruited from the British Isles and northwestern Europe,
and belonged to the agriculturalist class. By contrast, the new immigrants were primarily eastern and southern Europeans, who gravitated
towards urban areas and took industrial occupations. While the industrial centres of the United States attracted most of the newcomers, after
1900 Canada too became an important destination for labour migrants
from eastern and southern Europe, as the country's industrial expansion generated a constantly increasing demand for cheap labour.[6]

In Canadian statistics and other records of the time, Belarusans and
eastern Ukrainians usually appear as "Russians" – a term that had a
two-fold meaning in the early twentieth-century international vocabu-
lary. While it was commonly used as a label that could be affixed to
any native of the Romanov Empire (in the same way that "Austrians"
was applied to all immigrants from the Habsburg realm), it also had a
more ethnically pointed denotation limited to the three eastern Slav

peoples – Ukrainians, Belarusans, and Russians proper – who constituted the majority of Russia's population. In the ethnic taxonomy used
in Canadian immigration statistics after 1904, eastern Slavs from Russia passed as "Russians Not Elsewhere Specified" – a hazy category
that included all those who could not be defined as "Russian Jews,"
"Russian Poles," Finns, or Doukhobors. In addition to eastern Slavs, it
also included an indeterminable number of Russian subjects of non-
Slavic ethnic origins: Ossetians, Georgians, Latvians, Lithuanians,
Estonians, and others.

The tendency to label eastern Ukrainians and Belarusans as Russians
has survived to our day. The majority of immigration scholars in
Canada and the United States probably do not know that the immigrants they routinely call Russians were natives of Belarus or Ukraine.
In part, this usage owes its origin to the old difficulty of making a precise distinction between the territorial and ethnic meanings of the term
"Russian," particularly when available sources offer few clues about
the immigrants' ethnicity. But it also highlights an important dilemma
posed by the tension between the objective criteria of ethnicity (mother
tongue, ancestry, place of birth) and its subjective or, to use Benedict
Anderson's term, "imagined" elements.[7] The majority of Ukrainian
and Belarusan immigrants who came from the Russian Empire were
thoroughly Russified in their religion, language, and cultural orientation. This situation was typical for Eastern Europe, where the shared
ancestral roots of the Slavic population made the drawing of neat
ethnic boundaries difficult and where ethnic identity was much more
a question of choice between different political or religious loyalties
than a function of any innate characteristics. Imperial governments,
churches, and nascent ethnic elites competed with each other, attempting to inculcate Slavic peasants with a collective sense of belonging. After the beginning of mass emigration from Eastern Europe, Old World
identities and struggles were transplanted to the western hemisphere,
often persisting for decades.

The history and historiography of Ukrainians in Canada provides a
perfect example of imagined ethnic boundaries. Despite the sense one
may get from reading much of the existing literature on the subject, the
notion of the Ukrainian community in Canada or the United States has
never been coterminous with the collectivity of individuals with Ukrainian surnames who spoke the Ukrainian language. In early twentieth-
century Canada, it mattered little whether one was born in what today is
Ukraine. What counted was whether one considered oneself Ukrainian.

And this is precisely where Ukrainian immigrants from Russia were different from Galicians and Bukovynians. The ethno-political structure of the Habsburg monarchy, which granted Ukrainians a fair measure of cultural autonomy, represented a marked contrast to the Russian Empire, where all eastern Slavs were considered part of the Russian nation.[8] The Greater Russian identity among peasants was the direct result of the tsarist policy of Russification, which was carried out in eastern Ukraine and Belarus. Thus, eastern Slav immigrants from the tsarist empire not only entered Canada and the United States as "Russians," but they usually retained a Russian cultural orientation until the end of their lives. For many eastern Ukrainian immigrants in North America, the words "Ukraine" and "Ukrainian" were associated with Russophobia and "separatism" rather than with national pride. Together with Belarusans and other Russian-born immigrants who shared the same loyalties, they created their own network of fraternal associations, societies, socialist groups, labour unions, and ethnic (Russian-language) periodicals. Until the arrival of post-1945 displaced persons (DPS), "Russian" communities in the New World consisted largely of peasant immigrants from Belarus and eastern Ukraine. These russified Belarusans and Ukrainians constituted almost the entire membership of various Russian organizations as well as the main readers of the Russian-language press. The process of national awakening, which occurred in Soviet Ukraine and Belarus in the 1920s, had little effect on the pre-1914 generation of Ukrainian and Belarusan immigrants in North America, who largely remained "frozen" at the pre-national stage.

For an immigration historian, then, the question is how to balance the subjective and objective markers of ethnicity in demarcating the North American ethnic landscape. Group self-identity has been the dominant criterion to date for labelling an ethnic community and defining its boundaries. Canadian and American immigration historians (sometimes intentionally but often unwittingly) have thus tended to "essentialize" the boundaries of immigrant communities as they were "imagined" and constructed by ethnic elites. Works documenting the history of an immigrant group have too often been written in a teleological mode, presuming the inevitability of group evolution into a cohesive, nationally conscious community. The result is that little attention has been paid to persisting cultural subdivisions within immigrant communities and to minority groupings that did not fit the dominant pattern. It is here that we should look for the roots of the nearly complete absence of the pre-1914 immigrants from Russian Ukraine in the multiple renditions of the community's history. Beginning with early Ukrainian-Canadian historians, almost invariably connected to the Ukrainian nationalist diaspora in Europe and North America, the social boundaries of the early Ukrainian community in Canada have been charted in such a way as to include only "Ruthenian" immigrants from Galicia and Bukovyna, plus a handful of eastern Ukrainians who adopted a nationalist orientation.[9] Pioneering works such as Michael Marunchak's fundamental *Ukrainian Canadians* played an important data-gathering role, but they also constructed the meaning of "true Ukrainianness" and identified its enemies (socialists, Communists, "Russophiles,"[10] and all others who disrupted the community consensus or stayed away from the nationalist agenda). In these writings, immigrants from eastern Ukraine, who spoke a Russianized patois and usually shunned Ukrainian organizations, were either disregarded altogether or branded as sell-outs to Moscow.[11]

The new generation of professionally trained Ukrainian-Canadian historians that came of age in recent decades has rejected the politically motivated approaches of the early writers in favour of more balanced scholarly analysis. Even so, most scholars continue to subscribe to the established notion of Canada's early Ukrainian community as limited by and large to immigrants from Galicia and Bukovyna.[12] Ukrainian immigration from tsarist Russia has become something of a "grey area" for modern-day Ukrainian-Canadian historiography. On the one hand, historians seem to be aware that many immigrants disguised as Russians in early twentieth-century Canadian sources were of Ukrainian origin. On the other hand, standard accounts of Ukrainian-Canadian history that have appeared in the last decades tend to relegate Ukrainian immigration from the Russian Empire to an occasional sentence as numerically insignificant and thus of little importance.[13] Some works, both within and outside the field of immigration history, take the early twentieth-century ethnic descriptors for granted and mention "Russians" alongside Ukrainians without trying to probe their real backgrounds. The result is a curious historiographical paradox: while historians of Eastern Europe use the proper ethnic definition (Ukrainian) in regard to the eastern Slav population of Dnieper Ukraine, these same peasants turn into "Russians" when they appear in Canadian works on immigration. Although it is admittedly difficult to apply the term "Ukrainians" to people who often resisted being called that name, it is equally misleading to use ethnic self-identification as the only naming criterion – with no regard to ancestry, place of birth, or spoken language – since it obfuscates the true origins of early twentieth-century immigration from Russia.

The dearth of serious academic research on Slavic worker communities in early twentieth-century Canada is another reason why eastern Ukrainians remain invisible in Canadian historiography. Despite the works of Donald Avery and others, the image of early twentieth-century Slavic immigrants as agriculturalists who headed to the West still persists among the general public and, to some extent, in the academic community. One cannot but agree with historian Orest Martynowych, who pointed out over a decade ago that "Ukrainian frontier and urban labourers [had] failed to attract the attention of historians."[14] Although Ukrainian socialists figure as major players in a number of works on Canadian labour radicalism, there are no comprehensive academic histories of Ukrainian working-class communities in Montreal, Toronto, or Winnipeg.[15] Nor is there a definitive scholarly work on the Ukrainian socialist and labour movement in Canada.

Much of what has been said about eastern Ukrainians and their historical representations also applies to Canadian Belarusans – an ethnic group with a virtually non-existent historiography.[16] The major difference between the two groups is that Belarusans, whose ethnic territory lay entirely within the borders of the Russian Empire, had no cultural centre that could become the seedbed for a cultural *renaissance* and the formation of a nationally conscious elite in the same way that eastern Galicia was for Ukrainians. The city of Vil'na, which by the early 1900s became a gathering place for the small circle of Belarusan intelligentsia, could hardly emerge as a "Belarusan Piedmont" as long as Russification remained the official policy of the tsarist state. Depending largely on their religious affiliation (which was Russian Orthodox or, less commonly, Roman Catholic), Belarusan immigrants who came to Canada and the United States before 1914 reported themselves as Russians or Poles and continued to do so in the interwar period, when tens of thousands emigrated from Polish-ruled western Belarus. The nationally conscious segment of the community in Canada has always been extremely small, consisting primarily of Belarusan DPs who entered Canada after World War II. Their voice, attempting to raise public awareness of Belarusans as a distinct people, usually drowned among similar claims to recognition made by Canada's larger and more influential ethnic groups. Until 1971, Belarusans did not even appear as a separate group in the Canadian census.[17]

This study thus ventures onto little explored terrain in its attempt to provide a history of early twentieth-century labour immigration from Russia's western borderlands. It revises traditional assumptions about emigration from tsarist Russia as being primarily a movement of politically and religiously oppressed minorities, and demonstrates that Ukrainian and Belarusan peasants constituted a substantial portion of immigrants who arrived in Canada from the Russian Empire. By analyzing two neighbouring regions of the Russian Empire, the book seeks to illuminate the similarities and differences in the configuration of migrant flows that connected various parts of the European continent with Canada, along with their social, economic, and cultural causes. The following chapters examine the temporal and spatial dimensions of the migration process, the backgrounds and social profiles of the migrants, and their insertion into Canadian society as transient labourers and sojourners. Nearly 2,800 personal files of Ukrainian and Belarusan migrants drawn from the records of Russian imperial consulates in Canada provide the main source for the book (see Appendix for a detailed description of the files and research methodology).

Some of the central questions which are raised below – who emigrated, who stayed behind, and why were choices made? – have occupied historians at least since the dean of North American immigration historiography Marcus Hansen published his 1940 classic study of trans-Atlantic population movement.[18] The large amount of subsequent Canadian scholarship on continental European immigrants has not made these questions less relevant. We still know surprisingly little about why people in some areas of Europe, including the Russian Empire, migrated to Canada while their neighbours either went to the United States or did not emigrate at all. The majority of Canadian authors who investigate the experiences of eastern and southern European immigrants first meet their protagonists at the point of entry into Canada.[19] In these studies, written within the matrix of Canadian ethnic history rather than the history of international migration, chapters dealing with the world immigrants left behind usually serve as mere prefaces to the Canadian part of the story. There is also a need for a better understanding of the interconnections between overseas migration and other types of population movements (both internal and external), which can only come through transcending the boundaries of North American history and applying a transatlantic perspective. With few exceptions, such as the work of Bruno Ramirez, we have yet to move beyond the Canadian version of the "To America" framework to a more panoramic approach, which would view European migration to Canada in conjunction with international and locally specific patterns of population mobility.[20]

This book is a study of *migration* rather than *immigration*. Instead of focusing entirely on the receiving end of the migration process, it seeks to bring together the New and the Old World contexts in which the transoceanic moves of Ukrainian and Belarusan peasants occurred. My analysis draws on theoretical models from the recent works of historians and social scientists who apply a systems approach to the study of international migrations. At the centre of this approach is the concept of the migration system, which Dirk Hoerder defines as a "distinct cluster of spatial moves between a region of origin and a receiving region" that occurs over a period of time within a multi-level framework of social, economic, and political relationships. In Hoerder's words, the systems approach to migration combines "analysis of the position of a society of origin in the global order, its structures, the regional specifics, selection and self-selection of migrants from a reservoir of potential leavers and persisters, the process of migration itself, and – within the receiving society's structures – the insertion into partly internationalized labour markets, the formation of ethnic enclaves or of transcultural networks, and the interaction with new social values and norms."[21] This study views Russia's western frontier as the easternmost segment of the Atlantic migration system, which extended from the west coast of the American continent eastward to the Dnieper Basin, linking the European agrarian periphery with the North American industrial core, and serving as a conduit for transferring a large surplus workforce from East-Central Europe to the United States and Canada.

The phenomenon of migrant sojourning is another important theme that runs throughout the book. The vast majority of Ukrainians and Belarusans whose lives are described here came to Canada as temporary migrants and did not intend to make this country a permanent home. With the possible exception of Montreal, "Russian colonies" in pre-1920 Canada were an archetypal example of sojourning communities with all their characteristic features: a definitive predominance of men over women and children, a high degree of transience, and an undeveloped community life. The lack of stability and permanence in the lives of these labouring men shaped the entire range of their experiences as migrants – from residential patterns and living conditions to attitudes towards work, leisure, and religion. It also explained the tenacity with which most of them sought to maintain ties with the old country and their families.

Defining the boundaries of Belarus and Ukraine in a period when neither existed as an independent political entity, I follow the common practice of using administrative divisions that existed in tsarist Russia before 1917. For the purposes of this study, Belarus encompasses the territory of the empire's five northwestern provinces: Grodno, Minsk, Vil'na, Vitebsk, and Mogilev. Ukraine comprises nine provinces: Podolia, Volhynia, Kiev, Chernigov, Poltava, Khar'kov, Kherson, Taurida, and Ekaterinoslav. The only change I made to the standard definition of Ukraine was the inclusion of Khotin District of Bessarabia Province in the Ukrainian territory. Populated mostly by ethnic Ukrainians, Khotin also served as a major emigration donor.[22] The terms "Right-Bank Ukraine" and "Left-Bank Ukraine," which frequently appear in chapters 1, 2 and 3, refer to the empire's Ukrainian territories that lay west and east of the Dnieper River, respectively. No historian of Russia's western borderlands is likely to achieve a perfect demarcation of their chessboard-like ethnic landscape, and I certainly do not claim to have accomplished such a task. While the focus of this book is on ethnic Ukrainians and Belarusans, it is not always possible to consider them in isolation from Russians proper or from emigrants of other nationalities (such as Poles or Lithuanians) who also occasionally passed as "Russians." The ethnically diverse character of the population on the empire's western frontier resulted in a high incidence of mixed identities and in a typical borderland phenomenon which political scientist Josef Chlebowczyk has called "genetic bilingualism."[23] In addition, in the early 1900s Eastern European nations and national identities were still in the process of congealment. These complexities are reflected in the sources, which – especially when they mention a group of "Russians" as a whole – often contain few leads that would enable the historian to tell a Pole from a Belarusan or a Belarusan from a Ukrainian.

I

Economy, Society, and Migration on Russia's Western Frontier

All peasant migrations in late nineteenth- and early twentieth-century Europe had their roots in the economic and class structures of the donor societies. In each region, the local sets of social relationships associated with the dominant economic systems produced peasant responses specific to that particular area. Geographic factors – the proximity of ocean ports, major transportation junctions or large industrial centres, which served as safety valves for excess rural labour – could each have had an impact on migration processes, lending them a distinctive regional configuration.

Like other forms of population mobility, transoceanic emigration from East-Central and Southern Europe developed in areas sharing particular socio-economic characteristics.[1] Rural overpopulation and the resulting scarcity of natural resources available to the peasantry have been universally linked to emigration, as have the structures of landholding in the donor areas. Josef Barton argued, for instance, that emigration was heaviest in regions with widely distributed property and less pronounced gradations in income and social status, and minimal in areas characterized by sharp class cleavages and the existence of large manors.[2] Low urbanization and the lack of industrial employment in the donor areas are also commonly considered to be factors that facilitated emigration. On a more general level, the growth of overseas migration from Eastern and Southern Europe was related to the modernizing effects of capitalism and the market economy that began to change traditional modes of life and work in these parts of the continent. According to John Bodnar's oft-cited remark, late nineteenth- and early twentieth-century labour emigrants were the "children of capitalism."[3]

To see whether this interpretive framework holds true for eastern Ukraine and Belarus, this chapter will examine the demographic, social, and economic structures that existed on Imperial Russia's western frontier by the turn of the twentieth century. Such examination is all the more necessary because economy and society in the two regions have rarely been studied from the standpoint of a migration historian. Our main purpose is to establish the relationship between social change in Ukrainian- and Belarusan-populated territories of the Russian Empire and the extent of geographic mobility exhibited by the rural population. An analysis of this relationship will bring us closer to an understanding of the "push" factors that triggered various local types of peasant migrations, which eventually extended in scope to North America.

The early twentieth-century Russian Empire was a country in transition. Still deeply rooted in tradition, it was profoundly affected by social and economic changes brought about by capitalism and modernization – two concurrent forces that had increasingly shaped its evolution after the abolishment of serfdom and the other "Great Reforms" of the 1860s and 1870s. Shaken by the humiliating defeat in the war against Japan and the ensuing revolutionary upheaval of 1905, Russia seemed to have regained its lost momentum and enjoyed the world's fastest rate of industrial growth by 1913. Industrial modernization was complemented by large-scale agrarian reforms initiated by Prime Minister Peter Stolypin in 1906, whose goal was the elimination of all remnants of the feudal order in the Russian village and the introduction of a capitalist market economy. The liberalization of the political regime after the 1905 revolution, including the establishment of a consultative parliament (*Duma*), represented a step towards constitutional monarchy, narrowing the gap between autocratic Russia and the bourgeois democracies of Western Europe.[4]

Russia's modernization, however, proceeded at an uneven pace. Pockets of industrialization, urbanization, and technological advancement coexisted with the most backward forms of social and economic organization. As historical sociologist Teodor Shanin put it, "Russia was not quite Europe and yet Europe it was, a ballast for and a shadow over the brisk business and rational liberalism of the nineteenth-century West."[5] On the eve of World War I, the Russian Empire was still an overwhelmingly rural country. Out of 128 million inhabitants recorded by the Russian imperial census of 1897, more than 100 million (78 per cent) were peasants. A mere 13 per cent of the population lived in cities and towns, and many of the latter, despite their official status, were little more than large villages. According to the census data, approximately 75 per cent of the empire's population were employed in agriculture, and even the majority of industrial workers were peasants by origin, who still retained close ties to the village.[6] In this respect, however, Russia was similar to much of East-Central Europe. In Galicia, Transcarpathia, and Serbia – all major emigration areas – the percentage of population engaged in agricultural pursuits was even higher (in Transcarpathia, for instance, it was 93.6 per cent).[7] It was the sheer size of Russia's peasantry, coupled with the archaic ways of social and economic organization, that gave the country its well-known reputation as the mainstay of agricultural backwardness on the European continent.

The abolition of serfdom in the 1860s, which emancipated the peasantry and put Russia on the road to modernization, produced a string of long-term effects on the economic and social life of the village. An almost double increase in the rate of population growth was one of its most significant consequences. Between 1858 and 1897, the rural population of Russia's European provinces grew by 69.3 per cent.[8] Although Russian cities also experienced substantial growth during the post-emancipation period, they could only absorb a small part of the increasing rural population. The low level of Russia's industrial development prevented most urban centres from becoming significant outlets for the rising congestion in Russia's villages.

Population growth in the Ukrainian and Belarusan provinces of the empire substantially exceeded the average figures for European Russia. Between 1858 (the year of the last pre-emancipation rural census) and 1897, the rural population of Right-Bank Ukraine (Podolia, Volhynia, and Kiev provinces) increased by 92 per cent and reached almost 7.5 million.[9] During the same period, the peasant population of Belarus shot up by 108.1 per cent. Part of this statistical increase can be explained by the arbitrary decisions of the tsarist government, which chose to eliminate several previously distinct categories of its Belarusan subjects, such as Old Believers and *odnodvortsy* (descendants of the seventeenth-century frontier servitors with hereditary land ownership), by assigning them to the peasant estate.[10] Still, the rates of population growth on the western frontier were among the highest in the empire. In 1897, there were 9,567,010 people in Right-Bank Ukraine and 5,342,237 in west-central Belarus (the provinces of Vil'na, Grodno, and Minsk) – two areas that would supply the majority of overseas migrants.[11]

The population explosion west of the Dnieper was almost exclusively caused by high natural increase rather than by in-migration. Changed peasant expectations about the future, the increased productivity of peasant agriculture, and noticeable improvements in health care all contributed to the population boom. Demographers have found that Ukraine was characterized not so much by exceptionally high fertility as by lower mortality rates than elsewhere in the empire, probably due to a better and more stable food supply.[12] Although the Right-Bank territories had experienced some earlier inflow of migrants from the empire's northeast, internal migration to the area was no longer significant by the second half of the nineteenth century. The 1897 imperial census revealed that the overwhelming majority of rural residents in the region lived in the same district *(uezd)* where they had been born. As Table 1 demonstrates, men showed somewhat higher territorial mobility than women, but the general picture emerging from the census figures is that of a fairly sedentary peasant population. Until the mid-1900s, out-migration from Ukraine and Belarus to Asiatic Russia (across the Ural Mountains) was also low. In 1897 only 1.1 per cent of Belarusans and 8.8 per cent of Ukrainians lived outside Russia's European provinces.[13]

The rural population increase west of the Dnieper may also have been stimulated by the comparatively lenient policy of the tsarist government towards Ukrainian and Belarusan peasantry, which was regarded as an ally against the untrustworthy Polish landlords. After the emancipation, local peasants received larger land allotments and lighter obligations compared to former serfs in the empire's heartland.[14] According to an early twentieth-century estimate, the total acreage of peasant landholdings in Right-Bank Ukraine actually grew by 18 per cent after the emancipation, while in central Russian provinces it underwent a significant decrease.[15]

The density of agrarian population increased at an especially fast pace in areas with high soil fertility. In some parts of northern Bessarabia and Right-Bank Ukraine, population density was among the highest in Europe. According to the 1897 census data, the most heavily populated territory in the region was Kamenets District in Podolia with 115.6 persons per sq. km.[16] The figures for several other rural districts in Podolia, Kiev, and Bessarabia provinces were only slightly lower. In central and northern Volhynia and in west-central Belarus, where soil was poorer and the average size of landholdings was larger, population was much less dense, averaging 47.4 persons per sq. km in Volhynia, 47.3 in Grodno, and a modest 26.8 in Minsk Province.[17]

Table 1
Territorial mobility of rural population in Right-Bank Ukraine and
west-central Belarus, 1897

	Rural Residents Living in the District of their Birth (%)		
Province	Male	Female	Average
Volhynia	87.9	92.0	89.9
Kiev	92.8	94.4	93.6
Podolia	94.3	95.8	95.1
Vil'na	92.3	93.8	93.0
Minsk	92.5	95.0	93.7
Grodno	88.4	94.8	91.5
Total	91.4	94.3	92.8

Source: Pervaia vseobshchaia perepis' naseleniia Rossiiskoi Imperii 1897 goda (St Petersburg,
1897–1905), vol. 4 (Vil'na), 96; vol. 8 (Volhynia), 36–7; vol. 11 (Grodno), 42–43; vol. 16 (Kiev),
36–7; vol. 22 (Minsk), 38–9; vol. 32 (Podolia), 8.

The changing demographics of Russia's western lands put heavy
pressure on the natural resources. As a peasant saying had it, "Every
hand that held the sickle also held the wooden spoon." By the late
nineteenth century, agrarian overpopulation and the shortage of land
became serious problems for most parts of European Russia. Right-
Bank Ukraine, particularly its southwestern part, was characterized by
an especially high concentration of land property and by deep inequali-
ties in economic status within rural society. A favourable combination
of soil and climate in this region put a premium value on arable land
and created wide possibilities for the development of commercial agriculture. While grain remained the staple crop for the local peasantry,
the local agricultural economy was increasingly oriented towards the
production of sugar beets and other highly profitable cash crops. These
crops were produced mostly on large estates owned by Russian and
Polish nobility, which were quickly turning into modern capitalist enterprises employing large numbers of hired labourers, recruited from
the poorer classes of the peasantry.[18]

The profitable character of large-scale commercial agriculture in
Right-Bank Ukraine resulted in less decline in noble landholding here
as compared to other regions of European Russia, where the nobility
generally struggled to adapt to the post-emancipation conditions. Between 1877 and 1905 (the years of two general land surveys), Russian
nobility on the whole lost control of 30 per cent of its land, whereas in

Right-Bank Ukraine it only relinquished 16.5 per cent of its posses-sions.[19] In 1905, local nobles still held 75.4 per cent of all privately owned land.[20] In Bessarabia, the decrease of noble ownership during the same period was somewhat more substantial.[21] Most of it, how-ever, occurred in the sparsely populated southern parts of the province, while in the north the general agricultural conditions and the patterns of noble landholding were similar to those of Right-Bank Ukraine. In the northernmost Khotin District, which provided one of the largest contingents of labour emigrants, nobles in 1905 owned 75 per cent of private land – more than anywhere else in the province.[22]

The peasants did not share in the economic success enjoyed by the landed aristocracy in the empire's southwest. On the contrary, their economic condition grew progressively worse, cancelling out the ad-vantages that had been received during the emancipation. As Table 2 shows, by 1905 the average size of peasant land allotments (i.e., plots they received at the time of emancipation) in Right-Bank Ukraine had significantly declined compared to that of a quarter-century before, producing an army of dwarf-holders and landless peasants. Peasant land hunger was especially acute in northern Bessarabia and in Podolia, where the decrease was nearly 50 per cent. General and local statistics on surplus agricultural workforce exhibit considerable variations de-pending in part on each author's methodology, but these numbers were substantial by any count. According to the data compiled by a 1901 government commission, over 50 per cent of the rural population in European Russia could not be gainfully employed in either agriculture or industry.[23] Using the same source, M. N. Leshchenko placed the to-tal surplus rural population in the nine Ukrainian provinces at 68 per cent, or 7.3 million.[24]

The practice of partible inheritance, which existed in the villages of Ukraine and Belarus (as well as "Great" Russia), further contributed to the fragmentation and diminishing of peasant landholdings. Tradition-ally, the partitioning of family property occurred before the death of the head of the household, as nuclear families emerging within it began to claim their independence. As a rule, the result was an equal division of household property and land between all adult sons.[25] This custom of equal land apportionment differed substantially from the method practiced in neighbouring Poland, where the senior son usually inher-ited all family land and paid off his siblings in cash or farm stock.[26] Some authors have suggested that the equal division of land and prop-erty among male children tethered the heirs to the land, thus creating

Table 2
Peasant landholding in the Ukrainian and Belarusan territories of the Russian Empire,
1877-1905

Province	Average Size of Peasant Allotment, 1877 (acres)	Average Size of Peasant Allotment, 1905 (acres)
Bessarabia (Khotin District only)	13.8	9.2
Podolia	18.4	10.3
Kiev	19.4	15.7
Volhynia	33.8	21.3
Minsk	46.4	24.6
Grodno	40.5	44.6
Total	28.7	21.0

Source: Statistika zemlevladeniia 1905 goda, vol. 3 (Bessarabia), 45; vol. 8 (Volhynia), 51; vol. 11 (Grodno), 43; vol. 16 (Kiev), 53; vol. 22 (Minsk), 43; vol. 32 (Podolia), 51.

favourable conditions for temporary labour migration, while the practice of impartible inheritance encouraged the permanent emigration of non-inheriting children.[27]

Patterns of rural economy in the Belarusan provinces were different from those of Right-Bank Ukraine in several important respects. Lower seasonal temperatures and poorer soils, interspersed with vast stretches of forest and marshland (especially in the Polesie region), pushed down the value of land, hindering the growth of commercial agriculture in this part of the empire. Compared to Ukraine, Belarus was characterized by less obvious disparities in economic endowment between various classes of rural population. In 1905, the average size of peasant household allotments in Minsk and Grodno provinces was substantially larger than in the empire's southwest (see Table 2). In Grodno, it even showed a slight increase since 1877. The concentration of land property in Belarus was also considerably lower. The average noble estate in Grodno Province was only fourteen times larger in size than the average peasant holding.[28] In Minsk Province, which had the highest proportion of large estates in Belarus, the difference between the two was more significant but still much smaller than, for instance, in Podolia, where the average-size manor equalled 118 peasant allotments.[29] Agrarian overpopulation in Belarus, though substantial, also took less acute forms. According to V.P. Paniutich, only 32 per cent of the rural population in the five Belarusan provinces could be classified as surplus.[30] Yet these differences were only differences in degree of poverty. The lower fertility of most Belarusan soils, the abundance of wasteland, and the larger size of peasant households (9.5 inhabitants per average household compared to 7.7 in Right-Bank Ukraine) – all these factors made the lot of Belarusan peasants hardly better than that of their Ukrainian counterparts.[31]

If west-central Belarus and Right-Bank Ukraine were not exactly like each other in their rural organization, they had many common characteristics, which set both regions apart from imperial provinces east of the Dnieper River. The most important of these was the hereditary type of peasant land tenure. The emancipation measures of the 1860s preserved Russia's two historical types of peasant landholding (hereditary and communal), which defined – each in its own way – the entire complex of economic and legal relationships between the households and the peasant commune as well as the character of the commune itself. Most European regions of the Russian Empire, including Left-Bank and southern Ukraine, were characterized by the prevalence of communal land tenure. In peasant communes with this type of land tenure, the communal assembly could use the majority vote to redistribute the land among the households, usually according to the number of their resident members. As a result of such reallotments, larger households received additional land, while those with fewer members could be forced to part with some of their holdings. The house-and-garden plots, livestock, and other personal property were not subject to repartition, nor were the pastures, forest, and other non-arable lands, which were reserved for common use under the supervision of the communal assembly. Although few peasant communes in Russia continued to practice repartition on a regular basis by the end of the nineteenth century, communal tenure seriously hindered the development of individual farming and served as a powerful mechanism for preserving the egalitarian and communalist nature of the Russian village.[32]

Russia's western provinces owed their hereditary system of peasant land tenure to the period when they were part of the Polish-Lithuanian Commonwealth or (in the case of Bessarabia) the Principality of Moldavia. In Minsk and Grodno provinces, communal tenure did not exist at all, while in the three Right-Bank provinces it encompassed only 6 per cent of the households.[33] Bessarabia had a significantly higher percentage of communal tenure, limited mostly to villages populated by former State peasants.[34] In peasant communes with hereditary tenure, arable land was assigned to individual households in heredity and was excluded from periodic repartitions. While hereditary tenure was not legally equivalent to private property, economic interdependence within peasant communes that practiced this system was not as complete as in those with communal tenure, and the measure of control exercised by peasant families over their land was somewhat greater (thus, peasant land could be bought and sold with fewer obstacles). Most household allotments, however, consisted of several strips of land (at times only 3–4 metres in width) interspersed among other similar holdings, hindering the development of individual farming in this part of the empire. As a result of the strip system (*cherespolositsa*), all peasant households in a village were locked together in a common three-field crop-cycle, which was also necessitated by the existence of undivided communal land such as pastures and forests, used and administered jointly by the commune.[35] Under this system of cultivation, peasants were as effectively prevented from using advanced agricultural techniques and equipment as they were under communal tenure. Building and other improvements were also normally done with communal consent and assistance. As several authors have pointed out, in its daily functioning the Ukrainian peasant commune (*hromada*) in the Right Bank and the Belarusan *hramada* differed little from the better-known Russian *mir*.[36]

Nonetheless, hereditary tenure had important effects on peasant economy. On the one hand, it conserved economic inequality among peasant families, whose plots could not be increased as a result of repartition as they could in villages with communal tenure. On the other hand, it stimulated the development of capitalist agriculture in the region by forcing peasants to buy or rent land, while also creating a vast supply of wage labourers recruited from the poorer strata of the rural society. It was only a matter of time before the annual movements of these temporary labour migrants crossed international borders, eventually extending overseas. By making peasants less dependent on the commune as a source of well-being and creating a permanent legal tie between the family and its land, hereditary tenure also reinforced the individualist elements in the peasants' worldview and encouraged social mobility and the spirit of entrepreneurship.

Since the socio-economic function of the commune in Right-Bank Ukraine and Belarus was already weak, the Russian agrarian reforms of 1906–1911 (known as the Stolypin Reforms) did not have such a revolutionizing effect here as they had in areas east of the Dnieper River. The transfer of land title from the commune to individual holders – one of the key reform measures – did not apply to territories with hereditary tenure, where land was already divided among peasant families. The consolidation of peasant land strips into single plots, decreed by a government *ukaz*, met with fewer difficulties in areas with hereditary tenure than it did elsewhere. In Right-Bank Ukraine and Belarus, the majority of peasant families who had physically consolidated their holdings broke away from the commune and established individual farms *(khutory)*. In all other regions the dominant form of consolidation was *otrub*, when a peasant family joined its land strips into a single plot but did not move onto an isolated farmstead.[37] Although a recent study of the reforms cautions against exaggerated views of peasants' enthusiasm for the destruction of the commune,[38] its demise could not fail to bring an increased level of economic and social individualization in the Ukrainian and Belarusan village. New laws limiting the administrative jurisdiction of the peasant commune reduced its supervisory functions and ability to control the lives of individual members. The *ukaz* of 5 October 1906 stripped elected peasant officials and the heads of households of their rights to control the issuing of internal passports and to prevent adult members of the commune from changing their place of residence. The earlier elimination of the commune's joint responsibility for tax payments and other public obligations *(krugovaia poruka)* also expanded the boundaries of individual choice in peasant life, stimulated further erosion of the commune, and led to greater social and geographical mobility.[39]

Simplified legal procedures regulating the sale of old hereditary allotments were another important consequence of the 1906–11 reforms.[40] Land-hungry peasants in Right-Bank Ukraine and Belarus – both before and after the reforms – tried to improve their economic status through buying land from the aristocracy. The State Peasant Bank, established in 1883, facilitated such purchases by providing low-interest loans to the peasants. The percentage of peasant ownership in the total acreage of individually owned land increased from 1.4 per cent in 1877 to 5 per cent in 1905 in Right-Bank Ukraine, and from 4.5 to 5.7 per cent in Bessarabia.[41] Until the mid-1900s, peasant communes and co-operatives remained the main buyers of land, allowing peasants with lesser means to increase holdings by pooling their resources.[42] After 1906, and especially in 1909–1914, there was a slow but steady growth of individual land purchases through the Peasant Bank, which reflected the progressive erosion of communalist elements in the peasant economy.[43]

However, the gradual increase in peasant land ownership could not keep pace with the demographic boom and did comparatively little to alleviate the problem of rural overcrowding. Only a relatively small fraction of the peasantry (primarily the better off) could afford to purchase land, either individually or as members of a cooperative. Moreover, the price of land in most of Right-Bank Ukraine in the early 1900s and later was becoming prohibitive for the average peasant. In Podolia, for instance, it rose by almost 150 per cent between 1895 and 1910, reaching 93 rubles per acre.[44] As one moved north, land became cheaper. In Minsk Province, an acre in 1910 cost only 18 rubles.[45] These regional differences explain the greater extent of peasant land acquisitions in Belarus: while land acquired by peasants in Right-Bank Ukraine accounted for only 11.8 per cent of their total 1905 holdings, the corresponding figures for Minsk and Grodno were 19.9 and 13.8 per cent.[46] Even so, allotments received at the time of emancipation continued to form a far greater proportion of peasant landholdings in both regions.

Peasants also had the option of renting land, but high commercial demand for arable land in the Right Bank made it scarcely less difficult than buying. Landowners preferred to lease land to large renters, such as sugar companies, which could pay as much as 10 rubles per year for an acre of prime land. As a result, peasant households in Right-Bank Ukraine in 1905 rented only about 5 per cent of their plough-land.[47] Like purchasing, renting was easier in west-central Belarus, where in the early 1900s peasants rented 12–15 per cent of their arable land at the yearly rate of approximately 0.9 to 2.8 rubles per acre.[48] Meadowland was also rented on a large scale. Although monetary rent became prevalent in both regions by the late nineteenth century, pre-capitalist forms of land renting, such as sharecropping, survived until 1917. In some cases, rental obligations were fulfilled by working on the owner's land. As several studies have demonstrated, the patterns of renting both reflected and further sharpened the growing economic differentiation within the peasant class. The largest percentage of renters consisted of better-off peasants, who sought to expand their holdings and to increase the household income. For middle-class peasants, renting was simply a way of survival as independent cultivators. The poorest were usually not lessees but lessors. They rented out their minuscule allotment plots to their more successful co-villagers and then hired themselves out as farm hands, filling the increasing ranks of rural proletarians.[49]

The late nineteenth and early twentieth centuries saw an enormous rise in the numbers of landless peasantry and dwarf-holders, whose economic survival depended on external income obtained mainly from

agricultural or industrial work. The advent of the money economy required the peasant family to have at least minimal cash reserves to pay
taxes, rent, or mortgage, thus forcing most peasants to seek wage work
outside the village. The increased accessibility of industrial merchan-
dise, including previously unaccessible luxuries such as city garments,
also whetted peasant hunger for cash. Many peasants had already been
engaged in various home-based crafts and trades, which provided their
households with some extra money (such as pottery, carpentry, iron
work, weaving, etc.). Despite the progress of Russia's industrial development, these crafts survived into the twentieth century, albeit under
harsher competition from mass-produced goods. An analysis of 1897
census data shows linen weaving, carpentry, and shoemaking as the
leading peasant trades in Belarus and Ukraine. A substantial number of
peasants who owned horses also earned cash as teamsters.[50]

Working as craftsmen for a small local market, however, could not
provide most peasant households with sufficient extra income. This is
why every spring thousands of peasants (primarily, but not exclusively,
men) left their overcrowded villages in search of temporary wage
work. *Otkhodnichestvo* (a Russian term for leaving the village for
temporary work) had begun in Ukrainian and Belarusan villages long
before they were drawn into continental and, subsequently, transatlantic labour markets. No reliable statistical data on these internal migrations are available; in fact, it is unlikely that any statistics would
capture the short- and long-distance movements of millions of people
who criss-crossed Russia's western and southwestern lands every year.
In Belarus alone, the annual number of *otkhodniki* (seasonal peasant
migrants) was estimated at 400,000, or 13 per cent of the total adult
rural population.[51]

Destinations of these migrants varied from the nearest estate, where
work was always available during harvest time, to factories and mines
in central Russia and southern Ukraine. As in other parts of the continent, seasonal agricultural labourers employed on nearby estates or
farms belonging to rich peasants were the earliest and largest category
of rural wageworkers in Ukraine and Belarus. Most peasants hired
themselves out as day or seasonal labourers (the latter usually worked
from March to October), but there were also true rural proletarians –
permanent agricultural workers, who relied on wage work as their only
source of income and constituted the lowest status group in rural society. Due to the higher development of agricultural capitalism in Right-
Bank Ukraine and west-central Belarus (Vil'na, Grodno and Minsk

provinces), together with the existence of a larger class of dwarf-holding and landless peasantry, hired labour was used here more widely than in most other parts of European Russia. The surplus of rural population, however, kept wages low even in periods of high labour demand. In 1913, the nominal wages of agricultural day workers at harvest time in Right-Bank Ukraine and Belarus were, respectively, 19.5 and 15.5 per cent below European Russia's average.[52]

The predominantly agricultural character of the economy in Right-Bank Ukraine and Belarus meant that their excess rural population could not be siphoned off by the local industry. According to the 1897 imperial census, the size of the population employed in industry was meagre throughout both regions, ranging from 7.5 per cent in Grodno Province to 10.5 per cent in Volhynia.[53] In 1908, Ukraine possessed only 1,252 industrial establishments, which had a total of 106,218 workers (less than half of the population of the city of Kiev in 1897).[54] The levels of urbanization in Right-Bank Ukraine and west-central Belarus were among the lowest in the empire. In the former region, only 9.6 per cent of the population in 1897 lived in urban areas (compared to 11.2 in the Left Bank and 21.0 in industrially developed southern Ukraine).[55] In Minsk, Vil'na, and Grodno, the official proportion of urban residents stood at a somewhat higher 13 per cent.[56] But even those settlements officially designated as cities, including administrative centres of districts (uezdnye goroda), usually had fewer than 10,000 inhabitants and differed from the surrounding countryside only in being focal points for local trade and home for a significant population of Jews.[57] Poverty and unemployment that reigned in the towns of the Jewish Pale of Settlement, where petty merchants and artisans tried to eke out a living in a tiny market, further limited the prospects of urban employment for the local peasantry. Short-range rural-urban migrations (both permanent and seasonal) were thus less common here than they were in Russia proper, where, as Robert Johnson and other authors have shown, thousands of peasant-workers circulated annually between rural areas and industrial centres such as Moscow and St Petersburg.[58] In Belarus and Right-Bank Ukraine, with their lack of virtually any industry except the processing of agricultural products, the overwhelming majority of the peasantry remained tied to the countryside. Kiev with a population of 247,723 and Vil'na with 198,007 (in 1897) were the only truly urban centres between the Dnieper River and Russian Poland, but even they had little industry. In their low rate of rural-urban migration, these territories differed not only from the

Russian provinces but also from much of Eastern Europe, where increasing numbers of rural inhabitants were streaming into the cities.

Some Ukrainian and Belarusan peasants did travel in search of work to the industrial centres of northern and central Russia, but on the whole labour migration from the empire's western rim to its industrial core by 1900 was not significant.[59] Moscow, Ivanovo, and St Petersburg had their labour demand filled primarily by the local (Russian) peasantry.[60] It was more common for Belarusan peasants to find work as longshoremen in Riga or Libava, or in the Baltic timber industry. High wages paid in railway construction, especially in eastern Russia and Manchuria, also attracted many Belarusan and especially Ukrainian peasants, who crossed more than half the continent for seasonal employment on the Amur and Trans-Baikal railways – the newest additions to Russia's transcontinental railway system. But the majority of Ukrainian and Belarusan peasantry in the early 1900s headed for work in the southern direction. By the turn of the century, the rapid industrial development of southern Ukraine (also known as Novorossia or the Steppe) combined with the development of commercial grain growing to make it Russia's most dynamic region and the breadbasket of Europe. The high rate of economic growth in this part of the empire led to a steady demand for wage labour in both industry and agriculture, which could not be filled by the relatively sparse local population. The influx of agricultural workers to the South (Kherson and Ekaterinoslav provinces, and southern Bessarabia) took on especially large proportions at harvest time. From July to September, a day labourer in Kherson Province could expect to earn 1.23 rubles per day – a far cry from the average wages of no more than 72 kopeks in Volhynia and Podolia.[61] Many agricultural migrants sought employment from prosperous German colonists in the South, because they often paid their farmhands more and fed them better than the landowners back home. Others went to the Donets Basin area to work in the booming steel and mining industries, where wages were substantially higher than in central Russia, or travelled further to Odessa – Russia's main commercial port on the Black Sea – where seasonal jobs were always plentiful. Although migration from Left- and Right-Bank Ukraine to the Steppe did increase by 1914, most workers in the local industries came from the ethnically Russian provinces.[62] Besides their larger numbers, Russian workers generally possessed higher industrial skills, developed throughout a longer history of rural-urban migrations, and therefore enjoyed a competitive advantage over the Ukrainians.[63]

Demographic pressures, however, were beginning to be felt even in the thriving South. By the end of the first decade of the new century, the expansion of labour markets in southern Ukraine could barely keep pace with the spiralling growth of surplus workers being pushed out of the empire's villages. High competition for well-paying jobs, especially in the agricultural sector, forced thousands of migrant peasant-workers to wander throughout the southern Ukrainian steppe in search of work. Every summer, thousands of these migrants spent weeks at town marketplaces waiting to be hired as farmhands. Sometimes, only a few hundred of them managed to get jobs, while others resumed their desperate journeys.[64]

Moving to Siberia was another alternative for landless Ukrainians and Belarusans. Spontaneous peasant movement beyond the Urals, already on the rise in the last quarter of the nineteenth century, saw a dramatic increase after 1906 when the Russian government made internal colonization a strategic priority.[65] Nearly 2.8 million people relocated to Siberia (primarily to its southeastern part) between 1906 and 1913 under Russia's largest ever government-sponsored migration scheme.[66] This massive transfer of peasant population gave rise to the popular perception in the West that Russian peasants preferred to explore settlement opportunities at home even when they were given a chance to emigrate.[67] But, as the figures in Table 3 demonstrate, few Siberia-bound colonists came from the empire's western frontier. While peasants from Left-Bank Ukraine and eastern Belarus more willingly embraced the prospect of free land in the east, in Right-Bank Ukraine and west-central Belarus (especially Vil'na and Grodno) Siberian colonization never developed into a mass movement. Thus the Dnieper River, which separated the imperial heartland from the western periphery, also formed most of the boundary between the Russo-Siberian and the Atlantic migration systems.[68]

What factors accounted for the difference in migration patterns west and east of the Dnieper, and why did local peasants show little interest in the Siberian option? Apart from the enormous distances that separated the Right-Bank territories from Siberia, much of the explanation should probably be sought in the history and cultural orientation of Russia's western lands. Acquired as a result of the late eighteenth-century partitions of Poland, Right-Bank Ukraine and west-central Belarus were among the latest additions to the Romanov realm. A century later they still remained much less integrated into the empire, less affected by Russification, and more exposed to European cultural and

Table 3
Peasant migration to Asiatic Russia from selected provinces and regions of the Russian Empire, 1896–1913

Province or region	1896–1909	Rate of migration (per 1000)	1910- 1913	Decrease compared to 1896-1909(%)	Total 1896-1913
Podolia	51,190	17	28,443	44.4	79,633
Kiev	152,288	43	39,898	73.8	192,186
Volhynia	40,392	14	18,776	53.5	59,168
Left-Bank Ukraine*	653,483	86	168,856	74.2	822,339
Southern Ukraine**	281,829	45	178,071	36.8	459,900
Minsk	76,781	36	11,430	85.1	88,211
Vil'na	34,831	22	3,412	90.2	38,243
Grodno	20,382	13	6,338	68.9	26,720
Eastern Belarus***	313,669	99	53,905	82.8	367,574
Total	1,624,845		509,129	32.3	2,133,974

* Includes the provinces of Chernigov, Poltava and Khar'kov
** Includes the provinces of Taurida, Kherson and Ekaterinoslav
*** Includes the provinces of Vitebsk and Mogilev
Calculated from: N. Turchaninov and L. Domrachev, Itogi pereselencheskogo dvizheniia za vremia c 1910 po 1914 gg. (vkliuchitel'no) (Petrograd, 1916), 8–9, 10–11, 30–1, 32–3, 34–5; M.A. Iakymenko, "Orhanizatsiia pereselennia selian z Ukraini v roki stolypins'koi ahrarnoi reformy (1906–1913 rr.)," Ukrains'kyi istorychnyi zhurnal 1974 (7): 37; 1897 census, vol. 4, part 1, 1; vol. 8, 3; vol. 9, 4; vol. 16, 4; vol. 22, 5; vol. 32, 3.

economic influences than any of the tsar's possessions further east. For many peasants in the region, Siberia doubtless seemed a remote and unknown land, vastly different in climate and social customs from their home areas. Furthermore, it was not until 1911 that imperial provinces west of the Dnieper were granted self-government assemblies (zemstva), which were so crucial in other parts of Russia to organizing the Siberian colonization and providing assistance to the colonists.[69] Finally, the tsarist government itself was ambiguous about moving the Russian Orthodox population from the western borderlands. Dealing with the problem of agrarian overpopulation west of the Dnieper, the imperial authorities never lost sight of the potentially dangerous political effects of a massive peasant exodus across the Urals, which threatened to reduce the Slavic-Orthodox presence on the ethnically diverse western frontier. Prime Minister Peter Stolypin and director of the Main Administration for Agriculture V. Krivoshein agreed in 1911 that an "excessive weakening of the density of Russian population in Russia's western belt [...] is hardly desirable either politically or economically [because] Russia would surrender its western positions for a German advance, and mass out-migration would open numerous pores and apertures, which would be quickly filled with foreign colonists."[70]

Limited colonization movement from both Right-Bank Ukraine and west-central Belarus did occur, but any interest in Siberia that existed here was soon eclipsed by the irresistible lure of America. Among 212 persons from Podolia who moved across the Urals in June 1911, not a single one was a native of Kamenets District (the largest donor of Canada-bound emigrants from Ukraine). In April 1912 there was only one resident of Kamenets among 366 colonists.[71] A contemporary survey of peasant migrations from Volhynia showed that the total number of overseas emigrants from the province in 1910 was only 20 per cent smaller than the number of peasants who left for Siberia the same year. Five of the province's twelve districts actually had more emigrants than colonists. Emigration reached especially large proportions in the northernmost district of Kovel', where there was only one colonist for every ten emigrants.[72] But contrary to what many early twentieth-century commentators and modern-day historians have believed, the relationship between emigration and internal colonization was not always an inverse one.[73] In some Right-Bank districts (such as Novograd-Volynsk and Zaslav), peasants eagerly pursued both options. While more research on the topic is needed, it appears that each locality had its own dynamics of peasant mobility, which depended on a variety of circumstances: previous migration traditions of the peasantry; the experiences of earlier migrants; the existence of information networks; the attitudes of the zemstvo and the local administration, etc.

By the first decade of the twentieth century, conditions on the western rim of the tsarist empire were ripe for the development of transcontinental labour migrations. Large, though geographically scattered, territories in Right-Bank Ukraine and west-central Belarus were rapidly becoming the easternmost labour-supplying periphery for the North-Atlantic industrial core. Though different in several important ways, the socio-economic systems in both regions of the Romanov Empire were characterized by the inability of a large part of the peasantry to maintain an acceptable standard of living by remaining on the land. Diminishing landholdings (in Right-Bank Ukraine and northern Bessarabia) or barely cultivable soils (such as existed in many areas of Belarus) forced some peasants to seek additional income from home-based trades and pushed others out of the villages. Seasonal work migrations had already become a familiar phenomenon for rural communities in most of these areas. In the early 1900s these migrations began to extend across Russia's borders.

Through a combination of geography, economy, and ethnic diversity in this part of the empire, which lay at the meeting point of different cultures and ways of life, Russia's Ukrainian and Belarusan territories west of the Dnieper became the first to be drawn into the vortex of transoceanic labour migrations. While eastern Belarus, Left-Bank Ukraine and the Steppe remained more closely tied to Eurasian migration routes, Russia's western borderlands (culturally and geographically more distant from the imperial heartland) were quickly developing strong connections with the Atlantic economy.

2

The Anatomy of Migration

Human migration is never a random process. Even within relatively compact geographic areas, let alone such vast territories as Russia's western borderlands, it always exhibits variations in size, momentum, and the composition of the migrant stream. While emigration from certain localities on the empire's frontier developed as early as the 1890s, in others it did not take off until the eve of World War I and in most places remained nearly or fully absent. Areas where emigration proceeded at a relatively constant pace were interspersed with those where it showed sudden fluctuations. Migration trajectories, including the choice of travel routes and destinations, also displayed regional differences. As soon as the exodus of population from a particular area reached a certain level of intensity, locally specific migration chains developed, exerting a strong influence on the travel itineraries and overseas destinations of new migrant cohorts.

To a Canadian observer, Eastern European immigrants disembarking at Halifax or Quebec probably looked like a faceless crowd of sheepskin-clad "Polacks," but the real social portrait of the early twentieth-century immigrant labourer was, needless to say, more complex. More importantly, it was never simply a mirror image of the general population in the places of origin. Because emigration seldom recruited people with "typical" or "average" social profiles for a given area, aggregated population data on the donor territories can tell us little about who the migrants were. To understand how emigrant selection worked, the profiles of the migrants need to be compared with the demographic and social characteristics of the origin sites. Only in this case can we come closer to answering one of the central questions of any study in human migration: how different were people who chose emigration as a response to social and economic pressures from their less mobile neighbours, and what were the reasons underlying this difference?

Most of the data in this chapter, which dissects the social structure of the migration process that brought thousands of Ukrainians and Belarusans to Canadian shores, are drawn from a computerized sample of 2,743 immigrant files located in the papers of the Russian imperial consulates in Canada (known as the Li-Ra-Ma Collection). These files, described in more detail in the Appendix, contain two types of serial documents: application forms (questionnaires) used by immigrants who intended to return home and needed a Russian entry permit, and affidavits submitted by individuals seeking certificates of Russian citizenship. Both types of documents contain extensive personal and demographic information on their subjects (place and year of birth, occupation, marital status, family size, religion, ethnicity, year of immigration, places of residence in Canada, and others).

GEOGRAPHIC ORIGINS

The first Slavic immigrants to arrive in Canada from the western frontier of the Russian Empire were religious dissenters and political activists persecuted by the Russian authorities. Thus Semion Prokopenko from Sumy, Khar'kov Province, was forced to leave Russia in 1899 because of his conversion to Leo Tolstoy's pacifist teachings, which had been outlawed by the tsarist state. "I would have remained [Russian] Orthodox had I not realized that the so-called Orthodox faith was just one of many *sects*, only a dominant one," he explained to the Russian consul in Montreal.[1] He arrived in Canada with a wife and four children and settled in the Doukhobor village of Kamenka near Kamsack, Saskatchewan. Like Prokopenko, the majority of those who left Russia for religious reasons went to the Prairies and settled on the land, but some took up urban occupations. Petr Kuzmin, an adherent of the Old Believer sect, came to Canada with his wife in 1912 by a circuitous route, having spent twelve years in Argentina, and opened a small tavern in Sudbury.[2] Among the few Russian radicals of Ukrainian origin who found refuge in Canada was Savva Fedorenko, a Socialist Revolutionary militant charged with the murder of a policeman in Kiev Province. Support for Fedorenko, whose extradition was demanded by the Russian government in 1909, became a rallying point for Canadian labour and socialist organizations.[3] Military deserters, outlaws, and various kinds of adventurous souls completed the picture of the early immigrants. Aliaksandr Pilipchyk from Minsk Province, for example, managed to escape from prison, where he was serving a two-year sentence for a crime committed during military service, then went to Chicago and subsequently moved to Canada.[4]

It would take several years before the thin stream of non-conformist types fleeing the tsarist regime would be replaced by the increasing flow of ordinary peasant migrants. The sampling of migrant files from the Russian consular records points to 1905–07 as the years that signalled the beginning of labour immigration from Russia's western frontier. During the next eight years, especially 1912–14, thousands of Ukrainian and Belarusan peasants left their villages in pursuit of the Canadian dollar. As Figure 1 demonstrates, Belarus was drawn into the orbit of transoceanic population movements earlier than Ukraine. 16 per cent of Belarusans who reported their dates of arrival in the sampled files came before 1910, compared to less than 7 per cent of Ukrainians. However, after 1910 Ukrainian immigrants outnumbered Belarusans in both absolute and relative terms. While Belarus continued to produce thousands of peasant emigrants, the vast majority of them went to the United States.[5] The Russian Immigrant Home in New York reported in July 1913 that among the 6,677 immigrants it had received since 1908, approximately 55 per cent were born in Belarus and only 24 per cent in Ukraine.[6] Due to New York's prominence as the main port of debarkation for America-bound immigrants, these figures may be seen as representing the general pattern of Slavic immigration from tsarist Russia to the United States.

Peasant emigration from Belarus to Canada developed primarily in its northwestern and central parts, which included the imperial provinces of Vil'na, Grodno, and Minsk. Natives of Vil'na – one of the most ethnically diverse territories in the entire empire – were especially prominent among the early migrants. Local Belarusan peasants probably learned about "America" from their Lithuanian and Polish neighbours, who had begun to emigrate as early as the 1880s.[7] As elsewhere in East-Central Europe, informal migrant networks of kin, neighbours, and friends supplied information and resources to new cohorts of fortune-seekers in the form of remittances, loans, and prepaid tickets. Uladzimir Butkevich from the village of Pukhauka came to Toronto around 1906 on a prepaid ticket after his "friends in their letters praised this country and the abundance of opportunities to earn good money."[8] As emigration spread in the southeastern direction, Minsk and especially Grodno became the leading sources of

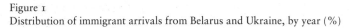

Figure 1
Distribution of immigrant arrivals from Belarus and Ukraine, by year (%)

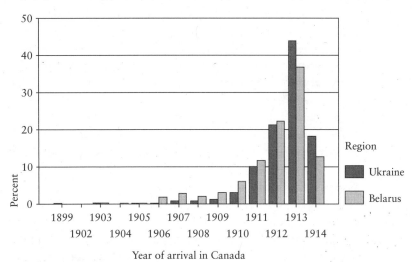

Year of arrival in Canada

Source: Li-Ra-Ma Sample

Belarusan emigration to Canada. In the end, Grodno sent by far the largest contingent of Canada-bound emigrants in all of Belarus.

Within each of the donor provinces, the intensity of emigration showed significant variations. The district *(uezd)* of Pruzhany, situated in the southwestern part of Grodno Province, was the birthplace of 63 per cent of all emigrants from that province and the source of approximately 42 per cent of all individuals of Belarusan origin for whom we have data on the place of origin.[9] It was probably the only place in Belarus where Canada attracted decidedly more emigrants than did the United States. Emigration to Canada was also significant in three other districts of Grodno Province – Kobrin, Brest, and Slonim – but not nearly as high as it was in Pruzhany. The lowest rates of Canada-bound emigration were in the westernmost areas of the province, where the majority of the rural population was of Polish origin. Within Minsk Province, peasants emigrated to Canada primarily from the southwestern districts of Pinsk and Slutsk, which together account for about 12 per cent of all the Belarusans in the sample.

Emigration from Russian-ruled Ukraine to Canada also had a geographically clustered pattern, being confined primarily to areas located west of the Dnieper River (Right-Bank Ukraine). The three Right-Bank provinces – Podolia, Volhynia, and Kiev, along with the northern part of Bessarabia – were the home of about 96 per cent of all sampled Ukrainian emigrants who reported data on their place of birth. Podolia stood as the largest donor province not only in Ukraine but also in the entire Russian Empire, with nearly 42 per cent of the Ukrainian-born emigrants reporting it as their place of origin.[10] Emigration from the province increased especially after 1910–11, leaving many villages with just a fraction of their male population. In 1911, Avraam Savchuk, an emigrant from the village of Hrynivtsi, received a letter from his sister, who reported that "[many] lads have gone to America, and Uncle Filipp's [son?] Tereshko has been away already for a year and a half, and has already sent money twice, and Uncle has already bought a couple of horses."[11]

Some peasants in Podolia learned about overseas migration alternatives during annual labour-seeking forays to southern Ukraine and the Black Sea region. Rumour had it that men from the village of Ivankivtsi had begun to emigrate to Canada around 1908–09 after Hnat Pychko, one of the village residents, met a mysterious "American entrepreneur" during his sojourn in Odessa – a major destination of seasonal migration for Ivankivtsi peasants. Soon after the fateful meeting Hnat set out on a journey to Canada, where he bought some land "in the city of Saskaton" [sic], "started a business," and eventually sent for his wife and four children.[12] Over the course of several years about half of the Ivankivtsi population caught the emigration fever, leaving behind mostly children, elders, and women.

Close cultural and commercial linkages between the southwestern part of Russian Ukraine and the neighbouring Austrian provinces of Galicia and Bukovyna played an important role in feeding information about Canada to the local peasantry and in shaping the direction of migration flows. As in other areas in Eastern Europe where state borders cut across ethnic lines, the boundary that separated the two empires had little significance for the daily lives of the local Ukrainian peasants. Circular movement across the border never stopped, with peasants crossing it in both directions to visit the nearest marketplace, to sell or buy goods, or even to track lost or stolen cattle. Many Galician peasants worked as seasonal farm labourers on large sugar beet estates in western Podolia.[13] The relaxed passport regime that existed in Russian territories adjacent to Galicia facilitated short-term trips across the border. A peasant who wished to go to Austria for the maximum of four weeks could do so by obtaining a so-called "legitimating pass" from the parish authorities.[14] The intermingling of population in the

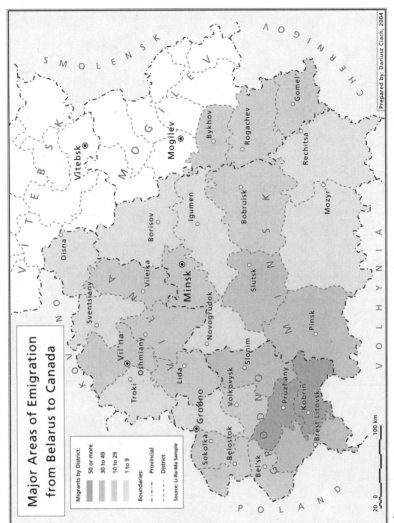

Major Areas of Emigration from Belarus to Canada

Migrants by District:
- 50 or more
- 30 to 49
- 10 to 29
- 1 to 9

Boundaries:
- —·—·— Provincial
- —·—·— District

Source: Li-Ra-Ma Sample

Prepared by: Dariusz Ciach, 2004

100 km

20 0

Map I

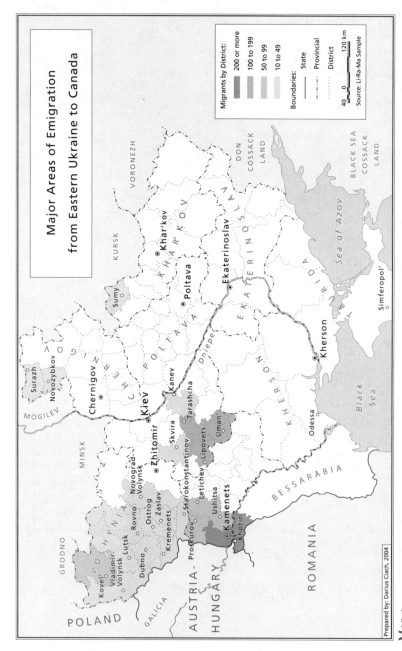

Major Areas of Emigration from Eastern Ukraine to Canada

Migrants by District:
- 200 or more
- 100 to 199
- 50 to 99
- 10 to 49

Boundaries:
- State
- Provincial
- District

Source: Li-Ra-Ma Sample

40   0   120 km

Prepared by: Darius Ciach, 2004

Map 2

border areas created transnational channels of communication, which carried information about new migration opportunities. Local market-places, which brought together large numbers of peasants and merchants from both countries, became particularly important venues for such information exchanges.[15] In March 1913, a leading Russian news-paper in Podolia complained that "residents of Austrian villages near the border come on market days to the market square [of Kamenets-Podol'sk, the provincial capital] and recruit peasants to cross the border without government passports."[16] Local peasants increasingly visited the square to hear the stories of recent returnees from "America." In August 1913 police had to be called in to disperse an unusually large crowd that had gathered around one of the storytellers.[17]

Given the multiple ties that connected Kamenets to neighbouring Galicia, it is little wonder that the district produced by far the largest Canada-bound migrant stream in all of Russian Ukraine. With less than 9 per cent of Podolia's total population, it supplied 70 per cent of its emigrants. In fact, every third Ukrainian immigrant that came to Canada from the Russian Empire was likely to be a native of Kamenets. The intensity of emigration from the district becomes even more obvious considering that Khotin – the second largest source district in Ukraine – was reported as the place of birth by only 12 per cent of all Ukrainians in the sample.

While in the overall count Podolia and northern Bessarabia were Ukraine's largest emigrant donors, they were not the earliest ones. Evidence from the Li-Ra-Ma Collection and other available sources does not bear out the view of Ukrainian emigration to Canada as progressively spreading in the eastward direction. Many of the first emigrants hailed from central and eastern Ukraine – especially the junction of Tarashcha, Lipovets, and Uman' districts and the environs of Kiev. Some even came from the Left Bank, otherwise little affected by emigration (see Map 2). The sample data show, for instance, that 9.4 per cent of all emigrants from Tarashcha came to Canada prior to 1911, while for the whole of Ukraine this figure stands at 6.5 per cent. A 1907 survey of a parish in the district found that over 400 of its male residents were "in America" as wage workers, and some had already sent for their wives and children.[18] In the local town of Tetyiv, so many peasants had been overseas by 1913 that, according to one commentator, it was "not surprising to see a man with a scythe in his hands wearing American shoes, a bowler hat, and a gentleman's suit."[19]

It was the exodus of Ukrainian Baptists, who began to leave for North America in the mid-1890s escaping the increasing persecution by the tsarist state and the Orthodox Church, which provided the needed catalyst for mass peasant emigration from Tarashcha and other districts with a Baptist population.[20] When Ukrainian Baptists discovered Canada as a migration destination, settlements composed of Baptist immigrants from the Russian Empire already existed in North Dakota, Virginia, Kentucky, and Pennsylvania.[21] Until 1914, small groups of Ukrainians of Baptist faith (perhaps no more than several hundred in total) continued to trickle into Canada. In April 1907, *Rada* – the leading Ukrainian-language newspaper in Russia – reported the departure of three Baptist families from the city of Kiev and six others from the nearby town of Borodianka.[22] Three years later, twelve more Baptist families from Kherson and Stavropol came to Canada and settled on homesteads near Monitor, Alberta.[23] In areas of Baptist emigration the words "America" and "Canada" doubtless became known to peasants much earlier than in many other localities, eventually prompting some of them to follow in the footsteps of the "sectarians."

The example of Tarashcha highlights the significance of ethnic and religious diversity in shaping local migration chains. As Josef Barton pointed out in his study of Slovak, Italian, and Rumanian immigrants in Cleveland, the "mixture of peoples – even within a single village – exposed different segments of the population to different economic and social pressures and also provided some individuals with special resources."[24] Like elsewhere in eastern and southern Europe, the diverse character of the population in Ukraine and Belarus facilitated the formation of inter-ethnic and inter-religious migrant networks. The persecuted and disadvantaged groups, or those with previous migration experience, usually left first, acting as conduits of information for their neighbours. While Baptists, Old Believers, Germans, or Poles could all serve as trailblazers, most peasants learned about "America" from the local Jews, who not only possessed a highly developed migration culture and well-functioning information networks but also constituted the majority of steamship and emigration agents operating in Eastern Europe. Many peasant emigrants would probably have agreed with the words of several Bessarabians who admitted in their letter to the Russian consul in Montreal that "as for Canada, we did not know that there was such [a country] on earth" until two Jewish agents came to their village in the summer of 1913.[25] The relationship between migration and the ethno-religious structure of the population in a particular area was not, however, a mechanical one. Thus Kiev District – another early sender of Baptist emigrants – never rose to the rank of a major donor area, probably due to the pull of the city of Kiev as an alternative destination for labour seekers.

Emigration to Canada from Left-Bank Ukraine, although not entirely absent, never reached the levels exhibited by the Right-Bank provinces. The largest and earliest emigration cluster east of the Dnieper emerged in the northern part of Chernigov Province, where the poor quality of the soil had long forced peasants to engage in peddling and other non-agricultural pursuits. According to local tradition, the first Chernigov peasant to discover America was Fedor Korotkii, a peddler who wandered into Poland around 1895 and met a group of emigrants who had just returned from the United States. Like thousands of others, he was captivated by "America stories" and joined the next group of Polish emigrants heading for the United States. After three years of working at a steel factory in Pennsylvania, Fedor came back to his village as a rich "*amerikanets,*" only to return to America the next year with about a dozen other peasants. As letters and money orders began to flow back from America to Chernigov, more and more local peasants proceeded in the opposite direction.[26] Some of them found their way to Canada, although the United States remained the main destination for Chernigov emigrants until 1914.

With most villages of origin, the movement of peasants from eastern Ukraine and Belarus to Canada appears to have never passed the pioneer stage of individual or small-group migration. The 594 Belarusan and 1,908 Ukrainian migrants in the Li-Ra-Ma sample came, respectively, from 367 and 729 different villages (see Table 4). Villages of heavy migration (10 migrants and over) made up only 1.1 per cent of all places of origin in Belarus and 7.1 per cent in Ukraine. In most of the donor areas a small group of heavy-emigration villages coexisted with a much larger number of places where emigration was sparse. This pattern developed not only in the provinces and districts of minor or moderate emigration but also in those with the highest migration rates, such as Kamenets, Khotin, or Pruzhany. In other words, relatively few Ukrainians and Belarusans came as part of large village chains, with the exception of seven villages (four in Podolia and three in Kiev) that were each reported as places of origin by more than twenty migrants in the sample. Geographically, villages of heavy emigration usually formed compact clusters, which sometimes cut across district borders. Thus over two-thirds of the major emigration villages in northern

Table 4
Intensity of emigration from eastern Ukraine and Belarus by villages of origin

Village Chains	Percentage of the total number of emigration villages		Percentage of immigrants sent	
Villages with:	Belarus	Ukraine	Belarus	Ukraine
1-4 migrants	94.6	84.8	77.6	45.5
5-9 migrants	4.4	10.7	15.3	28.7
10+ migrants	1.1	4.5	7.1	26.2
Total	100 (367)	100 (729)	100 (594)	100 (1,908)

Source: Li-Ra-Ma Sample.

Bessarabia were concentrated in the western part of Khotin District within a radius of twenty-five miles. The same pattern can be observed in the south-central part of Kiev Province, at the junction of Tarashcha, Lipovets, and Uman'.

Official statistics of Ukrainian and Belarusan immigration to Canada prior to 1914 are lacking. The tsarist government never kept a record of emigration from the empire, while Canadian census and immigration data provide little help, lumping all Russian-subject immigrants of eastern Slav origin into a catch-all category of "Russians." The confusion of ethnicity with country of origin led to the habitual inclusion of non-Slavic immigrants among the Russians (most Prairie residents whose "racial origin" was recorded by the 1901 census as "Russian" were in fact Germans from Russia).[27] The high rate of return migration to Russia and remigration to the United States among Russian-born labourers further complicates the matter. Bruno Ramirez has recently shown that about 17.6 per cent (or approximately 65,000) of all *recorded* European-born remigrants to the United States during 1906–30 were natives of Russia, and 80 per cent of them went south before 1919.[28]

According to one – probably exaggerated – estimate, Canada already had 10,000 Ukrainians from the Russian Empire as early as 1908. Cross-tabulated data on the mother tongue and racial origin of Canadians, drawn from the 1921 census, suggest that Canada's eastern Slav population born in the Russian Empire amounted at the time to 35,000.[29] If one compares this data with the proportional representation of various nationalities in the Li-Ra-Ma sample, it can be estimated that in 1921 the number of Canadian Ukrainians born in the former territories of the Russian Empire was close to 25,000, while the population of Belarusans approached 9,000.

THE SOCIAL BACKGROUNDS

The majority of Ukrainians and Belarusans who set out on labour-seeking voyages were men in their twenties and early thirties (Table 5). At the time of emigration, 57 per cent of the men in the Li-Ra-Ma sample were married (Table 6). Significantly, the proportion of married individuals among the migrants was higher than in the general rural population in all provinces except Vil'na.[30] The greater propensity of married men to emigrate was not exceptional to Ukraine or Belarus but has been observed as characteristic of the early stage of labour emigration in other parts of East-Central Europe. Many young men obviously went to "America" shortly after marriage in the hope of coming back with a nest-egg and giving a head start to their families. Approximately 22 per cent of the married emigrants in the sample went to Canada prior to the birth of their first child. Due to their young age, the emigrating men seldom had more than two children, although a few had as many as six or seven. There is some evidence that many of the newly married men still lived with their parents prior to emigration and saw temporary work in Canada as a way to save money in order to establish a separate household.

While the majority of the men were married, few brought their families to Canada – suggesting that most migration from Ukraine and Belarus was intended to be temporary. In 1917–18 (the years in which the majority of Li-Ra-Ma files were created), only about 8 per cent of married migrants had families in Canada. Such individuals were more likely to be found among Belarusans and the early arrivals of both nationalities.[31] Men with resident families constituted over 42 per cent of those who immigrated in 1907, but only 2.9 per cent of those who came in 1913. The rates of family migration also show variations by province of origin – from 20 per cent among immigrants from Vil'na to a mere 4.5 per cent among the natives of Kiev.

The nature of the sources does not allow us to establish the gender structure of the migrant population with any degree of precision. According to Canadian immigration statistics, which classified immigrants by racial origin and sex, women constituted 15.5 per cent of all "Russians" who came to Canada between 1904 and 1914, but the real proportion of females among Ukrainians and Belarusans was probably

Table 5
Age of migrants at the time of arrival in Canada*

	Total number of arrivals (%)	
Age group	Ukraine	Belarus
Under 20	18.7	21.0
20-24	23.2	23.1
25-29	21.6	25.6
30-34	14.9	12.1
35-39	10.4	8.7
40 and over	8.7	9.0

N = 1674
Source: Li-Ra-Ma Sample.
* Excluding individuals who came to Canada after 1914.

even smaller, for many women recorded as Russian were doubtless of Russian-German and other non-Slavic extraction.[32] Significantly, the ratio of women in the immigration statistics on "Russians" decreased in the last years before World War I, reflecting a shift from settlement to labour migration. A similar picture of gender imbalance among the "Russians" also emerges from Canadian census records, which differ from the statistics of immigrant arrivals in that they include the Canadian-born children of the immigrants. According to the 1911 census, in the provinces of Ontario and Quebec – two leading destinations of Slavic labourers from Russia – females made up, respectively, 15.8 and 28.2 per cent of all persons whose ethnic origin was listed as "Russian."[33] The higher ratio of females in Quebec may reflect the position of Montreal as Canada's earliest and largest destination of Slavic migration from Russia, but, as with Canadian immigration reports, these figures almost certainly exaggerate the presence of women among eastern Slavs arriving from the tsarist empire. The marriage books of the Saint Peter and Saint Paul Russian Orthodox Church in Montreal show that only 23.6 per cent of eighty-five Russian-born men who married in the parish between 1917 and 1921 were able to find brides from their country. The lack of brides from Russia led many young Ukrainian and Belarusan men to marry Orthodox girls from Austrian-ruled Bukovyna or Galicia.[34] The majority of Ukrainian and Belarusan labourers in Canada were "men without women" – the archetypal migrant sojourners separated from their female kin.[35] Emotional and

Table 6
Marital status of migrants compared with marital status of the general population
in the provinces of origin (men 20–29 years of age)

Province	Li-Ra-Ma Migrants (%)		General Population outside Cities (%)	
	Married	Single	Married	Single
Bessarabia (Khotin District)	70.0	30.0	58.7	40.6
Grodno	61.2	38.8	45.1	54.5
Kiev	65.7	34.3	59.2	40.3
Minsk	56.3	43.8	53.2	46.3
Podolia	57.9	42.1	54.8	44.5
Vil'na	30.8	69.2	32.5	67.2
Volhynia	57.1	42.9	62.6	36.7
Average	57.0	43.0	52.3	47.2

N = 734
Sources: Column 1, Li-Ra-Ma Sample; Column 2, 1897 census, Table 5, "Distribution of Population
by Marital Status and Age Group", vol. 3 (Bessarabia), 31: vol. 4 (Vil'na), part 3, 12; vol. 8
(Volhynia), 28; vol. 11 (Grodno), 32; vol. 16 (Kiev), 28; vol. 22 (Minsk), 30; vol. 32 (Podolia), 32.

business ties with those left behind were maintained through letters, photos, and money orders, which did not cease to flow across the Atlantic even in the worst months of World War I.

The sample files give us a rare glimpse into the migrants' literacy level, not recorded in contemporary Canadian immigration statistics. The pre-emigration literacy of Ukrainian and Belarusan men can be assessed from Russian passports, attached to 671 Li-Ra-Ma files. Every emigrant who could not sign his or her passport was recorded in that document as illiterate. Comparing these data with those from the 1897 Russian imperial census (Table 7), we can conclude that the level of literacy among the emigrants was higher than in the general peasant population of the same age. Given that the census defined literacy as the ability to read, which is normally learned before writing, the gap between emigrants and those who stayed behind was probably even wider.[36]

That the emigration movement recruited the more educated and more astute among the peasantry is hardly surprising. Literate men had access to more sources of information about the world beyond the village and were more inclined to venture into the unknown. The ability to read and write (if only in Russian) also made an emigrant less vulnerable to swindling and abuse. It was even more important in the early

Table 7
Literacy of migrants compared with literacy of the male peasant population
in major provinces of origin (men 10–29 years of age)*

Province	Passport File Data (%)	Li-Ra-Ma Sample Data (%)	1897 census (%)
Grodno	54.1	71.2	53.2**
Kiev	59.1	71.3	36.2
Minsk	50.0	75.2	28.3
Podolia	58.8	67.1	33.1
Volhynia	54.8	65.9	32.1
Average	55.4	70.1	36.6

Sources: Column 1, Passport File, Li-Ra-Ma Collection; Column 2, Li-Ra-Ma Sample; Column 3, 1897 census, Table 9, "Distribution of Population by Literacy, Education, Social Estate and Age Groups", vol. 8 (Volhynia), 54; vol. 9 (Grodno), 60-61; vol. 16 (Kiev), 54; vol. 22 (Minsk), 54; vol. 32 (Podolia), 60.
*   Other provinces of origin are represented in the Passport File or the Li-Ra-Ma Sample by too few cases to provide a reasonable level of statistical significance.
** The unusually high literacy of the peasant population of Grodno is probably due to the high proportion of Poles, who tended to have higher average literacy than Belarusans, particularly if the latter were of the Orthodox faith. According to my crude estimates, the literacy rate among Grodno's Belarusan population between the ages of 10 and 29 did not exceed 30 per cent.

stages of emigration, when few community support networks existed in the country of destination. The sample data also suggest that the level of elementary literacy among the migrants had a tendency to increase after several years spent in Canada. This is demonstrated by the proportion of individuals who were able to sign their completed applications for entry permits. The need to function in a foreign environment and to perform new tasks such as signing a job contract, depositing money into the bank, and sending money orders and letters to the family created the need to learn the basics of reading and writing, which had not been as urgent in the old country. Living for months in a company bunkhouse next to more educated compatriots provided a good opportunity to learn. Some men may have attended Sunday courses organized by Frontier College or by various religious missions proselytizing among foreign workers, even though the migrants' itinerant way of life was hardly conducive to that type of learning. The correspondence between the migrants and Russian consuls also contains evidence that some of the former illiterates indeed learned to write during their Canadian sojourn. In his August 1918 letter to the Russian consul general, Adam Shpyruk from Volhynia apologized for his poor grammar, "because [it is only] here [that] I have learned a little writing."[37] The increase in literacy appears to be higher among Belarusans than it was among Ukrainians, probably due in part to the earlier beginnings of Belarusan immigration and hence the greater number of years spent in Canada by the average immigrant.

The ethnic backgrounds of the migrants generally reflect the population structure in the territories of origin. The analysis of personal names in conjunction with other "objective" ethnic indicators shows that persons of Ukrainian and Belarusan ethnicity, respectively, constituted an overwhelming majority of emigrants from Ukraine and Belarus. Poles were the largest minority group in both parts of the empire. As in the general population, they tended to have a larger proportion of town residents and skilled tradesmen than either Ukrainians or Belarusans. Lithuanians, who were second in numbers to Poles among emigrants from Belarus, all hailed from the north-western districts of Vil'na Province, where they made up the bulk of the population.

Significantly, the ethnic self-identification of many emigrants was different from the picture obtained through the "objective" criteria of ethnicity. When asked to indicate their ethnic origin on the consular application forms, 75 per cent of the respondents identified themselves as "Russians," 11.6 per cent as "Little Russians" (malorossy), 4.1 per cent as "White Russians" (belorusy), and the rest as Poles or Lithuanians. Only eight individuals in the sample considered themselves to be Ukrainians. The others apparently did not understand the very concept of "nationality," which had little relevance to the life-worlds of East European peasantry, who interpreted the question in more familiar religious terms by reporting themselves as "Christian," "Orthodox," or "Catholic." The high proportion of persons who identified themselves as Russians suggests that the official tsarist concept of the "Russian nation" comprising Great, Little, and White Russians continued to persist in the peasant mind even after the demise of the monarchy in February 1917. Most Ukrainians and Belarusans from Russia (and some assimilated individuals of other origin) seem to have arrived in North America with a more or less articulated sense of "Greater Russian" identity, superimposed on local and regional identities. While a "Little Russian" or "White Russian" (as opposed to simply "Russian") identity might in some cases point to a somewhat higher degree of ethnic self-awareness, more often it was probably an illustration of multiple identities. As Robert Magocsi has noted, this phenomenon was common to Ukrainians in Imperial Russia, who usually considered themselves both

"Russians" and "Little Russians" or sometimes "Russians from Little Russia *(russkie iz Malorossii)."* These notions were not arranged in a rigid order of preference, since their usage depended on the situational context.[38] A similar kind of self-identification was also common to Belarus, where the national consciousness of the peasantry was, if anything, even lower than in Ukraine.

The religious affiliations of the migrants generally followed ethnic lines, notwithstanding some overlap, particularly in Belarus. Table 8 shows a definite predominance of Russian Orthodox believers among the migrants of both nationalities. Almost all Roman Catholics who came from the Ukrainian provinces were of Polish origin. The Ukrainians were overwhelmingly Orthodox, with a sprinkling of Protestant sectarians. The higher proportion of Roman Catholics among migrants from Belarus reflects the greater ethno-religious diversity of the region. Catholicism was practised here not only by Poles but also by Lithuanians and by many ethnic Belarusans living in Vil'na and parts of Grodno Province.[39] Not surprisingly, Catholics made up over 50 per cent of migrants from Vil'na but only 7 per cent among natives of Minsk.

Virtually all Slavic emigrants who arrived in Canada from the Russian Empire were recruited from the peasant class. Even those who reported themselves as "townsfolk" *(meshchane)* – the official state category that included lower-rank town and city dwellers – were often agriculturalists by primary occupation. Only a handful of the migrants came from large cities or belonged to the industrial working class (apart from seasonal work). Exceptions certainly occurred, but they were rare. Thus, Iosif Pyl' from Grodno and Iosif Rabizo from Vil'na worked as mechanics in Moscow and St Petersburg prior to emigration.[40] An examination of police registration stamps in Russian internal passports attached to a number of Li-Ra-Ma files shows that a small number of peasants had experience as railway construction workers in European Russia or the Far East, or as metal workers and miners in the factories of Ekaterinoslav, Odessa, and Donetsk. A few others had ventured to Riga and Poland. But these men were still far from crossing the line that separated a seasonal peasant-worker, essentially embedded within the rural mode of life, from an urban proletarian.

Unfortunately, systematic data on the economic standing of individual migrant families (such as the amount of immovable property or livestock owned) are lacking. From the evidence scattered through the migrants' correspondence with the Russian consuls and family from home, it appears that the majority were drawn from the middle or

Table 8
Religious affiliations of migrants

| | Region | | |
Denomination	Belarus (%)	Ukraine (%)	Total
Russian Orthodox	87.3	90.8	89.9
Roman Catholic	9.5	5.4	6.4
Other*	3.2	3.8	3.7

N = 2435
* Includes various Protestant denominations, Old Believers, and those who defined themselves as "Christian."
Source: Li-Ra-Ma Sample.

lower-middle class peasantry. They came from families that owned a house with a back garden, several acres of land, and one or two horses or oxen but still operated within the boundaries of the subsistence rather than the profit economy. An analysis of internal passports, some of which have data on their holders' occupations in Russia, showed that 62.3 per cent of the migrants were recorded as "agriculturalists," 30.9 per cent as "general labourers," 4.8 per cent as artisans, and 1.1 per cent were employed in "service."[41] There were also one teacher and two musicians.

These median figures, however, hide significant regional differences in the proportions of "agriculturalists" and "general labourers." While only 44.1 per cent of Ukrainians were recorded as "agriculturalists," among emigrants from Belarus they made up 80.6 per cent, with "general labourers" constituting 45.7 and 16.1 per cent respectively. The lower percentage of agriculturalists and the higher proportion of labourers among Ukrainian emigrants may have partly reflected the reality of greater social differentiation within the Ukrainian peasantry and the existence of a larger class of agricultural labourers compared to Belarus. But these statistics should be interpreted with caution. With seasonal wage work being a normal part of life in both Ukrainian and Belarusan villages, the lines between "agriculturalists" and "labourers" were generally less than clear-cut. Depending on the judgment of the local clerk or on the self-identification of the passport applicant, peasants of roughly the same economic standing could probably be classified as either "labourers" or "agriculturalists." The line between the rural artisans and the rest of the peasant population was drawn somewhat more precisely. Even though many of the artisans were also likely to own land, the skilled and well-rewarded nature of these men's work placed them in a separate category and usually allowed them to live off their craft.

Contemporary reports from areas of heavy emigration in Right-Bank Ukraine confirm a significant representation of artisans and tradesmen among the emigrants. "It is mostly artisans that are emigrating: carpenters, blacksmiths, weavers," a *Rada* correspondent wrote from the village of Chemyrivtsi in Kamenets District.[42] The village of Kniazhpil' in Proskurov District lost so many of its artisans to emigration that those in need of their services had to travel to neighbouring villages.[43] Not only were artisans prominent members of the migrant contingent, but they were also likely to leave first – a phenomenon observed in many other parts of Eastern Europe.[44] Although the absolute numbers of emigrating artisans were always small, they were significantly overrepresented among the early arrivals. After 1910, as emigration expanded both horizontally and vertically, the proportion of artisans in the emigrant stream declined.

The overwhelmingly peasant character of labour emigration from the western rim of the Romanov empire could not be altered by the presence of a very small number of lower gentry *(dvorianstvo)* among the emigrants. These were petty nobles, predominantly of Polish origin, many of them as ill-educated and probably as impoverished as the majority of their fellow peasant emigrants. Having little to lose at home, they were ready recruits for any adventure that could wrench them from poverty. Anton Zalesskii, a nobleman from Pruzhany District, whose brother worked on the Siberian railways, came to Vancouver in 1914. Lukian Rakhalskii immigrated to Montreal in 1913 from the town of Bershad' in Podolia, having crossed the border illegally like many of his peasant counterparts. Iosif Surent worked in Canada as a carpenter after leaving his native city of Vil'na in 1911.[45]

One of the most salient features of Ukrainian and Belarusan emigration from the Russian Empire, which would have important ramifications for the history of these communities in North America, was the lack of an educated or professional class in the migrant population. In this respect Russia was different from Galicia, Poland, Slovakia, or Italy, where emigration included a thin but visible stream of school-teachers, priests, and other ethnic intelligentsia, who quickly became the chief promoters of national consciousness among fellow emigrants. The explanation of this difference lies in the ethno-social structure of the Russian Empire, where Ukrainians and Belarusans were considered an organic part of the "Russian people" and lacked even such limited political, cultural, and religious self-expression as Poles, Finns, Germans, or Jews were allowed to have.[46] The result was not only a low sense of national consciousness among Ukrainians and Belarusans but also the lack of an ethnic elite capable of providing leadership in the process of national consolidation either at home or abroad. The several dozen Russian Orthodox priests who were present in Canada by 1917 were poor candidates for the role of ethnic community leaders, even when they came from Ukrainian or Belarusan backgrounds, for the Russian Orthodox Church served as a major agency of Russification and promoter of official Russian nationalism. Besides the clerics, the educated stratum among the migrants from Ukraine and Belarus was largely limited to a handful of revolutionaries and socialists who came to Canada in search of political freedom, but these were mostly ethnic Russians or russified Jews. Ukrainians or Belarusans were few in number among them and usually identified themselves with Russia at large. Like their revolutionary comrades back home, they showed little interest in taking up the cause of national consolidation.

MAKING THE CROSSING

For all emigrants, the journey to Canada began with crossing the Russian border. According to the Li-Ra-Ma data, 76 per cent of Ukrainians and Belarusans left Russia without passports in formal violation of the law. Some emigrants who lived near the Austrian border used "legitimating passes" to leave the country. The place and time of the crossing was determined by steamship agents and their local connections. It was usually safer for an emigrant to take the route offered by the agent than to travel on his own in an attempt to save money. In addition, few peasants had access to alternative sources of information, which would allow them to consider other travelling options. "Crossed secretly" and "crossed with the help of an agent" are the two most common answers found in the Li-Ra-Ma citizenship affidavits. Small border towns of Novoselytsia, Hukiv, Husiatyn, and Brody were the busiest crossing points for Podolians and Bessarabians on their way to western European ports and further to Canada. Peasants from Kiev and Volhynia usually travelled through Russian Poland, leaving the empire's territory near Myslowice, Sosnowice, or Prostkow, as did Belarusan emigrants from Grodno and Minsk.

By the early 1900s, transporting emigrants across the border had become a flourishing black market trade on the empire's western rim. Thousands of fortune seekers, assisted by hired guides, slipped through the loosely patrolled borderline. The guides were usually provided by the steamship agent or recruited from the local population, who knew the topography of the area and the workings of the border police. According to a 1913 report, in some areas of western Podolia local residents had almost entirely given up smuggling goods from Austria and turned to the more lucrative business of smuggling emigrants. In Kamenets, one could hire a guide to cross the Zbruch River, which formed the boundary between Russia and Austria, for six to ten rubles per person.[47] Every night, dozens of emigrants waded across the shallow waters of the Zbruch, carrying bundles of personal belongings on their shoulders. Others crossed the border in carts and wagons, hiding under heaps of hay or flour bags. The most ingenious method of deceiving border guards was probably practiced in Grodno Province, where emigrants placed their overcoats across the sand-covered security belt and used them to roll over to the other side without leaving footprints. Local agents, who reportedly invented this curious procedure, charged their clients eight rubles for the "roll-out" and two for the "roll-in" (for returning emigrants).[48]

On the other side of the border, the guide turned the emigrants over to an Austrian or German agent, who provided them with railway tickets to the port of departure and a contact address where they would receive steamship tickets. Hundreds of agent networks, organized in a chain-like fashion, functioned along the Austro-Russian and German-Russian borders.[49] The tight organization of the smuggling business usually ensured safe passage, but it did not make the crossing completely risk-free. According to one source, there were about 100 incidents every year when Russian border guards shot at trespassers.[50] Emigrants heading to the border also became victims of local racketeers or got caught up in conflicts between rival groups of agents, who settled their scores by reporting each other's emigrant parties to the police. Occasionally a guide would try to press his clients for more money by threatening to abandon them before the crossing was accomplished.[51] Most of the emigrants, however, crossed the border without much trouble.

If the crossing was successful, the emigrant proceeded to a major German and Dutch port or sometimes to the Adriatic port of Trieste. Those travelling through Germany to sail from Hamburg or Bremen had to report to one of the many "control stations" set up by the Prussian authorities along the Russian-German border. At these stations, emigrants were placed into barracks, inspected by doctors, divided into parties, and shipped to the port of departure on special trains. One of the largest stations of this kind was located in Myslowice on the Russian-German border. It was run by the large steamship agency of Max Weichmann, who was reported to employ about 500 sub-agents in the empire's western provinces.[52] Port inspection cards attached to some of the Li-Ra-Ma files show Hamburg and Bremen as the most popular ports of embarkation for Ukrainian and Belarusan emigrants travelling to Canada. Most of this traffic was carried by two German steamship giants – Hamburg-America Line (HAPAG), which operated out of Hamburg, and the Norddeutscher Lloyd, which ran passenger service between Bremen and Quebec. A large number of emigrants also took the Uranium Line, which was purchased in 1910 by the Canadian Northern Railway and began regular sailings between Rotterdam and Quebec continuing to New York. The Uranium probably had the lowest level of comfort and the poorest service among major European lines, but it also offered some of the cheapest third-class and steerage rates to Canada and the United States. The Uranium's reputation was damaged, however, by the deadly fire that occurred in October 1913 on its steamer *Volturno*, claiming about 150 lives.[53]

While western European ports drew the majority of Russia's illegal travellers, the legal emigrant traffic to Canada was channelled primarily through the Baltic port of Libava (Liepaja) on the ships of the Russian America Line, operated by the Russian East Asiatic Steamship Company. Before 1912, the majority of emigrants booked to Canada landed at New York – the final destination point for Russian America Line steamers – and headed north by land. This, however, was soon to change. In the spring of 1912, the Russian America Line was "approached by several Canadian Firms who informed [it] that the Canadian Railroads were in want of about 60,000 labourers, *preferably Russians*, and [was] asked if possible, to send over up to 1,000 per month by [its] steamers."[54] The interest in the proposed undertaking was mutual. The Russian America Line, which operated with meagre profits, had long been looking for opportunities to expand its business in the North Atlantic transportation market. For Canadian railway companies, an increased influx of Russian emigrants meant more passenger traffic and a new pool of navvies. In the spring of 1912, Halifax was made a transit stop for Russian America Line steamships sailing from Libava to New York. On 3 March the first Russian passenger ship, the *Lithuania*, pulled into Canadian waters. In late June, the first trial party of 100 labourers (apparently on pre-arranged employment) arrived in Halifax on the SS *Russia*, soon followed by 800 others.[55]

The opening of steamship service between Libava and Halifax allowed
Russian emigrants to travel directly to Canada at the moderate price of
60 rubles ($30). It was accompanied by a vigorous recruitment campaign
launched by the Russian America Line, and plans for translating and dis-
tributing Canadian promotional materials among prospective emigrants
were well underway by the fall of 1912.[56] A circular issued by the Russian America Line management instructed its agents to guarantee "immediate employment at Halifax" to all passengers booking their passage
with the company.[57] Advertisement posters distributed by the line emphasized its advantages as the only non-stop steamship service between
Russia and North America, allowing travellers to reach their destination
without frustrating changes of ship and repeated medical examinations.
A promotional poster issued by the company assured prospective passengers that they would enjoy the comfort of travelling in a familiar cultural
environment, "where everyone speaks Russian and where food caters to
Russian tastes and habits."[58] The brochure "How Do I Travel to America," produced by the Russian America Line in 1912, explained in detail
the booking procedures, services, and amenities provided onboard the
ships (even sample menus were not forgotten), as well as American and
Canadian admission regulations. Third-class and steerage passengers
awaiting departure were encouraged to use the company's newly opened
Emigrant House in Libava, where they could stay free of charge for five
days and enjoy the convenience of a library, a children's playground, hot-
water baths, and other facilities. For an additional fee, Russian America
Line officials helped emigrants without passports to obtain them from
the governor of Kurland Province.[59] Travellers were also invited to purchase insurance, which protected them against financial loss in case of
rejection at the destination port.[60]

The promotional measures paid off. By 1913, many Russian America Line ships probably had more Canada-bound passengers than travellers destined for the United States. "[F]or the present we have about
1,800 passengers lying here, out of which 1,400 are for Canada, so we
shall be able to fill the *Birma* with Canadian passengers alone," the
general manager of the Russian America Line reported to his superiors
in March 1913.[61] Statistics of emigrant departures from Libava in
1912–1913 compiled by the Russian authorities (see Table 9) demonstrate that the port's "catchment basin" included most Belarusan provinces as well as northern and central Ukraine. The figures supplied by
Russian statisticians correspond with data obtained from the Li-Ra-Ma
files, some of which contain information on the migrants' points of
exit. They show that Belarusans and Ukrainians from Volhynia and

Table 9
Emigration movement through the port of Libava, 1912–1913, by province of origin

Province	1912	1913	Total
Minsk	8,370	11,251	19,621
Volhynia	6,867	9,224	16,091
Grodno	7,018	7,130	14,148
Kiev ⟋	4,090	5,991	10,081
Saratov	5,949	3,492	9,441
Kovno	3,582	4,815	8,397
Vil'na	2,711	4,412	7,123
Samara	4,126	2,182	6,308
Mogilev	2,350	2,640	4,990
Chernigov	1,777	3,092	4,869
Podolia	1,113	2,058	3,171
Tersk	881	1,350	2,231
Total	48,834	57,637	106,471

Source: B. Kurchevskii, O russkoi emigratsii v Ameriku (Libava, 1914), 14–15.

Kiev reported Libava as their port of departure much more often than emigrants from the southwestern provinces, who preferred to use Bremen, Hamburg, Rotterdam, or Trieste.[62] Since it was possible to sail from a European port without a Russian passport, it is not surprising that the proportion of illegal emigrants in the southwest was much higher than elsewhere. According to the sample data, the average rate of legal emigration for the whole of Ukraine and Belarus was close to 23 per cent, but in Podolia it stood at 8.2 per cent and in northern Bessarabia at a mere 1.5 per cent. While channels of illegal emigration existed everywhere, peasants from provinces adjacent to the Austrian border had greater access to resources that enabled them to avoid passport hassles and to cross secretly to the other side.

After landing in Halifax, Quebec, or Saint John (depending on the chosen carrier), the immigrants were inspected by doctors, checked for the possession of the required minimal amount of money ($25 in the summer and $50 in the winter), and shipped into Canada's interior by one of the major railways. Under agreements concluded between the Russian America Line and Canada's two largest railway companies – the Canadian Pacific and the Grand Trunk – Russian passengers landing at Halifax were, until early 1913, divided evenly between the GTR and CPR. Both companies paid the steamship line a ten-per cent commission for each forwarded passenger.[63] Grand Trunk tickets could be purchased in advance through steamship agencies in Russia. In Russian-language flyers distributed to the passengers, the Grand Trunk was advertised as the "world's longest two-track railway under one management" and "the only two-track railway in Canada reaching all main destinations in the provinces of Quebec and Ontario."[64] By the end of 1912, negotiations about the sale of CPR railway tickets in Russia were also underway, but the fledgling cooperation between the two companies was brought to an end by the CPR's January 1913 withdrawal from the Atlantic Conference – the world's largest shipping syndicate, also known as "the Continental Pool."[65] After the negotiations were terminated, all passenger traffic originating in Libava was routed through the Grand Trunk, which did not own steamship lines and thus did not pose a threat to the Russian America Line.[66]

Russia's western frontier was among the last areas in Eastern Europe to become drawn into the Atlantic economy, but in the years prior to World War I it quickly became an important reservoir of unskilled labour for Canadian industries. Hundreds of villages in parts of Right-Bank Ukraine as well as western and central Belarus were affected by emigration, and some developed intensive migration chains leading to various Canadian destinations. The Dnieper River emerged as the geographical divide between the Atlantic and Russo-Siberian migration systems, although limited migration from areas further east also occurred.[67]

The migrant population was by no means a mirror image of the rural society in the donor areas. Examination of the socio-demographic structure of the migrant stream highlights the significance of age, literacy, marital status, and family size in the process of migrant selection. Although the social and demographic profiles of the migrants varied depending on the area of origin and time of emigration, most Ukrainians and Belarusans who set out on a transatlantic voyage were young married men, usually with one or two children. Women, either as individual migrants or the men's wives, constituted only a small fraction of the migrant total. Drawn primarily from the ranks of small landholders and agricultural labourers, most of the men who left their villages in pursuit of the dollar used temporary migration as an economic strategy that could allow them to avoid slipping into the inferior category of landless rural proletarians. Fulfilling their goal of building the family nest egg, however, would turn out to be a more challenging undertaking than most had expected.

3

An Airtight Empire?

When the first Ukrainian and Belarusan peasants reached Canada in the early 1900s, emigration in tsarist Russia was considered a marginal phenomenon, limited to the territorial and ethno-religious fringes of the empire and having little to do with the Slavic Orthodox population (the so-called "indigenous Russians"). Russian Jews began to emigrate in the early 1880s, soon followed by Poles, Lithuanians and Finns, but the masses of Slavic peasants east of Congress Poland remained outside the continental and transoceanic migrant streams. Mennonites and Germans from Volhynia, southern Ukraine, and the Lower Volga region were the only ethnic groups in the empire's heartland that provided substantial numbers of emigrants before 1900. At the turn of the century, they were joined by Russian and Ukrainian religious dissenters – Doukhobors, Molokans, and Baptists. Until the revolution of 1905, political emigration from the empire was also relatively small.

Prior to the 1900s, there was little official interest in emigration and scant public discussion of it. The imperial government kept no national tally of its emigrating subjects; only in semi-autonomous Finland and Poland did local authorities and public organizations collect some emigration statistics. The closest the Russian authorities ever came to recording emigration at the imperial level were the annual reports on the movement of people across the imperial borders, published after 1828 by the Customs Department of the Russian Ministry of Industry and Trade. These reports, however, made no distinction between emigrants and other travellers, nor did they classify them by ethnic or social background.[1] In fact, such a distinction was impossible, for emigration as a legal concept did not exist in tsarist Russia.[2] Anyone going abroad was *a priori* considered to be leaving the country temporarily and to all intents and purposes remained subject to Russian law. Even though emigration as such was not forbidden, Russian penal law contained harsh sanctions against any attempt to leave the country permanently or for an indeterminate period of time without first obtaining permission. Articles 325–327 of the 1903 Code of Punishments forbade "unauthorized abandonment of the homeland," which included staying abroad more than five years. Naturalization in a foreign country required the consent of the Russian authorities and prior release from Russian citizenship. Until the late 1900s, any propaganda of emigration on the imperial territory was considered a criminal activity punishable by arrest, exile, or disfranchisement.[3] However, the stringency of the juridical norms that regulated the procedures of border passage and temporary residence abroad was more a natural vestige of the autocratic system of government than a conscious policy aimed at restricting the outflow of the population. As will be demonstrated below, these legal provisions were routinely ignored in the real administrative practice of the late nineteenth and early twentieth centuries.

The unwillingness of the imperial government to develop a general policy on emigration was consistent with the underlying politico-legal doctrine of the Russian monarchical state, which rejected the notion of universal rights in favour of a complex system of duties and privileges specific to each category of its subjects. The emigration of certain classes of population such as religious minorities was handled on an *ad hoc* basis in accordance with the current political priorities of the Russian monarchy rather than with any general set of principles. This approach was applied, for example, to Jews – the largest and earliest group of Russia's emigrants. When the first wave of Jewish emigration began in the early 1880s, it caught the government without a clear policy on the issue. St Peterburg officials never objected in principle to the exodus of the Jewish population, since they were considered an alien and inassimilable minority, but as David Vital put it, Jews were granted "no explicit licence to leave the empire."[4] Like everyone else, they were the subjects of the tsar and therefore part of the human resources of the Russian state. By the early 1890s the pro-emigration attitude apparently recruited more supporters in the imperial capital. They argued that the permanent removal of the largest contingent of the empire's non-Christian population could be beneficial both politically and economically, as it would not only help eradicate the major source of ethno-religious tensions (and allegedly left-wing radicalism) but also reduce extreme overpopulation in the towns of the Jewish Pale. Guided by these considerations, the government in 1892 granted a charter to the Jewish Colonization Association (JCA), established by Jewish philanthropist Baron Maurice de Hirsch, to facilitate Jewish resettlement from Eastern Europe to other countries. According to the charter, Jews leaving Russia under the auspices of the JCA were exempt from paying hefty passport fees and received a preferential train fare to the Russian border.[5] However, these privileges came at a price: the emigrants had to renounce their Russian citizenship and were prohibited from returning to the homeland. Jews who emigrated on their own were not subject to these restrictions and could return to the empire if they so wished.

Similar policies were adopted in regard to group migration of persecuted Christian sectarians, such as Doukhobors and Molokans. Having failed to break the faith of these religious dissenters by repressive measures, the government lifted its long-standing objections against their permanent emigration from Russia. Probably the best-known enactment of this policy occurred in 1898–99, when approximately 7,700 Doukhobors were allowed to leave their homes in the southern provinces of the empire and move to Canada. In a confidential letter to the Ministry of Internal Affairs, the civil governor of the Caucasus Count Golitsyn wrote that mass Doukhobor departure "would facilitate the resolution of the Doukhobor question, for the removal from our territory of such a troublesome and dangerous element would seem very desirable."[6] Like the Jews leaving through the JCA, the Doukhobors too were barred from returning to the territory of the empire under the threat of "exile to remote localities."[7]

By the early 1890s, the Russian government was forced to deal with the first large class of transnational economic migrants – agricultural labourers from Russian Poland, who went for seasonal work to Germany and, to a lesser extent, Sweden and Denmark. Responding to numerous requests from the Berlin Government, which was interested in a steady supply of cheap labour for German Junkers, St Petersburg officials established special regulatory procedures for this class of migrants. In 1894, residents of Russian Poland who lived within three miles of the German border received the right to go to Germany for seasonal work on special free permits issued by the local police. After 1909 this privilege was extended to all Russian subjects going abroad as temporary agricultural labourers, regardless of their territorial origin (although it seems that few emigrants in the imperial heartland used this legal option).[8] According to another regulation, residents of Russian imperial territories bordering on Austria could travel there on personal business with special short-term permits known as "legitimating passes" *(legiti-matsionnye bilety)* that were valid for four weeks.[9]

The rest of the population were subject to the general provisions of the Passport Statute, which allowed individuals seeking to leave the country for up to five years to apply for a passport to the government of the province where they lived. Cumbersome and time-consuming, the application process had undergone little change since the mid-nineteenth century and involved a daunting number of bureaucratic formalities. First, all peasant applicants had to seek permission to emigrate from their village communes and to obtain proof that they did not owe the state any taxes. Following that, the local police captain had to certify that the passport seeker was not under criminal investigation or liable to military service. Women could not receive passports without written permission from their husbands. A similar procedure existed for town residents.[10]

Applicants for passports were also required to pay a ten-ruble processing fee plus an additional charge of five rubles, which went to the Russian Imperial Red Cross Society.[11] With the cost of application forms, the total fee amount reached seventeen rubles (approximately $9) – a sum which nearly equalled the average monthly earnings of a Russian farm labourer in 1913. If the passport (which was only valid for six months) expired while its holder was abroad, it had to be renewed at the nearest Russian consulate upon payment of another ten rubles.

Neither the Russian legislation nor the government was prepared to handle the increasing mass of economic emigrants streaming out of the country by the early 1900s. As a result, most emigrants spent months on passport hassles before setting out to America. Added to this were the red tape, corruption, and inefficiency that flourished at the lower levels of Russian government, turning a seemingly routine administrative process into a frustrating experience. Not surprisingly, many emigrants found it too demanding to comply with the passport regulations. "However bad it may be without a passport, with one it is even worse," peasants in Volhynia were often heard to complain.[12] A contemporary Russian author P. Tizenko estimated that the process of obtaining a passport could take up to six months, especially when the government offices were far from the emigrant's place of residence. According to other accounts, the total expenses incurred by the average passport seeker (including fees, postage, and travel expenses) amounted to over thirty-three rubles (approximately $17).[13]

If Russian authorities had attempted to consistently enforce passport and other regulations restricting the movement across the empire's borders, mass emigration from the empire would have become all but impossible. However, the usual failure of Russian law to keep pace with social change and the resulting discrepancy between legal norms and everyday administrative practices fully extended to emigration. By the early twentieth century – through a combination of bureaucratic negligence and attempts to reduce application backlogs – many regulations described above (including those imposing penal sanctions on emigrants travelling without a passport) had become a dead letter.[14] Emigration acquired a sort of quasi-legitimacy and was increasingly regulated by administrative precedent, which differed from the obsolete nineteenth-century statutes. As we have already seen, thousands of emigrants simply ignored passport law, slipping through the loosely patrolled imperial borders. According to contemporary estimates, illegal emigration from early twentieth-century Imperial Russia amounted to 75 per cent of the total.[15] If an illegal emigrant wished to return to the homeland, he simply declared his passport lost or stolen and applied to a Russian consul for a one-time entry permit, which was issued for a small fee after a routine check of the applicant's citizenship.[16]

Many officials in various levels of the government were aware of the archaic character of Russia's passport system, but change was slow to come. In 1906 the Ministry of Foreign Affairs admitted, in a typically heavy bureaucratic jargon of the time, that "the continued legal view of the passport as a document *permitting* a particular individual to reside abroad rather than as a certificate of one's identity, along with the complexity of passport-issuing regulations and high fees, leads to a situation of insurmountable difficulty for those Russian subjects who wish to regularize their passport status."[17] Some officials and public observers suggested eliminating passports altogether and replacing them with emigration permits to be issued for a nominal fee at the emigrant's place of residence.[18] Russian consuls, who had to deal with masses of illegal labour migrants lining up for entry permits in order to return home, also supported advocating simpler passport procedures. Mikhail Ustinov, who held the post of Russian consul in Montreal in 1912–13, advised the Russian Ministry of Foreign Affairs to "give free passports to all Russian workers who are going to Canada."[19] Some Russian Orthodox clerics in North America felt the same way, probably viewing easier emigration as a way to increase their flock. Rev. Theophan Buketov, who had served for one year in the Russian Orthodox parish in Montreal, wrote in the *American Orthodox Messenger* that emigration to America had a "civilizing" effect on the Russian peasantry and should be stimulated by the authorities rather than restricted by inefficient pass-port regulations.[20] By the early 1910s, the old emigration laws had few supporters left in either the government or among the general public.

Calls for the liberalization of Russia's passport system were part of the growing public discussion of the emigration question, which had been slowly gaining in strength since 1906–07. When Canadian and American immigration statistics first began to report quickly increasing numbers of "Russians," emigration finally began to attract the attention of the governing elite, social critics, economists, and all those who came into contact with population movements by virtue of their intellectual interests or professional duties. Assessing the latest trends in the emigration movement, a prominent agrarian economist N. Oganovskii wrote in 1914 that "the earlier emigrant types – the Jewish emigrant fleeing the pogroms in panic fear, [and] the marginalized politician – have been replaced by the common village workfolk, induced [to emigrate] by an agent of some legal or clandestine emigration bureau skilfully painting the picture of high pay in the United States or the vast land resources in Brazil."[21]

The motives that led the "Russian peasant" to leave his plot of land and seek a fortune in America began to concern Russia's educated class. The emigration theme had already inspired the imagination of at least one prominent Russian writer. In 1902, Vladimir Korolenko (1853–1921) published a short novel *Bez iazyka* (*Without the Language*). Based on Korolenko's personal impressions of emigrant life during his 1893 trip to America, the book described the dramatic story of Matvei Lozinskii, a Ukrainian peasant from Volhynia, who set out to America with his sister and a co-villager only to encounter mockery and abuse because of his foreign manners and inability to speak English.[22]

The lines of argument in the unfolding discussion on emigration were largely defined by Russia's post-1905 political discourse with its conflict between two dominant ideological orientations, which may be broadly defined as liberal-constitutionalist and national-monarchist.[23] For Russian liberals, who played the role of "loyal opposition" to the tsarist monarchy and advocated a broad program of reform, the growing labour emigration from the empire's western rim was first and foremost another proof of the poor state of the Russian peasantry, which required attention from both the government and the society at large. From about 1910 until 1914, publications on peasant emigration, ranging from brief reports to long analytical articles, increasingly appeared in the leading national journals of liberal orientation and in various liberal and *zemstvo* organs in the provinces.

According to the prevailing liberal view of emigration, peasants were pushed out of the country by the same economic forces that had long driven them to seek extra income outside the village.[24] For Oganovskii, the main liberal writer on emigration, the latest peasant exodus was little more than a new phase in the history of rural-urban labour migrations, which, if properly managed, could prove beneficial for both the peasantry and the entire nation. In a lengthy article written for the leading liberal newspaper *Russkie vedomosti*, he argued that "for Russia this work migration is a definite plus: we do not lose the emigrants – they return home with money and some knowledge of foreign culture."[25] Oganovskii also pointed to the fact that "American money" allowed a growing number of peasants in the western provinces to raise their economic status and to increase their landholdings.[26] Konstantin Voblyi, economist and author of the first major Russian study of the emigration question, discerned a similar connection between emigration and economic inequality. He argued that emigrants could have a positive impact on the sending country, especially if they kept "their nationality, their tongue, their mores and customs."[27] According to Voblyi, emigrants who remained loyal to their homeland would never align themselves with its enemies and would contribute to the development of international commerce. Therefore, he insisted, any country with high emigration should concern itself with the maintenance of economic and spiritual ties with its emigrants.[28] Publicists affiliated with Russia's transportation interests concurred with Voblyi's views, believing that the influx of emigrant money into Russia was a source of economic growth and better trade relations with the Western hemisphere.[29]

For the liberals, emigration was a complex phenomenon, and its short- and long-term effects still awaited a thorough analysis. Aside from pointing to the economic benefits of American cash flowing into the country, a number of liberal-oriented authors also argued that emigration had a strong "civilizing" effect on Russia's rural society. They noted approvingly that peasants returning to their villages after a two- or three-year stint in the United States or Canada possessed more energy and initiative than those who had elected to stay put. The returnees were also reported to be more polite, more respectful, and less addicted to drinking than their neighbours. Even Russian government officials, whose attitudes to emigration were normally less than friendly, occasionally admitted that exposure to American values transformed the peasants' work ethic, resulting in greater industriousness and discipline.[30] Some of the emigrants became more interested in education and self-improvement. Thus M. Volkov, a peasant from Tver' who settled in Michigan in 1907, wrote home that he was attending evening courses in agriculture after a day's work at the factory. Volkov's letters, published in one of the local *zemstvo* bulletins, extolled American agricultural practices and called for their introduction in Russia.[31] The liberals evidently hoped that returning "Americans" such as Volkov could become an important source of the new enlightened class of peasants for the modernization of Russia.

The government's slowness in tackling the question of peasant emigration led many liberal writers to consider the *zemstvo* as a possible source of assistance to the emigrants. The *zemstvo*'s recognized expertise in peasant economy seemed to lend itself to understanding the entire complex of issues related to peasant migrations. Many *zemstvo* councils had already been co-operating with the central government in carrying out a massive program of peasant resettlement across the Urals, which had become the cornerstone of tsarist agrarian policies after 1906. Social commentators of the time believed that the provision of emigrant aid and the collection of emigration statistics were a logical part of the *zemstvo*'s responsibilities, especially since the *zemstvo* employed a statistical system that was in many ways superior to that of the tsarist state. *Vestnik Novouzenskogo zemstva*, for instance, saw "no reason to doubt that zemstvo workers [...] if they were to include emigration in their work, would make it as orderly as they have already made [Siberian] colonization."[32]

The provincial *zemstvo* of Chernigov was among the first to bring the emigration question to public attention. In 1904 its monthly journal carried an article entitled "Novozybkov Peasants in America," which told its readers about the emigration of peasants from the district of Novozybkov, located in the province's north.[33] In later years, as more and more Ukrainian peasants caught the "America fever," other local *zemstvo* branches followed suit. Materials on peasant emigration began to appear regularly in *zemstvo* bulletins, although most of these were short reports chronicling emigration from a particular district or exposing dishonest steamship agents. An important role in facilitating the public discussion of emigration was played by the South-Russian Regional Resettlement Organization (SRRO), an association formed in 1908 by several provincial *zemstvo*s in Ukraine and southwestern Russia with the goal of promoting peasant colonization of Siberia. From 1911 to 1914, its journal published more than twenty articles related to emigration.[34]

The challenge that emigration was thought to present to the cause of Siberian settlement was a matter of concern for many *zemstvo* commentators. Even though emigration was not openly condemned and emigrating peasants received sympathetic treatment, moving to a farm in the homeland was considered a better and more natural alternative to the alleged tribulations of a transient labourer in a foreign country. One author hoped that emigration would abate if peasants were better informed about "the conditions of resettlement to Siberia, where they can always rely on the support of both the government and the *zemstvo*."[35] Another writer believed that the peasants simply lacked reliable information about what awaited them in America: "If only a portion of [the government's] expenses [spent on colonization] went towards acquainting those going to America with the arduous conditions of work overseas, it would probably direct some of the needed human resources to Siberia."[36]

By 1911–12, some publications in the Russian liberal press began to include practical information for prospective emigrants: travelling tips, brief descriptions of the economy, wages, immigration regulations of major destination countries, and the like.[37] This was hardly promotional literature of the kind that existed in other European countries, for its primary goal was to protect emigrants from the potentially harmful consequences of misinformation or idealistic expectations. Some works tried to convey their message in terms adapted to the Russian reader, including an article on Canada, which described that country as "the most suitable place for wage work in North America [...] A common peasant labourer makes three rubles a day in Canada, and one who knows a trade [makes] twice as much."[38] In an article called "How to Go to America for Work," written for a leading agricultural journal, F. Kryshtofovich, official agent of the Russian Ministry of Agriculture in North America, praised Canada as a country suitable for both settlement and wage labour: "For those who wish to settle in Canada its western part is more fitting. For those who seek work its eastern, more populated part [is better], primarily the province of Ontario with the cities of Toronto, Hamilton, St Thomas, and others. Winters in Canada in their severity resemble those in Perm' or Viatka. Its westernmost province, British Columbia, is much warmer but humid. In the western provinces there is plenty of free government land, which is allotted to settlers free of charge as homesteads, which are 50 desyatins [135 acres] each."[39]

But if Kryshtofovich portrayed Canada in generally favourable terms, he also cautioned his readers that "work in America has to be done quickly and strenuously, without losing a minute."[40] He warned

Russian peasants, whom he clearly thought to be sluggish and inert, that they should be prepared for the high intensity and strict discipline of industrial labour in North America. The cautionary tone was even more explicit in his other article, where cold Canadian winters, which "make window glass crack" and which had apparently ruined many Doukhobor settlers, were mentioned as something to be remembered by anyone intending to farm in Canada. After all, moving to Siberia might still be a better option for the land-seeking peasant: "Why go to Canada, when Russia has more than a few places similar to Canada? Many of them are both warmer and better."[41]

Many *zemstvo* publications lamented the lack of a national policy on emigration, which was blamed for the emigrants' continued misfortunes on their way to America. The *zemstvo* repeatedly attempted to draw the government's attention to the need for recording and studying the emigration movement. P.M. Novoselov, a professional statistician who had spent over a year in the United States, submitted a report to the 1912 conference of the SRRO, which revealed a poor state of national emigration statistics and a general neglect of the emigration question by Russian authorities. The report concluded that "neither the government nor the *zemstvo* [had] yet taken any serious steps towards the study of overseas emigration – this extremely important phenomenon in Russia's national life."[42] As a first step, Novoselov suggested the appointment of a Russian government agent on Ellis Island and the signing of an agreement with the United States that would provide for the collection of statistics on Russian immigrants.[43] The conference submitted an official petition to the Main Administration of Land Organization and Agriculture in St Petersburg, urging the government to begin recording and studying peasant emigration.[44]

While the *zemstvo* played a pioneering role in discussing peasant emigration and its impact on rural society, its interest in the subject by 1914 remained still very much at the data-gathering stage. With the exception of one attempt to establish a credit association for emigrating peasants, *zemstvo* officials had done little in the way of providing any direct assistance.[45] Nor did they have much time to develop practical measures, for when World War I broke out, mass peasant emigration from areas east of Russian Poland (except for a few localities) still had a very short history.

Emigration attitudes of Russian liberals and the *zemstvo* had much in common with those of Russia's nascent Ukrainian and Belarusan intelligentsia, which also stood in political opposition to the tsarist monarchy.[46] The growing proportion of Belarusan peasants in the emigrant stream attracted the attention of the empire's leading Belarusan-language newspaper *Nasha niva*, published in Vil'na since 1906 by a small circle of nationally conscious *littérateurs*.[47] Between 1906 and 1914, it featured some thirty publications on the emigration and life of Belarusans in America, including several pieces of poetry written by the Belarusan national bard Ianka Kupala and authors of lesser stature. Since Canada attracted a relatively small share of Belarusans compared to the United States, it was only rarely mentioned in the newspaper. The longest article on Canada, published in July 1912 by N. Charnotski, was devoted mostly to the discussion of its settlement opportunities. Prospective land seekers were advised to go to the Canadian West, where "one still can get good land of one's choice ... although far from the city, in the back country."[48] Though different in tenor and content, all of these materials expressed a sympathetic attitude towards the emigrants and emphasized the economic causes of the peasants' increasing flight off the land.

Like Russian liberals, most *Nasha niva* authors saw the overall impact of emigration on the peasant economy in positive terms. In a 1911 article "Emigration to the USA," the newspaper's editor Aliaksandr Ulasau estimated that "American money" accounted for at least three-fourths of all peasant capital in Belarus. Descriptions of hard emigration conditions and deceitful practices of steamship and labour agents were another prominent theme in *Nasha niva* publications. According to Ulasau, agent swindling could be prevented if the government closely supervised the emigration process and emigrants were better educated about what awaited them abroad.[49]

In Ukraine, peasant emigration was often discussed in the pages of *Rada* – the leading publication of nationally conscious Ukrainians in the Russian Empire, edited by Ievhen Chykalenko.[50] Despite the ambivalent attitude of Ukrainian activists towards the *zemstvo*, which they regarded as a vehicle of Russification, a number of *Rada* publications called upon *zemstvo* officials to take the initiative in organizing assistance to emigrating Ukrainian peasants. A July 1913 editorial described emigration from Russian Ukraine as a movement whose desirability and effects on the peasantry could be debated, but which required immediate government and public attention. "At present," the *Rada* editor observed, "our emigrants are left to themselves; they have no reliable information about the travel routes, the conditions which await [them] in America, or the American wages. As a result, [they] are being killed by guardsmen at the border, swindled by emigration agents, turned back from America, [and] heavily exploited by American entrepreneurs. It is obvious that if not the government, then at least the *zemstvo* should come to the peasants' aid. The time for this has come, for it has become clear enough that [emigration] is not a temporary but a long-term movement."[51]

Chykalenko called for a regional association of Ukrainian *zemstvos* for emigrant assistance, modelled after the South-Russian Resettlement Organization. Such an association, he hoped, would send its agents to each of the heavy-emigration provinces and to the main Russian seaports and American cities. Such agents could then provide the emigrants with necessary information, help them to find work, and protect them from mistreatment and abuse. Another publication commended the government on its recently announced plans to introduce a new emigration law, bringing organization and state supervision into the hitherto spontaneous movement.[52]

Canada enjoyed a much more prominent place on the pages of *Rada* than it did in *Nasha niva* – a natural consequence of the larger presence and much more vibrant cultural life of Ukrainians in that country. Notes about the life of Canadian Ukrainians, including reprints from *Kanadyis'kyi farmer* (*Canadian Farmer*) and other Ukrainian-Canadian periodicals, regularly appeared in the section "Ukrainians in America" along with less numerous reports from the United States. Most of these publications carried no promotional message, but there were exceptions such as the 1908 article by Iaroslav Kupins'kyi, reprinted in full from the Lviv paper *Hromads'kyi holos*, which praised Canada as a place with superior employment prospects for Ukrainian emigrants and a more developed Ukrainian community life compared to the United States. Kupins'kyi exhorted all Ukrainian emigrants "who set out to seek [their] 'fortune beyond the seas' [...] to choose one way – to Canada."[53]

Education of prospective emigrants was also carried out through the network of *Prosvitas* – Ukrainian cultural associations modelled on the Galician prototype. In 1908 the Kiev *Prosvita* produced a pamphlet entitled *Canada: What Kind of Land It Is and How People Live in It*. The publication contained a detailed overview of Canada's geography, history, political system, and economic development as well as advice for those wishing to settle or work there. A special section – "How Working People Live in Canada" – described the social conditions of Canadian farmers and farm workers as something that "our peasants cannot even dream of."[54] Written in an accessible style, the pamphlet was clearly intended for a peasant audience as well as for the rural intelligentsia (teachers, priests, etc.). V. Korolev's *Ukrainians in America*, which appeared a year later, was also written with a prospective emigrant readership in mind. Like most Russian and Ukrainian intellectuals, Korolev believed that while temporary emigration could benefit the peasantry, permanent settlement in America "weaken[ed] the native land," draining it of the most industrious workers.[55] The history of Ukrainian emigration to Canada and Ukrainian-Canadian community life occupied about half the volume. While Ukrainian farm settlements in the West received most of the author's attention, short term money-earning opportunities offered by Canada were also mentioned. The reader could learn, for instance, that miners and sawmill workers in labour-short British Columbia made as much as 10 rubles ($5) per day.[56] Practical recommendations for those considering emigration to "America" were also included:

Do not believe various crooks that wander through our villages.

[Before leaving] seek advice from well-informed people and find out everything in detail.

Do not go by yourself, it is better to leave together with other fellow villagers ...

People who are weak or ill should not go to a foreign country.

You should get good advance knowledge of the laws that are presently in force in this or that state.

Naturally, those who know the language of the country where they are going will earn more money.[57]

In contrast to the Russian liberals, who by and large held to the official doctrine of the "single Russian nation," Ukrainian and Belarusan political activists saw the emigration question not only as an opportunity to press for social reform but also as an important avenue for reaching out to the millions of Ukrainian and Belarusan peasants with the goal of awakening their national consciousness. This was done, for instance, by explaining to the emigrating peasants the value of mutual aid and national associations, which were deemed essential for survival in the foreign land. Aliaksandr Ulasau urged Belarusan emigrants in America to form fraternal societies along ethnic lines "in the same way as it is done [...] by Galician Ruthenians."[58] Another Belarusan author wrote that while "a steam plough in a co-operative can, of course, equally serve a Belarusan, a Ukrainian, a Lithuanian, or a Pole [...] each people needs its own songs, schools, and libraries."[59]

Around 1912, Belarusan political activists set up what they apparently hoped was a practical demonstration of the value of a national association: the Vil'na branch of the Warsaw-based Society for Assistance to Emigrants. Although little information has survived about the activities of this organization, it is known to have published the only emigrant guidebook in the Belarusan language before 1914. Entitled *Rady dlia emihrantou, katorye eduts' u Ameryku* (Advice for Emigrants Who Are Going to America), this sixty-four-page brochure contained extensive travel information, American immigration regulations, addresses of various agencies providing help to immigrants, a chart showing train fares from major US ports to various cities, including Montreal, and a Belarusan-English conversation aid. Like scores of other emigrant guides produced in early twentieth-century Europe, it warned the readers that "overseas one can achieve anything only through hard work," cautioning them against believing the stories of an American El Dorado told by steamship agents and often repeated in peasant "America letters."[60]

If liberals and ethnic activists approached emigration primarily from an economic perspective, Russian national-monarchist organs focused on its political and moral effects. The national-monarchist camp in early twentieth-century Imperial Russia comprised a motley assemblage of political groups, writers, and thinkers held together by a common adherence to the official doctrine of Russian statehood with its triadic formula of autocracy, Orthodoxy, and nationality.[61] The nationalists believed that emigration drained the country of its Russian-Orthodox population, destroying the peasant's mystical connection to the land and leading to the erosion of the patriarchal and communalist values of the Russian village. Such views were regularly aired in Russia's leading national-monarchist paper *Novoe vremia* and echoed in its counterparts in the western and south-western provinces: *Kievlianin, Podolianin, Severo-Zapadnaia zhizn'*, and others. Russian nationalists in the empire's multi-ethnic western provinces were especially vocal, fearing that a mass exodus of "Little Russian" and "White Russian" peasants to America would increase the proportion of Jews, Poles, Germans, and other "foreign elements" in the local population. Lamenting what it saw as the morally degrading effects of emigration, *Podolianin* went as far as to call it a "psychic disease of our peasant, which manifests itself in an excessive lust for money and 'gold'."[62] A correspondence from Proskurov District in Podolia, entitled "Flamboyance and Hooliganism," rebuked local peasants for their increasing preference for urban dress and lifestyle, which was explained, among other things, by their voyages to America.[63] The nationalists were quick to blame the new social evil on the mischievous "agent," who scoured the villages of Belarus and Ukraine, inducing the gullible peasants to desert their country. This kind of "conspiracy theory" was certainly not invented by Russian nationalists: in neighbouring Poland, for instance, it had been enunciated as early as the 1880s by the conservative gentry, who saw emigration as a threat to the survival of the Polish nation.[64]

"Agent-bashing," laced with Judeophobia, became one of the central themes of Russian nationalist writing on emigration. The deceit and swindling commonly practiced by emigration agents, most of them indeed of Jewish origin, were portrayed as qualities inherent to the "Jewish tribe." "Our peasants should not trust greedy agents (Jews), painting a rosy picture of American life," warned *Podolianin*.[65] Warnings of a similar kind could be found in many other right-wing periodicals, which widely exploited one of the favourite bogeyman images of Russian nationalists on the empire's western frontier – the ingenious and shifty Jew taking advantage of the honest but simple-minded Russian peasant.[66] Attached to communitarian values and convinced of Russia's predestination as the moral saviour of the Christian world, the nationalists portrayed "America" as a land of rampant commercialism, pragmatism, and individualism, where "religion and morality [were] nil."[67] The roots of all difficulties experienced by Russian emigrants in the New World were believed to dwell in the difference between the communalist and spiritually driven Russia and the individualist and pragmatic West. While such views were more common among the national-monarchists, in less Manichean forms they also extended to other parts of Russian society. Thus, a publicist disguised as S.R. wrote in the liberal *Vestnik Novouzenskogo zemstva* that for the "Russian character" the main purpose of human life lies "not in the pursuit of the dollar, but in that 'poetry of life', which Russian people (even Russian Jews) do not find anywhere outside the borders of their homeland."[68]

But even the nationalists had to admit that, while "emigration abroad is, of course, an *unnatural* and *undesirable* phenomenon which should not be encouraged [...] it is erroneous to think that [it] can be stopped or even reduced by police measures aimed at making border passage or the sale of steamship tickets more difficult."[69] Instead of trying to turn the clock back, they focused on pressing for government control over emigration as the only way of protecting emigrants from swindling and abuse at the hands of Jewish agents. "There is no doubt

that the absurd 'fortune-seeking' would have ceased long ago, had our
Russian authorities noticed this 'America fever' in time. In fact, they
still remain silent. The public sounds the alarm, but as for the government, it keeps calm," wrote *Kievlianin*.[70]

Circulating heart-rending stories of the hardships endured by "Russian workers" in America was one way in which the national-monarchist
press attempted to deter peasants from deserting the homeland. "Do
Not Go to America," "American 'Happiness'," "Tragedy at the Border" – these headlines, common to the right-wing writing on emigration, provide a sense of the general sentiment of these publications.[71]
While reports on the poor conditions of Russian emigrants also appeared in journals of other political orientations, the national-monarchist organs invariably told the same stories in a strong didactic tone,
instructing peasants to stay home and resist the lure of the American
dollar. The beginning of the worldwide economic recession in the summer of 1913 seemed to lend more credence to the right-wing position.
Accounts of unemployment and destitution among immigrant workers
in America spread throughout the Russian press and raised the pitch of
the nationalist emigration bashing ever further. Sometimes they included extensive quotations from letters, reportedly written by emigrants
who appealed for help or attempted to advise their correspondents
against emigration.[72]

Canada was often featured in these admonitory publications. In a series of travel notes from Canada published in July-August 1913 by
Kievlianin, Russian journalist M. Bernov described the scandalous treatment that many Russian workers received there. His correspondence
from Montreal told the story of sixty Russians swindled out of their
money and forced to walk from Quebec to Montreal.[73] Four of the victims were reported to have committed suicide by drowning themselves
in the St Lawrence River shortly after the incident. Obviously aston-
ished by the number of fellow Slavs he had met in the country, Bernov
exclaimed in his next letter from Canada: "You cannot imagine what a
great mass of Russian people Canada has! And every new ship arriving
from Europe brings more emigrants from Russia, mostly peasants from
the southern and south-western provinces – Podolia, Volhynia, and
others. All of them come to Canada lured by the big money, having
heard that wages here are two, three, four times higher than those in
Russia."[74] While some of these arrivals managed to find work, many
others, according to Bernov, filled the growing ranks of the unemployed
and "curse[d] the day when they came to Canada."[75]

The story of the sixty Russians became one of the most sensationalized accounts of this type in the contemporary Russian press, reverberating for several weeks in both regional and central newspapers, at times in what seem to be deliberately inflated versions. Thus, in the rendition that appeared in *Podolianin*, the number of the workers robbed of their wages somehow rose from sixty to two hundred.[76] The reprints were usually accompanied by indignant commentaries and renewed appeals for better government protection of Russian subjects working abroad. Hardly any of these publications, however, went on to suggest concrete measures for improvement.

The anti-emigration fervour of *Podolianin* and other local papers had its reasons: by 1912–13 Podolia had become the single largest area of peasant emigration in all of Russian-ruled Ukraine. Peasant exodus to "America" began to alarm the large local landlords, who suddenly found themselves threatened with a shortage and rising costs of agricultural labour.[77] In yet another attempt to stem the emigration tide, the same newspaper published in April 1914 "A Warning to Those Emigrating to Canada," reported to have come from the Russian consul in Montreal. Written in a condescendingly paternalistic style, the article described the emigrant workers as "Papuans of our south-western provinces," individuals "of low mental development" whose docility and ignorance made them a "desirable element for the local quasi-liberal and [quasi-] humane exploiters of white slavery."[78] The author urged the government to take immediate steps to inform all "unfortunate seekers of daily bread" intending to emigrate of the worsening situation in the Canadian labour market. The government of Podolia heeded the advice, circulating his message across the province.[79]

Public discussion of emigration in early twentieth-century Imperial Russia revealed a variety of reactions to the growing exodus of the country's Slavic peasantry. Attitudes to emigration ranged from outright condemnation to cautious acceptance, more often than not in keeping with the general political orientations of the exponents. Common to all, however, was the conviction that a national emigration policy was the order of the day, even though the motives for advocating such a policy were different.

By the early 1900s, the higher echelons of the Russian government were slowly coming to grips with the need to regulate emigration from the empire. The first signs of the government's intention to create new emigration legislation appeared even before the matter caught public attention. In 1905, at the initiative of the Division of Commercial

Navigation of the Ministry of Industry and Trade, a tsar's decree established a committee on emigration, which included representatives of seven ministries – Industry and Trade, Internal Affairs, Foreign Affairs, Finance, Transportation, Defence, and the Admiralty. Large steamship companies and the Jewish Colonization Association were also invited to participate. The creation of the committee was almost entirely a response to the increased pressure of Russian steamship interests engaged in the transportation of emigrants from Russian to European ports and, from 1906, directly to the American continent. Sharp competition from the more powerful German, Dutch, and British steamship lines, which carried the bulk of the migrant traffic, forced Russian shipping companies to appeal to the imperial government for protectionist measures. Russia's main players in the Atlantic transportation market included the Russian East-Asiatic Steamship Company (REASC), controlled by Danish and German capital, and the state-owned Volunteer Fleet.[80] In view of the opening of the direct line between the Russian Baltic port of Libava and New York, scheduled by the Volunteer Fleet for June 1906, government support of the Russian marine interests was regarded as especially crucial. Through a combination of state-authorized incentives and restrictions, the steamship companies hoped to draw part of the emigrant traffic originating in Russia away from Western European ports and redirect it to Libava and Riga – Russia's two main gateways to the Atlantic. One of the key changes advocated by the steamship lobby was an easier and more efficient passport system, which was expected to decrease the number of emigrants who avoided Russian ports because of passport hassles.[81]

In the summer of 1906, as the first Russian steamships cast anchor on Ellis Island, the emigration committee began its deliberations on the proposed draft of the emigration law. Prepared by the Division of Commercial Navigation, the document demonstrated considerable progress made by the tsarist authorities on the way to a formal recognition of the right of Russian subjects "to settle in a foreign state for an unspecified period of time."[82] The law also proposed a much simpler passport procedure (passports were to be issued free of charge within twenty-four hours of application), and established the imperial government's responsibility for protecting Russian subjects staying abroad. However, it also revealed the limitations of the imperial response to emigration, which clearly favoured the interests of the state and the steamship industry over those of the emigrants. Having granted a number of privileges to emigrants travelling through Russian ports, the law imposed restrictions on those who left the continent through European ports and proposed to ban foreign transoceanic steamship lines from selling tickets on imperial territory.[83] Such an approach reduced the government's policy to little more than a set of administrative regulations intended to suit Russia's shipping interests. No attempt was made to deal with the larger social implications of emigration or to consider providing assistance or information services to the emigrants. The proposed law, however, fell victim to a rift that developed between the Ministry of Industry and Trade and the Ministry of Internal Affairs over the control of emigration matters, and by the fall of 1907 the work of the committee had come to a standstill.[84]

The failure of the government to create a comprehensive legal framework for regulating overseas emigration was somewhat compensated by a number of piecemeal measures that effected a partial liberalization of Russian emigration procedures. Although rather limited, they demonstrated that the Russian authorities were becoming increasingly aware of the new reality of global migrations. In 1906, the government partially lifted the ban on emigration propaganda. In the revised version of the Code of Punishments such propaganda was no longer a crime in itself, and sanctions were to be imposed only in cases of knowingly spreading *false* information.[85] Some adjustments were also made in the passport system. Soon after the opening of direct steamship service between Russia and North America, the government of Kurland Province, which held jurisdiction over the port of Libava, was allowed to issue passports to any Russian subjects departing overseas regardless of their province of origin.[86] In November 1907, yielding to the pressure from Russian steamship companies, the government allowed them to open ticket agencies on the empire's territory to serve the growing emigrant clientele.[87] Previous requests to authorize these agencies had invariably fallen on deaf ears on the grounds that Russian commercial law contained no formal definition of such business operations.[88]

The Russian East-Asiatic Steamship Company took better advantage of the new opportunity than its main competitor, the Volunteer Fleet, which was forced to close its Russian-American line in 1908 due to financial losses. The REASC continued to offer a direct service between Libava and New York, carrying increasing numbers of America-bound emigrants. The company's more stable position in the transatlantic shipping market was due both to better management and to its membership in the Atlantic Conference. As a member of this steamship cartel, the REASC was guaranteed 2.5 per cent of the annual passenger

traffic from Europe to America and 3 per cent of the return traffic.[89]
Despite the REASC's relative success, its passenger lines operated with
substantial annual losses that were only covered by profits from commercial freight shipping. Searching for ways to remedy the situation,
some Russian writers connected to steamship interests called for the introduction of government-subsidized tickets and preferential train fares
for all emigrants leaving through Russian ports.[90]

While the interests of the Russian steamship industry continued to
dominate tsarist emigration policy by the late 1900s, other considerations were becoming just as important. The continuing spread of emigration from the outer limits of the empire to its interior, inhabited
primarily by Slavic and Russian-Orthodox peasantry, posed new challenges for the Russian authorities. As shown in the previous chapter,
the mass peasant exodus from the country, particularly from its ethnically diverse western provinces, went against the strategic interests of
the Russian monarchy, since it threatened to weaken the "Russian element" and to increase the political and cultural influence of ethno-
religious minorities (Jews, Germans, Poles, etc.). Some officials in
St Petersburg feared that the declining settlement opportunities in
Siberia would divert potential migrants abroad. A. Orlov, a senior em-
ployee of the Ministry of Industry and Trade, wrote in 1913 that "[i]f
so far there has been no causal link and relationship between external
migration and internal colonization, at the present time, with the satu-
ration of colonisable land east of the Urals, the labour-seeking emigration movement of the Russian peasantry from Russia's interior to
Europe and across the ocean is beginning to grow and will inevitably
continue to increase in the future."[91]

Amidst growing public awareness of emigration issues, the committee on emigration resumed its work in early 1910 under a new chairman – Deputy Minister of Industry and Trade P.I. Miller. This time it
was assigned the task of creating legislation regulating not only overseas emigration but also seasonal migration to European countries.
Temporary labour emigration became the primary focus of the committee's deliberations.[92]

In January 1910, the Ministry of Industry and Trade conducted a
comprehensive survey of emigration from various parts of the empire.
Provincial governors were asked to report on a wide range of questions:
causes of emigration, the ethnic and demographic composition and main
destinations of the emigrant population, the impact of emigration on the
economic and social life of the province, the number of returnees, etc.

While the survey results showed some variety in local emigration patterns, all the reports emphasized that labour emigrants were primarily peasant men between the ages of twenty and forty, who intended to spend two to five years in the United States, Canada, or South America before returning to their villages. Permanent emigration, according to the survey data, was limited primarily to the Jewish population.[93] As the governor of Volhynia remarked, "[a]mong the indigenous Russian population one does not observe a desire to emigrate forever."[94] Many of the reports acknowledged the economic causes of emigration, although such acknowledgment often went hand in hand with the familiar denunciation of the "agent." Assessments of return migration varied from 20 per cent in Podolia to 90 per cent in Minsk Province.[95] Most governors stressed the positive impact of American money and culture on peasant economy and morality, but the governor of Grodno also warned the government that some returnees brought back a "certain free thinking spirit," which "through the insufficient level of [their] intellectual development" had already led in several cases to "undesirable excesses."[96] Although the nature of the "excesses" was not specified, one suspects that it was a euphemistic reference to the radical views brought into the village by the peasants, some of whom became exposed to socialist agitation during their American sojourn.

The first part of the emigration law, which dealt with overseas migration, was approved by the Council of Ministers in February 1914 for submission to the Russian parliament (the Duma). The proposed law signalled important changes in Russian official thinking on emigration. Under certain conditions emigration could now be regarded as "favourable to the economic interests of the country," thanks to the influx of capital and knowledge from abroad. At the same time, permanent emigration was explicitly declared undesirable. All labour emigrants were assumed to be leaving the country temporarily, retaining the obligations – but also the privileges – of Russian subjects.[97]

According to the proposed law, general supervision of labour emigration was to be placed in the hands of a special Council on Emigration within the Ministry of Industry and Trade. The council was responsible for appointing emigration inspectors to the provinces and establishing government-run emigration agencies, which were to replace private agents and thus reduce exploitation and swindling. Special emigration commissioners, whose role was to provide information and protection to Russian-subject emigrants, were to be dispatched to major immigration centres in the United States, Canada, and elsewhere. It was also the intention of the imperial government to create a network of state-supervised labour and money exchange offices in all foreign countries with significant concentrations of Russian subjects.[98]

One of the most significant changes stipulated in the new law was the replacement of the notorious passports with five-year emigration permits, which could be issued by village or town police for a nominal fee. To be eligible for a permit, an emigrant had to leave through a Russian port and travel by a Russian steamship line. Those using the services of foreign carriers were required to apply for regular passports and to pay the requisite application and renewal fees.[99] This qualification, obviously inserted to protect the interests of Russian steamship companies, largely neutralized the positive effects of the changes in passport regulations: it was clear that illegal emigration would continue as long as travelling through European ports remained cheaper than departing from Libava.

The new law, however, was not fated to come into effect. The outbreak of World War I drastically changed the government's priorities, relegating emigration to a position of minor importance. The proposed legislation was shelved and never received a parliamentary hearing. By 1917, Russia still did not have an emigration law.

While a small cohort of lawmakers in the imperial capital wrestled with the emigration question, the government's day-to-day emigration policy continued to be guided by an inconsistent and often contradictory mixture of old and new approaches. Local tsarist administrators as well as higher officials within the Ministry of Internal Affairs regarded as suspicious anything that could be even remotely construed as promoting emigration among "indigenous Russians." Although the authorities seldom interfered with Jewish emigration societies, private suggestions to establish similar agencies for "Russian" peasants met with resistance from provincial governors and their superiors in Internal Affairs. In February 1913, the governor of Saratov Province refused to grant approval to the proposed opening of two private emigration agencies on the grounds that emigration from the region was "already considerable."[100] The governor of Podolia went even further when he insisted in August 1913 that even officially authorized Russian steamship agencies in the province's rural areas should be closed, for they caused "serious damage to state interests" by inducing local Ukrainian peasants to emigrate.[101] Apparently frustrated with the government's inaction, he tried to recruit the help of the Orthodox clergy in warning local peasants about the perils of emigration.[102]

Even such seemingly innocent suggestions as providing emigrants with officially authorized information about a destination country made the imperial authorities uncomfortable. Nicholas Passek, whose brief tenure as Russian consul general in Canada (1912–13) coincided with the heaviest wave of labour immigration from Russia, produced a pamphlet in 1913 entitled "Advice and Suggestions for Russian Immigrants Arriving in Canada." The slim brochure was handed out to Halifax-bound passengers of the Russian America Line along with copies of Canadian immigration and labour regulations. It warned Ukrainians, Belarusans, and Poles arriving in Halifax not to trust "Jewish agents" and urged them to use the services of the Russian vice-consulate, which could "provide the newcomers with various aid and full assistance."[103] Obviously pleased with the pamphlet, the management of the Russian East-Asiatic Steamship Company suggested that it also be distributed among the general population in areas where emigration to Canada was substantial. At this point, however, the Ministry of Internal Affairs, always on guard against emigration propaganda, sounded the alarm. Its Police Department strongly objected to the idea, pointing out that such a pamphlet would lead peasants to believe that "in Canada employment for foreign workers is guaranteed [and would] only serve to increase the outflow of our workers to America, which has already reached immense proportions in the last years."[104]

The Russian government might not welcome too much initiative on the part of its consular officials, but it increasingly recognized the importance of the consulates as the main vehicles for supervising hundreds of thousands of Russian labour emigrants across the western hemisphere. By 1917 the Russian Ministry of Foreign Affairs had seven consular missions in the United States, one in Mexico, three in South America, and three in Canada. The first Russian consulate in Canada was established in 1899 in Montreal, with Nicholas Struve as consul. A memorandum from the Ministry of Foreign Affairs cited "a considerable and ever growing influx of Russian emigrants to the country" as one of the key reasons for opening the Montreal consulate.[105] In Halifax, Canadian businessman Henry Mathers was retained as honorary consul, primarily to deal with matters of commercial shipping. It was not long before the increasing immigration from Russia caused Struve to suggest that another consulate be opened in Winnipeg.[106] Nicholas Passek and especially his successor Sergei Likhachev, probably the most competent of all Russian imperial consuls in Canada, continued to broach the subject with their superiors, but no progress was made until 1915, when the growing amount of Russian-Canadian trade in the Pacific led to the opening of a consulate in Vancouver.[107] The newly created consular district included British Columbia, Alberta, and the Yukon. Dealings with Russian subjects residing in Saskatchewan, Manitoba, and eastern Canada remained the responsibility of the Montreal consulate.

Russian consuls abroad were charged not only with issuing travel papers and providing information and assistance to Russian subjects who lived within their jurisdictions; they were also increasingly called upon to monitor their political orientations. Russia's new Minister of Foreign Affairs S.D. Sazonov made the efficiency of the consular service one of his priorities. In a January 1912 circular from St Petersburg, Russian consuls across the world were reminded of the need to take "care of the interests of Russian subjects in foreign countries and [give them] protection when necessary."[108] The circular defined the consul's position as that of the "head *(glava)* but by no means the superior *(nachal'nik)* of the Russian colony in his district" and instructed the consuls to display "personal accessibility" and "an attentive and considerate attitude" to the concerns of their clients.[109]

Despite these good intentions, the quality of consular assistance received by emigrants continued to depend on the professional competence and personal aptitude of the tsarist diplomats. Many consuls, especially old bureaucrats like Nicholas Passek, were recruited from the ranks of the nobility and treated their peasant clients in a condescendingly paternalistic manner, believing that they had brought their troubles upon themselves through gullibility and lust for money. Russian journalist M. Bernov wrote from Montreal that mistreated Russian workers had nowhere to turn for help, because Passek was "never in his office and obviously [had] his own understanding of service so far away from the eyes of his superiors."[110] It was apparently common for the consuls to regard their illiterate and rough-mannered visitors as annoying intruders in the smooth bureaucratic routine of their institutions. A 1906 digest of annual consular reports to the Second Section of the Ministry of Foreign Affairs mentioned that Russian Jews, "characterized by pushiness and insolence," were seen as a particular nuisance by some consuls.[111] When a consul was more amenable to dealing with his peasant and working-class clientele, insufficient funding and inadequate personnel usually limited his ability to provide proper assistance to them. According to the Russian newspaper *Novoe vremia*, the Russian consulate general in New York received only $500 a year from St Petersburg for the purpose of assisting destitute emigrants.[112]

Complaints of the indifference shown by Russian consulates to the plight of their needy compatriots were not uncommon, and sometimes they reached the Russian public and even the members of the Duma. In March 1914, following a number of disturbing press reports of massive unemployment among emigrants in the United States, forty-three Duma deputies made an official inquiry to the Ministry of Foreign Affairs about the measures taken to provide help to destitute Russian subjects abroad.[113] The Ministry admitted its knowledge of the problem, but maintained that aid could only be granted in exceptional cases: "There is such a great mass of emigrants that our consuls cannot help all of them in such a way as one would desire."[114] In January 1915, the subject was raised again in the Duma budget committee during the discussion of the annual appropriations for the Foreign Service.[115]

Mass emigration was a relatively new problem for Russia in the early twentieth century, and both public and official attitudes to it displayed a mixture of conflicting approaches. On the one hand, repeated attempts to create universal legislation regulating emigration from the empire were a definite sign of change. Although these attempts were foiled by bureaucratic inertia, an instinctive fear of any political innovations and, finally, the onset of war, they nonetheless showed a slow movement within the Russian state towards a monarchy based on the rule of law rather than a tangled fabric of group-specific privileges and obligations. On the other hand, a significant part of the educated class and the governing elite continued to view people as "human capital," a sort of state property necessary for the economic health and cultural survival of the nation. For them, emigration was a social evil or at best something that could only be tolerated because there seemed to be no effective way to prevent it.

The availability of vast colonisable lands in eastern and southern Russia made it different from other European countries. As a result, many naturally saw the solution to the problem of rural overpopulation not in terms of emigration but in the redistribution of the peasantry within the country, first of all through the colonization of Siberia. In these circumstances, emigration as a way of resolving socioeconomic tensions could hardly become a viable alternative to internal resettlement, as was the case, for instance, in mostly Ukrainian-populated eastern Galicia. The roots of ambivalent attitudes towards emigration also lay in the intellectual precepts and stereotypes of a traditional agrarian society, which tsarist Russia basically retained until 1917. Although modernization and urbanization had made some inroads into traditional culture, the belief in the intrinsic tie between the Russian peasant and the land was still well entrenched in early twentieth-century Russian thinking. Emigration may have been acceptable as long as the peasant returned home with American money and continued to till his farm. However, it became a problem at the point where it threatened to completely sever the peasant's connection with the land and transform him into an uprooted wageworker.

As statesmen and political commentators debated emigration, hundreds of thousands of Russian subjects were voting for it with their feet with little regard for the punitive laws, which increasingly existed only on paper. Mass emigration, primarily economic in its nature, could not be stopped – and the most far-sighted of Russian politicians realized that. If Russia had ever been an airtight empire, by 1914 it certainly was no more.

4

"So Close to Being Asiatics"

On 19 March 1909 the Ottawa *Free Press* carried a short article with a title that must have caught the attention of some readers and mystified others: "Russian Moujiks for G.T.P. Work."[1] It reported the landing of a group of "Russian labourers" at Vancouver for employment in the construction of the Grand Trunk Pacific (GTP) Railway. A few weeks later, an article in the Vancouver *Evening Post*, entitled "Russian Invasion Next," predicted that Canada was on the threshold of a massive inrush of "Slavs from Siberia." Quoting an unnamed passenger who had just arrived from Japan, a major transit point for Russian immigration to North America, the writer opined that after the Chinese, Japanese, and Hindus, the "next immigrant invasion [to Canada] will be of Russians."[2] Increasing numbers of Russian emigrants, apparently dissatisfied with the "unsettled conditions" in the tsar's realm, were reported to be gathering in the Far Eastern ports and waiting for an opportunity to proceed to Canada.

Prior to the spring of 1909, "Russians" was a word that was seldom if ever mentioned in Canada in the context of labour immigration. As a generic term referring to all subjects of the tsar regardless of their ethnic origins, it was often applied, collectively or individually, to Russian-born Jews, Germans, Poles, or even Finns – in short, to all groups which constituted the early immigration from the Russian Empire. This time, however, it seemed as if "Russian labourers" had made their first appearance on the Canadian horizon as a distinct group.[3] As we will see below, the 1909 episode would have a considerable impact on Canadian policies with regard to the "Russians," who would soon become one of Canada's largest groups of immigrant workers.

The influx of foreign labour into early twentieth-century Canada was a corollary of the unparalleled economic expansion that had begun in the late 1890s. Agriculture and resource industries (such as mining and lumbering) enjoyed particularly high rates of growth. The rapid settlement of the West, along with the demand for improved infrastructure created by the fast pace of industrial development, led to a railway construction boom. Canada's second and third largest railway companies (the Grand Trunk and the Canadian Northern) were building two new transcontinental lines in addition to the Canadian Pacific. Only 30 per cent of immigrants who came to Canada between 1896 and 1914 immediately took homesteads in the West. The rest headed for the cities or found employment as unskilled labourers in resource industries, railway construction, and agriculture.[4] Labour immigration shot up despite the fact that Canada's official immigration policy, as formulated by Clifford Sifton, Minister of the Interior in 1896–1905, explicitly favoured non-industrial categories of immigrants: agriculturalists with means sufficient to run a homestead, farm workers, and domestic servants. Under Sifton, the source areas of Canadian settlement immigration expanded to include not only the traditional "preferred" countries such as Britain, Germany, or Scandinavia, but also eastern and central Europe, particularly Galicia and Bukovyna. Tens of thousands of Galician and Bukovynian Ukrainians entered Canada in the late nineteenth- and early twentieth-century and settled on the Prairies. While mass Ukrainian immigration to Canada had already begun in 1891, it assumed especially large proportions during Sifton's tenure.[5]

In contrast to late nineteenth- and early twentieth-century Slavic immigration from Austria-Hungary, which was driven largely by Canadian settlement opportunities, few farmers were coming from areas east of the Austro-Russian border. The abundance of farmland in Siberia, the stringency of laws regulating land tenure, and obsolete passport laws made settlement in North America a difficult option for Russia's peasants. Furthermore, neither the Canadian government nor the Russian public made any effort to advertise the Canadian West in Russia. The history of Canadian immigration demonstrates that a movement of settlers from non-traditional donor areas, particularly those inhabited by "non-preferred" races, rarely occurred without the help of emigration promoters in the country of origin (Jozef Oleskow, who opened Canada to Austrian Ukrainians, is a good example). Such promoters, however, could hardly appear in tsarist Russia, where the ruling elites considered Siberia the best destination for land-hungry peasants west of the Urals (religious sectarians, whose emigration raised few objections, were an exception).

Rare voices calling to promote settlement immigration from Russia failed to find the support of Canadian policy makers. An unsigned 1890 memorandum to the Minister of Agriculture argued that peasants from northern Russia would be the best settlers for Canada's Northeast: "I think that the Dominion government should by all means have an agent in Russia. The North-West can be populated by the British Races easily but [the Northeast] should be opened up also and no race is better fitted for it than are the Russians."[6] But without any interest coming from Russia, the Canadian government was unwilling to tread the risky path of recruiting immigrants in a country known for its prohibitive emigration laws, unwieldy bureaucracy, and the general backwardness of its peasantry.

Although in the late nineteenth century the majority of Russian subjects who came to Canada were of Jewish and German origin, there were signs of a growing awareness of Canadian settlement and employment opportunities among Russia's Slavic peasantry. The Department of the Interior (which was responsible for immigration between 1893 and 1917) commissioned University of Toronto professor James Mavor to make a trip to Eastern Europe in 1900 with the goal of studying potential new sources of immigration to Canada. A recognized expert in Russian affairs and an active champion of the Doukhobor cause, Mavor visited several regions of the tsarist empire, including Ukraine and Belarus. In a confidential report submitted to the Department of the Interior, he mentioned "several thousand Russian peasants" from Minsk Province, who had reportedly approached a ticket agency in Finland that shipped emigrants to Canada. Mavor also had a meeting with Prince Khilkov, a known Russian dissenter and devoted supporter of the Doukhobors, who informed him that "some 1400 peasants, part of them from [his] estate near Kharkov, might migrate to Canada."[7] Many of these peasants probably belonged to the pacifist religious sect of Pavlovtsy, which held views similar to the Doukhobors and had a large following in Khar'kov Province.

There is no evidence that Mavor's report prompted any official action to promote peasant emigration from Russia. Nor did Canadian immigration authorities seriously contemplate attracting Slavic peasant settlers from the tsarist empire in later years. Among Canadian promotional materials translated into a dozen languages and distributed across Europe by immigration and steamship agents, there was not a single pamphlet in Russian (few Ukrainian peasants in Russia at the time would have been able to read Canadian booklets printed in "Ruthenian" for Galician and Bukovynian immigrants). "The Canadian government as such takes absolutely no part in the propaganda of emigration in Russia," Russian consul Nicholas Struve concluded in a 1910 report to St Petersburg.[8] Russian Germans and Mennonites, who had established a reputation in Canada as first-class farmers, were the only Russian subjects sought out by Canadian immigration authorities.[9] W. T. R. Preston, chief inspector of Canadian immigration agencies in Europe, paid a brief visit to Russia in 1899 to survey the possibilities of bringing new parties of German settlers to Canada.[10]

When the Canadian government finally began to discover Russia as a possible source of peasant settlers, it was too late to undertake any promotional efforts. On 22 July 1914 Lloyd Roberts, an official in the Immigration Branch, called the attention of his superiors to an American report which praised the Russian peasant as a "worthy settler" and encouraged Washington to promote agricultural immigration from the Russian Empire. "At present we [also] ignore [the Russian peasant], not even having a Russian pamphlet," Roberts wrote, suggesting that the current policy be reviewed.[11] Two weeks after Roberts's memorandum, however, Canada entered World War I.

While Canadian authorities did not attempt to promote mass peasant emigration from Russia, agents of private Canadian land companies made their own bid to attract settlers from some areas of the tsarist empire. In 1913, several peasant families from Bessarabia were induced by a Jewish agent to leave their village and settle near Canora, Saskatchewan on the property of Canada Lands Company, where they found "nothing but forest, marshes, water, and stones."[12] There were also a number of private schemes designed to bring Russian religious sectarians to Canada, but aside from the 1899 immigration of Doukhobors none of these plans came to fruition. One such scheme was conceived in 1913–14 by A.M. Azancheev, a Vancouver entrepreneur of Russian origin, who formed the Russian Colonization Syndicate with the intention of settling some 4,000 Russians on British Columbia and Alberta lands belonging to the Grand Trunk Pacific Railway. The majority of the initial settlers were to come from the Russian dissenter sect of New Israelites, who would then be followed by other land seekers.[13] Azancheev's project failed when the New Israelite leaders rejected Canada in favour of Uruguay. But his other idea – the establishment of direct steamship service between Vancouver and Vladivostok in order to stimulate Russian immigration – proved to be more in tune with the times.[14] Russian steamship interests were already contemplating the opening of a Pacific route to Canada, and in October 1914 the Russian Volunteer Fleet began regular sailings between Vladivostok and Vancouver.[15]

Virtually all Russian, Ukrainian, and Belarusan immigrants from the Russian Empire came to Canadian shores as labourers rather than as Clifford Sifton's sheepskin-clad farmers. Formally, Ottawa discouraged the immigration of industrial workers, particularly from "non-preferred" countries such as Russia or Austria. The Alien Labour Act of 1897, adopted largely to accommodate the interests of Canadian labour unions, specifically prohibited the importation of contracted foreign workers into Canada.[16] Government policy became even more selective under Sifton's successor Frank Oliver, who headed the Department of the Interior until 1911 with the help of the new director of the Immigration Branch W.D. Scott. In 1908, reacting to the arrival of large numbers of East Indian immigrants on the West Coast, the government passed an order-in-council (PC 27) introducing the "continuous journey requirement," which granted the Department of the Interior the right to reject immigrants who did not come directly from their country of birth or citizenship. Another order-in-council (PC 28) stipulated that every immigrant entering Canada (with the exception of those going to pre-arranged farm or domestic employment, or having family or kin capable of providing support) had to possess $25 ($50 if coming between 1 December and 15 February).[17] Both provisions were subsequently incorporated into the new Immigration Act of 1910, which, as Ninette Kelley and Michael Trebilcock pointed out, substantially increased the discretionary powers of the executive branch of the government in the area of immigration policy.[18] In practice, however, the Immigration Branch rarely took a firm stand against labour immigration from Europe. As Donald Avery has demonstrated, Ottawa was usually willing to accommodate the labour demands of Canadian industries and interpreted the laws regulating the entry of industrial workers in a rather flexible way.[19]

By the mid-1900s, the largest demand for immigrant labour in the Canadian industry came from the country's major railway companies, which employed tens of thousands of foreign workers through dozens of contracting and sub-contracting firms.[20] Throughout the early 1900s Canadian railway interests continued to apply pressure on the government in order to obtain a relaxation of admission policies.

Ample evidence of these efforts can be found in the archives of the Grand Trunk Railway, then Canada's second largest railway company. W. Smithers, the chairman of the Grand Trunk, wrote to the company's president E.J. Chamberlain in October 1912: "I hope you have taken up the question of obtaining labour in the North West, and I think whether the Government consents to a relaxation of their regulations or not, you should write them your views on the subject in order to have it on record that we have done all that is possible to press for the introduction of more men."[21]

As we have seen, limited migration to Canada from areas east of Russian Poland occurred as early as 1905–06 (and probably earlier), but it was not before the 1910s that peasant-workers of eastern Slav origin (primarily Ukrainians and Belarusans, but also ethnic Russians from Saratov and Samara provinces) became a dominant group among Russian-born immigrants. In their search for new sources of cheap labour, Canadian industrial companies were increasingly turning to the untapped Russian market. In 1906 and 1907, two Canadian pulp-and-paper companies inquired with Russian consul in Canada Nicholas Struve about the possibility of obtaining "Russian and Polish workers."[22] In the fall of 1906, the Grand Trunk Pacific Railway attempted to negotiate an agreement with the Russian government about bringing a party of 10,000 navvies to Canada on a temporary basis. The idea was put forward by Consul Nicholas Struve, who apparently saw it as a way to reduce growing unemployment in Russia. As Struve explained to GTR general manager Frank Morse, the plan would involve the recruitment of groups *(arteli)* of skilled workers in Russia on twelve-month contracts. A special agent in Russia was to oversee the recruitment operations and serve as the liaison between the Russian authorities and the Grand Trunk management. The GTR was to assume the cost of the workers' transportation and subsequently deduct it from their Canadian earnings. Struve was careful to point out to Morse that the workers' stay in Canada would be strictly temporary, as permanent emigration could "not possibly correspond to the views of the [Russian] Imperial Government."[23]

The GTR initially responded to Struve's proposal with enthusiasm, but several encounters with Russia's state bureaucracy were enough to dampen its interest in the idea. In addition to an array of logistical difficulties (such as the need to get the plan approved by the Russian Council of Ministers), Struve and Morse found it difficult to agree on the workers' wages and other conditions of their contracts. Although the project was eventually dropped, the GTR maintained a strong interest in Russian labour. Three years later, the company again raised the question of labour emigration with St Petersburg officials, this time on its own initiative. Louis Kon, head of the GTR labour department and himself an immigrant from Russia, wrote to the Russian Ministry of Internal Affairs about the shortage of railway labour in Canada and requested permission to recruit workers in Russia on two- or three-year contracts. He assured the Russian authorities that the company would provide the workers with "good meals, lodging, care and supervision," and would also pay for their return transportation to Russia.[24] The outcome of this scheme remains unknown, but it likely met the same fate as the 1906 project.

Not surprisingly, an increasing number of large Canadian employers found clandestine recruiting a much more efficient way of obtaining Russian labour. According to Edmund Bradwin, author of *The Bunkhouse Man*, "a trusted Russian" went back to his native village in 1911 with money advanced by a railway sub-contractor and returned with sixteen "stalwart countrymen."[25] The Canadian Dominion Iron and Steel Corporation (DISCO) hired labourers in Russia, using its London office as a base for European recruitment operations and reportedly paying its agents a commission of $3 for each contracted worker.[26] Canadian coal mining companies, faced by a series of strikes in 1912–13, attempted to recruit scabs in various Russian provinces.[27]

There is also some evidence that the Canadian Pacific Railway was showing an increasing interest in Russia's Pacific rim. In 1911, the Russian press reported that two CPR agents known as Perelstruz and Kashnitsky had set up a steamship office in the Manchurian port of Dairen (then part of Russia), offering transportation to Canada, Australia, the United States, and Hawaii through Yokohama, and advertising employment opportunities in these countries.[28] L. de Lara, who presented himself in Russian newspapers as the "Steamship and Railway Agent of Canada," ran a network of associates in Vladikavkaz, Khar'kov, and other southern Russian and Ukrainian cities, spreading information about the high demand for labour in Canada and guaranteeing a daily wage of $2.50.[29]

The arrival of fifty Russian labourers in Vancouver in March 1909 was probably the result of de Lara's recruiting activities. The coming of the "Russians" put Canadian immigration authorities under pressure to define their attitude towards this new class of immigrants. In view of high labour demand in British Columbia, J.H. MacGill, the government

immigration agent at Vancouver, decided to overlook the newcomers'
indirect passage to Canada and arranged their employment with
MacDonald and Gzowski, a large contractor firm for the Canadian
Pacific Railway.[30] But when several smaller groups of immigrants followed the first party, British Columbia immigration officials, always
wary of any "undesirable" foreigners, rang the alarm bell. MacGill reported to W.D. Scott, head of the Immigration Branch, that the CPR
"had been approached with regard to the transportation from Japan to
Canada of about 10,000 Russians" and asked for instructions.[31]

Ottawa's hasty consultations with British diplomats in Japan failed
to produce information about any secret schemes to import Russian labour.[32] What *was* discovered, however – and discovered with obvious
concern – was that some of the incoming "Russians" appeared to be
"Turks, Circassians, and other Caucasian tribes" (in reality, they were
Ossetians and Georgians – terms which early twentieth-century Canadian immigration officials would not have known).[33] This troubling
fact immediately added a racial dimension to the discussion of Russian
immigration, as Canadian officials struggled to find a proper place for
these newcomers in the ethnic classification system used by the Immigration Branch. MacGill wrote to Scott that he foresaw "considerable
difficulty in distinguishing the European or Asiatic origins of this Slav
immigration [sic], whose passports will all apparently be issued at their
point of departure from the Russian Empire."[34] The major cause of
concern, aside from the traditional view of Russia as not quite part of
Europe, was the impreciseness of the term "Russians." As noted above,
it was often used as a label of convenience for all subjects of the tsar,
including those that might happen to fall within the "Asiatic" category
by virtue of their place of birth. In addition, there was little in the physical appearance of the Ossetian immigrants that would enable Canadian immigration inspectors to easily identify their "Asiatic" origins.
Attempting to dispel the government's concerns regarding the racial
suitability of the immigrants, W.M. Stitt, CPR's general passenger agent
for eastern steamship lines, described them as "white men having been
employed on farms and at other work in Siberia, [who] will make desirable settlers for our west, both for the harvest fields and public
works."[35] The vigilant Immigration Branch gatekeepers, however, were
not easily convinced. Racial prejudice and the fear of stirring up anti-
Asiatic sentiments on the Pacific Coast were pushing Ottawa towards
an exclusionary attitude.[36] In November 1909, as the matter continued
to be broached, Scott wrote to Frank Oliver that the arriving Russians

"may be technically European, but they are so close to being Asiatics that I think we would do well to regard them as such. I do not regard them as good immigrants for Canada and I think that the movement ought to be discouraged as soon as possible."[37]

The racial composition of trans-Pacific immigration from Russia was not the only motive that drove Canadian immigration authorities to take restrictive measures. As if unsure of the validity of its racial argument, the Ottawa government soon found another reason to stop Russian immigration via the Pacific. In March 1911, Assistant Superintendent of Immigration L.M. Fortier wrote that "one of the reasons why Canada does not favour the immigration of people from Siberia is the fact that that part of the Russian Empire is used as a sort of penal colony and we would be likely to get among the immigrants quite a percentage who were really of the criminal class."[38] According to Fortier and Scott, exceptions could only be made for "bona fide" Russian agriculturalists.

Attempts to block the movement of Russian subjects to the Pacific Coast demonstrated not only the persistence of racial prejudice in early twentieth-century Canadian policy-making but also exposed the Canadian officials' poor knowledge of world migration routes and socio-economic realities in countries that served as major emigrant donors. Fortier was obviously unaware of the fact that Siberia had long ceased to be a mere dumping ground for criminals and misfits. Nor did Immigration Branch officials appear to realize that labour emigration from Russia was channelled primarily through Atlantic ports and that the relatively few Russian subjects who did come via the Pacific used Siberia mainly as a transit point on their way from Ukraine or southern Russia to North America. Ironically, when the supposedly "Asiatic" Ossetians and Georgians arrived in Halifax (as most of them did), they usually entered Canada without a ripple. After the opening of direct steamship traffic between Libava and Halifax, Canadian immigration inspectors even praised the arriving "Russians" as "the finest lot of foreigners ever landed by a foreign line."[39] Canada's Chief Medical Officer Dr. P. H. Bryce also complimented the Russian America Line for the high quality of its steamship service.[40]

After the 1909 incident, ambiguous attitudes towards "Russians" remained deeply entrenched among Canadian officials and soon resurfaced in connection with the question of relaxed admission for immigrant workers. In the summer of 1910, with the Canadian industrial boom at its peak, railway interests pressured Ottawa into lifting the $25 minimum requirement for labourers coming from continental

Europe, leaving only the medical requirements in place. Between July and December 1910, and again in the spring and summer of 1911, all healthy immigrants going to work in railway construction (with the exception of "Asiatics") were exempt from both the money and the continuous journey requirements.[41] However, alarmed by the resultant influx of thousands of "Galicians," "Polacks," and Italians, the Immigration Branch soon called a retreat. When the question of a money requirement was raised again in early 1912, Scott insisted on returning to a more selective approach. In March 1912 the exemptions were limited to immigrants from Western and Northern European countries, although they were later extended under pressure from big business to "Scandinavians, Finns, Poles and Austrians, desirable and suitable for railway labour."[42] When G.T. Bell, assistant manager of the Grand Trunk, asked whether the amended regulations included "Russian workers," Scott dryly replied that "the relaxation refers only to the classes specifically mentioned in the circulars," making Finns and Poles the only eligible Russian subjects.[43]

The Immigration Branch's opposition to the free admission of "Russians" would eventually be defeated by the strange alliance of Canadian railway businesses, Russian steamship interests, and St Petersburg officials. In March 1912, Robert Christiansen, general manager of the Russian America Line, sent a letter to Lord Strathcona, Canada's High Commissioner in London and past president of the CPR, asking him to "consider whether it would not be possible to extend the exemptions, now valid for emigrants from Northern and Western Europe, also to comprise labourers from Russia."[44] Christiansen also briefly mentioned the possibility of signing an agreement between Russia and Canada, similar to the existing Russian-German and Russian-Danish treaties. Such an agreement, he explained, would legalize the recruitment of labourers in Russia and perhaps even allow them to emigrate without having to obtain passports.[45] He also wrote to St Petersburg, asking the Russian government to bring the subject of exemptions to the attention of the Canadian authorities. The Russian Ministry of Foreign Affairs instructed Mikhail Ustinov, then Russian consul in Montreal, to "enter into communication with the appropriate authorities with a view to obtaining a cancellation of the restrictions existing in the local immigration law for Russian subjects going to Canada for work."[46] The consul immediately contacted W.J. Roche, recently appointed as Minister of the Interior in Robert Borden's Conservative government.[47]

The Canadian Pacific, then still a member of the Atlantic Conference and a business partner of the Russian America Line, also did its share of lobbying. The London office of the Russian East-Asiatic Steamship Company, the parent company of the Russian America Line, assured Christiansen that "Mr. Brown of the C.P.R. is ... very much interested [in extending the relaxation to the Russians], and with the valuable aid of Lord Grey, we hope to get the Canadian government to move in the matter."[48] But the Immigration Branch held its ground, continuing to apply the regular immigration procedures to "Russians" throughout the summer of 1912. It was only by the early autumn that Scott began to relent. On 25 September he notified Pickford and Black, the official agents of the Russian America Line in Halifax, that "Russian labourers already ticketed to assured employment via Russian America Line will be admitted on the same terms as those coming from the United States."[49] In March 1913, "Russians" and all other European immigrants with sufficient means and "definite employment" were again allowed to freely enter the country.[50]

However, with the economic recession already on the horizon, Ottawa was soon forced to revert to the old restrictive procedures. Beginning on 1 July 1913 the monetary qualification for European labourers of all nationalities was gradually reinstated in all seaports and on the Canadian-US border territory.[51] In May 1914 Scott informed the new Russian consul Sergei Likhachev that in view of the "economic difficulties" the only classes that should be encouraged to immigrate to Canada were farmers, farm labourers, and female domestics.[52] Likhachev forwarded Scott's letter to the Second Section of the Russian Foreign Ministry, adding that he too considered the arrival of Russian workers to Canada undesirable at the present time.[53] St Petersburg did not have time to react to the message. World War I, which broke out two weeks later, put a stop to the movement of labourers from Russia to Canada and made the issue of admission restrictions irrelevant.

For early twentieth-century Canada, *immigration* was obviously a problem of much greater dimensions and political importance than *emigration* was for tsarist Russia. In both countries, however, population mobility became closely linked to larger issues of national development. Different as they were in their origins, sources of legitimacy, and doctrines of governance, the Russian and Canadian states displayed essentially similar views of people as "human capital" necessary for the economic growth and cultural survival of their nations and acted as managers of this capital. Just as the Russian imperial elites showed themselves reluctant to embrace the idea of permanent emigration of its "true Russian" subjects, who were needed to people the vast lands of Siberia and serve as a bastion of Orthodox culture, immigration officials in Ottawa imposed economically and racially motivated restrictions on the admission of labour immigrants, attempting to filter out those who were considered unfit to become "true Canadians." Notably, the main opposition to mass migration of Russian labour to Canada did not come from St Petersburg, but from Ottawa, which struggled to reconcile in its policy-making the considerations of racial suitability with the interests of Canadian industries, which favoured an open-door immigration policy.

5

Frontiersmen and Urban Dwellers

If the majority of Galicians and Bukovynians headed to the Prairies to become agricultural settlers, Ukrainians from the Russian Empire migrated primarily to the resource frontier or large urban centres of eastern Canada, as did their geographical neighbours from Belarus. Here they joined the growing polyglot army of immigrant workers, many of whom floated across the country – or even across the Canadian-American border – in search of job opportunities. While much of this movement may seem spontaneous, by 1914 distinctive migration patterns specific to Russian-born workers began to emerge. Transnational networks of kith and kin, as well as the activities of labour agents and middlemen, directed Ukrainian and Belarusan immigrants to specific locations within Canada, primarily in Ontario and Quebec. In some of these locations, such as Windsor, they may have even formed the majority of the non-Anglo-Celtic population.

GENERAL IMMIGRATION PATTERNS

The Li-Ra-Ma files are an indispensable source for the presence of eastern Ukrainians and Belarusans in various Canadian provinces and cities. Because most files contain both the migrants' places of origin and their Canadian locations (often including even street addresses), we can identify, with a reasonable degree of accuracy, a number of regionally specific migration chains that linked Belarus and eastern Ukraine with Canada. Of course, these data are not flawless and probably do not present a mirror image of the migrants' distribution in Canada because residents of various Canadian provinces may not be equally represented in the records. It is also obvious that the term "territorial distribution," relatively unproblematic in the case of agricultural settlers, loses its definitiveness when applied to transient migrant sojourners, who often changed places of residence several times in the course of a year. Due to the carelessness with which many migrants listed their places of residence, the Li-Ra-Ma files are not always useful for establishing the number of years that a given individual spent at a certain location. However, most studies of labour migration show that while individual labourers could travel across the destination country in search of better jobs, regional migration patterns remained relatively constant, sustained by transoceanic networks of family, neighbours and friends.

Statistics in Tables 10 and 11, computed from the Li-Ra-Ma sample, illustrate major similarities in migration destinations between Belarusans and Ukrainians, but they also show important differences grounded in locally specific migration networks. A much higher presence of Belarusans in British Columbia is particularly noticeable. They were found almost exclusively in the Crow's Nest Pass area, where they worked in the coal mining industry. A Russian traveller who visited "the Pass" in 1913 noted that "peasants from Grodno and Minsk provinces are the majority [among the 'Russian' miners], although there are also Little Russians from Podolia Province."[1] According to the writer, lucrative employment opportunities available in western Canada's coal mining industry were well known in southwestern Belarus, where peasant families had been sending their men to work "on the coal" for a number of years. Belarusans, usually disguised as Russians or Poles, formed one of the largest contingents of Eastern European miners in the Fernie area (according to Allen Seager, Eastern Europeans constituted 22 per cent of the Crow's Nest Pass entire workforce in 1911).[2] Some Belarusans and eastern Ukrainians also lived on the Alberta side of the Pass in the mining towns of Coleman and Hillcrest.

Northern Ontario was another region where Belarusans figured more prominently than eastern Ukrainians, both in relative and absolute numbers. Here too they worked mostly as miners in the South Porcupine and Sudbury districts. Timmins – the gold-mining capital of Canada – had a particularly large population of Belarusans. At the same time, relatively few of them appear to have gone to the mining districts of Nova Scotia.

The figures in Table 11 suggest that Ukrainians were more likely than Belarusans to gravitate towards urban areas. Although the largest number of immigrants of both nationalities lived in Montreal and

Table 10
Distribution of migrants in Canada by province*

Province of Residence	Belarus (%)				Ukraine (%)				
	Grodno	Minsk	Vil'na	All Belarus	Bessarabia	Kiev	Podolia	Volhynia	All Ukraine
Ontario	49.6	41.3	28.7	45.8	32.2	52.1	44.3	34.6	43.4
Quebec	25.5	39.0	64.3	32.0	62.3	25.7	43.8	41.9	41.5
Manitoba	5.3	1.6	4.8	4.3	0.5	7.7	2.1	14.9	5.5
Saskatchewan	2.0	2.4	–	2.0	–	8.4	2.8	4.7	4.2
Alberta	4.4	2.4	–	3.6	1.4	2.3	2.7	2.2	2.3
British Columbia	12.6	10.6	2.4	11.2	0.5	2.3	2.7	1.1	2.0
Nova Scotia	0.9	2.4	–	1.2	3.3	0.8	0.6	0.7	1.0
New Brunswick	–	–	–	–	–	–	–	0.4	0.1

N = 2607
* Percentages do not add up to 100 due to rounding.
Source: Li-Ra-Ma Sample

Table 11

Cities with largest concentrations of eastern Ukrainians and Belarusans by province of origin*

Province of Residence	Belarus (%)				Ukraine (%)					
	Grodno	Minsk	Vil'na	All Belarus	Bessarabia	Kiev	Podolia	Volhynia	All Ukraine
Montreal/Lachine	24.9	39.2	64.3	31.6	61.9	24.9	42.6	40.0	40.4
Toronto	10.9	19.2	11.9	13.0	5.6	22.8	20.1	12.0	17.3
Hamilton	14.5	10.0	–	12.2	3.7	13.8	5.9	7.3	7.9
Timmins	7.1	0.8	–	5.0	–	2.6	0.7	2.2	1.4
Sudbury	2.4	–	2.4	1.8	1.4	2.1	1.8	1.1	1.7
Parry Sound	2.7	–	–	1.8	–	4.6	0.6	0.4	1.5
Sarnia	0.6	–	–	0.4	–	0.5	3.3	1.1	1.7
Windsor	0.3	–	–	0.2	17.7	–	1.2	1.1	3.2
Winnipeg	3.3	1.7	4.8	3.0	0.5	5.1	1.6	8.4	3.5
The Pas	1.8	–	–	1.2	–	2.6	0.3	4.7	1.6
Fernie/Michel	8.0	1.7	–	5.8	–	–	0.1	–	0.1

N = 2053

* Percentages do not add up to 100 due to rounding.

Source: Li-Ra-Ma Sample

Toronto, residents of these two cities constituted a smaller proportion among Belarusans than they did among Ukrainians. Ontario as a whole attracted roughly similar ratios of Belarusans and Ukrainians, but the former went mainly to the Timmins-Sudbury area whereas the latter preferred the Great Lakes region. Windsor, Brantford, St Catharines, London, Galt, and other small industrial cities each had from several dozen to several hundred Slavic workers from Russia. After Toronto, the largest recipient of Russian-born workers in Ontario was Hamilton, which had an estimated "Russian" population of 1,500 in 1917.[3] Hamilton was also the only city in southwestern Ontario that attracted comparatively more Belarusans than Ukrainians. The construction of the new Welland Canal, which began in 1913, together with the growth of the munitions industry around the Great Lakes after 1914, opened up vast employment opportunities for immigrant workers from all across Europe. The influx of immigrant labour to Windsor increased dramatically after Ford Motor Company opened an assembly plant there in 1904. In 1915 the local "Russian" population, composed largely of Ukrainians from Bessarabia and Podolia, was estimated at close to one thousand.[4] Many other small cities in southwestern Ontario were also centred on one dominant industry, which employed the majority of the local immigrant workforce. In Parry Sound, for instance, nearly all Russian-born immigrants worked for the Nobel Chemical Company, which produced explosives for the Allied armies during the war.[5]

Differences in destination choices existed not only *between* Ukrainians and Belarusans, but also *within* each of the two groups. A good example is the different proportions of "frontiersmen" among Belarusans from Grodno, Minsk, and Vil'na. Most of the Belarusans who toiled in the gold, copper, or coal mines of northern Ontario and the Crow's Nest Pass came from the district of Pruzhany in Grodno Province. Natives of Minsk and Vil'na provinces showed a stronger preference for an urban environment, heading mostly for Montreal or Toronto. Similar variations in residential preferences can be observed among Ukrainians. Bessarabians exhibited a particularly interesting pattern of territorial distribution. Over three quarters of them lived in just two Canadian localities – Montreal and Windsor – and almost none were found west of Ontario. They were also three times more likely than other Ukrainians to settle in Nova Scotia.[6] At the same time, immigrants from Kiev and Volhynia chose Prairie destinations much more frequently than those from other Ukrainian provinces. In contrast to the Belarusans, however, there appeared to be no single major concentration of eastern Ukrainian workers in the West. Although some did go to the Crow's Nest Pass, the majority were scattered among the small rural communities and logging and railway construction camps of Manitoba, Saskatchewan, and Alberta, with perhaps one or two thousands living in Winnipeg, Calgary, and other Prairie cities. An especially large percentage reported living in the Battleford district of west-central Saskatchewan, which emerged as a popular Prairie destination for Russian-born immigrants of various nationalities and religions. Along with Orthodox and Baptist farmers and workers from eastern Ukraine, it also had a large Doukhobor colony and several Russian-German settlements.

"ROUGHING IT" ON THE RESOURCE FRONTIER

The majority of Belarusan and Ukrainian labourers arriving in Canada from the Russian Empire streamed into industrial frontier occupations. The rapid growth of the mining and forest industries and the unprecedented expansion of Canada's railway network generated an insatiable demand for unskilled labour, filled primarily by immigration from continental Europe. Like other eastern and central Europeans, "sturdy" and "strong-limbed" peasants from Belarus and Ukraine were ideal candidates for the arduous and usually low-paying jobs in railway construction, logging, or mining, which held little appeal for native-born Canadians (especially those of Anglo-Celtic origin).[7] Some immigrants alternated industrial employment with working as farmhands, especially during the harvest season.

Working as railway navvies provided most Ukrainians and Belarusans with their first source of income and their first experience in the Canadian labour market. Thousands of Belarusan and Ukrainian immigrants toiled on the construction of multiple additions to the Canadian Pacific Railway network and on the building of the new Grand Trunk and Canadian Northern transcontinental lines. At the height of the railway boom in 1912–13, hundreds of immigrants were hired immediately after their landing at a Canadian port, crammed into specially provided coaches attached to regular trains, and taken to construction camps in the country's interior. To prevent "contract jumping," immigrants were often locked up and watched by the company's armed guards until the end of the journey.[8] Not surprisingly, the labourers resented such treatment, which they had hardly expected in a supposedly free country, and some attempted to protest. In an indignant letter to the Russian consulate, Ivan Humeniuk, a labourer from Volhynia, bristled as he described his first experiences in Canada following his arrival in Halifax on 29 March 1913:

At debarkation, Canadian immigration authorities charged each of us ten dollars for railway transportation through Canada to the place of our work, and gave us some sort of tickets, which later turned out to be contracts. There were over a thousand immigrants, but nobody knew that they cheated us this way into taking contracts. We were carried locked up in the cars like criminals; at the stations where the train stopped, CPR policemen with handguns and other arms surrounded the train and did not let anyone out, and those who did come out were beaten like criminals with handguns and some other arms and driven back into the car. They carried us this way for five days and brought us to a parkway in Saskatchewan, and there they divided us into work gangs.[9]

On at least one occasion the CPR's treatment of navvies from Russia produced a public scandal. In late March 1913, the Montreal *Gazette* reported (probably referring to the same event as reported by Humeniuk) that a great number of "Russian workers" were transported in boxcars without food. When several men managed to escape near Boharm, Saskatchewan, the guards opened fire and wounded them.[10] The apparent seriousness of the incident led to the intervention of the Russian consul in Montreal Nicholas Passek, who wrote for the particulars to the Department of the Interior.[11] The department ordered the government immigration agent in Winnipeg to conduct an investigation, which revealed that seventeen Russian labourers, incited by "their fellow countrymen," had jumped from the moving train, thus forcing the guards to stop the train and fire "a revolver into the air to intimidate them."[12]

The report claimed that statements regarding the lack of food and other "improper action" were "entirely unfounded" and that nobody was hurt as a result of the shooting. The government's interpretation of the events, which absolved the CPR of any responsibility for the disorder, did not convince Passek. Somewhat unusually for a foreign diplomat, he decided to appeal to Canadian public opinion. In a letter to S. White, the editor of the *Gazette*, the consul angrily denounced "the drastic measures taken by the officers of the CPR Co. in the case [...] which [recall] not only those taken in South Africa against the Chinese coolies, but even the old days of lash in the Black Slave Trade."[13] The Moose Jaw

Trades and Labour Council (TLC) also reacted to the incident: its letter
to the Department of Justice accused the CPR of violating the Alien
Labour Act and inhumanely treating its workers.[14] In the House of
Commons, W.E. Knowles, MP for Moose Jaw, questioned the Borden
government whether it was aware of the shameful conditions under
which the CPR transported Russian navvies.[15] Borden responded by or-
dering the Minister of Labour T.W. Crothers to investigate the matter. In
his 28 May report to the House, Crothers dismissed the "allegations" of
the Russian consul and the TLC as "entirely inaccurate," and confirmed
the earlier official version of the incident that laid all the blame on the
workers.[16] Passek chose not to press the matter further.

In most cases, railway contractors advanced the train fare to the
hired workers, who rarely had more than a few dollars in their pockets,
and then deducted it from their paycheque. "Greenhorns," who knew
nothing of the advance fare system and read no English, easily became
victims of unscrupulous employment agents, who charged them for
"transportation" that was already covered by the employer. The fraud
was usually not discovered until the first payday, when the deducted
wages appeared on the worker's account.[17] Keeping the navvy from deserting his job before the fare was fully repaid often presented a challenge to the contractors, but any losses incurred from desertions were
far surpassed by the profits received. Train fare deductions were not
the only ones that affected the navvies' pay: they were also charged
sixty to seventy cents per day for bunk and board, and about $1.25 per
month for medical and mail services.[18]

Slavic workers from Russia usually entered the railway construction
industry as members of "extra gangs," whose task was to ballast the
railway bed and to repair the tracks. They also worked in grade camps,
cutting rock and shovelling clay to prepare the roadbed for the laying of
tracks. Only a few immigrants achieved the rank of gang foremen and
fewer still managed to land the more skilled and better-paying jobs of
conductors or telegraph operators. The wages received for unskilled
work could sustain a single labourer, but they could hardly provide a living to a family or secure the desired savings – the main object of a Slavic
worker's arrival in Canada. In 1915 Peter Leshchuk, who worked on the
construction of a CPR line near Success, Manitoba, was paid only $1.50
per day. Roman Daniliuk made $1.75 per day working in a CPR extra
gang near Sudbury in 1913. Workers in grade camps received up to
$2.50 per day.[19] Still, after all the deductions were made, most navvies
could hope to pocket no more than $25–$30 per month. If a worker

stayed on the job longer than several months (usually three to six), he could receive a small daily bonus and a free one-way railway pass at the end of the contract.[20] Even these wages, however, were earned by back-breaking work and often at the expense of the workers' health. During the depression years (late 1913 to mid-1915), contractor firms used the constant threat of unemployment to raise the pace of work to a level that could hardly be sustained even by men accustomed to hard physical labour. Arnold F. George, a government immigration agent sent to investigate the complaint of thirty Winnipeg "Russians" discharged for "unsatisfactory" work by the contractor firm of McMillan Bros, wrote in his report that "it is not a question of how skilful the work such men can do, but of how much. At the time when these men were dismissed as unsatisfactory, thousands of men were roaming the line looking for work, while Le Pas is also full of them. Under such conditions, a pace is invariably set for the labourers, which requires the discipline of a constant discharge of some of the men to speed the others up."[21]

To increase earnings, more experienced labourers often formed their own gangs (usually from three to five men but sometimes as many as twenty) and contracted themselves for "station work" – a type of employment that in some ways resembled the old Russian tradition of *arteli* – small communes of itinerant workmen, who owned their own tools and travelled long distances in search of employment. "Station men" leased stretches of land ("stations"), which had to be graded for the laying of tracks. They were required to supply themselves with shelter, tools, and food, usually purchased at exorbitant prices from the contractor, who might charge $6 for a bag of flour that normally cost $2. Many contractors kept recycling used tools and equipment abandoned at the stations by previous gangs.[22] The need to pay back the resulting debt, coupled with the sojourner's drive to earn the most money in the shortest possible time, proved a far better incentive for hard work than the watchful eye of a foreman ever did. This self-motivation made the station system very cost-effective for the railway companies. Unlike regular navvies, station men set their own hours and were paid by the amount of earth or rock removed rather than by the time spent on the job. Pay schedules could vary significantly depending on the location and the hiring company. Labourers working on Vancouver Island in 1915 for McKenzie and Mann received 95¢ per cubic yard of solid rock and 26¢ for any other material removed. A gang of twelve Russian-born station men, who worked the same year on the construction of the Hudson's Bay Railway in Manitoba, were paid 40¢ per yard for clay and $1.35 for rock.[23]

While station work offered the alluring prospect of higher pay, it also had many pitfalls – especially for less experienced labourers, who frequently miscalculated the degree of its difficulty and their own skills. A formally larger measure of control over the work process allotted to station labourers often turned out to be illusory. Bad terrain and rainy weather could significantly slow down the workers and jeopardize the chances of fulfilling the contract. To get fair pay, company engineers who assessed the amount of work done by a gang usually had to be "oiled" – that is, paid off in the form of liquor (a widespread practice in other industries as well).[24] Workers who refused to participate in the bribing could find their paycheques slashed by as much as several hundred dollars. In 1913–14 Russian-born station men working in western Manitoba regularly dispatched one of their own to The Pas, located over 200 miles from the worksite, to buy liquor for the engineer (and, one suspects, for the workers' own consumption). Since alcohol was banned in and near construction camps, the "couriers" often had to sneak much of the way with a load of whiskey in their bags, trying to avoid a police patrol.[25] If all went well, the stationers might net $500, $600, or even $800 per season. But in the worst-case scenario, they were fortunate to break even. Contractors and company engineers who oversaw the work often tried to take advantage of the workers' illiteracy or lack of experience. Thus a group of fourteen station men on Vancouver Island discovered after the completion of their work that, in addition to the charges for equipment, tools, and horses, the contract they had signed required them to assume a debt of $1,500 left by an "Austrian gang" that had attempted and given up the same work earlier. With the help of a sympathetic lawyer, the men pleaded their case before the Supreme Court of British Columbia – only to fall victim to the nativist prejudice of the judge, who could "not see how we are to build railways in British Columbia, unless we make these sort of people live up to their contracts."[26]

After railway construction, the mining industry was the second largest employer of Russian-born immigrants in early twentieth-century Canada. The collieries of the Crow's Nest Pass and the Hollinger gold mines in Timmins employed the largest numbers of Russian-born miners, although "Russians" were also found in copper and nickel mines around Cobalt and Sudbury, in asbestos mines in Thetford, Quebec, and a few even managed to find their way to Cape Breton. By 1914 some Russian-born miners in Fernie had already made several trips to Canada, returning each time for a new pocket full of "coal dollars."[27]

Like other Slavic miners across Canada, most "Russians" worked at unskilled jobs – as surface workers or underground as muckers, trammers, or machine helpers.

In contrast to railway construction, logging, or farm labour, mining was less subject to seasonal fluctuations and thus provided a greater measure of stability for the workers. Of all the low- and unskilled frontier occupations in early twentieth-century Canada, it also brought the highest day wages. In 1913 Russian-born miners in Fernie averaged $3 per day, and more experienced workers earned up to $3.50. A series of strikes that occurred in the Crow's Nest Pass during the war (along with war bonuses) nearly doubled the wages: in 1919 skilled miners working at the coal face received up to $7.50 per day and even help boys could earn as much as $3.85.[28] In 1915 Hollinger paid its low-skilled workers $60–80 per month depending on seniority and the nature of the work. Machine operators received $3.50, helpers $3, and muckers $2.75 per day, with 75 cents deducted for board and other services.[29] As in other frontier industries, the labour turnover in mining was high: thus in 1917 only 10 per cent of the male population of Timmins were permanent residents, and at least half of the remaining 90 per cent stayed in the town for only three to four months of the year.[30] The arduous working conditions and health hazards of mining work forced many to quit after a few weeks or even a few days. Yet it was not uncommon for miners to remain in the same job for four, five, or even more years – something that rarely occurred among loggers or railway navvies. By 1914 a handful of Russian-born miners in northern Ontario had begun the transition from sojourning to permanent residence. An old-time resident of Timmins recalled that in the spring of that year Danil Shumovich, one of the few Belarusan miners to build his own permanent home before the war, brought over his wife Daria, who reportedly became the first "Russian" woman in the still nearly all-male town.[31]

While navvies and loggers in early twentieth-century Canada inhabited temporary bunkhouse camps, miners usually lived in small company towns (of which Fernie and Timmins were typical examples), scattered across the resource frontier. In Fernie they built rough wooden frame shacks, shared by five or more tenants, who slept on bunk beds covered with straw mattresses and crude blankets. The centre of the shack was occupied by a stove used for heating, cooking, and washing. The Fernie *Free Press* complained in 1910 about the unsanitary conditions among the Russians and urged the town authorities to take action to improve them.[32] As historians have pointed out, early twentieth-century Canadian mining towns were socially and ethnically segregated communities.[33] In the Fernie area, "Russian" workers lived in a shanty settlement ironically named "New York," which was nestled on a mountain slope and separated from the rest of the town by the Elk River. Italians, French Canadians, and Scandinavians populated the opposite end of the shantytown, while the English and Scottish managers of the Crow's Nest Coal Company inhabited comfortable houses across the river, equipped with sewage and other amenities.[34]

Frontier occupations usually presented a greater hazard for workers than urban employment. According to the Department of Labour statistics, logging, mining, and railway construction together employed about 9 per cent of Canada's working population, but they accounted for 46 per cent of all fatal industrial accidents recorded between 1904 and 1923.[35] Railway navvies received most of their injuries from dynamite explosions and tumbling piles of rails or ties. Mishandled dynamite was also a common cause of injury and death among miners. Many miners were crippled by falling coal and rock, hit by cars, and poisoned by seeping gas. Silicosis – a lung disease caused by inhaling tiny particles of silica dust – claimed the lives of many Slavic workers in Timmins and other places. Many Slavic workers lost their lives and property during the devastating fires that blazed through the Porcupine district in 1911 and 1916, destroying much of Timmins and other settlements. In Fernie, when the wind blew from the coke ovens located near the miners' shantytown, the air became filled with flakes of soot that covered the buildings and polluted the town's wells. Falling trees were the leading cause of industrial accidents in the logging industry. The inability of many immigrant loggers to communicate verbally with their co-workers made coordinated operation of machinery difficult and increased the chances of injury. In logging as in other industries, employers were rarely prepared to admit their fault in the accident and often accused their victims of malingering. Foma Mel'nychuk, who was hit by a falling tree because he could not understand a French Canadian assigned as his workmate, was told by his contractor that he knew the trade well enough to be able to get out of the tree's way.[36] Iakov Mazur, who had his arm broken as a result of a similar accident, also failed to obtain compensation from his employer, the Lake Superior Paper Company. The company doctor, who failed to set the bone properly, not only considered Mazur fit for "any kind of work" but also rebuked the injured worker for thinking that "because he had been hurt somebody ought to maintain him ..."[37]

By 1916, laws providing some degree of protection to victims of industrial accidents were in place in all Canadian provinces except Prince Edward Island. If employer negligence could be established, the workers were entitled to a one-time payment, weekly disability pension, or a combination of both. In Nova Scotia, large coal and steel companies established their own insurance funds regulated by special legislation. Obtaining compensation under the industrial disability laws was, however, a costly and often frustrating experience even for native-born workers, not to mention immigrant labourers. In some provinces, workers employed in the forest industry, agriculture, fisheries, and domestic service were not covered by this legislation and could proceed only under the common law. In Quebec, foreign-born workers without resident families could not claim benefits under the provincial *Loi des accidents du travail*, and under the Manitoba law the dependents of a deceased worker could receive an indemnity only if they resided within the British Empire. Ontario was the first Canadian province to take disability protection away from the courts and place it in the hands of a government-appointed body. Under the Workmen's Compensation Act, introduced in April 1914, a special board composed of three commissioners dealt with all claims involving death or injury in industrial accidents and determined the amount of compensation. According to the act, non-resident families of foreign workers could receive an indemnity equivalent in value to that accorded them by the laws of their home country. Where such laws did not exist, the amount of the compensation was left to the discretion of the commissioners. Immigrant workers received still better protection in the 1915 British Columbia law, which in most respects emulated the Ontario legislation but made no distinction between Canadians and "foreigners."[38]

With the adoption of government-regulated disability protection plans in Ontario and British Columbia, immigrant workers injured in industrial accidents that occurred in the two provinces were spared the costly and often fruitless procedure of suing their employers for damages. Elsewhere, they still had to initiate lawsuits under the common law or the provincial disability act in order to obtain compensation. This was exactly what some Ukrainian and Belarusan labourers attempted to do. They hired interpreters and lawyers and attempted to turn the law to their advantage. While organized labour militancy in early twentieth-century Canada has received detailed attention in Canadian historiography, we have yet to explore the extent and significance of litigation as a form of *individual* protest used by workers (including immigrants) to confront mistreatment and overexploitation. The Li-Ra-Ma records suggest that legal action by Russian-born workers against their employers or labour agents was far from exceptional, even though it was difficult to bring to a successful end due to the plaintiff's poor knowledge of English, unfamiliarity with Canadian legal procedures, and the double burden of class and ethnic prejudice.[39] Proving employer negligence in court usually presented the greatest challenge. Because of the high mobility of migrant workers and the typically late institution of legal proceedings, few plaintiffs could produce witnesses of the accident. Given that most employers knew better than to testify against themselves, many such cases were dismissed by the courts. Time was also a crucial factor: according to the law, lawsuits initiated more than six months after the accident could be accepted by a court only in exceptional circumstances. High fees charged by lawyers and interpreters (sometimes amounting to several hundred dollars) often left their clients penniless without increasing their chances for a successful verdict. A security deposit of another two or three hundred dollars was required if the plaintiff decided to appeal an unfavourable verdict in a higher court. When a successful outcome of the appeal seemed probable, some lawyers advanced part of the expenses to their clients, but the latter still had to raise the bulk of the money.

Occasionally, Ukrainian and Belarusan immigrants brought their complaints against employers and labour agents to the Russian consulates in Montreal and Vancouver. Usually such assistance was sought as a last resort, after other ways of obtaining redress failed to bring results. The operational files of the two consulates contain over a hundred cases involving compensation of damages suffered from industrial accidents.[40] After fruitless encounters with Canadian legal bureaucracy, many injured workers regarded the consuls as their only remaining hope for justice. To prick the conscience of the supposedly cold-hearted tsarist bureaucrats, they employed the same strategies that were used by peasant petitioners back home: from purposely hyperbolic descriptions of their misery to personal flattery and straightforward offers of monetary rewards.[41] In a typical letter of this kind, Ivan Bespal'ko from Kiev Province described the circumstances of his injury and asked for help in obtaining an indemnity from his employer:

Your Excellency, I beg for your help in an accident [...] I worked for the Canadian Copper Company at Creighton Mine and I was injured by a dynamite explosion so badly that I have been disabled for six months – my whole right side was injured, my right eye was completely blown out and I also lost two teeth. My right cheek is all black from gunpowder. Therefore I want some aid from the company. Let it pay me for the lost eye and give me a good job, because now I cannot do any hard work. So I have to suffer now, for I cannot get a job at another company. I have become a cripple for my whole life, and therefore I ask that I be given some allowance.[42]

By 1914, the Russian government began to pay greater attention to protecting its subjects in foreign countries. The ongoing transformation of the Russian monarchy into a state based on the rule of law was bringing with it an understanding that every subject of the tsar should, at least in theory, be entitled to an equal measure of protection. Around 1913, the consulate general began to use the services of the reputable Montreal law firm of Dessaulles, Garneau and Vanier to handle the skyrocketing number of requests for legal assistance. Occasionally the lawyers acted as direct representatives of the injured workers, but usually their role was limited to finding out the details of the case and providing the plaintiff with legal advice. In some cases, such intervention facilitated settlement, but it made little difference if no witnesses could be located or if employer negligence seemed impossible to prove. Reporting to the Russian Ministry of Foreign Affairs in March 1915, Consul Sergei Likhachev wrote that most victims of mistreatment applied "for consular assistance too late and, moreover, [could not] provide the needed information."[43] When no compensation could be obtained, the consulate sometimes stepped in with small one-time allowances (usually not exceeding $10–$15), but these were rare and reserved only for the most destitute. It is clear that both the industrial accidents legislation and consular intervention could only provide a modicum of protection for Ukrainian and Belarusan labourers, exposed on a daily basis to the risks and hazards of the frontier occupations.

As Orest Martynowych put it, "insecurity and uncertainty were the only constants in the lives of Slavic frontier labourers."[44] Their work and life cycles usually revolved around the irregular rhythm of the resource economy, which heavily depended in turn on the vagaries of the climate and the market. After working for eight or nine months on the frontier, most workers converged on the nearby cities during the cold season, where they lived off their quickly dwindling savings or took up occasional jobs. Here they entered the emerging ethnic enclaves, which by 1914 were a permanent fixture on the Canadian urban landscape.

THE "URBANITES:" THE CASE OF MONTREAL

Like the frontier camps, the fledgling urban communities of Ukrainian
and Belarusan workers were composed mostly of single men. Their
size and composition fluctuated in unison with the seasonal and long-
term economic cycles. In the late autumn and winter months, the number of Russian-born labourers in such cities as Montreal, Toronto, and
Hamilton could swell to several thousand, while in the spring and summer it probably shrank to a few hundred with the arrival of the new
railway construction and farming season. Before 1914, only a relatively
small proportion of Ukrainian and Belarusan workers, primarily those
with skilled jobs or resident families, remained in cities on a permanent
basis. For the majority, the boundary between the city and the resource
frontier was never a fixed one, as they alternated short urban stints
with longer periods of "roughing it in the bush."

Of all early twentieth-century Canadian cities, Montreal was by far
the largest recipient of immigrants from Russian Ukraine and Belarus.
The size of the city's "Russian colony" and its relatively well-documented
history make it a good model for exploring the social experiences of urban labourers.[45] Toronto, Winnipeg, and Hamilton – other popular
destinations for immigrant workers from Russia – were in many ways
smaller replicas of the Montreal community, with similar patterns of
settlement, work, and leisure.

As a bustling metropolis which produced 17 per cent of Canada's to-
talindustrial output in the early 1900s and served as its largest commercial port, Montreal exerted a strong pull on immigrants from central,
eastern, and southern Europe. A municipal census conducted by the
YMCA in 1915 found 102,000 "people of foreign speech" within the
city limits, including 55,000 Jews, 17,500 Italians, 12,500 "Ruthenians
and Poles" as well as smaller numbers of Bulgarians, Greeks, Chinese,
and others. By 1917, some observers believed that the city's foreign-
speaking population had increased by at least another 5 per cent.[46]

Peasant immigration from Russian Ukraine and Belarus to Montreal
began around 1903–04 and assumed such large proportions during the
last pre-war years that the Labour Gazette, which rarely paid attention
to specific ethnic groups among immigrant workers, felt compelled to
note in August 1913 that "this season a large number of Russians have
been added to the labour population of the city and suburbs."[47] The
federal census of 1921, which found only 2,067 "Russians" living in
Montreal (still an approximately two-fold increase compared to 1911),

doubtless missed a large army of transient migrants, who flooded into the city at the end of every year only to leave it again in several months.[48] The estimated figure of 5,000 "Russians," which appeared in 1915 in the Russian-American newspaper *Novyi mir*, seems to be much closer to the reality.[49] The first Ukrainian and Belarusan immigrants to arrive in Montreal were natives of Volhynia, Kiev, Minsk, and Mogilev provinces.[50] After 1910, they were joined by an even larger wave of labour migrants from the new donor areas – Podolia, Bessarabia, and Grodno.

Montreal's Ukrainians and Belarusans exhibited largely similar residential patterns, although the rate of dispersal for the Belarusans was somewhat higher (see Table 12).[51] The earliest area of eastern Slavic settlement in the city emerged in Point St Charles, whose primarily Irish and Francophone working-class character was undergoing rapid changes in the early 1900s (see Map 3). Point St Charles was also the first site of Montreal's Russian Orthodox parish, founded in 1907 and housed in a small rented building on Soulanges Street.[52] By the early 1910s, the role of Point St Charles as the centre of the Slavic colony began to decline, with more and more immigrants settling in the large downtown area along St Lawrence Boulevard, the city's main thoroughfare, which formed the dividing line between its English- and French-speaking sections. Over 60 per cent of Montreal's immigrants from Russian Ukraine and Belarus, along with thousands of other Eastern and Southern Europeans, were huddled into the so-called "immigrant corridor" – an area that extended from Ontario Street in the north to Craig Street (now rue St Antoine) in the south, and from St Denis Street in the east to Bleury Street in the west. Most Ukrainians and Belarusans lived within the rectangle formed by St Urbain, Craig, Sanguinet, and St Catherine streets. St Dominique and Cadieux (now de Bullion) streets had particularly dense concentrations of Slavs. The availability of cheap boarding-houses, owned mainly by Jewish families, and the abundance of small garment, cigar-making, and food-packing factories, drew thousands of these migrant sojourners to the Centre area, which one author described as "a cosmopolitan Mecca where the Jew predominates."[53]

A third concentrated area of Ukrainian and Belarusan settlement in early twentieth-century Montreal sprang up at the western edge of Hochelaga, north of Ontario Street and east of Iberville. As Table 12 demonstrates, it was especially popular with the Belarusans. The 1916 decision of the ss Peter and Paul parish to move to a new church on

Table 12
Major Ukrainian and Belarusan settlement areas in Montreal, ca 1920

| | Origins | |
Areas	Belarus (%)	Ukraine (%)
Centre	51.0	66.2
Hochelaga	26.0	14.4
Point St Charles	14.4	16.1
Other	8.6	3.3

N = 471
Source: Li-Ra-Ma Sample

Cartier Street (which never materialized) reflected the changing geography of Slavic immigrant settlements in Montreal, now centred on the downtown and Hochelaga districts.

Smaller groups of Ukrainians and Belarusans were also found in other city areas, especially in Côte St-Paul (on Notre Dame Street West and adjoining streets) and in Montreal's numerous satellite towns and suburbs. In Beloeil, about a dozen miles southeast of the city, the Canadian Explosives Company employed a number of "Russians," while in nearby Laprairie they toiled in road construction and at the local brick manufacturing plant.[54] But the largest Slavic colony on the city's outskirts emerged in Lachine, where hundreds of "Russian" Ukrainians lived next to the even more numerous Bukovynians, together occupying the area known as the Dominion Park. Lachine, however, attracted relatively few Belarusans and so remained a predominantly Ukrainian enclave. By 1909–10, the town's Orthodox community was large enough to establish its own Orthodox parish.[55]

Socially and geographically, eastern Slav workers who came from Russia to Montreal were not divided across ethnic lines. They settled in the same neighbourhoods, shared the same boarding-houses, frequented the same stores and labour agencies, and belonged to the same parishes and immigrant organizations. Although natives of the same villages and districts tended to cluster together within certain blocks, it was also common for an immigrant from Minsk to live in a boarding-house with several Ukrainians or vice versa. The social geography of Montreal's Ukrainian and Belarusan communities proves the validity of Robert Harney's insightful remark that "ethnic enclaves are rarely made up uniformly of one ethnic group, [nor] does consensus within

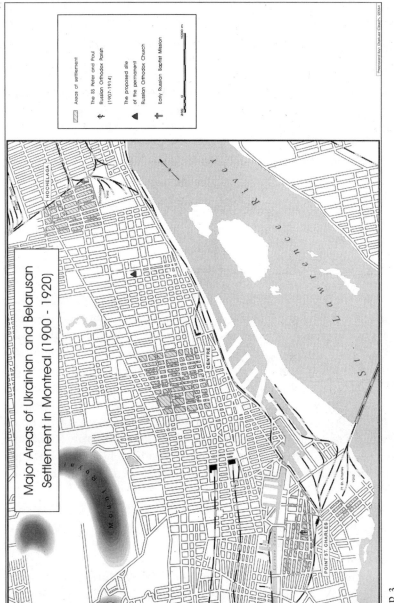

Major Areas of Ukrainian and Belarusan Settlement in Montreal (1900 - 1920)

Areas of settlement

The SS Peter and Paul Russian Orthodox Parish (1907-1914)

The proposed site of the permanent Russian Orthodox Church

Early Russian Baptist Mission

250   0   1000 m

HOCHELAGA

St Lawrence River

Mount Royal

CENTRE

POINT ST. CHARLES

N

Map 3

the group necessarily follow from shared ethnicity."[56] A weak or non-existent national consciousness was typical of early twentieth-century Eastern Europeans, preventing the creation of socio-cultural barriers between various ethnic groups that the rising nationalist elites were eager to erect. The social identities of immigrants from eastern Ukraine and Belarus were defined by their country of birth, common religious and political loyalties, and shared "high language" (Russian). To all intents and purposes, they were "Russians" and regarded themselves as members of the city's "Russian colony" – a rather amorphous polyethnic formation, which also included Russians proper, Russian-speaking Jews, as well as some Poles, Armenians, and others.

Like other "Russian" immigrant communities across North America, the "Russian colony" of Montreal had no clearly drawn ethnic boundaries, reflecting the absence of a commonly accepted understanding of what it was that made one Russian. In this regard, "Russian" communities abroad were very much a mirror image of the homeland, where, as historian Theodore Weeks pointed out, no clear definition of any nationality – Russian or non-Russian – was ever formulated.[57] Due to cultural assimilation, many non-Russians born in the tsarist empire not only knew enough Russian to function easily in both the larger "Russian colony" and their own communities but also adopted Russian as their primary identity. There was also intermingling between "Russians" and Orthodox Ukrainians from Galicia and Bukovyna, many of whom regarded Russia as their cultural focal point. The surviving records of the ss Peter and Paul Russian Orthodox parish reveal a high degree of intermarriage among Orthodox Slavs from Russia and Austria. The scarcity of marriageable women from home led young immigrant men searching for a spouse to turn to the more numerous Bukovynian and Galician women. Out of the 110 marital unions recorded in the church's metric books between 1917 and 1921, only twenty-eight united spouses who were both Russian-born.[58] Marriages with Greek and Roman Catholics occurred as well, but these seem to have been the exceptions.

Montreal's immigrant neighbourhoods differed little from those of other large North American cities as far as living conditions were concerned. According to historian Paul-André Linteau, overcrowding was less rampant in the city's working-class quarters than it was in American metropolises but in certain areas of the downtown core it still appears to have reached significant proportions, especially following the prewar immigration boom.[59] When in 1917 Methodist social workers

conducted a survey of one immigrant block on an unidentified downtown street, they found 333 men and sixteen women packed into sixteen boarding-houses with a total of eighty-four rooms, where the
average room measured 10 by 8 feet.[60] Unsanitary living conditions
and lack of sewage were a serious problem in such buildings, causing
some of the continent's highest rates of infectious disease and child
mortality.[61] Like the majority of migrant sojourners, Ukrainians and
Belarusans were prepared to sacrifice personal comfort for the sake of
accumulating larger savings in order to return home, send money to the
family, or bring it over to Canada in the shortest possible time. In addition, running water and in-house bathrooms were amenities deemed
expendable by all but very few Eastern Europeans, who had not been
familiar with these luxuries of modern civilization in the Old World.
Only a few long-timers and men with families owned or rented their
own homes; the majority were content with living in the numerous
boarding-houses that lined the streets of the immigrant neighbourhoods. Run mostly by Jewish families from Eastern Europe, these
cramped dwellings provided their tenants with a bed in a shared room
and with daily meals as well as the comfort of a familiar cultural environment. The boarding-house keepers could also supply a "greenhorn"
immigrant with precious information about the city, its amenities, and
employment opportunities. But even such uncomfortable lodgings
could prove a burden on one's finances. The unwillingness of Montreal
city authorities to regulate the housing market, combined with the constant influx of new immigrants, pushed up rents in working-class
neighbourhoods, which in 1914 averaged between $10 and $16 a
month, or about one third of an unskilled worker's earnings.[62] As far
as housing costs were concerned, Ukrainians and Belarusans in Lachine,
who usually inhabited their own shanties built of scrap wood and
metal, were in a better situation than their fellow workers in Point
St Charles, Centre, and Hochelaga districts.

With the exception of the recessions of 1907–08 and 1913–15, early
twentieth-century Canadian cities offered plenty of jobs to be filled by
Slavic, Italian, and other European workers. Most of these jobs required little or no skill. Of the 501 Montreal immigrants who reported
their Canadian occupation in the Li-Ra-Ma files, 417 (83.2 per cent)
chose the broad category of *chernorabochii*, which in Russian means
"one who performs black (i.e. unskilled) labour." This figure obviously represents the respondents' own view of their occupational status, but given that the definition of skill has always contained socially

constructed elements, there is no reason why it should be accepted as less valid than the data provided in contemporary censuses or social surveys.[63] Various sources indicate that many Ukrainians and Belarusans who held unskilled jobs worked in road construction. An especially large number of Slavic workers were employed digging the railway tunnel under Mount Royal, one of the city's most labour-intensive projects on the eve of World War I. Others worked on the construction of new streetcar tracks. The "immigrant corridor" along St Lawrence Boulevard, with its plethora of employment bureaux, served as the main distribution point for these labourers. Being on the municipal payroll brought higher wages than working for private contractors: in 1914, construction workers employed directly by the city earned $2.25 per day compared to the $1.75–$2.00 offered by private firms.[64] According to the Li-Ra-Ma records, the immigrants also worked as freight handlers, coal drivers, general helpers, night watchmen, waiters, or window cleaners. The fast growth of Montreal's munitions industry after 1914 generated still more demand for unskilled and low-skilled labour.

Numerous factories, plants, and shops clustered along the Lachine Canal not only employed a large foreign workforce but also shaped the geography of immigrant settlement. Many of the first Ukrainians and Belarusans who settled in Point St Charles, for instance, were attracted by the employment opportunities offered by the nearby Redpath Sugar Refining Company.[65] The Grand Trunk railway yard, the Northern Electric and Canadian Steel Foundries companies, all located in Point St Charles, also hired large numbers of Slavic immigrants. Similarly, the opening of the CPR's Angus shops in 1904 helped turn the Hochelaga district into a major centre of Slavic and east European settlement. Other large employers of immigrant workforce in the area included the CPR railway yard, the Montreal Locomotive Works, and the Montreal Light, Heat and Power Company – the city's main supplier of electricity.[66] In Lachine, there was work to be found at Canada Car Turcot, Dominion Copper Products, Dominion Bridge, or Dominion Engineering.[67]

Among those in the Li-Ra-Ma sample who held jobs requiring at least a minimal level of skill, the majority were carpenters, ironworkers, and mechanics. Interestingly, among Belarusans the proportion of workers who reported their jobs as other than "general labourers" was almost two times higher (27 per cent) than among Ukrainians (14 per cent). While this may be partly explained by the slightly higher average literacy of Belarusan immigrants, it was probably their longer presence in the city that made the key difference. The Li-Ra-Ma data reveals a correlation between the nature of employment held by an immigrant and the number of years spent in the country. Among persons who came to Canada before 1911, the proportion of "general labourers" was only 67 per cent compared to the 85 per cent of those who arrived in later years.[68] Being an "old-timer" was likely to increase a migrant's chances of breaking out of the endless cycle of exhausting low-end jobs and finding more skilled employment, which provided a higher income and greater economic stability. In many cases, it also sped up the transition from sojourning to permanent settlement: the percentage of individuals with resident families was significantly higher among skilled workers and artisans than it was among "general labourers" (19 per cent compared to 11 per cent). By the war's end, a few of the earlier immigrants were able to establish themselves as small entrepreneurs. Around 1917, Vasyl Hutsuliak, who came from Ukraine in 1908, opened a grocery store at 86 St Dominique.[69] Aliaksei Skapets, a Belarusan immigrant from Vil'na, owned a business (the nature of which he did not specify) at 92 St Lawrence Boulevard. Another "old-timer," Ryhor Milouskii from Mogilev, ran a restaurant on de Montigny Street.

Many Ukrainian and Belarusan immigrants found their first jobs through friends or relatives who had come to the city earlier. Labourers without the advantage of such connections resorted to private labour agencies, which proliferated in pre-World War I Montreal. In 1912, the city had twenty-six licensed employment bureaux and hundreds of unauthorized labour agents.[70] Some agencies catered to a multi-ethnic immigrant clientele, supplying employers with workers of the nationality they preferred. "Send us the Order and we will send you the Men. Describe the Work and State Wages Paid, also what Nationality is preferred," read the advertisement for the Dominion Labour Bureau, which offered services in Russian and seven other languages.[71] Others, like the "Russian-Bulgarian Agency" located on St Antoine Street, had a more specific ethnic orientation. Ethnic steamship agents, grocers, and other entrepreneurs also ventured into this lucrative market, attempting to supplement their main income by acting as middlemen between employers and job seekers. Multi-functionality was common for immigrant businesses, which often operated as a combination of a general store, bank, ticket agency, labour exchange, and translation and interpretation office. Many such establishments also served as a sort of postal outlet, where their peripatetic clients picked up mail.

But if ethnic entrepreneurs met many vital needs of the immigrants, they could also be notorious for their fraudulent practices. The history of Slavic immigration to early twentieth-century Montreal is full of co-lourful characters who made a comfortable living off the credulity and misfortune of their "greenhorn" clients. Esther Slobodsky, the owner of a grocery store on St Urbain, was somewhat unusual since she suc-ceeded as both a woman entrepreneur and one of the city's most influ-ential "shadow" labour agents. In 1914, when Eastern European workers were among those hardest hit by the economic recession, the enterprising Mme Slobodsky became infamous far beyond Montreal for her scam job placement schemes. In collusion with several company foremen, she charged her Ukrainian, Belarusan, and other clients $10 for providing them with jobs. After earning his money back, the worker was fired under a false pretext, only to be immediately replaced by another unsuspecting job seeker.

The scheme seemed to work smoothly until March 1914, when about fifty victims, represented by George Alexander, a Russian-speaking law-yer of Armenian origin, initiated a lawsuit against MmeSlobodsky.[72] Alexander himself had a somewhat shady past. After leaving Russia in the late 1890s and spending several years in Europe, he came to Canada in 1902 and served as an interpreter, labour agent, and lawyer for Russian and Armenian immigrants in various Canadian cities, occasion-ally running into troubles with the law. Around 1913, he turned up in Montreal, where he immediately set out to endear himself to the Russian consul (then Nicholas Passek), posing as a defender of the "Russian people" in Montreal against an alleged legion of Jewish swin-dlers. Alexander's personal interest in the Slobodsky case was thinly veiled: by toppling Slobodsky, he hoped to establish himself as the city's most influential Russian-speaking agent. While Alexander did not make much headway with the ailing and nonchalant Passek, he received more sympathy from the new consul Sergei Likhachev, who helped obtain a provincial licence for his newly opened "Russian-Slavic Agency." The consul's enthusiasm, however, quickly cooled after Alexander impli-cated a consular official in his financial machinations and began to un-lawfully advertise his agency as authorized by the consulate.[73]

The fact that most businesses catering to Slavic urban workers were run by Jews (or other non-Slavs) highlights the extent to which the East European ethno-social divisions were reproduced in North Amer-ican immigrant communities. This was especially true of such metrop-olises as New York and Montreal, where many thousands of Slavs and

Jews shared the same neighbourhoods. It was far from uncommon for a Ukrainian or a Belarusan immigrant on the streets of Montreal to run into a Jewish pedlar or tavern-keeper from his native town. Inevitably, the legacy of Old World ethno-religious prejudices and tensions also followed the immigrants across the ocean. Morris (Moishe) Tatarinsky, well known among the Russian-born immigrants of Montreal as the proprietor of a boarding-house and a labour bureau on de Montigny Street, complained to Likhachev in February 1915 of being pursued by an immigrant gang out to rob him. Tatarinsky claimed (but did not convince the consul) that the real cause of the trouble lay in his Jewish roots and, given the opportunity, "such types would have organized a pogrom under the leadership of their own kind …"[74] Overall, the degree of popular Judeophobia in Slavic immigrant communities seems to have been relatively low, although more research is needed to reach any definitive conclusions. Some Russian Orthodox hierarchs in America and Russian-American nationalist newspapers occasionally made appeals to keep "Yids"[75] away from "true Russians," but they achieved little success. Even some of the most vicious Judeophobes grudgingly acknowledged the fact that Jews were an economically vital element of "Russian colonies" and usually provided better service than Slavic entrepreneurs.[76] With their usually superior knowledge of English and business connections, Jews were also prominent as interpreters and negotiators in legal disputes between Slavic workers and their employers. "To hire a Jew" and "to hire an interpreter" meant the same in immigrant parlance. In addition, Jewish boarding-house keepers and small proprietors sometimes took care of their sick or injured Slavic tenants, providing them with food and, sometimes, a few dollars to get back on their feet.

The "Russian" presence in Montreal peaked during the last years of World War I, when the end of the railway construction boom and the expansion of munitions industries drew many frontier workers to the city. As we shall see in the following chapters, it was also the heyday of the city's Russian Orthodox church, Russian Protestant missions, and (in 1917–1918) Russian socialist groups. The "urbanites" might have enjoyed a larger circle of social contacts and better access to community support networks, but most of them essentially remained temporary sojourners, who, like their fellow workers on the frontier, had to face the mental and emotional tests of sojourning life.

6

Sojourners and Soldiers

Like thousands of other labour immigrants from eastern, central, and southern Europe, the majority of Ukrainians and Belarusans who came to Canada from the Russian Empire were temporary sojourners – "birds of passage," who did not intend to settle in Canada for good. By the eve of World War I, only a few of the earlier arrivals had completed the transition from sojourning to settling. The Li-Ra-Ma files show that some labourers, still primarily engaged in industrial occupations, acquired plots of land with the apparent goal of putting down roots in Canada. Yet even by 1917–18 their number, by all indications, was small. The majority of the migrants continued to float across the country in search of employment and nurtured plans of returning home as soon as conditions permitted. Sociologist Paul Siu's concept of the sojourner as an individual who regards his stay in the host country as a "job" to be finished in the shortest possible time and organizes his life accordingly is a useful framework for explaining the mindset and behavioural patterns typical of eastern Ukrainian and Belarusan labour migrants in early twentieth-century Canada.[1] As sojourners, most Ukrainian and Belarusan migrants interacted with the host society only to the extent that enabled them to reach their target of accumulating enough financial resources to return home. The continued use of the old-style Julian calendar, often found in the migrants' correspondence, may be a small detail but it reveals much about the writers' mentality. As one Russian-American commentator put it, the migrant worker from Russia felt like a tenant in a "squalid hotel, where you wake up, get rid of bedbugs, and go about your business trying to think as little about this hotel as you can."[2] Forming permanent communities or putting down roots was difficult and made little sense as long as one's primary-group affiliations and loyalties remained elsewhere.

Sojourning created many emotional and mental challenges: loneliness, lack of stable social contacts, separation from family and friends, and cultural alienation. Most migrant men reacted to these challenges by falling back on certain gender-specific behaviours that lent the "culture of sojourning" a recognizably masculine flavour: rowdiness, shows of physical strength, excessive consumption of alcohol, gambling, and, frequently, sexual profligacy.[3] But the brutalizing effects of sojourning alone cannot explain the large extent of violence among the migrant labourers, for we also need to take into account the Old World cultural roots of such conduct.[4] In the popular culture of Eastern European peasantry, brawn and boisterousness had long been considered normative qualities of masculinity.[5] Heavy drinking and ritual group fistfights were part of village life, occurring most frequently on Sundays and major holidays as well as at weddings.[6] Transplanted across the ocean, these forms of socializing reflected the migrants' yearning for the familiar in a foreign cultural environment and were used as ways of fostering male camaraderie.

Of all the leisure activities, drinking was probably practiced most by both Ukrainian and Belarusan labourers. Following the Old World pattern, paydays, Sundays and religious holidays turned into major occasions for excessive use of alcohol (usually beer and whiskey, which were often consumed together). The migrants' resourcefulness in adjusting to a foreign diet did not exclude even the consumption of liquor: unaccustomed to the taste of whiskey, Belarusan and Ukrainian workers in the Crow's Nest Pass mixed it with chilli pepper to eliminate the "unpleasant smell."[7] The arrival or departure of a comrade was also accompanied by spontaneous drinking parties. The intemperate habits of Slavic workers made them a constant source of profit for bar owners and bootleggers. One immigrant recalled that on paydays the owners of Fernie hotels (known more for their bars than for their lodging facilities) drove to the workers' quarters in their automobiles handing out free liquor. "Warmed up" this way, the labourers immediately proceeded to the hotel to continue the feast, squandering hundreds of dollars in a matter of days.[8] After the introduction of prohibition in wartime Canada, the sale of hard liquor moved underground to boarding-houses and immigrant-owned stores, which soon attracted the attention of the police. Belarusan immigrants Paraskeva and Andrei Shumovich, owners of a boarding-house in Sault Ste Marie, were arrested and fined twice for the illegal sale of liquor in addition to other charges, which included obstructing a police officer and maiming a cow by cutting off its tail.[9] Drinking often triggered brawls, followed by the arrival of the police and fines for disorderly conduct. In the Li-Ra-Ma affidavits, which required their subjects to disclose their criminal records in Canada, drinking and disorderly conduct were the two most commonly listed offences (failure to carry identity papers during the war was the third most frequent infraction). At times, drunkenness brought more serious consequences, as it did in the case of Andrei Lesnik, who was inebriated when he stabbed his boarding-house keeper to death after the latter attempted to prevent him from making improper advances to his wife.[10]

Alcohol could also aggravate ethnic and cultural divisions that were normally dormant between various groups of workers. When the war began in 1914 and suddenly pitted "Russians" against "Austrians," drunken fights between the two groups became increasingly common, even though the majority of participants on both sides were Ukrainian. Some Russian-born immigrants in wartime Montreal used their status as subjects of an Allied state to start rows with "the Galicians" – and then happily watched the police arrest the troublemaking "enemy aliens." Similar incidents flared up in other places. What began as a baptism celebration at a Russian immigrant's house in Saskatoon soon turned into a debate with several Galician guests over "whose tsar will win" before ending in a drunken brawl and the arrest of ten people.[11] In London, Ontario a street fight between "Austrians" and "Russians" broke out after the former made a scornful remark about the Russian army as they walked past the line of Russian boarding-houses. Deploring such outbreaks of popular chauvinism, the Russian-American socialist newspaper *Novyi mir* wrote sarcastically that "all week Russians and Austrians live together peacefully, and only on Sundays, under the impact of alcoholic fumes, do they turn into patriots."[12]

Gambling and playing pool were two other favourite pastimes, and it was far from uncommon for a luckless labourer to leave a whole month's wages at the card table. Cardsharps and various crooks preyed upon the immigrants, especially the younger and less experienced ones.[13] Immigrants fortunate enough to land good jobs were often disoriented by the sudden transition from Old World poverty and the monotony of village life to the sudden state of relative financial security, so they found the temptation to indulge in sensual pleasures hard to resist. Young bachelors, unburdened by the obligations of supporting a family, were apparently more susceptible to the lure of the gambling table and the beer parlour, whereas married men usually showed more frugality and self-discipline. Bachelors were also the main frequenters of

brothels, which proliferated both in the cities and on the resource frontier, often operating under the roof of boarding-houses. For instance,
Moishe Tatarinsky, owner of a boarding-house and a large labour
agency in Montreal, was also said to run a brothel filled "with Russian
and Austrian prostitutes."[14]

Short periods of time between work and leisure were usually spent
writing or dictating letters to relatives and friends in the old country.
Maintaining a connection with kith and kin was an essential part of the
sojourning culture: a migrant was "not typically a sojourner unless he
[had] maintained his homeland tie."[15] Apart from its practical purposes, it helped relieve the psycho-emotional stress of what Robert
Harney called the "suspended animation" of the sojourner's life.[16] Despite the gradual decline of Eastern European peasant culture with its
traditional anti-individualism and communitarianism, family obligations remained central to peasant cosmogony. Failure to conform to the
socially prescribed spousal roles, disrespect for the elders, or some other
intentional violation of traditional norms of conduct could result in the
loss of one's social standing in the village. After all, it was precisely the
strong sense of familial duty that provided one of the most compelling
motives for peasant men to go overseas for temporary work. That said,
we should not generalize too easily about the migrants' family values.
As William Thomas and Florian Znaniecki pointed out in their classic
study of the Polish peasantry, emigration often recruited individuals
less wedded to traditional peasant culture and, in turn, further contributed to the latter's erosion.[17] In addition, the migrants were a demo-
graphically heterogeneous group, which included single and married,
young and old individuals, as well as persons with and without children.
Searching for socio-cultural explanations of the migrants' behaviour,
we should also remember the impact of individual psycho-emotional
characteristics on family relationships. Like any human beings, early
twentieth-century peasant men differed in the strength of their attach-
ment to their spouses, parents, and children, not to mention the obvious fact that some individuals tended to feel the psychic stress of
separation more keenly than others.

Most Ukrainian and Belarusan labourers tried to maintain a regular
two-way communication with their families. This correspondence, occasionally accompanied by photographs, was not simply the only way
for early twentieth-century immigrants to exchange information but
also a medium for reasserting their sense of belonging and renegotiating
relationships with their kin.[18] Exactly how frequent the communication

was depended on the psycho-emotional dynamics of each relationship. Hryhorii Studilka from Podolia sent nine letters (and remitted $115) to his wife over a period of eight months, while Prokop Podorozhnyi only wrote twice before he broke off all communication.[19] While few letters written by immigrants from eastern Ukraine and Belarus have survived, many Li-Ra-Ma files contain what is often called "reverse" letters written between 1912 and 1920 by wives, parents, and occasionally other relatives of the immigrants. These letters, which often contain indirect voices of the other party, provide a precious glimpse into the impact of sojourning on family relationships.

Like peasant letter writers in other parts of Eastern Europe, Ukrainians and Belarusans followed a certain writing ritual, in which showing respect for the members of the family was of utmost importance. As a rule, the letters opened with "bows" from the writer to each of the readers (leading Thomas and Znaniecki to call such correspondence "bowing letters"[20]), sometimes accompanied by other standard forms of greeting such as wishes of good health or "success in the deeds of your hands." The writers rarely went beyond the events and accidents within the household and the village (deaths, births, marriages, fires, comings and goings of the co-villagers, etc.), and even major social and political happenings such as the war and the revolutions of 1917 were seldom mentioned. Family business was the dominant theme in the majority of the letters, suggesting that many men remained closely involved in the management of the household even years after emigrating (one letter from Bessarabia, for instance, discussed the purchase of a new ox cart[21]). Wives and parents took special care to provide their husbands and sons with detailed accounts of the current state of the family economy: acreage occupied by various crops, harvest prospects, current agricultural prices, livestock sold and bought, etc. The money received from Canada was accounted for with particular diligence.

The modicum of economic security brought to peasant families by the emigration of their male members was often purchased at the cost of considerable social disruption. The departure of husbands and fathers altered the fragile structure of power relations within peasant households and rural communities, placing the remaining members of emigrants' families in vulnerable positions.[22] The longer the husband's absence, the stronger the likelihood that his wife would be mistreated by senior relatives, particularly in-laws, whose authority was buttressed by tradition and custom. Economic power in the family, including control over the money received from Canada, was one of the main issues behind these conflicts. At the same time, the temporary role of household managers (which turned out in some cases to be permanent) gave emigrants' wives the leverage that they had lacked before. Some women even tried (not always without success) to defy the hostile elders: thus, after numerous conflicts with the in-laws whose house she shared, the wife of Iustyn Hedz', an immigrant from Podolia, reported to her husband that she had started building a separate house for the young family.[23] Endowed with this new power, the women felt that they were not only entitled to fair treatment by the relatives, but also had the moral right to hold their absent husbands accountable for failing to stay in touch or provide enough support for the family. Natalia Shkiruk from Podolia wrote to her husband: "I don't have any food for the children now. You only sent me enough money to pay the debts, but not for my expenses. I am struggling to feed the children here, and you are there all by yourself."[24]

In her study of the effects of male emigration on Polish women, Mary Eleanor Cygan has argued that, far from enjoying their autonomy, the emigrants' wives typically saw their situation in rather glum terms and encouraged their husbands to return.[25] By and large, the reading of letters from eastern Ukraine and Belarus bears out this conclusion. Frustrated by years of trying to maintain a normal appearance of family life under the adverse circumstances of the war and, later, revolution and civil unrest, the women used various ways of persuading their husbands to come back: from threatening them with public shame ("people are laughing at how you are shirking your family") to trying to melt the men's hearts by appealing to their fatherly feelings.[26]

The theme of spousal infidelity – an inevitable danger in any long-distance relationship – loomed large in the emigrant correspondence. Adultery was common among male immigrant sojourners in North America, and Ukrainian and Belarusan men were no exception. Forced and voluntary sexual liaisons between male boarders and the wives or daughters of boarding-house keepers occurred on a regular basis, and visits to "houses of ill fame" were such a normal part of the sojourners' lives that they almost ceased to be regarded as serious moral offences. Despite the long distances, information about the men's indiscretions travelled home by way of gossip and stories passed on through village and kin networks. However, patriarchal peasant society subjected male sexual transgressions to far less scrutiny and moral condemnation than female infidelity. Nor was it easy to exercise the usual forms of community pressure such as public shaming, when the perpetrators were thousands of miles away. As historian Jeffrey Burds has shown, it was hard enough for the peasant commune in Russia to enforce moral control over seasonal migrants working as far away as the nearest city.[27] It was usually left to the woman herself to try appealing to her husband's sense of spousal duty. Thus Vasil' Astapchuk, a native of Pruzhany, had to face unpleasant questions from his wife and teenaged children: "Maybe you want to forget about us? We hear that you are having a good time there, like a bachelor. All of you there have forgotten your wives and children, and you all pretend to be single men …"[28] Some women went so far as to raise openly the question of divorce. Paulina Hushcha, also from Pruzhany, pressed her husband Andrei to tell her whether he intended to "live with [her] as before" or else to send her divorce papers so that she could remarry.[29] When pleas and moral pressure did not work, the more determined of the women wrote to the local authorities in Ukraine or Belarus complaining about their husbands' misdeeds. After passing through the many circuits of the tsarist bureaucracy, some of these petitions reached the desk of the Russian consul in Montreal but, as might be expected, they seldom brought results. In the rare cases when the man was located (a tall order for the consuls given the migrants' transience), he often turned the tables on the woman, casting aspersions on her moral character. Serhii Asaulenko, who had emigrated in 1908 from Kiev Province, wrote to Consul Struve that he would not send his wife any money despite her pleas, for she had always led an immoral life, repeatedly turned down his attempts to bring her to Canada, and eventually left the village, abandoning their small children.[30]

These counter-accusations were not necessarily unfounded. Although a detailed discussion of sexual practices in early twentieth-century Ukrainian and Belarusan villages would require a separate volume, adultery and illicit sex appear to have become increasingly common among both peasant women and men. As elsewhere in Europe, the outbreak of the war shook the patriarchal foundations of peasant society in eastern Ukraine and Belarus, which had already been affected by modernization and secularization. The passage of Russian troops through a village sometimes resulted in sexual liaisons between local women and soldiers billeted in peasant homes, increasing the number of illegitimate childbirths.[31] Unlike the extra-marital adventures of their emigrant husbands, female infidelity was much more likely to be noticed (especially if followed by pregnancy) and publicly condemned. As Christine Worobec has pointed out, in the male-dominated Ukrainian peasant society women were seen as temptresses possessing insatiable sexual urges and prone to moral laxity.[32] A married woman who remained away from her husband for a long time, even through no fault of her own, usually found herself frowned upon by the peasant community, and her chastity became the subject of village gossip. Many peasant men working in the mines of Fernie or in the logging camps of northern Ontario must have suspected that their wives back home were not always leading virtuous lives. Real or suspected "improprieties" committed by the wives and fiancées of the migrants were promptly reported to Canada by parents, friends, neighbours, or new arrivals from the village. Mykola Korsak received a short note from his friend, apparently written with the sole purpose of informing him that a man from Mykola's village had "gotten into the habit of [...] pleasing" his girlfriend.[33] Sometimes such reports led to tragic consequences. A miner in Fernie, who had been working hard to pay off the mortgage on his recently acquired land, collapsed and died of a heart attack after learning from a newly arrived co-villager that his son had passed away and that his wife had eloped with a soldier. Another miner was rumoured to have killed his unfaithful wife and her illegitimate child after returning home.[34] The women defended their honour (or perhaps hid their misdeeds) as best as they could, trying to dispel their husbands' suspicions. Thus Ahafia Koval' from Davydkivtsi, Podolia, assured her husband Opanas in an affectionate and emotional letter that she was "free from any crimes and improper acts of which your father probably thinks I am guilty."[35]

If letters helped preserve the emotional tie between the migrant and his kin in the old land, the economic connection with the home village was sustained through money remittances, sent in the form of postal or bank money orders, or passed on in cash with returning co-villagers. As emigrant family letters demonstrate, it was common for migrant men to send money not only to wives and parents but also to siblings, cousins, and other members of the extended family. Female relatives, especially younger sisters, also received small gifts from "America" in addition to money allowances (such as kerchiefs, which were the most coveted). Remarkably, some migrants even sent money orders to their brothers who were fighting on the battlefields of World War I.[36] Most immigrants began to send money home as soon as they found their first full-time jobs, with the first remittances normally used to pay back the loans made to finance the sender's voyage. The amount and frequency of the remittances depended on the man's earnings, frugality, and sense of

moral duty. The Li-Ra-Ma files, some of which contain money order re-
ceipts, show that the value of individual remittances sent by Ukrainian
and Belarusan migrants varied from $5 to about $400. While small cash
infusions had the purpose of simply helping the family stay afloat,
larger sums were sent with a view of accumulating savings, although
rampant wartime inflation and the post-1917 collapse of the Russian
economy thwarted these intentions. Pavel Harbelik, an immigrant from
Minsk, sent eleven money orders between 1913 and 1917 with a modest total of $326. By contrast, Antin Zapotochnyi transferred $577 to
his family in Podolia in just two years.[37] In some cases (usually when
the emigrant was a bachelor who had lived with his parents), the family
had to wait months or even years before receiving the first remittance.
Anton Ialets, for instance, was told off by his parents for not sending his
first $25 until four years after leaving his native Grodno.[38]

As Ewa Morawska put it, immigrant remittances that circulated in
the early 1900s between the two continents (including cash carried by
returning migrants and enclosed in letters) represented the "lower cir-
cuit" of the transnational movement of capital.[39] On the eve of World
War I, the amount of immigrant money annually remitted to Russia
was in the millions of dollars. According to the statistics of Canada's
Post Office Department, between 1 March 1913 and 31 January 1914
Russian immigrants sent home 43,074 money orders with a total value
of $1,864,735.[40] In the absence of direct postal exchange between
Russia and Canada, money was sent through British banks and post offices, which charged an additional six-cent commission for every $24
(the project of a Russian-Canadian postal convention was discussed in
1914 but never materialized). Immigrants from Russia sent such a large
amount of money through the post in Montreal that in the autumn of
1914 Consul Likhachev suggested to Canada's Postmaster General that
a Russian interpreter be attached to the city's main post office.[41]

To send money to the homeland, many Ukrainians and Belarusans
also turned to immigrant-owned banking and steamship agencies,
where they could be served in Russian or another familiar language. In
each Canadian province or large city, the business of handling immigrants' transactions with Russia was concentrated in the hands of a few
large operators. Many Russian-born labourers in Ontario sent money
through the Louis Gurofsky Company, which had its head office in
Toronto and branches in Hamilton, Sudbury, Timmins, Parry Sound,
and Sault Ste Marie. In Montreal they usually patronized the George
Rabinovitch agency, located on the northeast edge of the downtown

"immigrant corridor." But dealing with immigrant bankers could be a risky business. One of the worst cases of banking fraud that affected hundreds of Russian immigrants happened in August 1914, when Louis Mednik, the owner of Montreal's International Bureau, declared bankruptcy and disappeared with several thousand dollars of his clients' money.[42] Canada's chartered banks and express mail companies – Dominion Express and Canadian Express – usually presented a safer alternative, but they had the drawback of not offering service in Eastern European languages. Some immigrants found a reliable way of sending money through the Russian consulates. As early as 1908, several young Bessarabians working near Gaspé asked Consul Nicholas Struve for the favour of forwarding money to their parents.[43] Struve's successors at the consulate occasionally continued to act as a conduit for immigrant money remittances, which were transferred to the recipients through the Foreign Ministry's Second Department and later through the provincial governors' offices.[44] From 1916 Russian consulates in North America also housed special overseas branches of the Russian State Savings Bank, established with the goal of channeling emigrant savings into the faltering Russian economy. The "Special Financial Department for Transfers and Deposits of Money to the State Savings Banks" in Montreal opened its doors in June 1917 in the consular building on St Nicholas Street. It offered its clients an opportunity to convert Canadian dollars into Russian rubles and to deposit them into a savings account with the bank.[45]

The outbreak of World War I in August 1914 marked a turning point in the lives of thousands of Canada's immigrant workers. By thwarting their plans of returning home, the war eventually prompted many to ponder permanent settlement, establish more stable communities and, ultimately, move towards a greater degree of integration into Canadian society. While the wartime experiences of Russian-subject workers were in many respects similar to those of other continental Europeans, they were also characterized by important differences arising from the status of Russians as nationals of a major allied power. There were some instances of mistreatment, prejudice, and even occasional internment, but generally Russian-subject Ukrainians and Belarusans fared much better during the war than Ukrainian immigrants from Austria, who bore the stigma of "enemy aliens" and suffered from a variety of legal restrictions. Only in 1918 did things take a turn for the worse. The end of the war in November 1918 brought little relief to the thousands of former subjects of the tsar. The beginning of the civil war in

Russia following the Bolshevik coup of October 1917 continued to keep eastern Ukrainian and Belarusan workers trapped in Canada, gradually diminishing their prospects of reunion with their families.

As Russian subjects of military service age, most Russian Ukrainians and Belarusans during the first weeks of the war had to confront the dilemma of returning to fight for the "Faith, Tsar, and Fatherland" or remaining in Canada to face the risk of hefty penalties and public condemnation back home. Reactions to the war in Canada's "Russian" colonies were mixed. Cooler heads questioned the wisdom of sacrificing the comforts of life in Canada on the altar of the decadent Romanov monarchy, while socialist organizations denounced the war as imperialist and having nothing to do with the interests of the international working class. The Russian Progressive Club of Winnipeg at its August 8 meeting passed a resolution of protest against the war. Anti-war meetings were also held in other cities. Russian patriots in Montreal who tried to exhort their fellow countrymen to go home and fight were expelled from a large workers' rally convened by socialist and labour organizations.[46] On the whole, however, popular chauvinism, which ruled the day in all belligerent nations, also seemed to dominate the "Russian colonies" in the opening months of the conflict. Letters from wives and parents urged immigrant men to come back and join the Russian army to avoid being branded as cowards.[47] In the first two months of the war, 1,267 Russian-subject immigrants (most of them Ukrainians and Belarusans from Montreal) voluntarily signed up at the consulate to be shipped to the front at the first call of the Russian military authorities.[48] Sometimes as many as ten to twelve men from the same Montreal boarding-house came to the consulate asking to be sent to fight the Germans. Throughout the fall and winter of 1914–15, dozens of loyalist addresses and letters poured into the Russian consulate general. Danylo Bobyk, a Bessarabian living in Windsor, Ontario wrote, for instance, that he wanted to become a pilot in order to "be of some use to Russia."[49] The mayor of Vancouver T.S. Baxter telegraphed Consul Likhachev that many Russian-subject residents of the city were zealous to enlist in the Russian army. Similar communications came from Sudbury, Edmonton, and other cities.[50]

Patriotism was not the sole reason why many Russian immigrants wanted to return to the homeland. The economic recession, which hit Canada in mid-1913, drove many Ukrainians, Belarusans, and other Russian-born workers into destitution, forcing them to look for ways to leave Canada. Persistent rumours that the Russian government had promised to cover the cost of return passage for persons liable for mobilization doubtless led many immigrants to pose as ultra-patriots in order to receive a travel allowance. In the late summer and fall of 1914, the Russian consulate was flooded with requests to be shipped to Russia at government expense. An experienced bureaucrat, Likhachev was not easily convinced by the patriotic rhetoric that often accompanied these letters. "I can say with some certainty," he reported to Petrograd in March 1915, "that the desire to enlist in our army was not the only or main one for those who applied [for travel subsidies]. The hope of leaving Canada at the time of poor job prospects played a major role".[51]

Going back home during the war was difficult but not impossible, provided an emigrant had a stable job in the midst of an economic recession and could save enough money to buy a steamship ticket. The common assumption that the outbreak of the war put a stop to transatlantic population movements is only partially true, for even after August 1914 there was substantial return migration to Europe.[52] Although major German and Dutch ports were no longer accessible, steamship communication with Europe was maintained via the North Sea despite the increased risk of sea travel. The Scandinavian-American Line, which operated under the flag of neutral Denmark, offered Russian passengers safe passage from New York to Christiania (Oslo) and then by rail to Petrograd. For $60, one could also take the Cunard Line from New York to Liverpool or travel to Finland by the White Star Line, which sailed under the American flag and thus was deemed (until 1917) less vulnerable to German submarine attacks.[53] After a short interruption in August 1914, the Russian America Line also resumed regular sailings to New York, using Archangel (on the North Sea coast) as the port of origin instead of German-occupied Libava. Finally, returning immigrants could use the relatively safe Pacific route – from Vancouver or Seattle through Yokohama to Vladivostok.

In the first two years of the war, there was little change in the passport and visa regulations pertaining to Russian subjects in Canada. Unlike nationals of enemy states, Russians could freely leave the country as long as they had the required papers. According to the Russian regulations of 1912, which remained in force until late 1916, returning subjects of the empire had to possess a valid passport or apply to the nearest Russian consulate for a one-time entry permit (*prokhodnoe svidetel'stvo*). An affidavit signed by a priest or two proven Russian subjects who knew the applicant was normally accepted as sufficient proof of citizenship. According to the figures which Likhachev provided to Prime Minister Robert Borden in January 1917, the two consulates in Montreal and Vancouver had issued nearly 3,500 entry permits and validated some 100 passports since August 1914.[54] Another 300 Russian-subject immigrants hired themselves out as crew members on Canadian transport vessels carrying shipments of horses to Britain as a way to travel back to Europe (several of these vessels were torpedoed en route by German U-boats).[55]

It is not possible to establish how many of these 3,900 individuals actually reached Russia, for the fact of possessing a travel document cannot serve as proof of successful return. It is also likely that many others who *did* return had either neglected to contact the consulates for entry permits or obtained them from Russian consular missions in the United States or Sweden – the main transit point for returning Russian immigrants. But these statistics do show that migration back to Russia continued even during the worst months of the war, although it never approached the mass return of recruits and reservists that was expected by the Russian government. The proof of such migration can also be found in emigrant family letters dated 1915–17. Within days of returning to their home villages, most men were drafted and sent to the trenches.[56]

By the fall of 1916, increased security concerns led the tsarist government to start limiting admission to the empire's territory. The new entry regulations, adopted by the Russian Council of Ministers in late October, annulled all previously issued passports and required Russian subjects who wished to return to the homeland to submit detailed personal and family information on a special questionnaire along with proof of citizenship and two photographs, all of which were forwarded to the Russian Ministry of Foreign Affairs for an identity check.[57] However, it was only in January 1917 that Russian consular missions finally received detailed instructions (known as Circular 630) explaining the new procedures. Putting the regulations into effect thus became the responsibility of Russia's new Provisional Government, but the post-revolution turmoil and various more pressing concerns delayed their introduction until July 1917. As soon as the new permits were available, the Russian consulates in Montreal and Vancouver were swamped with applications. Answers provided on line 19 of the questionnaire, where the applicant was asked for a "precise indication of the trip's purpose," were usually standard, especially when a clerk at a ticket or labour agency had completed the form. While these answers should not always be taken at face value, they are nonetheless our only available source on the motives for wartime return migration to Russia (unlike the US government, Canadian authorities did not keep the statistics on emigration). The most commonly given reasons included "going back to my family" (25 per cent of the answers), "returning home" (21 per cent), "going to take care of my household" (15 per cent), and "returning after temporary work *(zarabotki)*" (14 per cent). Notably, about 45 per cent of the immigrants gave return destinations other than their native provinces; most of these individuals were Belarusans from the provinces of Grodno and Vil'na, returning to search for their refugee families scattered across central and eastern Russia. Although economic and family reasons for returning predominated, approximately 20 per cent gave "political" motives such as the desire to "serve the motherland" or "to fulfil my military obligation," and 4 per cent suffered from nostalgia. Some naturalized immigrants wanted to leave in order to avoid conscription into the Canadian army. One such man threatened with the draft was Tymofii Fedyk, the owner of a farm in Alberta, who wrote to the consul that he would rather sell his land and return to Russia than "suffer and die for the country of Canada for which I have no love."[58]

Given that the application process took about three months, there were probably few immigrants who received their entry permits by late October 1917, when the Bolshevik coup in Petrograd once again drastically changed the Russian political landscape. The installation of the Soviet government in Russia brought the review of applications by the Foreign Ministry to an end, leaving Russian consulates across North America (which did not recognize the new Soviet regime) with a backlog of unprocessed files. With Russia's political future unclear and anxiety among thousands of permit seekers high, in January 1918 the Russian embassy in Washington gave all Russian consulates in North America the green light to resume the issuance of permits to all persons who could prove their Russian citizenship. Between January 1918 and May 1919, the Montreal consulate furnished over 2,000 former Russian subjects of various nationalities with travel papers (the figures for the Vancouver consulate are missing), but it is impossible to ascertain how many of them actually managed to make the crossing.[59] The outbreak of civil war, followed by the Allied intervention and naval blockade of Soviet Russia, made travelling via the Atlantic for most of 1919 and 1920 next to impossible. Although Russia's eastern frontier was controlled by the White forces of Admiral Kolchak and remained open for most of the period, the unstable political situation in Siberia and the Far East could not guarantee a safe passage. Nevertheless, during 1918 and the early months of 1919 those most desperate to return did attempt to sail from Vancouver to Vladivostok via Yokohama. In March 1919, admission of returning emigrants through the Far Eastern ports was temporarily closed on the grounds of possible "Red" infiltration. It was resumed in several weeks with new entry regulations in place, which turned over the responsibility of issuing entry permits from the consulates to the embassies. To filter out possible Communist sympathizers, all applicants for permits were required to submit proof of their non-involvement in the Bolshevik movement.[60] In May 1920 (after the Kolchak government's demise) Russian consular missions in North America regained the right to issue travel papers. However, with the rapid disintegration of Russia's White movement, ex-tsarist diplomatic missions lost all financial support as well as their legitimacy in the eyes of both Russian immigrants and foreign governments.

Thousands of Ukrainians and Belarusans returned home during the war years, but most stayed in Canada by choice or necessity. For many of them, enlistment in the Canadian expeditionary troops became the only way to contribute to the Allied war effort and to achieve financial security at a time of rampant unemployment, which lasted until 1916. Although the tsar's decree of April 1915 allowed Russian reservists who could not return home for mobilization to enlist in the armies of Russia's allies, Canada was only added to the Allied list on 5 June 1915.[61] Many immigrants from Russia had already begun to enlist as volunteers in the Canadian Expeditionary Force (CEF), with little regard for (or knowledge of) Russian government regulations.[62] Decent salaries paid to Canadian soldiers (a private in the CEF received $33 a month) and generous separation allowances ($20 per month) for the wives, widowed mothers, and guardians of minor children of the volunteers were probably the main reason why many had signed up. Canadian military salaries were even high enough to attract Russian immigrants from the United States. 25-year-old Anton Gretzky, a native of Grodno and the grandfather of Canadian hockey star Wayne Gretzky, was one of the American arrivals. In August 1917, Anton left his job as "stationary fireman" in Chicago and came to Toronto, where he enlisted in the 1st Reserve Battalion of the Canadian Expeditionary Force.[63] When the volunteer's family was in Russia (as was the case with Gretzky and many others like him), it received Canadian separation allowances through the office of the British consul in Petrograd.

Thus enlistment not only provided an escape from destitution for many immigrant men but also allowed them to remain their families' breadwinners at a time when civilian employment was scarce.

The Russian consulates in Canada tried to monitor the enlistment campaign in order to prevent "enemy aliens" (especially Austrian Ukrainians and Poles) from enlisting under the guise of Russian subjects. The Russian government feared that nationals of enemy states might infiltrate the Allied forces due to the laxity of Canadian recruitment procedures. There was already mounting evidence of Ukrainians from Austria masquerading as Russians to avoid discrimination or to appear eligible for enlistment.[64] At the July 1915 meeting between Likhachev and Prime Minister Robert Borden it was decided that in all cases when the Russian citizenship of a volunteer could not be ascertained, the recruiting officer or the volunteer himself should contact one of the Russian consuls for identity verification. Despite instructions from the Department of Militia and Defence, recruiting officers were anxious to "snatch" anyone willing to serve and commonly accepted volunteers without a proper identity check.[65] There were instances when immigrant men signed recruitment papers under the influence of alcohol bought by an unscrupulous recruiter, or were led to believe that they were merely signing a "declaration of their Russian citizenship."[66] The majority, however, enlisted of their own free will.

The total number of Russian-subject immigrants of various nationalities who served in the CEF during the war remains unknown and can only be established through an exhaustive search of hundreds of thousands of archived military personnel files. A consular list, compiled between the end of 1916 and the beginning of 1917, contains the names and birthplaces of 124 Russian-subject soldiers affiliated with twenty various CEF units, including fifty-two men born in eastern Ukraine and thirty-five in Belarus.[67] Ukrainian-Canadian historians have accepted 2,000 as the probable number of Ukrainians from the Russian Empire who served in the Canadian army during the Great War.[68] If we assume that the relative proportions of Ukrainians and Belarusans shown in the consular list were typical of the whole Canadian Expeditionary Force, it may be estimated that the number of Belarusan volunteers was close to 1,300. The difficulty of establishing the extent of Russian nationals' representation in the CEF is increased by the fact that many non-Canadian volunteers had their names anglicized or mangled in other ways: thus, Grigory Petrikovsky became Harry Patrick and Filipp Titorenko was enlisted as Philip Titeronto. Still, various sources indicate that many Canadian battalions had significant contingents of "Russians." Two undated consular logs of enlisted Russian subjects show that at least seventy-eight battalions and several auxiliary units had Russian volunteers, including the 218th Battalion ("Irish Guards") with as many as 153 Russian-born servicemen and the 221st Overseas Infantry Battalion with seventy-one.[69] According to the testimony of its commanding officer, the 198th Battalion ("Canadian Buffs") boasted a whole "Russian platoon."[70] The enthusiastic enlistment of Russian subjects in the CEF even brought out proposals to create separate Russian battalions. Although the idea of ethnic units never caught on with Canadian military authorities, the number of Orthodox recruits in the overseas forces was so large that in September 1915 the Department of Militia and Defence enlisted Rev. Ioann Ovsianitsky, a Russian Orthodox priest from Quebec City, as a military chaplain with the 57th Battalion, which was then being trained at Valcartier. Ovsianitsky not only performed religious services for Orthodox volunteers but also vigorously promoted enlistment in the CEF through the newspaper *Russkaia zemlia* published by the Russian Orthodox mission in the United States. In August 1916, he sailed off to Britain to minister to Canadian soldiers waiting to be shipped to the front.[71]

While some Ukrainians and Belarusans signed up for military duty, others contributed to the war effort by working at Canada's numerous industrial establishments producing munitions and war supplies. In 1914–15, when the job market remained tight, Russian-subject workers in some localities were quick to turn the restrictions imposed on "enemy aliens" to their advantage by demanding the discharge of "Austrian" navvies and miners. In July 1915, a group of Russian-subject navvies working near Sudbury urged Consul Likhachev to help "drive these Austrian scumbags out of this [railway] section." Forty-three Ukrainian and Belarusan miners from Russia employed with the Mond Nickel Company signed a petition, claiming that "there are many Russians out of employment and unable to obtain work at the said Mines owing to the number of Austrians employed."[72] In June 1915 Russian, Italian, and Canadian-born miners in the Crow's Nest Pass held several strikes in protest against the employment of enemy aliens. After prolonged negotiations between the strike committee and the management, naturalized and married enemy aliens were allowed to return to work.[73] In 1916 the expanding war production replaced the stagnation of the previous two years with labour shortages and high wages. By mid-1916, workers who did not report for mobilization no longer had to fear punishment from the home country's authorities: in June of that year the Russian General Staff granted exemptions from mobilization to Russian subjects employed in Canadian industries deemed essential for the war (the definition of which was later expanded to include railway construction, shipbuilding, and agriculture). Beginning in the spring of 1917, these workers were required to obtain certificates of employment from their companies and to present them to the consulate for legalization.[74]

Economic difficulties aside, Russian-subject immigrants enjoyed a relatively trouble-free existence in Canada during the first three years of the war. Although they were occasionally mistaken for enemy aliens and sometimes even placed in internment camps, such instances seem to have been uncommon. The introduction of national manpower registration in August 1916, however, marked the first step towards increased government control over "friendly aliens" (the term applied to the subjects of the Allied countries). The fact that most Russian-subject labourers lived in Canada without documents and could not prove their citizenship began to pose significant problems after the Military Service Act was passed in July 1917, introducing selective conscription of male British subjects between the ages of twenty and forty-five. As foreign nationals, Russian-subject Ukrainians and Belarusans were not eligible for the draft, but their failure to immediately produce proof of Russian citizenship to the police or military authorities often resulted in detentions and fines for non-possession of identity papers.[75] By late 1917, with the Robert Borden government struggling to put more men in the field, Canada's "friendly aliens" were faced with a conundrum. They were increasingly seen as "slackers" profiteering from the war, since they were able-bodied men of conscription age who could not be legally forced to serve. By the end of 1917 and especially in 1918, instances began to multiply of Russian nationals being pressured into enlistment by their employers or the police. Nykyfor Shchur from Podolia wrote to Likhachev that he and several other Russian-subject immigrants in Welland, Ontario were "given two weeks to obtain passports from the Russian consul, and if we do not have them, they will send us to the Canadian army."[76] In response to such cases of unlawful treatment, Russian socialist organizations in several Canadian cities set up "committees for the defence of Russian citizens." These committees provided immigrants with legal advice regarding conscription and other wartime laws and helped them obtain certificates of citizenship issued by the Russian consulates in Montreal and Vancouver.[77]

The precarious situation in which thousands of Canada's Ukrainian and Belarusan migrant workers found themselves by the war's end was compounded by the growing strain of separation from their loved ones. Keeping in touch with the family was increasingly difficult because of the German occupation and the post-1917 turmoil of civil war, which was particularly brutal in Ukraine. Undelivered letters, returned or lost money orders, years spent without hearing a word from wives or parents – all this put the strength of the migrants' familial attachments to a severe test. Many migrants lost all contact with relatives who had fled from the German troops into Russia's interior, some as far as Siberia and Central Asia.[78] Those who managed to maintain communication received letters from their wives in which pleas to return were mixed with growing resentment and bitterness. Local Russian administrators often singled out emigrants' wives for the most arduous home-front duties such as digging trenches or clearing snow from the railways. Faced with such discrimination, some women blamed their absent husbands for all their misfortunes. The wife of Vasyl Dovhan' complained in a letter to her husband that "*soldatki* [soldiers' wives] are never sent to dig trenches, only *amerikanki* [American emigrants' wives] are. You are away, and I am suffering here because of you."[79] Ivan Kravchenko's wife fell ill and nearly died after shovelling snow from the railway tracks in cold weather.[80] Trapped in a state of permanent uncertainty, the migrants and their families struggled to stay in touch, despite the complete breakdown of postal communication between Canada and most of European Russia during 1918–20. Others gave up trying, as happy dreams of reunion were replaced first by frustration and despair and then by weariness and indifference.

By the war's end, many Ukrainian and Belarusan migrants found themselves at a point where crucial decisions about the future had to be made. Until 1920–21, most of them probably still harboured hopes of return. In his "Short Report on the Russian Colony in Canada," prepared in December 1918, Consul Sergei Likhachev wrote that "[t]he majority of Russia's natives living in Canada at the present time have made considerable savings and are only waiting for an opportunity to go back to the homeland."[81] However, with travel routes remaining closed and post-war economic recession setting in, these hopes were slowly waning. Like thousands of other migrant workers, Sylvestr Nechykhman grappled with the dilemma of staying or returning. In June 1917 he wrote to his sister in Ukraine that he needed another two years of work before he could buy a return steamship ticket, otherwise he "would probably have to settle here in Canada."[82] He also advised her not to make major investments in the family household, because her emigrant husband (his brother-in-law) was looking for ways to establish himself in Canada and send for the family.

Attitudes toward the new Soviet government also mattered in deciding whether or not to go back. While the desire to live in the world's first workers' state was hard to resist for those with strong pro-Soviet sympathies, others were discouraged from returning by ghastly rumours coming from the homeland. Dmytro Shvets, a CEF veteran, gave up hopes of ever seeing his native Ukraine again "because the Bolsheviks do not admit those who served in the Canadian army, and if someone comes home [...] he gets killed at night in his house by mobsters."[83] He decided instead to find a way to bring his family to Canada, hoping (like some other war veterans) that the Canadian government would assist him in covering the cost of their passage.[84]

We do not know if Dmytro's family managed to make their way to Canada. Nor do we know the general extent of individual or family migration from Soviet Ukraine and Belarus to Canada. In any case, such migration was unlikely to occur before 1921, when the storms of the war and the revolution had finally calmed down, reopening communication between Eastern Europe and North America. Until the late 1920s, the Soviet authorities generally allowed emigration on the grounds of family reunion, and there is scattered evidence that some of Canada's pre-war immigrants from eastern Ukraine and Belarus did bring over their families.[85] Emigration from western Volhynia and Grodno (which became part of the independent Polish state in 1921) or from northern Bessarabia (which was incorporated into Romania) presented even fewer difficulties, provided one had the determination and sufficient means to travel. But many men never saw their families again, eventually forging new marital alliances in Canada and leaving old relationships behind. For others, the "suspended animation" of sojourning never completely ended, as they continued to lead the lives of permanent bachelors in the ethnic slums of Montreal or Toronto, haunted by fading memories of the old land and unable to find a place they could call home.

7

A Difficult Constituency:
Priests, Preachers, and Immigrants

The relationship between immigrant workers and religion was more complex than it is often presumed to be. For cultural, social, or political reasons, not all immigrant groups displayed the same degree of religiosity and commitment to the church. Organized religion was a secondary concern for the majority of labourers from the Russian Empire, who viewed their presence in Canada as a temporary break in the village lifecycle and showed little inclination to expend their energy and savings on the creation of institutions they considered to be of little use. Such attitudes, partly rooted in intrinsic peasant pragmatism, were exacerbated by the lack of Old World experience in organized community life compared to such ethnic groups as Italians, Slovaks, Poles, Finns, Galician Ukrainians, and Jews. Village reading clubs and peasant benevolent societies, often headed by priests in other parts of East-Central Europe, were little known in eastern Ukraine or Belarus.

In contrast to Slavic peoples living under the Ottoman and Habsburg rule, whose status as minorities stimulated a feeling of "us against them" and provided an impetus for organization, in the Romanov empire it was the state itself that posed as the supreme protector of its Slavic Orthodox subjects – but only so long as they accepted their Russianness. The process of national awakening, which provided the vital bond for building ethnic parishes and community institutions among Galician Ukrainians and many other immigrant groups, had barely touched Russia's western frontier, where most nationalist movements in the early 1900s were either at the heritage-gathering stage (Belarus) or had just begun to embark on mass political agitation (Ukraine).[1] This explains why Ukrainians who came to Canada from the Russian Empire prior to 1914 produced hardly any prominent spokesmen of Ukrainian nationalism and why so few Belarusans were aware of their ethnic roots.[2]

The status of Russian Orthodoxy as the official church of the Russian state and a major pillar of Russian nationhood also had profound consequences for the shaping of the immigrants' ambivalent attitude towards organized religion. Although the Russian Orthodox Church did take some steps to accommodate the multi-ethnic character of its North American flock, it essentially saw all its eastern Slav adherents as part of a single national and spiritual community. While religious leaders emerged as one of the mainstays of the national movement among Poles or western (Greek Catholic) Ukrainians, Russian Orthodox priests in North America promoted official Russian nationalism and (until 1917) loyalty to the tsar as the ultimate protector of all Orthodox believers, regardless of their ethnic roots. Prior to 1917 this posture created few problems with Russian-born immigrants, who usually were loyal subjects of their monarch, but the situation changed drastically after the demise of the Romanov monarchy. The inability of the church to divest itself of its former ideological and political connections became a major reason for the decline of many Russian Orthodox parishes across the continent.

KEEPING "HOLY RUS" ALIVE

The Russian Orthodox Church first established a foothold in North America in the late eighteenth century after the Russian discovery of Alaska. Its first mission was organized in 1794 in Kodiak, Alaska, where it ministered to Aboriginal converts and a handful of Russian merchants and settlers. In 1870, the Alaskan parishes received the status of a separate Diocese of the Alaska and the Aleutians, and two years later the newly created episcopal see was transferred from Sitka to San Francisco. The beginning of mass immigration from Eastern and Central Europe in the 1880s provided the basis for an impressive growth of the church over the next quarter century, when dozens of Orthodox parishes and brotherhoods sprang up across the North American continent. In September 1895, a meeting of clergy and lay representatives of Orthodox brotherhoods in Wilkes Barre, Pennsylvania, established a federated Russian Orthodox Mutual Aid Society, whose weekly organ *Svit* (*The Light*) was published in a mixture of Russian and Ukrainian languages. In 1900, the name of the mission was changed to the Diocese of the Aleutians and North America. Five years later, in response to the shifting geography of America's Orthodox population, the episcopal seat was moved from San Francisco to New York.[3]

The earliest followers of Russian Orthodoxy in Canada were Bukovynian and Galician Ukrainians in Manitoba and the Northwest Territories. The first Orthodox service in Canada was held in 1897 at the Ukrainian farm settlement of Wostok in Alberta (also known as Limestone Lake) by a missionary priest dispatched by Bishop Nicholas Ziorov, then head of the Russian Orthodox Church in North America. The majority of Wostok inhabitants consisted of Greek Catholic (Uniate) Galicians who chose to adopt Orthodoxy.[4] In 1908, a separate Canadian deanery of the Russian Orthodox mission in North America was created under Hieromonk Arseny Chekhovtsev. Thirty-two of its thirty-three parishes were located in the West and were served by a mere seven priests, who had to spend most of their time on the road.[5]

By the early 1900s, the conversion of Uniate Galician immigrants to Orthodoxy became the most politically important task for the Russian Orthodox Church in Canada. The struggle between the Greek Catholic and Russian Orthodox churches for the souls of Ukrainian immigrants soon turned the Prairies into an arena of bitter religious conflicts between various factions.[6] Ukrainians from Russia, relatively few in number and almost entirely Orthodox, were rarely involved in these battles. The mission of the church among its Russian-born flock, as formulated by Rev. Chekhovtsev, was to keep the immigrants away from various "evil [Protestant] heresies and alien sects" and to spread the "spirit of patriotism and ... love for the dear fatherland."[7] The Russian Orthodox Church in Canada became the primary medium through which the Russian imperial state attempted to exert ideological and political control over its emigrant subjects. As far as the Russian Orthodox hierarchs in North America and their superiors in St Petersburg were concerned, patriotism was inextricably linked with maintaining allegiance to the faith of one's ancestors.

The number of immigrants from the Russian Empire in the rural Orthodox parishes of western Canada always remained small. Most congregations in Manitoba, Saskatchewan, and Alberta had few if any "Russians." With its largest population of immigrant workers from Russia in all of the Canadian West, Winnipeg was something of an exception, but even here the Russian-born were the clear minority among the Orthodox faithful. Church marriage and baptism registers show the predominance of Galicians and Bukovynians in both the rural and urban parishes of western Canada. According to the 1907 records of the Winnipeg Holy Trinity Russian Orthodox Church (established in 1904), immigrants born in Russia accounted for only about 16 per cent of its 316 parishioners – a percentage that remained relatively constant in later years.[8] Of the 507 baptisms performed in the church from 1913 to 1915, children who had at least one Russian-born parent constituted 17.2 per cent, and among the 352 persons who were married there in the same period, those from Russia made up 15 per cent (the proportion of couples where either or both of the spouses were natives of Russia stood at 22.7 per cent of the total). The majority of the Russian-born members of the church were Ukrainians from Volhynia and Kiev, with Belarusans and ethnic Russians (mostly from Saratov) each contributing about 15 per cent.[9] The parish had a school, where a small number of Ukrainian, Belarusan, and Russian children learned the Russian language, history, and the basics of the Orthodox faith.

Immigrants from Russia came to have a considerably larger presence in the Orthodox communities of eastern Canada, since most immigrant labourers gravitated towards the east. The first and largest Russian Orthodox congregation east of Manitoba – the parish of ss Peter and Paul in Montreal – was organized primarily by the natives of Volhynia and Minsk provinces. The founding of the Montreal parish followed the model typical of many North American immigrant communities: it began with the establishment of a fraternal society, whose role was to consolidate the community and to accumulate financial resources for building the church and supporting the clergy.[10] The parish began in 1905, when a group of Belarusans and Ukrainians, with the help of Russian consul Nicholas Struve, wrote to Archbishop Tikhon Belavin, head of the Russian Orthodox Mission in North America, asking him to send a priest to the "Russian Orthodox people" of Montreal. In March 1906 the mission responded by sending Rev. Alexander Hotovitzky, rector of the St Nicholas Cathedral in New York, to find out the needs of the city's Slavic Orthodox immigrants and to celebrate a liturgy.[11] After the service, Rev. Hotovitzky attended the founding meeting of a fraternal society, which named itself the Russian Orthodox Brotherhood of the Holy Trinity. Both the service and the meeting were held at the St Nicholas Syrian Orthodox church, housed in a remodelled factory building on Vitre Street.[12]

According to the surviving register of the Montreal brotherhood, about 80 per cent of its members were Ukrainian and Belarusan immigrants from the Russian Empire (Volhynia, Kiev, Podolia, Minsk, Grodno, Vil'na, and Mogilev). The remaining 20 per cent were Orthodox Ukrainians from Bukovyna and Galicia. The election of David Malevich from Minsk Province as secretary of the brotherhood and

Consul Struve as its honorary member emphasized the "Russian" character of the parish.[13] The brotherhood became a chapter of the Russian Orthodox Mutual Aid Society of North America, providing members with sickness and death insurance in proportion to paid dues.[14]

Composed primarily of male labourers, the parish had no resources to build a permanent church. The first temporary church hall, consecrated in 1907, was located in the Point St Charles area of Montreal in a small building on Soulanges Street, which also had a poolroom in the basement. The parish's first priest, Rev. Theophan Buketov, exemplified the more competent type of North American Russian Orthodox clergyman of the time: a young, energetic missionary born in Russian Ukraine, he went to the United States shortly after graduation from the Odessa theological seminary. Before his appointment to Montreal, Rev. Buketov had served in two Connecticut parishes, where he had helped bring a group of Greek Catholics into the Orthodox fold. Father Buketov only stayed in Montreal until 1908, when he was transferred to Brooklyn, New York.[15]

For several years the Montreal parish remained the only Russian Orthodox congregation in eastern Canada. It was only in 1911–12, when immigration of Orthodox Christian labourers to Canada reached its zenith, that small and unstable church communities, composed mostly of Galicians and Bukovynians, sprang up in Fort William, Ottawa, Lachine, Quebec City, and Sydney. The establishment of new parishes continued at a brisk pace after the outbreak of World War I, due largely to the energy of Alexander Nemolovsky, appointed in 1916 as the first Russian Orthodox bishop of Canada.[16] While the Prairies remained the Canadian stronghold of the Russian Orthodox Church, it was Eastern Canada with its substantial and increasingly radicalized migrant worker population that was becoming the focus of Orthodox missionary activities. Although Winnipeg was officially chosen as the centre of the Canadian bishopric, the diocesan chancellery was temporarily set up in Buffalo with a view of moving it to Montreal once a permanent church building had been erected in that city. A tireless traveller and dedicated missionary, Bishop Nemolovsky spent weeks touring eastern and central Canadian cities with significant Russian Orthodox populations. In October 1915, accompanied by the head of the Ontario deanery Iosif Dankevich, he visited southern Ontario to assess the prospects of organizing new parishes. In Toronto, Bishop Nemolovsky and Rev. Dankevich performed a liturgy in the Macedonian church and proceeded to Hamilton, where they only managed to gather about thirty people for a service in the local Serbian church. The bishop's impressions of the immigrants' religiosity were grim. "[R]ussians in Toronto have gone absolutely wild *(sovershenno od-ichali),*" he lamented in the pages of the *American Orthodox Messenger.* "In Hamilton, the state of Orthodoxy is even more horrible. There are up to thirty Russian families here and about 600 single [Russian] men, about 100 Serbs (fifteen families) and nearly 700 Bulgarians. The Russians have almost all turned to socialism."[17]

Bishop Nemolovsky's missionary efforts were not totally fruitless, however. Soon after his visit to Toronto, a small group of local Orthodox immigrants from Russia and Austria collected $6,000 to purchase an old Protestant church in the city's Junction area, at the corner of Royce and Edwin avenues; they also organized the St Michael Orthodox brotherhood, which joined the Russian Orthodox Mutual Aid Society.[18] On 24 September 1916 the bishop himself consecrated the new church, naming it the Russian Orthodox Church of the Resurrection of Christ. The Toronto *Globe,* which sent a reporter to the consecration, estimated that the ceremony had attracted some 700 people.[19] According to Rev. Mikhail Kaimakan, the first priest of the new church, the parish had only about 150 permanent members: 125 "Austrians" and twenty-five "Russians."[20]

Between 1914 and 1917, new parishes and missions also appeared in Hamilton, London, Oshawa, Windsor, Welland, St Catharines, Thorold, The Pas, Halifax, and even in the small industrial settlement of Thetford Mines in southwestern Quebec. Logging and mining communities on the West Coast were also not forgotten. In the summer of 1916, the Russian Orthodox Mission in New York sent the Galician-born priest Mikhail Prodan to organize a church in Vancouver – a city seen as a hotbed of "Ukrainophile" and socialist propaganda. Rev. Prodan also visited Nanaimo, Britannia Mine, and other far-flung mining towns throughout the province, holding services and attempting to organize church brotherhoods wherever possible among local Ukrainian and Russian miners.[21]

Most of the small and sometimes short-lived Russian Orthodox congregations that emerged after 1910 on Canada's industrial frontier could not afford to have their own church buildings and struggled with the lack of clergy and funds. Some parishes fared better than others: it was the size of the community and its material resources that often made the difference. In Windsor, efforts to organize a viable church community met with greater success than in many other places, since most local immigrants earned high wages with the Ford Motor Company, which rewarded sobriety, thrift, and discipline. In the summer of 1916, Windsor's newly organized Orthodox brotherhood purchased two lots in the area known as "Ford City" for the construction of a church building. The Windsor Orthodox parish of St John the Divine was officially opened in 1917. Its baptismal records for 1917–21 show that immigrants from the Russian Empire (primarily natives of Bessarabia) constituted about 58 per cent of the parishioners, who also included Bukovynians, Galicians, and a few Romanian and Serbian immigrants.[22] Despite the extremely high turnover of clergy during its first years, the congregation held on (and still exists today in the same location).

It is difficult to say with certainty what proportion of Russian Orthodox workers in early twentieth-century Canada were involved in organized religious life. The few surviving membership rolls and church registers of the time suggest that the constituency of the Russian Orthodox Church among urban and frontier labourers never amounted to more than a small fraction of Canada's total population of Orthodox Christians, which numbered in the tens of thousands. Even in Montreal, the membership of the church brotherhood never exceeded several dozen persons. Many members left the fraternal society after one or two years, while others were expelled for non-payment of dues, "improper behaviour," or other reasons. By late 1916, when the record of its activities ceased, it had fewer than twenty members.[23] The itinerant way of life of most immigrant workers and the extremely low number of families among them presented the greatest challenge to the urban and frontier parishes. As Robert Harney pointed out, "for most of the [immigrant] groups ... the presence of women was required to make ethnic parishes necessary."[24] The membership of Orthodox congregations in Canadian cities and their financial stability changed with every fluctuation of the economic cycle. As a result of the industrial recession of 1913–15, many migrants either left Canada or drifted away from the church to save their shrinking earnings. Still others waited only for the end of the war to return to their villages and were reluctant to spend their scarce money and time on church activities (the churches were usually full only on major holidays such as Easter or Christmas). Rev. Vasily Gorsky, who served in a small parish in Halifax, complained in early 1917 that the majority of about 150 Orthodox men living there spent their Sundays drinking and gambling rather than praying. While they regularly paid fines for drunkenness, "when you ask them to give to the church, it is hard to get anything."[25]

The immigrants' lukewarm attitude to the church can also probably be traced to the fact that peasant religion in much of Eastern Europe was based on the formal observance of prescribed rituals, buttressed more by social custom than by deep piety or a clear understanding of religious canons. When mechanisms of social control enforced by the village community were weakened through emigration, peasant men began to either avoid church altogether or see it from a purely utilitarian standpoint. Whatever authority the priest could command depended less on his role as a spiritual guide than as a sort of a middleman, who could write or read a letter, tell the latest news, or help find a job. Many priests were aware of this and attempted to use their function as intermediaries between the immigrants and the outer world as a way to maintain at least some form of connection between them and the church. They lent money to their parishioners, gave them food in times of need, and provided other services.[26] Rev. Mikhail Kaimakan, for instance, petitioned the Russian consul in Montreal on behalf of his Austrian-subject parishioners interned during the war at Kapuskasing.[27]

The specific nature of the relationship between church, state, and society in late Imperial Russia and the resulting popular attitudes towards institutionalized religion also need to be taken into consideration. In most of early twentieth-century Eastern Europe the church continued to retain close links to the state, but nowhere was it so subordinated to and dependent on secular authorities as in the Russian Empire, where religious affairs were governed through a state-appointed body – the Holy Synod – and where Orthodox Christianity was inextricably linked to the official doctrine of Russian nationhood with its triadic formula of "autocracy, Orthodoxy, and nationality." Orthodox priests, appointed to their parishes by the Synod, were not accountable to their flock for the administration of parish affairs. Lay initiative, let alone parish democracy, was not only unwelcome but often regarded with hostility as something beyond the competence of the rank-and-file faithful. The state guaranteed salaries (if not particularly lucrative ones) to the clergy and released congregations from the responsibility of shouldering the financial burdens of church membership.[28] The Orthodox priest in tsarist Russia "was severely handicapped [by the fact] that he had been compulsorily converted into a quasi-official and defender of the state."[29] As a result, the low esteem in which the peasantry held tsarist bureaucracy was easily projected onto the priesthood. The insufficient education and sometimes the dubious moral standards of village priests (known to be addicted to the bottle) did not improve their image either. Unlike most Eastern European congregations, rural parishes in Russia rarely became centres of organized social or cultural life. The modest number of Russian Orthodox fraternal societies in the tsarist empire serves as a good illustration of this fact. Of 715 such societies that existed in 1914 under the authority of the Russian Holy Synod, 275 (nearly 40 per cent) were in North America, where the majority of Orthodox believers hailed from Bukovyna, Galicia, or Transcarpathia. By comparison, the Diocese of Volhynia, which included territories with some of Russia's highest emigration rates, had only fifty-eight fraternal societies for the 2.2 million Orthodox faithful living within its borders.[30] The social inertia of Russian-born immigrants perplexed Orthodox priests from Galicia and Bukovyna. Rev. Panteleimon Bozhyk, who ministered to Ukrainian immigrants in Mundare, Edmonton, and Toronto, lamented that "very rarely do [Ukrainians from Russia] say a kind word about their priests in the Old Country. At the mention of priests, one notices their indifference. One does not hear them talk, as do Galicians, about priests in the Old Country organizing them into reading clubs or cooperatives, or siding with the [peasant] commune in taking the landlord to court."[31]

The North American situation, where priests and ministers depended on their parishioners for material support and had to share control of parish affairs with elected church committees, was a novelty to many Russian Orthodox clerics – particularly those with no record of service outside Russia. This frequently led to conflicts between Orthodox clergy and their congregations, which tested the authority of the priests against that of the church committees. The confrontation in the Montreal church of ss Peter and Paul was typical in this regard. It began after Father Vladimir Sakovich, an ambitious 31-year-old priest who had come to Montreal in October 1913, pressured the general meeting of the parish into removing the old trustees (members of the church committee).[32] The banished members complained to the Russian consul general, accusing Father Sakovich of wanting to "be the full master" of the parish and surrounding himself with people who "obey him in everything [...] Such an interpretation of Orthodox religion may have been all right in that village where Fr. Vladimir was something [sic] before his arrival in America, but it will not do in Montreal."[33]

The situation took a dramatic turn when the former trustees padlocked the church door and refused to give up the official seal of the parish along with access to its bank account. Religious services had to be temporarily held in the Syrian church until Consul Sergei Likhachev finally ordered the lock to be cut.[34] The "rebels" were completely defeated in 1915 when the act of incorporation of the parish, passed by the Legislative Assembly of Quebec, required them to turn in "all property ... whatsoever belonging to the ... congregation."[35] Such an outcome was hardly unpredictable in Catholic Quebec, where the authority of the parish priest was not to be questioned.

Financial instability was another problem that afflicted all Russian Orthodox parishes in Canada, especially urban and frontier ones. Although the Russian Orthodox mission in North America received an annual subsidy from the Holy Synod in St Petersburg and occasional donations from the tsar's family, these were not sufficient to cover anything but a fraction of the church's rising expenses.[36] To make matters worse, Russian ecclesiastical authorities ranked Canada far below the United States as a field for missionary work. The much larger numbers of Slavic immigrants south of the border (Rusyns, Ukrainians, Belarusans, Serbs, and others) ensured the priority of the United States over Canada and thus better funding of American Orthodox parishes. According to one source, in the years before 1914 the Russian Orthodox mission in North America spent less than 4 per cent of its annual budget of $70,000 on Canadian parishes.[37] In comparison, the Baptist Convention of Eastern Ontario and Quebec, whose proselytizing activities will be discussed below, spent $6,711 on Slavic missionary work in 1914 alone.[38] Direct appeals to the Holy Synod for subsidizing individual parishes rarely brought results. Even the support of Consul Struve failed to move the chief procurator of the Holy Synod to assist the Montreal parish in the purchase of a suitable church building. The request was rejected on the grounds that "parishioners [in North America] are getting used to taking the financial support from the Mission for granted, but they do not care about the church themselves and contribute nothing to it from their own earnings."[39] With only limited financial support from the diocesan authorities, the majority of urban Orthodox parishes struggled to survive on the contributions from their members – Ukrainian, Belarusan, Serbian, and Romanian labourers, whose earnings and generosity varied greatly from place to place. Many parishes became mired in debt in their attempts to build churches. By late 1917 the parish of ss Peter and Paul amassed a debt of $13,848, including $1,000 owed to the priest.[40] A few congregations even had to declare bankruptcy.

The poor financial state of the Russian Orthodox Church resulted in part from its being a small ethnic denomination with no connections to

mainstream Canadian churches. Unlike Greek Catholics, Orthodox believers in Canada did not have to struggle to stake out their claim to autonomy within an existing church organization, but they were also
devoid of the financial assistance that Canada's Greek Catholic parishes
received from the Roman Catholic bishops, interested in bringing eastern European immigrants under their control. The majority of Russian
Orthodox priests in early twentieth-century Canada lived in very modest material conditions, and some in outright poverty. In January 1917,
only twenty-four of the forty-three clerics in the Canadian diocese received salaries from their parishes (usually $15–$25 a month in rural areas and small cities and up to $60–$65 in larger cities like Toronto).[41]
Of the rest, nine received small allowances from both the parish and the
Russian Orthodox Ecclesiastical Consistory in New York, two were
paid only from the Consistory, and eight had no regular income at all.[42]
Understandably, some priests were tempted to supplement their meagre
earnings by charging illegitimate fees for various non-religious services,
such as providing immigrants with certificates of Russian citizenship (a
prerogative enjoyed by Russian Orthodox clergy in North America until
late 1916) or acting as intermediaries in obtaining travel passes from the
Russian imperial consulates in Montreal or Vancouver.[43]

High clergy turnover was another bane of most Russian Orthodox
parishes in Canada. The small mission parish of Welland, Thorold, and
St Catharines was deserted by three priests over a period of four
months, while the St John the Divine parish in Windsor had ten different priests between 1917 and 1921. The majority of priests, especially
those with large families, preferred the stability of the older and larger
American congregations to the insecurity of the Canadian missionary
frontier. In an attempt to deal with the shortage of clergy, Father
Vladimir Sakovich set up a winter theological seminary in his own
Montreal home, which trained three priests before it was forced to
close after Rev. Sakovich's departure.[44] The problem grew even more
acute with the onset of the economic recession. In October 1915
Bishop Nemolovsky was forced to appeal to his Canadian clergy, asking them to remain true to their calling and not "dream about the
brightly lit streets and various conveniences of life in the States."[45] The
plea produced little effect: less than a year and a half later, eighteen of
the forty-one diocesan priests still wanted to be transferred south of the
border. In a pastoral letter of September 1916, the bishop also asked
the faithful not to proceed with the organization of new parishes until
he had personally inspected the financial situation there.[46]

The authority of the Russian Orthodox Church in Canada was also increasingly challenged by socialist and anti-tsarist ideas, which by 1914 had begun to penetrate immigrant communities. Socialist agitation with its pointedly anti-religious message caused much consternation for Canada's Russian Orthodox clergy, who could not turn the authority of the state against the agitators as their fellow priests did in Russia. Within days of his assignment to Montreal, Rev. Sakovich wrote to the Russian archbishop in New York about the vicious activities of "the so-called Socialists-atheists, who have a great influence on the uneducated mass by their authoritative word."[47] In August 1914, a group of Russian radicals in Montreal attempted to disrupt a patriotic rally organized by the church brotherhood in support of the Russian war effort. During Sunday services, radical activists came to the church to distribute socialist literature, rousing the anger of the "patriots" who tried to drive them away.[48]

As the war drew on, the close association between the Russian Orthodox Church and the unravelling tsarist state made it especially vulnerable to socialist attacks. On his arrival in the small Manitoba town of The Pas, a shocked Bishop Nemolovsky had to endure the scorn and ridicule of the Russian-born workers there, who called Orthodox priests "robbers, obscurantists, and agents of the Russian government" and threw unpleasant questions in the bishop's face: "Why did you excommunicate Tolstoy? He is a genius of philosophy! Why jails? Why this war?"[49] Heated debates, which occasionally burst into skirmishes, broke out between supporters and opponents of the church in many of the newly organized parishes. Radical activists often purposely came to meetings called by priests to collect funds for the church with the goal of stirring up trouble.[50]

While among Russian-born workers it was socialism that emerged as the main threat to the authority of the church, many Orthodox Ukrainians from Galicia and Bukovyna increasingly resented its Russian nationalist orientation. Conflicting political and national loyalties, dormant in peacetime, came to the fore during the war, which pitted Austria-Hungary against Russia and caused a wave of popular nationalism. In May 1916, a group of Ukrainians interned in Edmonton began to sing Ivan Franko's patriotic song *Ne pora* ("*This is Not the Time*") when Rev. Panteleimon Bozhyk attempted to hold a religious service in the camp.[51] In many places, relations between Austrian- and Russian-born parishioners became tense. Father Ieronim Lutsyk, a "Russophile" priest from Bukovyna transferred to the nearly bankrupt

Fort William parish in 1915, complained to Evdokim Meshchersky, the newly appointed Russian Orthodox Archbishop in New York, that most of his parishioners were "roused by [the propaganda of] Ukraine, with the result that the difference between Galicians and Bukovynians has been erased."[52]

Even so, the troubles experienced by the Russian Orthodox Church in Canada prior to 1917 were nothing compared to the disastrous situation in which it found itself after the fall of the Russian monarchy and especially after the Bolshevik revolution. Spared the physical violence and destruction brought upon the parent church in Russia, it was heavily affected by the dwindling of its authority among the flock and the loss of financial support from Russia. With morale running low and the mood of uncertainty setting in, petty intrigues and plotting spread widely among the anguished clerics. Some unscrupulous priests travelled to other parishes to "poach" on the local flock by offering baptismal and other services at lower fees.[53] By 1918, the Russian Orthodox hierarchy in North America was also riven by bitter factional conflicts. Questions arose about the legitimacy of Bishop Alexander Nemolovsky, who had been appointed in early 1917 as temporary administrator of the archdiocese after Archbishop Meshchersky went to Russia to take part in the All-Russian church *Sobor* (Congress). A detailed analysis of the complicated strife within the Russian Orthodox hierarchy after 1917, which still awaits impartial scholarly treatment, goes far beyond the limits of the present study. It may be briefly noted, however, that Canada was the site of one of the central battles. In mid-1918 a group of Ukrainian-Canadian intelligentsia met in Saskatoon to establish a separate Ukrainian Orthodox Church. The 1919 Cleveland convention of the Russian Orthodox Church in North America recognized in principle the right of Ukrainians to have a national church, but Bishop Nemolovsky, acting in his capacity as head of the mission, took a hostile attitude to the idea. His famous phrase that Ukrainians were "not a nation but only a political party" spurred the Ukrainian activists to break away completely from the Russian Orthodox Church. On the other side, Archimandrite Adam Filippovsky of Winnipeg accused Nemolovsky as being too lenient with the "Ukrainophiles" and attempted to establish jurisdictional control over the Canadian diocese. In his quest for power Filippovsky was supported by Galician and Carpatho-Rusyn "Russophiles" in Canada and the United States, who distanced themselves from the Russian Orthodox hierarchy, while also opposing the creation of a separate Ukrainian church.[54]

Many urban and frontier Orthodox parishes in Canada were in a poor shape to weather the storm of the Russian revolution and the rising national and social movements, not to mention the proselytizing of Protestant churches, especially Baptists, who had established Russian and Ruthenian missions in Winnipeg, Toronto, Montreal, Hamilton, and other cities. Several newly organized parishes collapsed in 1917–19 under the double burden of mounting debts and shrinking flocks, and a few others became amalgamated into larger neighbouring congregations. The Resurrection of Christ parish in Toronto, whose church building was seized by creditors, became defunct by late 1918.[55] The Russian Orthodox parish in Vancouver ceased to exist in September 1917, within a year of its opening, due to financial woes and declining membership. When Rev. Mitrofan Poplavsky, head of the Seattle Deanery, came to inspect the parish, he found that the priest, Mikhail Prodan, "had no parishioners left except for Mr. Consul [Ragozin]" and was forced to use the church as his living quarters and to work as a longshoreman to support himself.[56] The Orthodox parish in Halifax managed to stay afloat somewhat longer, but it too was closed in 1923 and its property was auctioned off. The church iconostasis and furnishings were sold to the local Ukrainian Catholic church, and the building itself was purchased by Protestants.[57] The parish of ss Peter and Paul in Montreal was among the few urban congregations that survived despite a succession of weak priests who came and went, unable to command the support of the diminishing flock and manage the parish's daunting debt. In June 1919 Rev. Grigorii Glebov, who had served in the parish for about a year, kept sending futile requests for money to the Russian consulate in Montreal in order to satisfy creditors and to "fight the terrible virus of Bolshevism" among the parishioners.[58]

The Russian Orthodox Church in Canada never fully recovered from the shock of 1917. Its membership was heavily affected by the secession of Ukrainian, Serbian, Romanian, and other ethnic congregations, by the return of many immigrant workers to Europe after 1920, and by the growing apathy of those who stayed. "Russian people are becoming rare visitors to the churches. Orthodox churches in Canada are turning primarily into churches for Ruthenians and Carpatho-Rusyns," a Canadian correspondent complained in Russkoe slovo.[59] The left wing of the immigrant community continued to associate religion with obscurantism.[60] Only in the early 1920s, when the storm calmed down, did the membership of some Orthodox churches stabilize. In some places, old parishes were reconstituted under new names by small groups of the faithful. In 1921, a handful of Orthodox immigrants in Toronto began to hold services in a local Anglican church. The revived congregation was soon officially registered as the Russian Orthodox Church of Christ the Saviour.[61] Conditions also began to improve in Montreal with the arrival of Rev. Arkady Piotrovsky, who found only five cents in the parish treasury and had to rely on his own savings and voluntary donations to buy church supplies.[62] As before, most of the parishes retained their ethnically mixed composition that included Belarusans, Ukrainians from Russia and Austria, as well as a small proportion of Serbians, Romanians, and other Orthodox believers.[63]

SPREADING THE GOSPEL

Canadian Protestant churches increasingly challenged the influence of the Russian Orthodox Church among Slavic immigrants. Missionary work among "foreigners" was part of the large-scale social gospel movement, which encompassed most of the Protestant denominations in North America. Presbyterians, Methodists and Baptists moved into the field with particular zeal; Anglicans, who held on to their historical roots as an English church, were less active. Early twentieth-century Canadian social reformers sought not only to bring about a spiritual transformation of the "foreigners" but also to introduce them to the virtues of democratic citizenship and speed up their assimilation.[64] Slavic immigrants, presumably raised in the darkness of autocracy and spiritual slavery, were the evangelizers' primary targets. While Ukrainian and other immigrant farming settlements on the Prairies became the first arena for Protestant missionary activities, it was not long before preachers, ministers, and social workers followed the newcomers into the crowded urban slums and the far-flung bunkhouse camps of the Canadian resource frontier. By 1914 Methodist, Presbyterian, Baptist and, in some cases, inter-denominational missions were functioning in Toronto, Montreal, and Winnipeg. Such missions were also active in the smaller industrial towns of northern and southern Ontario, where they ministered to the rapidly growing numbers of foreign migrant workers. In these missions, religious services were combined with educational and social events, including English language classes, lectures, lantern slide shows, Sunday schools, sewing and cooking classes for the women, etc.[65]

Of all the major Protestant churches that tried to proselytize among Russian-born immigrant workers, the Baptists made the most sustained and successful effort. Unlike other Protestant denominations, Canadian Baptists put individual salvation before social reform, convinced that "if they could Christianize all (or at least most) of the individuals in society, [...] these individuals could then in turn be counted on to Christianize the social order."[66] The fact that the Baptists were the only Protestant church that had taken some root among the Slavic population of the Russian Empire (especially in Ukraine) gave the Baptist missionaries in Canada an important edge over other proselytizers. Small and close-knit groups of Ukrainians and Russians of Baptist faith had existed in most of the empire's western provinces since the mid-nineteenth century, when evangelist teachings had first reached local peasants through German settlers. As a result, Canadian Baptists could rely on a small but dedicated cadre of Russian-born preachers in their missionary work among the immigrants. Most of these preachers had been converted to the Baptist faith in the old country and had come to Canada to escape persecution by the Russian government and the Orthodox Church. A 1916 report on Baptist work among the Russians stated, perhaps too optimistically, that "'Baptist' to [the Russians] needs no explanation as does 'Methodist' or 'Presbyterian.' It is native to the Russian."[67] The importance of having missionaries able to speak the language of the immigrants and familiar with their customs was well understood by the Baptist Church, which traditionally placed great emphasis on personal contact between missionaries and their audience.[68]

Until the turn of the nineteenth century, Baptist missionary work was restricted mostly to German and Scandinavian immigrants. Only in the late 1890s did the Baptists begin to target Galician and Doukhobor settlers on the Prairies. As early as 1897 the Home Mission Board of the Baptist Convention of Manitoba and the Northwest (BCMN) sent George Burgdorff, a German missionary who knew some Russian, to preach the gospel to the Slavic immigrants.[69] Canada's first Baptist preacher of Slavic origin was probably Sylvestr Muzh, who was exiled from Russia in 1899 for his beliefs and began missionary work among the Galician Ukrainians at Stuartburn, the Dauphin-Sifton area, and later in Winnipeg.[70] The arrival of new groups of Baptist exiles from eastern Ukraine in the early 1900s broadened the Baptist immigrant constituency in the West and increased the number of preachers who could minister both to old adherents and to potential converts in their own language.

One such preacher was Ivan Shakotko, a native of Chernigov Province, who came to Canada with his family in the spring of 1903 and in the following year organized a Russian Baptist Church in Winnipeg. [71] In 1905, a church building was erected. Within five years, the membership of the congregation rose from fifteen to twenty-four, and a Sunday school was established with H. Hilton, a local Baptist missionary and reportedly a fluent Russian speaker, as the schoolmaster.[72] The BCMN quickly recognized Shakotko's dedication and organizing abilities, appointing him "missionary to the Russo-Ukrainian people of the West" with a monthly salary of $50. Shortly thereafter, he was sent to open new parishes in Saskatchewan, which by that time had become the main destination of Baptist immigration from Russia. Travelling across the western provinces, Shakotko preached to Doukhobor, eastern Ukrainian, and Ruthenian farmers (some of them already Baptist converts) in Eagle Creek, Canora, Rosthern, Blaine Lake, Lizard Lake, and other settlements. In 1909, the first "Russian and Galician" Baptist conference was held in Canora. It resolved to start a monthly Baptist paper in the Russian language, to increase the number of Sunday schools, and to seek the appointment of a "General Missionary to the Russian and Galician people" of Canada.[73] By 1912, there were five ordained Slavic missionaries and five organized Slavic churches in western Canada (one in Manitoba, one in Alberta, and three in Saskatchewan), with a total membership of 171.[74]

While Baptist work among Ukrainians and other Slavs had made some progress in the early 1900s, it was confined, with the exception of Winnipeg, to the rural areas of the Canadian West and rarely involved labour migrants. The vast opportunities opened by the growing numbers of foreign workers in Canadian urban centres, particularly in the east, were not lost on Baptist church leaders, but the shortage of Slavic-speaking missionaries hindered the expansion of their reach. In this situation, John (Ivan Alekseevich) Kolesnikoff, a 53-year-old preacher of Russian origin, who arrived in Toronto in 1908 from Pennsylvania, reportedly to survey the field for missionary work, was indeed a "man sent from God" to help Canadian Baptists in spreading their word among Slavic urban immigrants.

Kolesnikoff's name has made a few short appearances in Canadian ethnic historiography, primarily in studies of immigrant Toronto, but his full story still remains to be told.[75] A preacher of outstanding talent and dedication verging on fanaticism, he was probably the most successful Baptist missionary to the immigrants in early twentieth-century Canada. Born in 1855 in Kherson (southern Ukraine), he lost his parents at an early age and was placed in an Orthodox Church orphanage.

Planning to become a priest, he successfully graduated from a theological seminary, but after a conflict with the Synod hierarchy over the place of his first missionary assignment, he broke with the Church and joined an underground socialist group.[76] Kolesnikoff's conversion to the Baptist faith, which likely occurred around 1883, was the result of his meeting with a missionary, who introduced the young rebellious mind to the evangelical doctrine. After serving a prison term for preaching a forbidden religion, he moved to Odessa and helped organize a number of missions and preaching stations. Alarmed by the preacher's popularity, the authorities eventually forced him to move to Bessarabia. There he continued preaching the gospel, this time among the small sect of Russian Quakers, who enjoyed limited religious freedom in tsarist Russia. Four years later Kolesnikoff left Russia for good and spent thirteen years in Romania and Bulgaria. Working in partnership with the Bulgarian Baptist missionary Peter Doychev, he was reported to have brought more than 100 new converts to the church. In 1903, he emigrated to the United States with his wife and three children to work among fellow Slavs in Scranton, Pennsylvania, where he soon established a Russo-Ukrainian Baptist mission.

The day after his arrival in Toronto in late July 1908, Kolesnikoff could be seen preaching, singing Gospel songs, and reading from the Bible at the corner of Trinity Square and King Street, attracting dozens of curious listeners with his oratorical skill and remarkable ability to switch between at least four languages during a sermon. He spent all of August visiting the homes of several hundred Macedonian, Polish, Ruthenian, and Russian immigrants in the city's central ward and in the East End, combining his visits with regular outdoor sermons. By early September, the Baptist Home Mission Board was so impressed with Kolesnikoff's achievements that it appointed him missionary to the "foreign population of Toronto" with a monthly salary of $75.[77] In the autumn of 1908, two mission halls were set up – one on King Street East for Macedonians and Bulgarians (later turned over to the Macedonian preacher Michael Andoff), and the other on Alice Street for "Russians and Ukrainians." In 1913, a second Russian mission was opened in West Toronto on Dundas Street.[78]

The missions became centres of vigorous evangelical and social activities. Regular prayer meetings and Bible readings alternated with English language classes, "lantern lectures" on social issues (with topics varying from the prevention of tuberculosis to the stopping of liquor traffic), and Macedonian brass band concerts. A dispensary was open

at the King Street mission once a week, providing free medical treatment. All three missions also operated as labour exchange bureaux. In
1909, Kolesnikoff began to publish a sixteen-page semi-monthly called
The Witness of the Truth in the Ukrainian language, which was distributed across North America as well as in Russia and Austria. Hymn-
books and religious tracts in Russian and Ukrainian were also printed.
In their missionary activities Kolesnikoff and Andoff were assisted by
the Women's Baptist Home Missionary Society, which sent volunteers
to the Toronto Slavic missions to organize classes of sewing and
"household science," to teach night and Sunday school, and to visit immigrants' homes.[79]

Kolesnikoff was inspired by a vision of transforming the derided
"foreigners," compared by his own Canadian co-religionists to
"hordes of barbarians," into enlightened Christians.[80] While the
"Canadianizing" part of the missionary work was probably less important for him and for other Russian-born preachers than it was for native-born social reformers, he emphasized the civilizing effects of
Protestant Christianity on Slavic immigrants, whom he often called
"my people." For him, evangelization was the shortest road to their integration into Canadian society: "You English say, 'Scratch a Slav and
find a Tartar.' I want you to give them the Gospel. When they have the
Gospel, you will not say, 'Scratch a Slav and find a Tartar,' but 'Scratch
a Slav and find a Christian.'" These words, which were said to be
Kolesnikoff's last before he died in March 1918, are probably the best
summation of his life's work.[81]

From his headquarters in Toronto, Kolesnikoff travelled widely
across eastern Canada, seeking to establish new missions and acting *de
facto* as a General Slavic (Baptist) Missionary – the position he would
formally assume in early 1915. In July 1909 he sent Peter Shostak, a
missionary born in eastern Ukraine, to preach in Fort William with an
annual salary of $200 provided by the Baptist Home Mission Board.[82]
In subsequent years, Russian Baptist missions also sprang up in Hamilton, Welland, Berlin, Port Arthur, and London – all important centres
of Slavic immigration from the Russian and the Habsburg empires. The
missions in Welland and Hamilton were run by Kolesnikoff's two sons,
appropriately named Peter and Paul.[83] From Ontario, Baptist proselytizing activities expanded into Montreal, where a group of about forty
Ukrainians and other Slavic immigrants petitioned the Home Mission
Board "for a missionary who could speak the Polish and Ruthenian
languages."[84] In February 1912 Kolesnikoff was dispatched to Montreal

to train the new missionary Alex Naydovitch, a former labour activist and a recent convert to the Baptist Church. That same month, with the help of the First Baptist Church of Montreal, which supplied both furnishings and teaching staff for the night school, a mission for Russian and Ruthenian immigrants was opened on Brown Street, on the edge of a large Slavic and Lithuanian immigrant colony.[85]

Thanks to the efforts of Kolesnikoff and his associates, Baptists were well ahead of the other Protestant churches in missionary work among the Slavic immigrants in the urban centres of eastern Canada. In many Ontario cities, including Toronto, Baptist missions appeared earlier than Russian Orthodox or Greek Catholic parishes. In April 1915, when the city's Orthodox Christians still possessed no place of worship, the Russian Baptist congregation of Toronto had fifty-three members (consisting of Ukrainians and Belarusans, with a few Poles and Russians). Georgy Kurilovich, one of Kolesnikoff's lieutenants, was accepted at McMaster College to study for the ministry.[86] Through a network of Russian secret police agents in North America, reports of Kolesnikoff's proselytizing activities in Toronto reached the Ministry of Internal Affairs in Petrograd, which branded him a dangerous agitator spreading "anti-Russian propaganda under the guise of preaching the gospel."[87] The ubiquitous missionary also became a thorn in the side of Toronto's Russian Orthodox parish when it was finally established in mid-1916. Father Mikhail Kaimakan complained to the Russian Consul General that Kolesnikoff delivered anti-Russian and pro-German sermons at the corner of Royce and Edwin avenues, only steps away from the church. A police investigation conducted at Likhachev's insistence, however, found no anti-Allied statements in Kolesnikoff's sermons.[88]

What brought Ukrainian, Belarusan, and other East European immigrant workers to Baptist missions, and how serious was their commitment to Protestantism? Historian Lillian Petroff rightly observed that the vast majority of Macedonians in Toronto simply took advantage of the educational and work opportunities offered by the proselytizers without abandoning their faith or cultural heritage.[89] There is no reason to believe that the motives of Slavic immigrants from tsarist Russia were substantially different, with the exception of those few who had already adopted the Baptist faith in the homeland. If the numbers of formal conversions among the immigrants can be used as an indicator of success, the missions' performance was hardly stellar. In 1916, for instance, only four baptized converts were reported in Toronto and nine in Montreal, the figures for other years being similar.[90] Most of those who frequented the missions probably came for information or assistance, while others used them as an opportunity to socialize. For some, belonging to a Baptist congregation may have been a form of intellectual protest against the ritualistic practices and statist attitudes of the Russian Orthodox Church or merely satisfied intellectual curiosity. In any case, it seems that very few embraced the new faith wholeheartedly and irreversibly.

The fact that Baptist missions did not depend on financial contributions from their Slavic members gave them a short-term advantage over the traditional churches, particularly in times of economic trouble. It may not be accidental that the peak of the Baptist missionary work occurred at the time of the 1913–15 economic depression. Eventually, however, the progress of social adaptation and an improving economy began to draw many immigrants away from the missions, which increasingly experienced difficulties maintaining their membership, let alone recruiting new adherents. After 1915, the size of Russian Baptist congregations in large urban areas began to shrink. The departure of many immigrants to Europe after August 1914, both as war reservists and to escape economic depression, also cut deeply into the Baptist constituency, which could no longer be replenished by new immigration. When economic prosperity returned in late 1915, many of the old converts were lured away by high wartime wages and new employment opportunities, never to come back. The itinerant way of life pursued by most Slavic migrants, who were characterized by the Home Mission Board as people "of a restless, roving disposition," presented the same difficulty for the Protestant missions as it did for the Russian Orthodox parishes. The number of "non-resident members" of Slavic Baptist congregations began to grow: in 1919, only nine of the thirty-four members of the York Street mission in Toronto still remained in the city.[91] The death of Kolesnikoff at the age of sixty-three in March 1918 added to the mounting troubles. For about a year and a half, the city's Russian mission was headed by his daughter Sarah and his son-in-law Paul Ambrosimoff. After both missionaries left Toronto in September 1919, the mission went into further decline and was finally closed in May 1921, with a view of amalgamating all Slavic work in the city into a single mission hall in the Junction district.[92]

There was also increasing tension between immigrant preachers and Canadian-born missionaries assigned to Slavic work. In June 1917, the Home Mission Board had to admit that work in Montreal "was not making progress" because of "a constantly widening breach" between Alex Naydovitch and one Miss Owen, appointed as his assistant by the Women's Baptist Missionary Society.[93] While the precise causes of the misunderstanding were not specified, one wonders if the Russian-born preachers and their Slavic flock simply found it difficult to accept the paternalist attitudes of Anglo-Saxon Baptist workers and their inability (or perhaps unwillingness) to adjust to the specific socio-cultural environment of the immigrant missions. Three years earlier, similar friction had emerged between Kolesnikoff and his female Canadian assistant in the Toronto mission.[94] It is also possible that the members of the Russian congregations and their Russian-born leaders resisted the "Canadianization" that the Anglo-Saxon missionaries attempted to impose on them. This may be one of the reasons why in 1919 the Russian-born members of the Montreal mission demanded that their pastors be selected only from their own community, even if they had not been formally ordained.[95] Apparently, both Naydovitch and his flock also struggled with the notion of an unmarried woman as a church worker, since only nuns were acceptable in the Russian and East European tradition. According to the Home Mission Board's report, the Slavic members of the congregation were "unable to appreciate or comprehend the position and motive of an English Bible Woman, and her day to day activities suggest to their mind an improper familiarity on the part of the Bible Woman."[96] It was therefore decided to remove Miss Owen from the mission and to give her position on a part-time basis to Mrs. Naydovitch.

Ethnic and political antagonisms exacerbated by the war and European revolutionary and national movements also took their toll on Slavic Baptist communities. By late 1918, the Montreal Slavic mission was in the throes of another conflict – this time between its "Russian" and "Ruthenian" members, in which the use of the Russian language in the services was a major issue. Accused of favouring Russians over Ruthenians (in addition to the charge of financial manipulations), Naydovitch was finally forced to resign and leave Montreal. Conciliatory efforts by the Home Mission Board brought no results, and in 1919 the mission split into two separate – Russian and Ruthenian (Ukrainian) – congregations.[97]

Despite the efforts of the Home Mission Board, which was willing to accommodate to a certain extent the special needs of its ethnic parishes, Slavic mission work across Canada continued to suffer setbacks. After the First World War Slavic Baptist communities in eastern and northern Ontario struggled with financial adversity, diminishing membership, and the often hostile attitudes of the traditional churches.

Missions in some Ontario cities had to be closed altogether and their property sold off. In search of a solution, the Home Mission Board embraced a new strategy, shifting the emphasis from immigrant men to the slowly increasing urban population of Slavic women and children, thus giving more control over the Slavic missions to the Women's Missionary Society.[98] In sum, towards the early 1920s, Baptist "Slavic work" in Canada came to a crossroads, with opinions regarding its future widely divided.

Although other Protestant denominations in early twentieth-century Canada also tried to reach the "Russians" through missionary work, their efforts were less ethnically pointed and had a more sporadic character. Presbyterians, who could boast considerable success among Ukrainians on the Prairies, began to turn their attention to the "Russians" only in the mid-1910s. In November 1913, a Russian Presbyterian mission in Winnipeg with a reading room and regular lectures was added to the several Ruthenian missions that were already functioning in the city.[99] The mission was regularly visited by workers from Russia, attracted by free Russian-language journals and newspapers. It soon became a source of permanent concern for the nearby Russian Progressive Club, which could not afford the luxury of not charging fees for the use of the library.[100] In Toronto the Presbyterian Social Service Institute for Non-Anglo-Saxons, run from February 1913 by the Russian preacher Michael Sherbinin, served Ruthenians, Russians and other immigrant workers by holding Sunday and weeknight services, offering lectures, and providing reading facilities.[101]

Among twenty-three Methodist missions established for "foreigners" prior to August 1914, none catered specifically to Russians (compared, for instance, to no less than eight Italian Methodist missions that were operating by 1917).[102] Methodist social workers, however, reached some labourers from Russia through ethnically mixed missions, which welcomed all immigrants regardless of nationality. Annual reports of the All People's Mission in Winnipeg, run by prominent social reformer J.S. Woodsworth, regularly listed "Russian" children enrolled in its Sunday school as well as "Russian" workers attending night classes.[103] In the Sault Ste Marie area, with a population of several thousand immigrant labourers, the Methodist church established a mission for the "Finns, Russians, and Syrians," leaving the Italians to the Presbyterians.[104] The division of missionary work along ethnic or territorial lines between the two churches, which maintained friendly relations, existed in other places as well.

The Anglican Church in early twentieth-century Canada stayed away from active proselytizing among non-English-speaking immigrants. Some Anglican parishes, however, provided assistance or church space to local Slavic Orthodox immigrants, including Ukrainians and Belarusans from the Russian Empire. These acts of charity were grounded in the ecumenical contacts between the Holy Synod of the Russian Orthodox Church and the Church of England.[105] In contrast to other Protestant churches, these acts were not accompanied by any attempts at "soul poaching." On the contrary, the Anglicans displayed a surprising readiness to adjust as much as possible to Orthodox ways and customs and did not use aggressive evangelist rhetoric, which was probably the main reason for their success. A remarkable example of coexistence between an Anglican parish and a Russian Orthodox community occurred in Halifax, where Rev. V.E. Harris of the All Saints' Cathedral began in June 1914 to hold weekly Orthodox services for the local Russians "until such time as a priest of their own Church may be sent to minister to them."[106] By the end of the year, the services (initially held in English of necessity) were conducted "almost entirely in Russian," and sacraments such as baptisms and weddings were also performed. The parish even purchased a plot of land at the local St John's Cemetery to bury deceased Slavic members according to the Orthodox rite. In December 1914, student volunteers from Dalhousie College began to teach night classes for the local "Russian colony." Significantly, the classes had a purely educational character, with no religion taught.[107] Rev. Harris's efforts received the support of Consul Sergei Likhachev, who sent him money for the purpose of assisting needy immigrants. Such cooperation between Anglican clergy and Orthodox Christians in various Canadian cities would continue into the 1920s.

Several religious denominations in early twentieth-century Canada vied for the souls of Russian-born immigrant workers, attempting to organize them into viable church communities. In virtually every case, these efforts were inextricably linked to larger political goals. Maintaining an allegiance to Russian Orthodoxy was inseparable from a pro-Russian and, until early 1917, pro-tsarist orientation, while the adoption of a Protestant faith usually involved the renunciation of old-country heritage. Despite some isolated successes, attempts to harness the predominantly transient male labourers to the church and inculcate them with religious piety generally proved to be fruitless. While the decline of the Russian Baptist and the less numerous Presbyterian and

Methodist missions was largely due to the gap between the Protestant *Weltanschauung* and Eastern European peasant culture, the Russian Orthodox Church in North America fell victim to its close association with the tsarist monarchy, which by 1916 was in a state of irreparable crisis. Incapable of keeping the allegiance of its predominantly peasant subjects at home, the Russian tsarist state could hardly accomplish a similar task in the North American democracies with their free market of secular and religious teachings. Left without a clear political orientation after the double shock of the February and October revolutions of 1917, the Russian Orthodox mission in North America – the main arm of the Russian state in the emigrant diaspora – proved unable to muster either the sufficient moral authority or the necessary resources to keep thousands of itinerant Ukrainian and Belarusan peasant-workers in Canada in the Orthodox fold. In North America no less than in Russia, socialism had emerged as a powerful alternative to church and religion for all those who were too impatient to wait for eternal happiness in the other world.

8

Bolsheviks or Rebels?

Ukrainian and Belarusan labourers came to Canada from rural communities with no traditions of organized labour or socialism that could be transplanted to the New World. In the western provinces of the Russian Empire, where an industrial proletariat was all but non-existent, socialism recruited its ideologues and followers primarily from the ranks of the urban and small-town intelligentsia or progressive-minded nobility. Even so, the Ukrainian and Belarusan radical parties that began to emerge in the Russian Empire in the early 1900s were small and could rarely compete with their stronger and better-organized Russian counterparts. By the time of the 1905 revolution, Russia's two largest socialist parties – the Russian Socialist Revolutionary Party and the Russian Social-Democratic Labour Party – had established their branches on the empire's western frontier; however, their influence outside the predominantly Russian- and Jewish-populated industrial centres of Left-Bank and southern Ukraine remained minimal.[1] It was therefore the Russian socialist groups that usually made the first attempts to introduce Ukrainian and Belarusan villages to the basics of class consciousness.

This situation was very much the same in North America, where Russian socialist émigrés who were forced to flee from tsarist repressions soon discovered a growing number of potential followers composed largely of peasant immigrants from the Belarusan and Ukrainian provinces. Not necessarily of ethnic Russian origin, the majority of these activists regarded themselves and their fledgling organizations as part of the all-Russian socialist movement, viewing nationalist agendas as detracting from the principal goal of social and political liberation of Russia's proletariat. Although the political spectrum of Russian émigré socialism included some groups which called themselves "Russo-Ukrainian" rather than simply Russian, they made little consistent effort to mobilize their immigrant constituency along the lines of ethnicity. The pattern of Russian socialist parties as multi-ethnic organizations, usually open to any Russian-speaking native of the empire, was repeated in the United States and Canada throughout the first two decades of the twentieth century and, to a large extent, even in later decades.

The 1917 Bolshevik revolution in Russia and the ensuing "Red Scare" that swept through Canada and the United States in 1918–20 created a lasting image of "Russians" as an immigrant group especially susceptible to radicalism. In 1919, most Canadians were probably convinced that nearly every Russian-born immigrant was a member of some clandestine anarchist cell plotting a socialist revolution. Although the intensity of such perceptions waned in subsequent years, Canadian suspicions of "Russians" as a potential threat to Canadian democracy never completely disappeared. To what extent were these stereotypes grounded in historical reality? Were Russian-born immigrants in early twentieth-century Canada as prone to radicalism as they were portrayed? Who were the Russian émigré radicals, and how did they attempt to mobilize the immigrant masses?

PRE-1917 RADICAL GROUPS

The small cohort of Russian émigré socialists in early twentieth-century Canada could not claim the same authority and intellectual rigour as Lev Deich, Sergei Ingerman, Leon Trotsky, or Nikolai Bukharin, who were all affiliated at different times and for various periods with the Russian socialist movement in the United States.[2] In contrast to Western Europe and, to a lesser extent, the United States, Canada never became a major destination for political emigration from tsarist Russia. A remote and predominantly rural land with weak traditions of organized labour protest, it held little appeal for the "elite" Russian socialists, who preferred to settle in the warmer and more culturally hospitable climate of Switzerland, France, and England or at least in bustling New York and Chicago. Nonetheless, small numbers of political dissenters of lesser prominence did find their way to Canada, especially after the Russian revolution of 1905–07. The largest single group of Russian political expatriates that found a new home in Canada included the participants in the famous 1905 mutiny on board the Russian battleship *Potemkin*, who fled to Romania after the mutiny was suppressed. Among those mutineers who came to Canada were the Russians David Borodin, Vasilii Zverev and Pavel Peresedov, and the Ukrainians Karp Babchenko and Stefan Denysenko.[3] In 1912, several former *Potemkin* crewmen settled with their families on farms near Nelson, British Columbia, in the vicinity of a large Doukhobor colony. While some of them opted out of political activities, others decided to become involved in the Canadian socialist and labour movement.[4]

Before the time when immigrant radicalism began to be perceived as a threat, Russian political exiles generally enjoyed the sympathy of Canadians, and some of them received a good deal of publicity, helping to perpetuate the unsavoury image of tsarist Russia, already well entrenched in Canadian public opinion. On occasion, Canadian newspapers carried sensationalist stories of Russian revolutionaries who had escaped their Siberian exile and made their way abroad. In 1910, the Canadian public was stirred by a Manitoba court decision to extradite Savva Fedorenko, a Socialist Revolutionary militant of Ukrainian origin wanted by the Russian authorities for the alleged murder of a policeman in his native Kiev Province.[5] When the Winnipeg police arrested Fedorenko, Canadian socialist organizations, including the Socialist Party of Canada (SPC) and its Jewish, Ukrainian, and other ethnic branches, established a "League for the Defence of Russian Revolutionaries," launching an international campaign against his deportation. The League held numerous public meetings and fundraising events, collecting $2,600 in Canada and $2,500 in the United States to cover Fedorenko's court expenses.[6] The campaign received nation-wide press coverage, becoming an early example of working co-operation between ethnic and mainstream socialist and labour organizations in Canada. In December 1910 the Manitoba Court of King's Bench rescinded the deportation order on technical grounds (the extradition procedure was judged to be not wholly compliant with the 1886 Anglo-Russian extradition treaty), but the political motives behind the verdict were transparent. Fedorenko was released and quickly left Canada before the Judicial Committee of the British Privy Council upheld the deportation verdict in July 1911.[7]

While some Russian socialist exiles saw Canada only as a stop on their way to the United States or other preferred destinations, others remained in the country and made attempts to join Canadian socialist groups or to form their own organizations. A few Russian-born socialists of Ukrainian origin found themselves at home in the Federation of Ukrainian Social Democrats (FUSD), established in 1909 by a circle of

left-wing Galician intelligentsia and later renamed the Ukrainian Social
Democratic Party (USDP). Despite the USDP's primarily Galician origins, its members included some eastern Ukrainians conscious of their
Ukrainian identity as well as a few Russians, Poles, and other Slavs,
who lacked their own labour organizations before 1910. Pavlo Krat
(Ternenko), a romantic nationalist and social radical, was the most co-
lourful and the most controversial figure among the Russian-born émigrés who participated in the Ukrainian socialist movement.[8] Another
eastern Ukrainian, Matvii (Matthew) Shatulsky, a miner from the
Volhynian town of Bazalia, was one of the organizers of the socialist-
oriented Taras Shevchenko Self-Education Association in Edmonton
and a leading figure in the Ukrainian Labour-Farmer Temple Association (ULFTA).[9] Lev Mikhnevich, a native of Podolia and a founder of the
Sudbury branch of the USDP, had been involved in the Russian Socialist
Revolutionary movement since 1902. Sentenced to imprisonment for his
participation in revolutionary activities, Mikhnevich managed to escape
to Galicia for three years before arriving in Canada in 1911.[10] David
Borodin (one of the *Potemkin* crew) and Evgueni Volodin, both of Russian background, served in 1913 on the editorial staff of the Working
People's Publishing Association established by the FUSD.[11]

The first socialist groups bearing the word "Russian" in their names
started to appear in Canada by 1911–12, and usually they were no
match for their more numerous and better established Ukrainian counterparts. Yet on the eve of World War I, Russian radical circles representing various brands of socialism existed not only in the larger cities
of Toronto, Montreal, Vancouver, and Winnipeg, but also in smaller industrial centres such as Timmins. The majority of them (with the exception of those on the West Coast, where Russians and Ossetians
seemed to predominate) were composed mostly of Ukrainians and Belarusans. However, the significant presence of ethnic Russians and
Jews, so characteristic of Russian socialist parties in Ukraine and Belarus especially at the leadership level, was reproduced in Canada. The
radical émigré intelligentsia that led the Russian socialist movements in
Canada were almost exclusively of Russian or Jewish origin. Some
Russian-Jewish émigrés, fluent in both Russian and Yiddish, also
became involved in the growing Jewish-Canadian socialist movement.
Solomon Almazov, who came to Canada in 1913 at the age of twenty-
three and two years later began his studies in economics and philosophy at the University of Manitoba, was both a leading member of
Winnipeg's Russian Social Democrat group and the editor of *Die
Volksstimme*, a local Jewish socialist paper.[12]

Along with the more educated *intelligenty*, there were the "grass-roots" activists, who came to the socialist movement through personal encounters with capitalist exploitation or tsarist repression and whose peasant origin and lack of intellectual finesse were compensated by the ability to find the way to the mind of the rank-and-file labourer. This class of radical leaders was more likely to include ethnic Ukrainians and Belarusans, who were rarely found among the intelligentsia. Iosif Rabizo, a native of Vil'na Province and an organizer of the Russian Socialist Revolutionary group in Montreal, was one of these self-educated activists. After finishing a People's College *(narodnoe uchilishche)*, he spent several years as a steelworker in St Petersburg before arriving in Montreal around 1913. By 1915, Rabizo broke with the Socialist Revolutionaries over their support of World War I and joined the local Russian Social Democratic branch, only to leave Canada for Chicago after the branch collapsed the following year.[13]

Some of the the first Russian socialist organizations to emerge in North America were the anarcho-syndicalist "unions of Russian workers," which combined the rich tradition of Russian anarchism with the militant industrial unionism of the kind espoused by the International Workers of the World (IWW) and later by Canada's One Big Union. The anarcho-syndicalist doctrine with its emphasis on direct action held much appeal for unskilled Ukrainian and Belarusan migrant workers, who had been reared in the Old World traditions of peasant violence and could not understand the "bread and butter" unionism of the American Federation of Labour or the Canadian Trades and Labour Congress. The first "unions of Russian workers" began to appear in the United States around 1907–08. There is some evidence that by 1912, such a union existed in British Columbia – traditionally the main stronghold of Canadian militant unionism – but little information about it has survived.

It was, however, the Socialist Revolutionary groups that became the most numerous Russian socialist organizations in early twentieth-century Canada. Affiliated ideologically with the Russian Socialist Revolutionary Party, they advocated peasant revolution, abolishment of large landowners' estates, and a classless society of independent producers. The Socialist Revolutionaries' populist and agrarian orientation gave them a large following among the immigrant peasants-turned-workers. Before and during World War I, "Russian" and "Russo-Ukrainian" Socialist Revolutionary circles sprang up in Lachine, Brantford, Timmins, Hamilton, London, Galt, and Iroquois Falls, but the largest ones functioned in Toronto and Montreal. In 1915, the Toronto "Russo-Ukrainian Socialist Revolutionary Group" was reported to have sixty-two members, an active drama circle, and a library of 150 titles.[14] By the summer of 1914, Russian Socialist Revolutionary groups in Ontario established a "regional committee," modelled after similar *oblast* (regional) associations in Russia, to coordinate the work of the branches. A group of Montreal Socialist Revolutionaries who belonged to the moderate wing of the party were instrumental in organizing a secular benevolent association, which was founded in December 1915 as the Russian-Slavic Mutual Aid Society. At its height, the society had nearly 100 members eligible for sickness and death benefits and was able to rent a hall for social events, concerts, and dances.[15] Shunning the militant atheism of the more radical socialist groups, the society maintained an amicable relationship with Montreal's Russian Orthodox parish. Like the majority of moderate socialists in the homeland, it adopted a "patriotic" rather than an internationalist attitude during World War I. In early 1916, its members collected and sent to Russia some $50 for helping war refugees.[16]

Russian Social Democrats also began to form small groups in Canada around 1910–11. These organizations regarded themselves as offshoots of the RSDLP, whose revolutionary Marxist doctrine attracted primarily the support of Russia's urban proletariat. Winnipeg became the main gathering place for Russian Social Democrats in Canada, although its population of Russian-born workers was smaller than that of Montreal and probably even Hamilton. In 1912, a group of members of the local Russian Progressive Club (D. Kotliarenko, D. Leonidov and others) established the first Russian local of the Social Democratic Party of Canada (SDPC) with fifteen members.[17] Kotliarenko, who was a member of the RSDLP since 1902 and probably the most prominent Russian socialist ever to arrive in Canada, had formerly lived in Paris where he had worked for the Russian Social Democrat paper *Proletarii*.[18] Russian workers were urged to join the local on the pages of *Robochyi narod*, the organ of the Ukrainian Social Democrats, who provided their Russian comrades with moral support and access to the printing press.[19]

In the early 1910s, the SDPC became the main organizer of non-English-speaking immigrants in Canada. Unlike the cerebral and British-dominated Socialist Party, which had little time for the specific needs of its non-Anglo-Saxon members, the Social Democrats did not lose sight of the immediate demands of the working class and allowed the party's ethnic locals a substantial degree of autonomy.[20] Russian

Social Democratic groups also emerged in Toronto and Montreal, subsequently forming two short-lived Russian branches within the SDPC. The Montreal group held regular meetings in the city's Labour Temple Hall at 305 St Dominique Street and set up a "Self-Educational School" and a library, which subscribed to the Russian Social Democratic newspapers *Pravda* and *Novyi mir*. Montreal Social Democrats also established contact with the Russian writer and playwright Maxim Gorky, who sent his greetings and a shipment of books to the new Russian socialist organization in Canada.[21]

Before 1918, Russian socialist and "progressive" groups of different ideological stripes rarely operated in isolation from each other (aside perhaps from the most dogmatic anarchists). Doctrinal differences between the two main branches of the Russian socialist movement – the Social Democrats and the Socialist Revolutionaries – were mitigated by the spirit of class solidarity and the existence of a common enemy: the tsarist monarchy. The Socialist Revolutionaries, who had no printing press of their own until 1918 (and then only for a short time), often announced their activities in the Social Democrat organ *Novyi mir*, and it was not uncommon for local branches of the two parties to organize joint political events. Such non-partisan groups as the Society for Aid to the Political Victims of the Russian Revolution and the Society for Aid to Political Exiles in Siberia, whose first Canadian branches were founded in 1914, brought together socialists of various affiliations.[22] Russian "progressive clubs" in Winnipeg, Toronto, and Montreal were open to everyone who spoke or read Russian and became forums for heated debates between adherents of various socialist platforms. The largest of them was the Russian Progressive Club of Winnipeg, created in January 1912 by Social Democrat émigrés. Located on Main Street in the immigrant-populated North End, in March 1913 the club boasted seventy regular members.[23] The clubs established libraries and reading rooms, where for a moderate fee anyone could enjoy access to educational and socialist literature in the Russian language. In 1915, the Russian Progressive Library in Winnipeg held over 1,000 titles (a substantial number for the time) and received thirteen Russian periodicals of liberal-reformist and socialist orientation including *Russkoe bogatstvo*, *Sovremennyi mir*, *Pravda*, *Novyi mir*, and others. The Russian Progressive Library in Toronto was first located at 185 Queen Street West and later moved to 194 Spadina Avenue, where it remained into the early 1920s.[24]

Like other ethnic radicals in early twentieth-century Canada, Russian socialists employed a variety of methods to reach the immigrant masses. Outdoor meetings, public lectures, workers' picnics (modelled on Russian revolutionary *massovki*), folk concerts, and drama circles were all used to strengthen the faith of the converted and to recruit new followers. From 1911 to 1915, the Russo-Ukrainian Socialist Revolutionary Group in Toronto held 120 propaganda meetings and staged ten plays.[25] Ukrainian plays and folk songs were stock items of many Russian socialist organizations, which took into consideration the ethnic background of their immigrant audiences. In Timmins, where Belarusans made up the majority of labourers from Russia, Ukrainian plays were performed in Russian (Belarusan as a literary language was still in its formative stage).[26] Proceeds from the above events were often used to further the cause of the socialist and labour movement: they were sent to assist striking workers in Canada and the United States, or to support friendly organizations or political exiles in Russia.

Despite the efforts of these small cohorts of political activists, the influence of socialist ideas on Canada's Eastern European workers should not be overstated, especially in the years before World War I. While some immigrant groups such as the Finns had a well-developed socialist culture (made possible, among other factors, by their high literacy rate), the same could not be said of Ukrainians and Belarusans. Wedded to peasant culture with its mistrust of garrulous "city folk" and dreaming of a good-sized farm in the old country, Ukrainian and Belarusan immigrants were often suspicious of socialist agitators and their abstract-sounding speeches. In addition, the majority of Russian-born workers in Canada hailed from some of the least industrially developed regions of the tsarist empire, where an organized socialist movement was barely existent (unlike the radical hotbeds found in Left-Bank and southern Ukraine). "[These] thousands of peasants and workers from Grodno, Minsk, Volhynia etc., who lived in Russia during [the revolution of] 1905, have no idea of what was going on at that time. The revolution passed them by without having the slightest effect. Many have never even heard of it," a Russian émigré socialist complained in *Novyi mir*.[27] The effectiveness of socialist propaganda was also undermined by the doctrinarism of some émigré *intelligenty*, who looked down upon the "uneducated peasants" and lamented their low proletarian consciousness and addiction to drinking in the pages of the socialist press. Nor did the Jewish origin of many socialist proselytizers help spread the "progressive" word among the migrants, who heard from the priests that socialism was a Jewish conspiracy aimed at destroying Orthodox Christianity and the Russian monarchy. Before

1917, attempts to distribute Russian socialist literature in Slavic immigrant neighbourhoods often ran up against the indifference or scowl of the workers, who could not understand why they should spend their hard-earned cents on something as useless as a newspaper. When the socialist organizer Nikolai Romanov tried to call a political meeting of the few dozen Russian workers that he had found in Brockville, Ontario, many of them refused to go, thinking that Romanov wanted "to subvert the Russian state."[28] Socialist canvassers who had the temerity to appear at Slavic boarding-houses on Sundays were sometimes "greeted" with threats of physical violence from the inebriated tenants. Such organizations as the Society for Aid to Political Exiles in Siberia consisted almost exclusively of radical intelligentsia and thus held little appeal for the rank-and-file labourer.[29] Socialist Revolutionary and Social Democrat groups had a relatively broader support base, but they too appear to have included (especially before 1917) only a small percentage of the politically conscious immigrant population.

As elsewhere in North America, Ukrainian and Belarusan immigrant workers employed in the mining industry with its traditions of labour militancy were more susceptible to socialist agitation. The geographic isolation of most mining towns and their less itinerant workforce compared to railway construction and logging camps made miners a logical target for socialist propaganda, particularly when tension between the workers and the employers ran high. Thus, the South Porcupine branch of the SDPC was organized in January 1913 at the height of the district-wide strike of gold miners, most of whom were Slavic immigrants. After a political rally where one of the key speakers was Ukrainian socialist Vasyl Holovatsky, approximately forty miners decided to form a local of the Social Democratic Party. Although the branch did not seem to have a specific ethnic affiliation, migrant workers from Belarus and eastern Ukraine (Vasilii Krisevich, Mikhail Moroz, Makar Kudreiko, N. Plesko) constituted the majority of its leadership.[30] In other resource frontier towns, where immigrants could not be easily reached by the church and its patriotic sermons, socialist ideas were also finding their way to the masses of Russian-born workers. In The Pas, for instance, Ukrainian and Belarusan loggers and railway navvies regularly read the socialist newspaper *Novyi mir*.[31]

Russian émigré socialists of the day commonly regarded themselves as offshoots of the home country's socialist movement rather than as part of Canadian labour politics. The umbilical cord that connected European-born radicals to the old continent was further strengthened

by the ambivalent attitudes of Canada's mainstream unions and labour
parties to non-Anglo-Saxon workers and their organizations, which, as
one English-Canadian activist put it, were largely "strangers to each
other."[32] Moreover, Russian socialists, unlike their Jewish or Finnish
comrades, targeted immigrant worker communities which were neither
as large nor as class conscious. Regarding their stay in Canada as
forced exile, the Russian émigré radicals, as a rule, were more concerned with fomenting revolution in the homeland from the relative
safety of their Canadian abode than with addressing the needs of the
Canadian working class. They were revolutionaries in waiting, prepared
to jump at the first opportunity to overthrow the hated Romanovs.
Even the dissemination of socialist ideas among the masses of Russian-
born immigrants was done primarily with a view of moulding the future political vanguard of the Russian proletariat, for it was no secret
that the majority of the immigrant workers intended to return to their
villages in Ukraine or Belarus.

Many Russian socialist branches in Canada maintained not just
emotional but organizational ties with parent organizations in the
homeland. The Social Democrats, for instance, sponsored fundraising
drives in Winnipeg, Montreal, and Vancouver to support Social Democratic candidates to the Fourth Duma in 1912.[33] There were also well-
functioning clandestine channels of sending money and other donations
to Russian political exiles in Siberia. Shipments of Russian socialist
periodicals published in Europe went in the opposite direction. In
1915, several dozen copies of every issue of the Bolshevik party organ
The Social Democrat were regularly sent to four addresses in Montreal
and Winnipeg.[34] The agenda of socialist meetings and rallies was
shaped more often by Russian issues than by Canadian ones. Many
Russian socialist organizations, for instance, held meetings to honour
the victims of 9 January 1905 ("Bloody Sunday"), when police had
crushed a large demonstration of workers in St Petersburg.[35] In September 1912, the Russian local of the SDPC in Winnipeg held a mass
rally commemorating the tsarist trial of the Social Democrat deputies
of the Second Duma, which reportedly gathered an audience of 1,200.
The public was addressed by Grigorii Belousov, a Russian Social
Democrat and a former member of the Duma, who had been exiled to
Siberia in 1906 and afterwards fled to the United States.[36] The same
year, G.S. Kuznetsov, a Social Democrat member of the Fourth Duma,
spoke at a meeting organized by the Russian Progressive Library in
Toronto and attended "by migrant labourers from Russia and Galicia

numbering about 300."[37] Russian socialists in Canada also maintained friendly ties with their larger and financially better off counterparts in the United States.[38] The Russian Social Democrat organ *Novyi mir*, published in New York since 1911, had many readers north of the 49th parallel and frequently carried materials on Canada authored by Russian-Canadian socialist leaders.[39]

This is not to say that Russian radical groups, especially Social Democrats, were completely immune to the concerns of the working class in Canada and the United States. In March 1912, Russian Social Democrats in Toronto staged a concert and a drama performance in solidarity with the Eaton's tailors' strike and decided to boycott the company stores.[40] Fundraising events also occurred in support of large strikes in the United States, such as the 1913 general strike of garment workers in New York.[41] Some Russian-born labour activists attempted to organize workers across the lines of nationality. Members of the Russian Progressive Club in Toronto, for instance, were involved in establishing the first trade union at the local Massey Harris plant, which, however, was soon crushed by the company. Grigorii Kukhar, who lived in Toronto after escaping from Siberia and was involved in the Russo-Ukrainian Socialist Revolutionary Group, played an active role in creating the local carpenters' union in 1913, while M. Zaiarniuk tried to organize meatpackers at the local Swift plant.[42] However, Russian workers in Canada simply lacked the numbers to create their own ethnic unions that would match the strength of their American counterparts, such as the Russo-Polish Union of Cloakmakers in New York.

Within the politically active nucleus of Canada's Eastern and Central European working class, ethnic differences were muted by the sense of comradeship originating from shared social and class experiences as foreign workers in a predominantly Anglo-Saxon environment. Cultural and linguistic affinities, coupled with memories of common Old World struggles against the tsarist regime, also acted as a unifying force. In fact, it is difficult to separate the history of one ethnic socialist movement in early twentieth-century Canada from that of another. Russian, Ukrainian, Polish, Jewish, and other ethnic locals of the Social Democratic Party of Canada often staged joint political events, picnics, and May Day parades, which brought together migrant workers of various nationalities and were addressed by speakers in three or four different languages. It was common for Russian socialist organizations to use the facilities of their larger and better-funded Ukrainian or Finnish counterparts for political and cultural activities. Russian socialists in Timmins, for instance, held their drama performances, concerts, and lectures in the newly built Finnish Labour Temple.[43]

After the onset of the economic recession in 1913, Russian and other ethnic socialist groups held joint rallies in several Canadian cities, attempting to mobilize their polyglot population of unemployed workers. One of these rallies, convened in January 1915 by Montreal socialists, gathered a reported audience of about 800. Iosif Rabizo called upon Montreal workers of all nationalities to unite and demand the creation of municipally funded public works. The meeting ended in the formation of an "Organization of the Unemployed" with seventy members and an executive committee consisting of Russian, Ukrainian, Polish, Jewish, and other labour activists.[44] Later the same year, sixteen socialist and labour organizations of the city established an umbrella group called the Socialist Council of Montreal, which included the Russian Socialist Revolutionary Group, the Society for Aid to Political Exiles in Siberia, Ukrainian, Jewish, German, Italian, Lithuanian, and several English- and French-speaking locals of the Social Democratic Party, two locals of the Socialist Party, and several leftist labour unions.[45]

While Russian-born workers and their socialist leaders were largely spared the adverse effects of wartime anti-alien measures that decimated many Ukrainian socialist organizations in 1914–16, this did not make the task of mobilizing an army of itinerant sojourners any easier. The recession of 1913–15 increased the transience of the labour migrants, who traversed the country in desperate search of work, and left many socialist organizations struggling. Only thirty out of the seventy founding members of Montreal's "Organization of the Unemployed" came to its second meeting, which was held just three weeks later.[46] The membership of Russian socialist groups shrank as immigrants travelled across Canada, headed south of the border, or found their way back to Russia. Some branches collapsed altogether. Montreal's Russian Social Democrat group became one such victim of the recession. In June 1916, the Russian local of the SDPC in Montreal announced its closure "due to the departure of the members," with the few remaining activists joining the party's Ukrainian branch.[47] A Montreal correspondent of *Novyi mir* lamented in August 1916 that the local "Russian colony" was "in some sort of commotion: some are going home, others enlist in Canadian regiments [but] as for organization, there is none. There is not even someone who would explain to the confused what is going on …"[48] Russian socialist work in Winnipeg also fell into stagnation after some of the leaders of the Progressive Club went in 1915 to the United States to work as munitions inspectors – an act condemned by the uncompromising Solomon Almazov as a betrayal of the anti-militaristic principles of the socialist movement.[49]

Popular nationalism and anti-Semitism, stirred by the war, also had a negative impact on the strength and cohesion of some socialist groups. A group of Slavic members of Winnipeg's Progressive Club made an apparently unsuccessful attempt to rid the organization of Jews. In another example of thinly veiled anti-Semitism, Montreal's Russian Progressive Mutual Aid Society added the word "Slavic" to its name and barred persons of any other origin from membership.[50] To add to the socialists' troubles, in April 1915 the Canadian government took the advice of Russian consul Sergei Likhachev and placed two leftist Russian-American newspapers – *Novyi mir* and *Russkoe slovo* – on the list of periodicals prohibited from Canada on the grounds of their anti-war platform. Canadian labour organizations protested the decision, finding an unlikely ally in the US State Department, which attested to the loyalty of the two publications. As a result, in May 1915 both newspapers were back in circulation. The following year, however, the Russian government renewed its efforts to suppress the émigré socialist press. In August 1916, the Russian ambassador in Washington Yuri Bakhmetiev wrote to his British colleague, asking that the two papers be banned again. The request was passed on to Ottawa, sending *Novyi mir* and *Russkoe slovo* back on the black list. In late 1916, the ban on the more moderate *Russkoe slovo* was removed but the pro-Bolshevik *Novyi mir* remained prohibited for the duration of the war, although it was illegally shipped into Canada.[51]

THE IMPACT OF THE RUSSIAN REVOLUTION

The fall of the tsarist regime in February 1917 marked a turning point in the development of the Russian immigrant left in Canada. The revolution politicized the immigrant masses, breathing new life into the old radical organizations and giving rise to dozens of new "progressive" groups, which added their voices to the spirited debates about Russia's future. The *Sudbury Star*, for instance, reported in January 1918 that Russian labourers in the city often failed to appear for work and preferred instead to spend their time debating the merits of socialism and revolution.[52] Most of the Russian organizations created after 1917, however, turned out to be unstable products of spontaneous revolutionary enthusiasm, which lacked a clear political orientation and either disappeared or became amalgamated into other groups as quickly as they emerged. The year 1917 witnessed the resurgence of several semi-defunct Socialist Revolutionary circles[53] and the creation of others, including a large "Russo-Ukrainian Socialist Revolutionary Group" in Windsor. Led by Ivan Pereguda and Grigorii Kolodii, it was reported to have over 600 members, a night school, a choir, and a drama circle.[54] With its close connections to American socialists in nearby Detroit, Windsor soon became one of the main strongholds of Russian radicalism in Canada, causing growing anxiety for local businesspeople. In August 1919, when the "Red Scare" hysteria had reached its highest point, the president of the Border Chamber of Commerce F. Maclure Sclanders informed the Department of Immigration and Colonization that Windsor had "quite a number of Russians employed in our factories and among these there are a good many of very distinctly revolutionary tendencies who ... indeed are a general menace."[55] In other cities, Russian-born immigrants (Ukrainians, Belarusans, Russians, and Poles) began to organize "Unions of Russian Workers" (Soiuzy russkikh rabochikh), whose political colouration (Bolshevik, anarchist, Socialist Revolutionary, etc.) usually depended on the ideological affiliations of their leaders.[56] The Union of Russian Workers that appeared in Toronto in February 1918 claimed a membership of fifty-three and saw its goal as "fostering revolutionary class consciousness among Toronto's Russian workers for the direct struggle against capital and the government."[57] A similar organization established in Galt, Ontario, included fifteen out of seventy-five Russian-born workers who reportedly lived there at the time.[58]

Canada's "Russian colonies" also included a few moderate liberal-democratic groups, which exhorted immigrants to shun the radical political alternatives and to support the Russian Provisional Government. In September 1917, a handful of Russian-born intelligentsia in Montreal announced the formation of the Russian Democratic Union and called upon all Russian citizens in Montreal "regardless of nationality, party, or belief" to unite in support of a democratic Russia. The new organization was led by Zachary Zhenirovsky, ex-member of the short-lived Society for Aid to Political Exiles in Siberia, and by S. Akopian, an Armenian Socialist Revolutionary. The Russian Democratic Union was represented on the Central Committee of the United Russian Organizations in America (UROA), a New York-based umbrella association of moderately "progressive" immigrant groups that rejected political extremism.[59] However, like other Russian émigré groups that attempted to create a viable political centre, the Russian Democratic Union turned out to be stillborn. Towards the second half of 1917, the evolution of political orientations of Russian-born immigrants in Canada and the United States largely mirrored the change of political climate within Russia itself, where the concepts of parliamentary democracy and constitutionalism had little support outside the small strata of educated urban society. War-weariness and growing disillusionment with the Provisional Government, which had failed to accomplish most of its promised reforms (including the redistribution of land), were shifting popular sympathies in the "Russian colonies" towards the more radical groups, including the Social Democrats and their left-wing Socialist Revolutionary allies. Pro-Bolshevik sentiment, as usual, was strongest in western Canada. On 17 June 1917, the Russian Progressive Club of Winnipeg organized a mass meeting attended by 600 immigrants from Russia. The meeting passed a resolution of support for the Bolshevik-controlled Soviet of Workers' and Soldiers' Deputies in Petrograd.[60]

In one respect, the democratic changes in the homeland proved to be a mixed blessing for the Russian socialist movement in North America. The political amnesty declared by Russia's Provisional Government opened the way to the repatriation of many émigré socialists, thus weakening the leadership of Russian radical organizations abroad. In March 1917, the Russian Ministry of Foreign Affairs instructed all its consular missions to facilitate the return of former political exiles by providing them with passports and travel allowances. In most North American cities that had Russian consular missions, Russian and other ethnic socialist organizations established co-ordinating committees for assisting the repatriation of political émigrés. These committees compiled lists of persons eligible to be returned at the Russian government's expense and submitted them to the consulates.[61] The Russian "progressive" organizations of Montreal met in mid-April in the Labour Temple Hall on St Dominique Street to create the "Advisory Council for Assistance to Returning Political Émigrés."[62] The council appears to have primarily included members of the Russian-Slavic Progressive Mutual Aid Society of Montreal, which was dominated by moderate Socialist Revolutionaries.

Canadian seaports also served as important transit points for political émigrés returning to Russia from the United States. In June 1917 the Russian embassy in London, which was in charge of all Russian consulates in Canada, wired $10,000 to Consul Konstantin Ragozin in Vancouver in order to repay the loans he had secured from the Dominion Bank for the purpose of assisting political repatriates. In the spring and summer of 1917, the consulate provided financial support to over 150 persons belonging to the "political" category, including some from Canada.[63] One such returnee group, which was preparing to sail in May 1917 to Vladivostok on the ss *Empress of Russia*, caught the attention of Vancouver city authorities. The police officer dispatched to investigate the political views of the returning exiles anxiously reported that some of them had every intention of turning the ongoing fight against Germany into a war against the Russian government. He thought it "not very wise to let them have the privilege of going through the Dominion with such ideas."[64]

Vancouver police officials might not have known that Canadian naval authorities in Halifax, acting on the information from the British Admiralty, had detained a group of five prominent Russians less than two months earlier. One of the five was Leon Trotsky, who was allegedly carrying $10,000 raised with German help to "stir up trouble" in Russia. On 2 April, Trotsky and the others were removed from the Norwegian steamer *Kristianiafjord*, en route from New York to Christiania. They were placed in an internment camp near Amherst, Nova Scotia and released only a month later after the intervention of the Russian Ministry of Foreign Affairs, which was forced to act by the protests of socialist and labour organizations on both sides of the Atlantic.[65]

By the mid-summer of 1917, the movement of political repatriates to Russia came to a halt as funds dried up and the political situation in Russia became increasingly unstable. The alleged misuse of government money allocated for repatriation and the growing threat of left-wing radicalism dictated a change of Russian policy towards the returning exiles. In early August, the Russian Foreign Ministry cancelled the favoured visa regime for political repatriates and made them subject to the newly introduced universal passport regulations, which required Russian consular missions to verify the identity of each returnee with Petrograd before issuing travel papers.[66]

Like the majority of socialist organizations in Canada, most Russian socialists greeted the formation of the first Soviet government in Russia as a promise of freedom for the world's proletariat and as a model for emulation.[67] In December 1917, Russian Social Democrats in Winnipeg were strong enough to launch a pro-Soviet Russian-language weekly called *Rabochii narod* (*The Working People*). Edited by Michael Charitonoff, the new secretary of the Russian Progressive Club, the newspaper was printed with the press of the Ukrainian Social Democratic Party.[68] Three months later, left-wing Socialist Revolutionaries in

Toronto began to publish a bi-weekly newspaper named *Zemlia i volia* (*Land and Freedom*), which also adopted a pro-Bolshevik posture.[69] Not all socialist groups, however, rallied around the Bolsheviks. The right wing of the Socialist Revolutionary Party and other moderately "progressive" or avowedly non-partisan groups were much more reserved (if not openly hostile) in their attitudes to the new Soviet government. One such organization was Hamilton's Society for Aid to Russian Victims of the War, organized in late 1917 by Ukrainian and Belarusan workers from Russia. It protested the Bolshevik seizure of power and expressed its support of the Allied war effort.[70]

In early 1918, as the prospect of civil war in Russia became a reality, ideological polarization within the "Russian colonies" across the United States and Canada was a *fait accompli*. Two Russian immigrant congresses were held simultaneously in New York in February 1918, each claiming to speak on behalf of the entire community. The first gathering, convened by the UROA, was attended by delegates from some fifty moderately "progressive" organizations. Ilya Tartak, a lecturer in Russian literature at McGill University and a CEF veteran, represented the Russian Progressive Mutual Aid Society of Montreal. The congress condemned the Bolshevik coup and demanded an immediate transfer of power to the Constituent Assembly.[71] The parallel congress of eighty-four socialist organizations representing Russian-born immigrants of various nationalities (including Russian, Finnish, Latvian, Jewish, and other ethnic socialist locals and labour unions) declared full support for Soviet Russia and sent greetings to the Council of People's Commissars in Petrograd and to "the revolutionary Russian people."[72]

Political divisions among Russian-born immigrants in Canada continued to deepen in the following months. In February and March of 1918, Montreal's newly organized Society for the Defence of the Constituent Assembly held meetings of protest against the Bolshevik dissolution of Russia's Constituent Assembly and against the "shameful" treaty of Brest-Litovsk signed in March 1918. By mid-spring, the Russian-American press published reports of both pro- and anti-Bolshevik groups in Montreal recruiting volunteers for the Russian civil war.[73] Thousands of immigrants from Russia who had enlisted in the Canadian armed forces overseas were also not immune to the politicizing and divisive influence of recent events back home. When 135 Russian CEF soldiers were brought back from England in December 1918 to be included in Canada's Siberian contingent, the majority of them were rejected as "unreliable" and stayed in Canada as depot personnel. Still,

the Canadian Expeditionary Force in Siberia (CEFS) had at least fifty
ex-Russian subjects, including some World War I veterans such as Filip
Konowal, a native of Podolia and the only Ukrainian-Canadian to ever
receive the Victoria Cross. Five of the Russian soldiers deserted while
stationed in Siberia, probably using enlistment in the Canadian contingent as a way to return to the homeland.[74]

While Canada's "Russian colonies" were split in their attitudes towards Bolshevism and Soviet Russia, most Canadians, including
government officials, saw "Russian" as increasingly synonymous with
"Bolshevik." Amidst multiplying rumours of a Bolshevik conspiracy,
the Ottawa government began to implement a concerted program to
weed out all suspicious foreign groups regardless of their national, ethnic, or political labels.[75] The Russian-German treaty of Brest-Litovsk
increased Canadian resentment of Soviet Russia, which was now regarded as a traitor of the Allied cause. Russian socialist groups were
among the first to feel the strong hand of the Canadian state. Thus, in
October 1917 police broke into the meeting hall of Windsor's Russo-
Ukrainian Socialist Revolutionary Group and arrested its leaders Ivan
Pereguda and Grigorii Kolodii.[76] In March 1918, popular anarchist agitator Feliks Konosevich was arrested in Timmins after a socialist meeting held in the Finnish Labour Temple (although he was later acquitted
by the court).[77] But it was not until the late summer of 1918 that the
federal authorities attempted a true crackdown on Russian radicals and
other "dangerous foreigners." On 16 September, the Winnipeg police
searched the premises of *Rabochii narod* and a week later arrested its
editor Michael Charitonoff, who was charged with "having objection-
able literature in his possession" and sentenced to a fine of $1,000 and
three years' imprisonment. Charitonoff's arrest stirred up socialist organizations and labour unions in Winnipeg, which set up a special fund
to appeal the case.[78] The display of class solidarity won out:
Charitonoff was released on bail in early December. After a series of
appeals to Ottawa, he was cleared of all charges, although the publication of *Rabochii narod* was not resumed.[79] The meeting called by the
Winnipeg Trades and Labour Council on 22 December to protest the
repressive orders-in-council, the persecution of political radicals, and
the Allied intervention in Russia greeted Charitonoff's appearance with
loud applause.[80]

Russian socialist groups and their Ukrainian counterparts in
Timmins, Brantford, Montreal, and other cities were also raided in the
fall and winter of 1918–19, with some of their members arrested and

tried for seditious activities.[81] In mid-September 1918, the Department of Justice decided that it would be "advisable for the protection of the country against Bolsheviki [sic] propaganda and machinations" to obtain a full inventory of Russian citizens (with names, places of residence, etc.) from the Canada Registration Board.[82] The procedure took two months to complete, providing C.H. Cahan, director of the Public Safety Branch in Ottawa, with a list of 63,784 registered Russian nationals (Ukrainians, Finns, Jews, and others), organized by electoral sub-district.[83] Two infamous orders-in-councils (PC 2381 and 2384), enacted that same autumn, banned all publications and meetings in Russian and eleven other "enemy" languages with the exception of religious and scholarly purposes. They also prohibited a number of real and imaginary radical organizations including "the Russian Social Democratic party," "the Russian Revolutionary Group," "the Russian Social Revolutionists," and "the Russian Workers' Union." The following June, Section 41 of the Immigration Act was hastily amended to permit deportations of any non-Canadians advocating the "overthrow by force ... of constituted law and authority."[84]

Despite their apparent severity, the repressive measures failed to quash the Russian radicals. In May 1919, shortly after restrictions on Russian-language publications and organizations were lifted following the end of the war, Charitonoff and two other members of the Russian Social Democrat group began to collect funds for launching another Russian-language socialist newspaper called *Novyi vek* (*New Age*), which "would show the right way to the liberation of the working class."[85] It was to be distributed across both Canada and the United States, where the "Red Scare" was also in full swing. According to American intelligence sources, in June 1919, at the height of the Winnipeg General Strike, Charitonoff and his associates received $7,000 from Ludwig Martens, head of the Soviet Government Information Bureau in New York, to assist in the newspaper's publication. The money was allegedly delivered by "Fedchenko, a notorious Russian Anarchist of Pittsburgh, Pennsylvania, who ... was making frequent trips in June between Detroit and Winnipeg, carrying money and confidential documents."[86]

It is hardly possible to verify the credibility of this information, just as there is no evidence to support the US officials' allegation that some or all of this money was later turned over to the Winnipeg strike committee. We only know that Martens and his assumed contacts with Russian radicals in Canada, like the communications between American and Canadian "Bolsheviks" in general, indeed became a permanent headache for Canadian authorities.[87] The growing public fear of foreign radicals prompted the Royal North-West Mounted Police to raid the homes of several socialist leaders believed to have played a key role in the Winnipeg Strike. Of the eleven men arrested during the June 17 raid, five were "foreigners": Oscar Schoppelrei, Sam Blumenberg, and three Russian citizens – Solomon Almazov, Mike Verenchuk, and Michael Charitonoff, who was arrested for the second time in ten months.[88]

It was the government's intention to deal with the detained "aliens" by applying the newly amended Section 41 of the Immigration Act, which now authorized deportation on political grounds. Calls for the deportation of all alien (and, indeed, even naturalized) "troublemakers" found wide support in Canada among returning war veterans, businessmen, and law-enforcement officials even before the Winnipeg confrontation. In the words of Windsor entrepreneur Maclure Sclanders, "Deportation, if it is possible, would quickly and finally solve the problem [of foreign radicalism], because there is nothing people of the class in question dread more than to be sent from this great country back to their own lands."[89] After June 1919, such views became a stock item in the Canadian discourse on the "Bolshevist threat."[90] In mid-July, the five men arrested in Winnipeg (including the innocent Verenchuk) were brought before an Immigration Board of Inquiry presided over by Justice R. M. Noble. As Donald Avery pointed out, these hearings were of the utmost importance, for they could set a precedent and clear the way "for the deportation of hundreds of other immigrant agitators across the country."[91] The amended provisions of the Immigration Act, however, proved inadequate: of the five, only Schoppelrei, an American citizen, was deported (and then under a different section of the Immigration Act). Verenchuk was released after an unsuccessful attempt to question his sanity, Almazov was acquitted, and Charitonoff and Blumenberg, initially ordered deported, had their deportation orders rescinded following their appeal to the Department of Justice.[92]

As the widely publicized Winnipeg deportation hearings were coming to an end, a lesser-known series of cases involving Russian-born radicals was brought before the Immigration Board of Inquiry in Vancouver. In late July, as a result of Mounted Police spy work within Russian radical groups, the Vancouver police charged twenty-seven men with allegedly participating in an anarchist ring connected to the Union of Russian Workers. According to police evidence, the group held seditious meetings in two poolrooms owned by Elmurza Butaev, an Ossetian from Tersk Province, and Johan Kelt, a native of Estonia. Fedor

Riazanov, one of the anarchist leaders, was accused of planning to bomb the Russian consulate and the CPR's luxurious Vancouver Hotel. Pavel Semenov was charged with disseminating seditious propaganda among immigrant miners in the Crow's Nest Pass.[93] Despite a defence campaign organized by the Vancouver Trades and Labour Council and supported by other socialist groups, by mid-September all fourteen were ordered deported and placed in an internment camp at Vernon pending deportation arrangements.[94]

However, the war and the chaotic political situation in the territories of the former tsarist empire made the deportations of Russian radicals impossible. The collapse of the old order in Russia resulted in multiple border changes and a muddle of internecine conflicts that disrupted normal channels of diplomatic communication. In December 1919 the Canadian Department of Immigration attempted to arrange the deportation of sixty-one Russian immigrants through the former tsarist consulate in Montreal, which then represented the anti-Bolshevik government of Admiral Kolchak. Along with criminals, public charges, and the mentally ill, the deportee list included ten of the fourteen "agitators" arrested in Vancouver: Fedor Riazanov, Johan Kelt, Elmurza Butaev, Pavel Semenov, Grigorii Trusov (the secretary of the Union of Russian Workers), Fedor Golovin, Gapo Chekov, Bashir Dzukoev, Savva Kodovba, and Kasimir Medeikis.[95] Canadian immigration officials' intention to send the "Russian anarchists" home was not appreciated by the Kolchak administration and its short-lived successor governments, which had no desire to import Communist radicals into territories under their control. In February 1920 Consul Sergei Likhachev, following recommendations from the Russian embassy in London, refused to issue visas to the deportees and advised the Canadian government to send the "Red" agitators to Soviet Russia instead.[96] Having no contact with the Bolsheviks, Canadian immigration authorities continued searching for a way to deport the fourteen Russians, who were transferred in the meantime to the New Westminster Penitentiary. The search did not stop even after it became abundantly clear that the case was based on largely fabricated evidence. When by mid-December all possible options were exhausted, the Minister of Immigration James Calder was forced to parole the fourteen prisoners, whose release was triumphantly greeted by the socialist organizations of western Canada.[97]

The repressions and deportation attempts of 1919–20 had a depressing effect on Russian socialist organizations. Some were disbanded as their members became dispersed or lost interest in political activities, while others joined the much stronger and more financially secure branches of the Ukrainian Labour-Farmer Temple Association. The Winnipeg Russian Progressive Club merged with the Workers' Party of Canada, soon to be renamed the Communist Party.[98] After the revolutionary enthusiasm of 1917–18 had passed, many workers began to return from socialist meeting halls to saloons and poolrooms. Left-wing organizations were also weakened by the repatriation of their activists, which resumed in early 1921 with the lifting of the Allied naval blockade of Soviet Russia.

RETURN MIGRATION TO THE SOVIET UNION

Emigration from North America to Soviet Russia and Ukraine began in 1918–19 as an offshoot of the international working class campaign aimed at ensuring the survival of the world's first proletarian state. The campaign received much of its momentum from the return drive that spread among immigrants from the former Russian Empire after 1917. For these immigrants, Bolshevik Russia was something more than the land of their birth – it also symbolized a new future, free of landlords, capitalists, and religious oppression. Many Russian socialists and sympathizers abroad believed that they could help transform Russia from a symbol of economic backwardness into a world-class industrial power. The Soviet government well understood the important role that returning emigrants could play in Russia's economic revival, for America had turned these formerly rural dwellers into much-needed carriers of western technology and capital for the homeland, ravaged by years of war, revolution, and civil unrest. In May 1919 Ludwig Martens, head of the Soviet Government Bureau in New York, issued an appeal "To The Citizens of the Russian Soviet Republic in America," proposing a conference of Russian immigrant organizations interested in providing technical aid to Russia.[99] Even though Martens was deported from the United States in early 1921 on charges of seditious activities, the movement was already underway. The Society for Technical Aid to Soviet Russia (STA), organized in May 1919 with Martens's support by a group of Russian immigrants in New York, became the main conduit for sending technical assistance to the Soviet republics. The Society recruited immigrants into agricultural and industrial teams (communes), helped them buy the needed supplies, and arranged visas and transportation. By 1922, there were seventy-five STA branches across the United States and Canada with an estimated 6,000 regular members, primarily Slavs, Jews, and Finns from the former Russian Empire.[100]

The first Canadian branch of the STA was established in September 1919 by the Russian Socialist Revolutionary group in Montreal under the initial name of the "Union of Russian Engineers and Workmen." Its leader William Revenko was described by the RCMP as an able "public speaker [with] great influence among the foreigners."[101] The organization opened a Russian language school and offered evening classes where immigrant workers could learn how to operate a tractor or an automobile. By the early 1920s, branches of the Society for Technical Aid also existed in Toronto, Winnipeg, Vancouver, Ottawa, and several smaller cities.[102]

Other Russian socialist organizations in Canada established similar schools that invited would-be returnees to acquire the basics of general and technical education. Russian immigrants in Winnipeg, for instance, could take advantage of courses in arithmetic and electricity offered by the local Russian Self-Education Society.[103] The Russian Progressive Club of Toronto opened an evening workers' school (described by the RCMP as "thoroughly Bolshevistic"), which gave classes in the Russian language, arithmetic, algebra, geometry, and technical instruction.[104] Ukrainian-Canadian socialists also joined the technical aid campaign. Even though Galicians and Bukovynians constituted the absolute majority in Ukrainian-Canadian socialist organizations, they viewed the Ukrainian Soviet Socialist Republic (which did not include western Ukraine at the time) as their true homeland. In Winnipeg, the Society for Technical Aid worked in close cooperation with the ULFTA and used the Ukrainian Communist press to recruit Ukrainian and other Slavic workers into an agricultural commune, scheduled to leave for Ukraine in the spring of 1922. Each candidate was required to make a contribution to the communal fund (either $500 per member or $800 per family) and to show willingness to work for the benefit of the Russian revolution. Simultaneously, Russian socialists in Montreal were inviting fellow immigrants to join a mechanics' team that planned to work in one of the Soviet industrial factories. In early 1922, the Montreal and Winnipeg groups merged to form the First Canadian Agricultural Commune with a total of fifty-two (according to other sources, forty-two) members and the combined assets of $35,000. The commune purchased three tractors, two Ford trucks, several reapers and threshers, and equipment for a small power station. Clothes, kitchenware, and other household items were also procured to meet the Soviet requirement of complete self-sufficiency for all immigrant communes entering Russia.[105]

The First Canadian Agricultural Commune was one of the first North American immigrant collectives to leave for Soviet Russia as part of the technical aid campaign. In April 1922, the Baltic-American Line steamer *Lithuania* set sail from New York en route to Liepaja (Libava), carrying the first party of Canadian "communards" and two American collectives – approximately 200 men and women in total. About two months later, the Canadians reached their final destination in Ukraine: a Soviet state farm near the village of Myhaiv, some 100 km north of Odessa. Soviet archival records list thirty-one Canadians who arrived on the *Lithuania* – all of them men, primarily in their thirties, born in Galicia (53%), Bukovyna (13%), and the former Russian Empire (34%). All but two declared their membership in the Workers' Party of Canada (the forerunner of the Communist Party), the ULFTA, or the Society for Technical Aid to Soviet Russia. The group had no labour activists of national prominence, but it did include a few seasoned radicals such as Pavel Semenov, whom Canadian immigration authorities had attempted to deport two years earlier.[106]

In the spring of 1923 two other Ukrainian-Canadian agricultural communes, named the Grain Grower and the Workers' Field, settled on the steppes of southern Ukraine near the city of Kryvyi Rih. The Workers' Field, organized by the Montreal branch of the Society for Technical Aid, attracted primarily Ukrainian immigrants from the Russian Empire, who constituted the majority of Ukrainians in that city. The Grain Grower was the product of the Toronto branch, but its members came from places as diverse as Lethbridge, Ottawa, and Saskatoon.[107] In 1923–25, more parties of returnees came to join the pioneers. All told, about 350 men and women relocated in 1922–25 to the USSR as members of the three Ukrainian-Canadian agricultural collectives.[108] Approximately 150 Doukhobors also left Canada and moved to the USSR, believing the Soviet promises of religious freedom and vast land grants in southern Ukraine.

Return migration from Canada to Soviet Russia turned out to be a short-lived phenomenon, which began to slow down around 1923 and virtually stopped in 1926. The Roaring Twenties ended the unemployment and pessimism that had fuelled the movement, and letters from disillusioned returnees further discouraged those who still contemplated leaving. Also, American and Canadian labour organizations began to complain to Moscow about the exodus of their best cadres to the Soviet Union. In an ironic twist of events, the majority of Canadian Doukhobors who had left for Russia ended up returning to Canada in 1928, when the Soviet government broke its promise to free members of the pacifist sects from military service.[109] Of those returnees who remained in the USSR, probably more than half deserted the communes. A few years later Stalinist repressions struck, sending many "communards" into the Gulag.

The collapse of the Russian Empire in 1917 shattered the traditional foundations of Russian nationhood based on loyalty to the tsar and adherence to the Orthodox faith. The revolution also rocked the boat that held Canada's "Russian colonies" together. The ideological vacuum created by the sudden demise of the *ancien régime* was soon filled by a welter of various left-wing ideologies, which had heretofore existed on the fringes of the immigrant community, largely composed of illiterate peasants with little experience in political activism. The events in the homeland exerted a powerful mobilizing influence on Slavic immigrants from the tsarist empire, most of whom received their first political education through participation in Russian radical organizations that were mushrooming across North America towards the end of 1917. However, it would be simplistic to equate the spontaneous upsurge of political consciousness among the immigrant workers with a deep interest in or understanding of socialist doctrines. In this respect, Canada's "Russian colonies" were largely a mirror image of the peasant communities in Ukraine or Belarus from which they had sprung. For most immigrants, unable to grasp the intricacies of various "progressive" teachings, the meaning of socialism and revolution was reduced to a few slogans ("land to the peasants," "down with the war," etc.). In addition, Canadian public opinion, government agencies, and the immigrant press clearly exaggerated the real support that Russian radical organizations were able to muster from the thousands of ordinary immigrants whose voices are absent from the historical record. As it soon became obvious, even a social upheaval of such magnitude as the Russian revolution could not momentarily transform the average Ukrainian or Belarusan peasant into a revolutionary democrat or a class-conscious proletarian, notwithstanding the small minority that may in fact have accomplished the transformation. The political activism of the immigrant masses had more in common with the anarchistic peasant rebellion *(bunt)* spurred by hopes of a secular paradise than with an organized working class movement. Dissipated by the economic prosperity of the 1920s, riven by factional struggles and weakened by the emigration of the leading activists, the post-1917 Russian immigrant radicalism died away almost as quickly as it had emerged. To be sure, socialism would never again be relegated to the margins of Canada's Eastern European immigrant communities, but in the early 1920s its influence was clearly on the wane.

Conclusion

Between 1896 and 1914, Canada added over 3,000,000 immigrants to its population. While many came as agricultural settlers attracted by the promise of a free homestead on the Prairies, others filled the growing ranks of Canada's working class. Throughout the period, Britain and the United States remained the largest suppliers of Canadian immigrants, but it was the "strong-limbed" eastern and southern Europeans that came to be sought the most eagerly by prosperous Canadian farmers and industrialists searching for new reservoirs of cheap labour.

Ukrainian and Belarusan immigration from the Russian Empire was part of the massive transoceanic circuits of population and labour that firmly tied North America to the European agrarian periphery. This study has attempted to revise the popular version of immigration from tsarist Russia as consisting primarily of religious and political refugees. As we have seen, economic migrants, predominantly of eastern Slav origin, constituted the bulk of the migration stream originating on the western frontier of the Romanov Empire from about 1906–07. The opinions of historians who link the growth of mass emigration from tsarist Russia to the flight of the peasantry from army recruitment, political repressions, or the increased pressure of Russification do not find support in the sources, at least not in the case of Ukrainians and Belarusans. While such motives may have played a role for some emigrants, their numbers were not significant. The high incidence of return migration among Ukrainians and Belarusans also proves that economic rather than political considerations provided the main incentive for peasant emigration from tsarist Russia, just as they did for the majority of other Europeans who crossed the Atlantic during the era of great migrations.

The image of Clifford Sifton's stalwart Slavic peasants coming to till the land on the Prairies did not apply to the vast majority of Ukrainians and Belarusans who hailed from Russia's western frontier. Although small groups of these immigrants did settle on the land, most came to Canada as unskilled labourers and headed towards the resource frontier or urban centres. As temporary migrants, they had much less in common with early Ukrainian settlers from the neighbouring Austrian provinces of Galicia and Bukovyna than they had with the Italian "birds of passage," who have become a staple of North American immigration history.

Belarus was the first to develop labour migration to Canada, but Ukraine sent a far larger number of emigrants. By 1914, there were approximately three Russian-born Ukrainians for every Belarusan immigrant in Canada. In both regions, the topography of emigration to Canada was characterized by an irregular pattern, repeated at the district and village levels. While most immigrants came from villages of solitary or low emigration, almost a quarter of Ukrainians and about 7 per cent of Belarusans arrived in Canada from places that developed large migration chains. In these villages, emigration often claimed several male members of extended families (brothers, cousins, or even fathers and sons) and was beginning to have a significant impact on the local economic micro-structures and social relations.

The Dnieper River formed the geographical watershed between areas that developed considerable emigration to Canada and those other areas where it remained weak or non-existent. The few pockets of emigration from territories east of the Dnieper are exceptions that only prove the rule. Detailed answers (if they are possible) to the question of why the latter territories largely remained outside the pull of the Atlantic economy must await further studies, but some general hypotheses may be suggested. First of all, having been part of the Russian Empire for a longer period, Left-Bank Ukraine and eastern Belarus were more closely integrated into the imperial core than Russia's southwestern and northwestern borderlands, more exposed to the Great Russian cultural influences, and further removed, geographically and culturally, from the Atlantic world. This also explains the relatively large extent of colonization movement to Siberia from the former areas, which diverted a significant part of their migration potential in the eastern direction. In addition, the physical distance that separated these territories from the Atlantic made the extension of overseas migration networks across the Dnieper difficult. Whether the "America fever"

would still have penetrated here if World War I had not brought transatlantic migration to a halt will never be known. However, the examples of Russian peasants from the provinces of Saratov and Samara,
who around 1910 discovered Canada through local German emigrants, and the Black Sea Ossetians and Georgians, who began to
emigrate around the same time, serve as evidence in favour of an affir-
mative answer.

The case of Russia's western frontier shows that the Atlantic migration system is best conceptualized as a broad analytical category useful
for highlighting the general similarity in the structure and patterns of
migrant flows between Europe and America and within each continent.
On a more empirical level, it functioned as a combination of multiple
regional subsystems not necessarily coterminous with ethnic, religious,
or administrative boundaries. In each of these subsystems, routes and
destinations chosen by the migrants exhibited their own pattern. The
configuration of local migrant networks depended on a multitude of
factors specific to the given area: the proximity of areas and population
groups with a more developed migration culture; the availability of alternative migration options; and the exposure of the local peasantry to
outside contacts and influences. As a result of these factors, Belarusan
peasants from the district of Pruzhany, for instance, went overwhelmingly to Canada, while their neighbours from adjacent areas invariably
chose Pennsylvania or New York.

Economy, of course, had a major impact on emigration: overpopulation, meagre landholdings, or infertile soils all created conditions that
favoured population mobility. The hereditary system of land tenure,
which predominated in all heavy-emigration areas of Russian Ukraine
and Belarus, perpetuated rural poverty by preventing peasant families
from expanding their plots through periodic repartitions that were practised (albeit with diminishing frequency) in areas with communal tenure.
At the same time, the weakness of the commune on the empire's western
frontier created a peasant culture different from that of the heartland areas – one that left more room for individual initiative and entrepreneur-
ial spirit needed to make emigration an acceptable alternative.

In each of the two regions, economic pressures that acted as a stimu-
lus for emigration were played out in locally specific ways, but with essentially the same effect. A comparative analysis of the two regional
economies reminds us that, as a factor that contributed to emigration,
overpopulation should be interpreted not as a synonym of high population density but as a relationship between the number of residents in a

given area and the economic resources available to them. A simple comparison of aggregate statistics, which reveals a much larger size of peasant plots in Belarus coupled with lower population density than that in Ukraine, can tell us little about the real conditions of the peasantry in each of these regions. It is only through the analysis of such factors as soil fertility, family structure, and the organization of local agricultural economies that we can understand the essentially similar nature of the pressures faced by the rural population in west-central Belarus and Right-Bank Ukraine. While in Podolia, Kiev, and northern Bessarabia the impoverishment of the peasantry resulted from the domination of the local economy by large capitalist manors, in Grodno and Minsk poverty was largely caused by the poor quality of the soil and the larger size of peasant families, which cancelled out whatever advantages in the amount of landholdings that Belarusan peasants might have had over their Ukrainian neighbours.

And yet, however heavy the economic "push," the wheels of emigration were always set in motion by the forces rooted in human agency. As elsewhere in Europe, the vast migration potential of the empire's western frontier could be realized only through the creation of mechanisms that would supply future emigrants with information and resources needed for making an overseas move. Where such mechanisms did not emerge or were slow to come into existence, peasants continued to head for work, as they had done for years, to the nearest sugar beet estate, to a wealthy German farm in Bessarabia, or to a coalmine in Donbass. After all, peasant emigration from Belarus and especially "Russian" Ukraine (except for a few localities) never reached the same intensity which it had exhibited in such parts of Europe as Italy, Poland, or Transcarpathia, where many villages lost nearly all their male population. Even at its zenith, emigration in rural Russia could rarely compete, either in the numbers of migrants or in economic significance, with the much more extensive internal population movements. Moreover, before emigration could settle into a chain pattern, the conservative East European peasant – always averse to any radical break with traditional ways – required convincing proof of the worthiness of the overseas adventure, preferably in the form of money orders and first-hand accounts from pioneers. For the majority of peasants, emigration was never a "life or death" question but rather a conscious choice between a temporary spell as an industrial worker and permanent proletarianization. A few years of hard work in a Canadian mine or railway construction seemed a small price to pay for the preservation

of their status in a society that still valued land above all else. Contem-
poraries were quick to notice that as far as its economic purpose was
concerned, temporary emigration was largely an extension of the old
tradition of internal labour-seeking migrations, which had drawn millions of Ukrainian and Belarusan peasants into their orbit by the late
nineteenth century. Viewed from the emigrants' standpoint, labour emigration was intended to preserve the old social order, even though in
reality it usually led to a further weakening of traditional society.

For the majority of peasant families, emigration was a short-term
economic strategy aimed at achieving larger goals such as the extension
of family landholdings and property. Marriage played a crucial role in
opting for emigration: as we have seen, not only did married men (especially newlyweds) predominate among the migrants, but their relative proportion in the migrant cohort surpassed the proportion of
married men in the general rural population of the same age. In many
Ukrainian and Belarusan villages, emigration was doubtless seen as the
quickest way for a young peasant family to accumulate some starting
capital and to separate themselves economically from their parents'
households. To what extent such a strategy was successful is a different
– and difficult – question, which cannot be answered on the basis of the
available sources. In the long run, peasant families in eastern Ukraine
and Belarus proved to be much less fortunate than their counterparts in
the rest of Eastern Europe. The German occupation of 1914, two revolutions in a single year, and the catastrophe of the civil war which established Soviet rule over most of Ukraine and Belarus nullified
whatever economic gains emigration might have brought. From the
late 1920s onward, the very fact of having had an emigrant in the extended family could bring fatal consequences to all of its members.

Essentially a socio-economic phenomenon, labour migration can be
fully understood only in the context of the political and legal systems
of the sending and the receiving states. As this study has demonstrated,
the formal strictness of tsarist emigration laws was never matched by
consistency in their practical application, thus allowing hundreds of
thousands of people of various nationalities to leave the empire for as
long as they wished without much interference on the part of the authorities. The popular image of the Russian Empire as a giant prison
encompassing one-sixth of the world's territory should thus be seen as
having little to do with historical reality. The very failure of the Russian
imperial state to develop comprehensive legislation regulating emigration testifies to the fact that the issue was not seen as having extreme

political importance, although the possible weakening of the Russian Orthodox presence on the empire's western frontier did begin to cause some concern. So long as peasant emigration retained (as it largely did) a temporary character, it was perceived in some public and, increasingly, even government circles as a possible source of financial and intellectual capital for the state. As they began to realize the futility of their efforts to keep Russia's peasants at home, the tsarist authorities – more by intuition than by design – slowly turned their attention to the development of mechanisms that would maintain the emigrants' ties to Russia. At the other end of the migration stream, the economic interests of the rising Canadian industry largely outweighed public and state concerns about the racial unfitness of the arriving "Russians" and generally allowed the latter trouble-free entry into the country. In fact, the approaches of both the Russian and the Canadian governments towards labour migration followed the same unspoken rule: official responses to migration remained anti-interventionist as long as the estimated cost of its negative effects remained significantly lower than the expense involved in erecting effective control mechanisms.

The introduction of Ukrainian and Belarusan peasants into Canadian society occurred within two socio-economic contexts. The majority took lower-end occupations in the resource industries or railway construction, while others headed for the cities where they shared the same neighbourhoods with thousands of Jews, "Ruthenians," Poles, and other Eastern Europeans. Large urban centres served not only as places of permanent settlement for these Eastern European labourers but also – or even primarily – as regional labour exchanges. The boundary between the city and the frontier was a blurred one for the majority of the migrants, who followed the needs of the labour market and went wherever there were jobs to be found. Montreal and perhaps Toronto and Windsor were the only cities in early twentieth-century Canada where one could spot the emerging nuclei of permanent ethnic settlements composed of Russian-born Slavic workers. Even these settlements, however, lacked the necessary foundation of fully viable communities – the sufficient presence of women, families, and children. The lack of female immigration from Russia led single men of eastern Ukrainian and Belarusan origin to marry Orthodox (less often Roman or Greek Catholic) women from Galicia, Bukovyna, or Poland. The elasticity of early twentieth-century "Russian colonies," which lacked definite criteria of belonging except the use of the Russian language and, usually, adherence to Orthodoxy, allowed them to integrate members of other Slavic (and, on occasion, even non-Slavic) groups, but it just as easily led to the loss of their own members to these culturally affined communities. On the left wing of the Russian community, where religion had little or no integrative power, the sole markers of one's "Russianness" were one's language, self-identity, and country of origin.

The experiences of most Ukrainian and Belarusan migrants in early twentieth-century Canada are best described through the concept of sojourning, which highlights the lack of stability and permanence in their lives. Oscar Handlin's concept of "uprooted" immigrants wrenched away from their homes and prone to psychological distress may be inadequate as an overarching theoretical model, but it remains useful for describing the sojourning culture of Slavic workers who inhabited the numerous work camps and frontier towns of early twentieth-century Canada. For the majority of these men, as long as they held hopes of returning home, contact with the host society was limited to the economic sphere. To survive and succeed, one certainly had to grasp the workings of the Canadian labour market, but the world that made sense and had meaning lay beyond the sea, in the home village where their wives and parents continued to till the land, waiting for the money remittances from their husbands and sons. Maintaining contact with the homeland therefore assumed great significance: mentally, if not physically, the temporary migrant still remained embedded in the social networks of his village community. The fragility of these ties increased with every year, although it might not always mean greater integration into Canadian society. Gendered forms of leisure such as drinking, gambling, and brawling allowed the men to ease the stress of sojourning and create a substitute masculine culture modelled on their home village. However, due to the high mobility of the migrant population, social relationships formed as a result of such interaction had a temporary and tenuous character.

Although in most places religious institutions were the only type of association available to the immigrants, organized religion rarely played a major role in the lives of the migrant workers. The creation of viable parishes was possible only with the emergence of more permanent and more gender-balanced settlements, in which women could apply their tempering and stabilizing influence. Attempts of the Russian Orthodox Mission in North America to reach its Canadian flock were also thwarted by the geographic isolation of Canada's work camps and mining towns and by the transience of the migrant population. Since most of its followers (primarily Rusyns from Transcarpathia) were south of the 49th parallel, the Russian Orthodox Church in Canada remained a small, non-incorporated ethnic denomination with few resources and even fewer experienced clergy. In spite of these many handicaps, it did achieve a modicum of success by 1917, partly as a result of the Russian patriotism that swept the immigrant communities at the beginning of World War I. But, just as the church seemed to be making progress, the fall of the Romanov monarchy – followed in eight months by the Bolshevik revolution – dealt two crushing blows to Russian Orthodox communities all over the world.

The end of financial infusions from Russia was, however, a lesser problem compared to the growth of radicalism among the immigrant masses, which, like millions of peasants in Russia itself, rejected the prospect of salvation through faith in favour of a secular paradise promised by the slogans of October 1917. The nearly all-male world of the "Russian colonies" may have proven an obstacle to the creation of church institutions or benevolent societies, but it turned out to be fertile ground for revolutionary agitation (at least in the short term). Estimates of the number of Russian-born workers involved in radical organizations are bound to remain conjectural, but the public branding of "Russians" as Bolsheviks and anarchists did reflect the reality of a considerable short-term radicalization of the Russian immigrant population, even though its threat to the existing order was certainly exaggerated. A marginal force in immigrant communities before World War I, Russian and Russo-Ukrainian socialist organizations of all imaginable political colours suddenly moved to the centre stage for a few turbulent years, only to die away as quickly as they had emerged. The establishment of Soviet rule in much of the former Russian Empire by 1921 was a major reason for the decline of Russian socialism in America, for it removed the *raison d'être* for most of the radical groups, which were little more than overseas extensions of parent socialist parties in Russia with few connections to the Canadian labour movement.

As a postscript, a few words need to be added about the post-1920 history of Canada's "Russian colonies," which provide an instructive example of ethnic identity permutations that occurred among eastern Slav immigrants. Weakened by return migration, intermarriage, and the movement of some of their wealthier members from industrial occupations to farming, Canada's frontier and urban "Russian colonies" continued to shrink in size and vitality until the late 1920s. The records of what was once Canada's largest urban Russian Orthodox parish of ss Peter and Paul in Montreal show a marked decline in the number of sacraments performed and in the overall intensity of the parish's social life during the 1920s. Small groups of anti-Bolshevik refugees that trickled into Canada in the early 1920s did provide some revitalizing impulse to the flagging community, but their arrival in the existing parishes often created tensions with the old members, whose humble backgrounds and pidgin Russian-Ukrainian-English speech set them apart from the newcomers. Many Russian-born Ukrainians and Belarusans of the "progressive" type who maintained an interest in politics were drawn to the larger and stronger Ukrainian socialist organizations and eventually merged with the Ukrainian-Canadian community. Only with the arrival of a new cohort of Belarusans and Volhynian Ukrainians from Poland in the mid-1920s did the Russian community enter a period of revival. In contrast to Ukrainians from Galicia (also ruled by Poland between the wars), the majority of Ukrainian and Belarusan immigrants from the former Russian imperial territories continued to use Russian as their written language and held on to the Russian orientation, which they saw as an antidote to Polonization. The left-wing and atheistic leanings of many of these newcomers soon found their expression in the founding of Russian Workers' and Farmers' Clubs, whose structure and ideology reflected the strongly pro-Soviet bias of their members. In 1942, at the height of the wartime campaign to aid Russia, these clubs were amalgamated into the Federation of Russian Canadians, which claimed a membership of over 20,000.

Because Russian identity came to be associated in Canada with either the old tsarist imperialism or the pro-Soviet politics of the interwar immigrants, it was rejected by the majority of eastern Ukrainians and Belarusans who arrived in Canada after 1945 as displaced persons and war refugees. Unlike their parents, most of these post-war immigrants had grown up in an environment that favoured Ukrainian or Belarusan self-consciousness thanks to the Soviet state, which encouraged the development of non-Russian national cultures until the early 1930s. Others became inculcated with a nationalist and anti-Russian outlook while fighting against the USSR in various nationalist formations or living in the DP camps. As a result, the majority of this third wave of Slavic immigrants from what had once been the western frontier of the tsarist empire no longer thought of themselves as Russians, but rather as Ukrainians or Belarusans. For the first time most eastern Ukrainians were integrating into Canada's Ukrainian community, still composed primarily of persons with Galician or Bukovynian roots, while Belarusans began to form their own associations instead of joining Russian or Polish ones. These processes boded ill for the future of Canada's Russian community. Although the Russian population also increased after the coming of the post-1945 refugees, the extent of the increase was comparatively small (simply because there were relatively few ethnic Russians among the DPs). In addition, the new arrivals by and large formed their own organizations and parishes, rarely mingling with the pre-1945 peasant immigrants from tsarist Russia or interwar Poland. With the gradual passing of the old Russified generation of Ukrainians and Belarusans in the 1970s and 1980s, the boundaries of the Russian-Canadian community continued to shrink until the arrival of the post-Soviet immigrant wave.

APPENDIX

The Likacheff-Ragosine-Mathers Collection as a Statistical Source

The data on the geographic origins and socio-demographic profiles of Ukrainians and Belarusans who migrated to Canada from the Russian Empire were taken from the Passport/Identity series of the Likacheff-Ragosine-Mathers (Li-Ra-Ma) Collection. Available on microfilm at Library and Archives Canada, the series comprises approximately 11,400 personal files created by the Russian consulates in Montreal and Vancouver for Russian subjects who contacted them for various papers, primarily travel documents and certificates of citizenship. The majority of the files in the series are dated 1917–18, with smaller subsets created in 1916 and 1921–22.

PROVENANCE

The Li-Ra-Ma files fall into two main categories. The first contains applications for entry permits, submitted to the two consulates at various times, primarily in late 1917 and early 1918, by Russian-subject individuals who wished to return to the homeland. With some exceptions, these documents owe their origin to the passport regulations adopted by the Russian imperial government on 25 October 1916 and put into effect by the Provisional Government in July 1917. These regulations annulled old passports issued to Russian subjects prior to the First World War and replaced them with a uniform entry permit *(prokhodnoe svidetel'stvo)*, issued by Russian consulates and allowing its holder to be admitted to Russia in a legal fashion. To receive a permit, returning emigrants were required to provide detailed personal information on a special questionnaire *(oprosnyi list)*, which could be obtained by mail or in person from the consulate. They also had to attach two recent photographs of the primary applicant and dependents along with documentary proof of Russian citizenship. Such proof could include an expired Russian passport, a certificate of military standing, a copy of a baptismal or marriage record or – when none of the above was available – postmarked family letters from Russia. The questionnaire required the applicant to provide the following information: given names; family name; rank *(zvanie)*; occupation; place of registry and social estate *(soslovie)*; date and place of birth; marital status, the number of children (if any) and their names; military standing; year of summons to military service; current place of residence (number of years); names of parents and their places of residence; all places of residence during the last five years; religion; nationality; citizenship; citizenship of parents; changes of citizenship (if any); return destination in Russia; purpose of return and a list of documents proving identity; relatives in Russia and their places of residence; journeys outside Russia during the last three years and their purposes, with dates of departure and return. The form, which remained in use until April 1919 with minor modifications, was completed in duplicate. One copy was intended for the use of the Russian Ministry of Foreign Affairs, which verified the applicant's identity, while the other remained at the consulate. However, most of the files were never sent to Russia due to the Bolshevik coup, and both copies were archived by the consulates along with the originals of various documents attached to them.

The second class of files in the Passport/Identity series contains applications for consular certificates of Russian citizenship. The purpose of the certificates was to protect Russian nationals in wartime Canada from being mistaken for enemy aliens or pressed into enlistment in Canadian overseas forces as British subjects. Any individual claiming to be a Russian subject and wishing to obtain consular certification of his or her Russian citizenship was required to produce a Russian passport or, in the absence of such, swear an affidavit on a special form supplied by the consulate. The following questions had to be answered on the form: name; religion; native province, district, parish and town/village; marital status, names and address of wife and children (if any); names and addresses of closest relatives in Russia; military standing; criminal record in Russia and offences committed; documents proving identity; date, place and way (legal or illegal) of crossing the Russian border; direct or indirect (via the United States) entry to Canada, including the port of disembarkation; criminal record in Canada and offences committed; occupation in Canada; land or real estate ownership in Canada; and naturalization status in Canada.

A researcher dealing with the Li-Ra-Ma immigrant files as a source of statistical data is confronted with several methodological issues. Because the files were compiled neither by a systematic count (unlike censuses) nor by scientific sampling (unlike modern-day sociological surveys), the question of their statistical representativity inevitably comes to the fore. Even a perfunctory analysis of the collection shows that the Li-Ra-Ma Collection should not be used as a cross-section of Canada's migrant population with roots in the Russian Empire. As a general rule, immigrants who had obtained Canadian naturalization, or had purposely severed all connections to the old country, or had simply lived in Canada too long to feel any affinity with the Russian state, are all poorly represented. There are, for instance, few files belonging to religious dissenters such as Doukhobors, Mennonites, and Baptists or to Germans or Jews who came to Canada before 1900. Farmers are also few: obtaining a title to the land required naturalization, which usually brought along permanent settlement in Canada and the weakening of ties to the state of origin. The majority of the migrants who appear in the files are sojourning labourers, "birds of passage," who came to Canada with no intention of staying.

Because Ukrainians and Belarusans migrated to Canada from tsarist Russia almost exclusively as labourers rather than as settlers, the Li-Ra-Ma files are an invaluable source of information about them. Files belonging to persons of these two nationalities form about half the collection, accounting for about 5,700 cases – probably as many as 20–25 per cent of all *Russian-subject* men of Ukrainian and Belarusan origin who lived in Canada around 1917–1920 and about 15 per cent of the population of both sexes. The lack of reliable statistics on the ethnicity of the Russian-born population in early twentieth-century Canada precludes a more accurate estimate of the collection's representativity.

The Li-Ra-Ma files hold information found in no other Canadian or Russian statistical source: data on emigration areas within the Russian Empire (down to the level of village); migration routes and chains; the extent of illegal migration; comparative social and occupational standing of the immigrants in Russia and Canada; reasons for returning to the homeland, and other data. Since most of the migrants' individual characteristics (place of birth, age, religion, marital status, family size, occupation, etc.) are not related to the motives which brought them to the consulates, there is no reason to expect a significant over- or underrepresentation of any social or demographic group within the migrant population. Some exceptions do apply, however. First, there is the possibility that persons who lived closer to the two consular sites (Montreal or Vancouver) were more likely to come into contact with the consuls and are thus somewhat overrepresented. Secondly, one should be aware of the probability of an inverse relationship between the number of years a person spent in Canada and the likelihood of his or her appearance in the files. Thirdly, when using the files to estimate the gender composition of the migrant population, the historian needs to exercise great caution. Less than 1 per cent of the Ukrainian and Belarusan files belong to women, but many more women are "hidden" inside the files as wives of the primary applicants. Unfortunately, the questionnaires have to be discounted as a source of data on the presence of eastern Ukrainian and Belarusan women in Canada because these documents did not ask the applicants to report the current location of their dependents (even though some immigrants still did so by their own choice).

The reliability of personal information contained in the files is another important question. While we cannot totally exclude the possibility of misreported personal data, the reasons that compelled the immigrants to seek out the consuls were far too important and the cost of being denied an entry permit or citizenship certificate too high to suspect a high incidence of false reporting. Moreover, distorting personal information brought no real advantages, for after the fall of the tsarist monarchy the consuls' main concern was to filter out persons falsely claiming Russian citizenship, not to punish individuals who had past troubles with the Russian law (such as military deserters or illegal emigrants). On the whole, there seems to be no reason to doubt the veracity of personal information found in the Li-Ra-Ma files any more than one would question the reliability of such data in census or other serial records commonly used by immigration historians.

METHODOLOGY

At the first stage of my work with the Li-Ra-Ma files, I created a fifty-percent random sample of the partial spreadsheet database of the Passport/Identity series, which was made available to me by Library and Archives Canada. In making the decision about the size of the sample I was guided by two considerations: it had to be large enough to have a sufficient degree of representativity but also manageable by one individual within a reasonable time frame. The second step was a further reduction of the ethnic and territorial scope of the sample by excluding areas and population groups irrelevant to this study. In accordance with the focus of the book, I used the migrants' territory of origin as the main criterion of selection, limiting the sample to cases originating in Ukraine and Belarus and leaving out persons that came from elsewhere in the empire (even when they appeared to be of Ukrainian or Belarusan ethnicity).

Thus reduced, the sample still contained a substantial proportion of persons belonging to various non-eastern Slav nationalities who had once populated Ukrainian and Belarusan provinces. While Germans and Jews were easy to identify and exclude from the sample, Poles, Russians and Lithuanians presented a greater problem due to undeveloped ethnic identities, the overlapping of ethnic and administrative boundaries, and the presence of minorities interspersed within the dominant population. In some cases, the combination of a person's name, place of birth, and religious affiliation served as a sufficient clue but it still did not provide a perfect solution overall. After some deliberation, I resolved to keep all Ukrainian- and Belarusan-born persons of Slavic and Lithuanian origin in the sample, which in its final version included 2,743 cases.

The microfilmed copies of the above files were then examined for all quantifiable information about the individuals to whom they belonged. The retrieved data were coded (with the exception of personal and place names) and added to the initial set of data contained in the LAC database. The variables I used in the final version of the database include: (1) file number, (2) surname, (3) first and middle name, (4) sex, (5) year of birth, (6) province of origin, (7) district of origin, (8) parish, (9) village, (10) religion, (11) nationality, (12) marital status, (13) literacy, (14) number of children, (15) military standing, (16) year of arrival in Canada, (17) current Canadian residence, (18) port of exit, (19) port of entry, (20) Canadian address (for Montreal residents only), (21) destination of return trip to Russia, (22) stated purpose of return, (23) date of completion of the questionnaire, (24) possession of a passport when emigrating from Russia, (25) current location of the family, (26) occupation in Canada, (27) possession of real estate in Canada, (28) criminal record in Canada. Variables 1–10 and 12–20 were applied to all cases in the database; variables 11 and 21–23 were only used for cases containing a questionnaire; and variables 24–28 were only used for those containing an affidavit. Due to omissions in the original documents, the amounts of data for various cases differ considerably; in fact, there are relatively few cases that have information in all twenty-eight variable categories.

A separate and smaller aggregate file, referred to as the "Passport File," supplements the main sample described above. It consists of 671 sampled files that contain either an external or internal Russian passport. The passports yielded three categories of data that could not be obtained on a consistent basis from the questionnaires or the affidavits: the migrants' occupation in Russia, their literacy prior to emigration, and points of border passage.

The two databases were used to produce a large series of statistical data included in the text of this study or expressed in the form of graphs or tables. As a disclaimer, it should be emphasized that, although the Li-Ra-Ma files constitute a representative and irreplaceable source for the study of labour immigration from Russia, calculations based on the random sampling of the collection should not be treated as a mirror image of the migrant population. Rather, they are intended to illustrate the general trends of patterns of Belarusan and Ukrainian migration from Russia's western frontier between the early 1900s and 1914.

Notes

INTRODUCTION

1 Donald Avery, *"Dangerous Foreigners:" European Immigrant Workers and Labour Radicalism in Canada, 1896–1932* (Toronto: McClelland and Stewart, 1979).

2 The most recent historiographic reviews of Canadian literature on immigration and ethnicity are Franca Iacovetta, "Manly Militants, Cohesive Communities and Defiant Domestics: Writing about Immigrants in Canadian Historical Scholarship," *Labour/Le travail* 36 (Fall 1995): 217–52; and Anthony W. Rasporich, "Ethnicity in Canadian Historical Writing 1970–1990," in J.W. Berry and J.A. Laponce, eds, *Ethnicity and Culture in Canada: The Research Landscape* (Toronto: University of Toronto Press, 1994), 153–78. For an analysis of the earlier historiography, see Dirk Hoerder, "Ethnic Studies in Canada from the 1880s to 1962: A Historiographical Perspective and Critique," *Canadian Ethnic Studies* 26, 1 (1994): 1–18.

3 See, for instance, David Davies, "Canadian-Soviet Relations in Historical Perspective," in David Davies, ed., *Canada and the Soviet Experiment: Essays on Canadian Encounters with Russia and the Soviet Union, 1900–1991* (Toronto: Canadian Scholars' Press, 1994), 6–7.

4 A good example of this stereotype is Robert C. Williams, "Emigration from Russia," in Joseph L. Wieczynski, ed., *The Modern Encyclopaedia of Russian and Soviet History.* Vol. 10 (Gulf Breeze, FL: Academic International Press, 1979), 194–200. See also Barbara A. Anderson, *Internal Migration during Modernization in Late-Nineteenth Century Russia* (Princeton, NJ: Princeton University Press, 1980).

5 Although Finland and Congress Poland, which produced massive waves of labour emigrants, were also part of the Russian Empire, their history

has traditionally been studied separately from the history of other
imperial territories.

6 Donald Avery, "Canadian Immigration Policy and the Alien Question,
1896–1919: The Anglo-Canadian Perspective" (PhD Thesis, University
of Western Ontario, 1973); Avery, "Canadian Immigration Policy and the
'Foreign' Navvy, 1896–1914," Canadian Historical Association *Historical
Papers* (1972): 135–56.

7 See Benedict Anderson, *Imagined Communities: Reflections on the Origin
and Spread of Nationalism* (London: Verso, 1983). For another example
of the "constructionist" approach to ethnicity, see Werner Sollors, ed.,
The Invention of Ethnicity (New York: Oxford University Press, 1989),
"Introduction." For a useful theoretical discussion of ethnicity, see
Wsewolod W. Isajiw, "Definitions of Ethnicity," in Rita M. Bienvenue and
Jay E. Goldstein, eds, *Ethnicity and Ethnic Relations in Canada.* 2nd ed.
(Toronto: Butterworth, 1985), 5–18.

8 See Dominic Lieven, *Empire: The Russian Empire and Its Rivals*
(New Haven: Yale University Press, 2000), 175–90.

9 Michael Marunchak, *Ukrainian Canadians* (Winnipeg: Ukrainian
Free Academy of Sciences, 1970). Paul Yuzyk, member of the Senate of
Canada and holder of a doctorate from the University of Minnesota,
was among the few professionally trained historians in this group. His
main works include *The Ukrainians in Manitoba: A Social History*
(Toronto: University of Toronto Press, 1953) and *The Ukrainian Greek
Orthodox Church of Canada, 1918–1951* (Ottawa: University of
Ottawa Press, 1981), the latter based on his doctoral dissertation.
See also Olha Woycenko, *The Ukrainians in Canada* (Winnipeg: Trident
Press, 1967).

10 "Russophile" (less frequently "Moscowphile") was a term used in the late
nineteenth and early twentieth centuries by nationally conscious Ukrainians
to designate those natives of Galicia, Bukovyna, or Transcarpathia who
shared a pro-Russian orientation and viewed Russia as their spiritual and
cultural homeland. At times it was also applied to Ukrainians from the
Russian Empire in general.

11 See Yarema G. Kelebay, "The Ideological and Intellectual Baggage of Three
Fragments of Ukrainian Immigrants: A Contribution to the History of
Ukrainians in Quebec (1910–1960)" (PhD thesis, Concordia University,
1993), 53.

12 A list of the most important works on Ukrainian Canadians written before
1999 can be found in Frances Swyripa, "Ukrainians," in Paul Robert
Magocsi, ed., *Encyclopedia of Canada's Peoples* (Toronto: University
of Toronto Press, 1999), 1310–11.

13 The only existing English-language study which treats Ukrainians from the Russian Empire as part of the Canadian-Ukrainian community is Oksana Leshchenko, "Early Immigration from Eastern Ukraine to Canada: Background and Significance" (MA thesis, University of Waterloo, 1992). A number of works mention the emigration of eastern Ukrainian Baptists: Vera Lysenko, *Men in Sheepskin Coats: A Study in Assimilation* (Toronto: Ryerson Press, 1947), 68–9; Jaroslav Petryshyn, *Peasants in the Promised Land: Canada and the Ukrainians, 1891–1914* (Toronto: Lorimer, 1985), 135; Orest Subtelny, *Ukrainians in North America: An Illustrated History* (Toronto: University of Toronto Press, 1991), 20.

14 Orest Martynowych, *Ukrainians in Canada: The Formative Period, 1891–1924* (Edmonton: Canadian Institute of Ukrainian Studies Press, 1991), 534.

15 The best available source on Ukrainian urban communities in Ontario is a collection of short essays from *Polyphony*, the bulletin of the Multicultural History Society of Ontario, published as a single volume. See Lubomyr Luciuk and Iroida L. Wynnyckyj, eds, *Ukrainians in Ontario* (Toronto: Multicultural History Society of Ontario, 1988). For two dated but still useful sociological studies of Montreal Ukrainians, see Stephen W. Mamchur, "The Economic and Social Adjustment of Slavic Immigrants in Canada: With Special Reference to Ukrainians in Montreal" (MA thesis, McGill University, 1934); and Charles M. Bayley, "The Social Structure of the Italian and Ukrainian Immigrant Communities in Montreal" (MA thesis, McGill University, 1939).

16 The only book-length history of Canadian Belarusans is John Sadouski's *A History of the Byelorussians in Canada* (Belleville, Ont.: Mika, 1981). See also Raissa Zuk-Hryskievic, "Belorussians in Canadian Statistics," in *Slavs in Canada: Proceedings of the Second National Conference on Canadian Slavs, June 9–11, 1967* (Toronto: Inter-University Committee on Canadian Slavs, 1968), 127–34.

17 *1971 Census of Canada* (Ottawa: Supply and Services Canada, 1980), vol. 1, part 3: Population: Ethnic Groups, Table 2. Even after 1971, however, many Canadians of Belarusan origin continued to report themselves under other ethnic names.

18 Marcus Hansen, *The Atlantic Migration, 1607–1860: A History of the Continuing Settlement of the United States* (Cambridge, MA: Harvard University Press, 1940).

19 Some of the best studies of immigrants from eastern and southern Europe include John Zucchi, *Italians in Toronto: Development of a National Identity, 1875–1935* (Kingston, Ont.: McGill-Queen's University Press, 1988); Franca Iacovetta, *Such Hardworking People: Italian Immigrants*

in Postwar Toronto (Montreal: McGill-Queen's University Press, 1992);
Lillian Petroff, *Sojourners and Settlers: The Macedonian Community
in Toronto to 1940* (Toronto: Multicultural History Society of Ontario,
1995). A separate literature focuses on ethnic labour militancy. See, for
instance, Ruth A. Frager, *Sweatshop Strife: Class, Ethnicity and Gender in
the Jewish Labour Movement of Toronto, 1900–1939* (Toronto: University
of Toronto Press, 1992); Donald Avery, *"Dangerous Foreigners;"* Varpu
Lindstrom, *Defiant Sisters: A Social History of Finnish Immigrant Women
in Canada* (Toronto: Multicultural History Society of Ontario, 1988).

20 Bruno Ramirez, *On the Move: French-Canadian and Italian Migrants in
the North Atlantic Economy* (Toronto: McClelland and Stewart, 1991);
Ramirez, *Crossing the 49th Parallel: Migration from Canada to the United
States, 1900–1930* (Ithaca: Cornell University Press, 2001).

21 Dirk Hoerder, *Cultures in Contact: World Migrations in the Second
Millennium* (Durham: Duke University Press, 2002), 16, 19. See also his
"Changing Paradigms in Migration History: From 'To America' to World-
wide Systems," *Canadian Review of American Studies* 24, 2 (1994):
105–26. Other important works on migration systems include J.T. Fawcett,
"Networks, Linkages and Migration Systems," *International Migration
Review* 23, 3 (Fall 1989): 671–80; and Mary M. Kritz, Lin L. Lim and
Hania Zlotnik, eds, *International Migration Systems: A Global Approach*
(Oxford: Clarendon Press, 1992).

22 In 1918, Khotin and the rest of the province of Bessarabia passed under
Romanian control. It was incorporated into the Ukrainian Soviet Socialist
Republic in 1940 and has since remained part of Ukraine.

23 Josef Chlebowczyk, *On Small and Young Nations in Europe: Nation-
Forming Processes in Ethnic Borderlands in East-Central Europe*
(Wroclaw: Zaklad Narodowy Imienia Ossolinskich, 1980), 26.

CHAPTER ONE

1 Due to the large amount of literature dealing with the "push factors" of
labour emigration from continental Europe, it is impossible to mention
even a fraction of these works here. For two examples of studies that deal
with these issues in the most convincing and detailed way, see Julianna
Puskás, *From Hungary to the United States (1880–1914)* (Budapest:
Akadémiai Kiadó, 1982), 45–63; and Ewa Morawska, *For Bread and Butter: Life-Worlds of East Central Europeans in Johnstown, Pennsylvania,
1890–1914* (Cambridge, MA: Harvard University Press, 1985), chapter 1.
A good summary of scholarly arguments related to the causes of European

labour emigration is given in John Bodnar, *The Transplanted: A History of Immigrants in Urban America* (Bloomington: Indiana University Press, 1985), chapter 1.

2 Josef Barton, *Peasants and Strangers: Italians, Rumanians, and Slovaks in an American City, 1890–1950* (Cambridge, MA: Harvard University Press, 1975), 32–4.

3 Bodnar, *The Transplanted*, 1.

4 See, for example, Hans Rogger, *Russia in the Age of Modernization and Revolution, 1881–1917* (New York: Longman, 1983). The best recent social history of nineteenth- and early twentieth-century Imperial Russia is Boris Mironov (with Ben Eklof), *A Social History of Imperial Russia, 1700–1917*. 2 vols. (Boulder, CO: Westview Press, 1999–2000).

5 Teodor Shanin, *The Awkward Class: Political Sociology of Peasantry in a Developing Society: Russia 1910–1925* (Oxford: Clarendon Press, 1972), 9.

6 Ibid., 9–10.

7 Morawska, *For Bread and Butter*, 27.

8 A.M. Anfimov, *Krestianskoe khoziaistvo Evropeiskoi Rossii, 1881–1904* (Moscow: Nauka, 1980), 10–11; V.P. Paniutich, *Sotsial'no-ekonomicheskoe razvitie belorusskoi derevni v 1861–1900 gg.* (Minsk: Navuka i tekhnika, 1990), 45.

9 Robert Edelman, *Proletarian Peasants: The Revolution of 1905 in Russia's Southwest* (Ithaca: Cornell University Press, 1987), 37.

10 Paniutich, *Sotsial'no-ekonomicheskoe razvitie*, 46.

11 *Pervaia vseobshchaia perepis' naseleniia Rossiiskoi Imperii 1897 goda* (St Petersburg, 1897–1905), vol. 4 (Vil'na), part 1, 1; vol. 8 (Volhynia), ii; vol. 11 (Grodno), iv; vol. 16 (Kiev), iv; vol. 22 (Minsk), v; vol. 32 (Podolia), iii (hereafter *1897 census*).

12 Ralph S. Clem, "Population Change in the Ukraine in the Nineteenth Century," I.S. Koropeckyj, ed., *Ukrainian Economic History: Interpretive Essays* (Cambridge, MA: Harvard University Press, 1991), 237.

13 Anfimov, *Krestianskoe khoziaistvo*, 34.

14 Edward C. Thaden, *Russia's Western Borderlands, 1710–1870* (Princeton: Princeton University Press, 1984), 138; Geroid Robinson, *Rural Russia under the Old Regime: A History of the Landlord-Peasant World and a Prologue to the Peasant Revolution of 1917* (New York: Longmans, Green and Company, 1932), 85.

15 M.N. Leshchenko, *Ukrains'ke selo v revolutsii 1905–1907 rr.* (Kiev: Naukova dumka, 1977), 36. Government statistics gave even higher figures.

16 Calculated from *1897 census*, vol. 32 (Podolia), 1.

17 *1897 census*, vol. 8 (Volhynia), iii; vol. 11 (Grodno), iv; vol. 22 (Minsk), v-vi. The south-eastern part of Minsk Province and northern and north-western Volhynia were situated in the so-called Polesie region, abundant with dense forest and marshland. This led to a particularly low population density in these districts.

18 Edelman, *Proletarian Peasants*, 50–61.

19 Calculated from *Rossiia. Tsentral'nyi statisticheskii komitet. Statistika zemlevladeniia v Rossii 1905 goda* (St Petersburg, 1905–1907), vol. 8 (Volhynia), 39; vol. 16 (Kiev), 39; vol. 32(Podolia), 39 (hereafter *Statistika zemlevladeniia 1905 goda*).

20 Ibid.

21 Ibid., vol. 3 (Bessarabia), 33.

22 Ibid., 36.

23 Anfimov, *Krest'ianskoe khoziaistvo*, 24.

24 Leshchenko, *Ukrains'ke selo*, 84.

25 Shanin, *The Awkward Class*, 31.

26 William I. Thomas and Florian Znaniecki, *The Polish Peasant in Europe and America*. 2nd ed. (New York: Dover Publications, 1958), 160.

27 See, for instance, H.J. Habakkuk, "Family Structure and Economic Change in Nineteenth Century Europe," in Norman W. Bell and Ezra F. Vogel, eds, *A Modern Introduction to the Family* (Glencoe, IL: The Free Press, 1960), 167–8.

28 *Statistika zemlevladeniia 1905 goda*, vol. 22 (Minsk), 35. Interestingly, the largest landowners in Minsk Province were not nobles but merchants, although they owned only 3.9 per cent of the land. The average size of a merchant's landholding in the province was over 8,000 acres.

29 Ibid., vol. 32 (Podolia), 43.

30 Paniutich, *Sotsial'no-ekonomicheskoe razvitie*, 61.

31 Jeffrey Burds, *Peasant Dreams and Market Politics: Labour Migration and the Russian Village, 1861–1905* (Pittsburgh: Pittsburgh University Press, 1998), 36.

32 Anfimov, *Krest'ianskoe khoziaistvo*, 150; Robinson, *Rural Russia*, 74–6, 211–12. Robinson's discussion of types of peasant tenure is particularly useful.

33 In Podolia, only 0.4 per cent of households were on communal tenure, while in Volhynia and Kiev communal holdings constituted about 9 per cent. See *Statistika zemlevladeniia 1905 goda*, vol. 32 (Podolia), 53; vol. 16 (Kiev), 56; vol. 8 (Volhynia), 53. The proportion of communal tenure decreased and gradually disappeared as one moved westward from the Dnieper River.

34 Ibid., vol. 3 (Bessarabia), 47. Prior to emancipation, Russia's peasantry was divided into several legal categories, the largest of which were private serfs, State peasants, and those belonging to the imperial family.

35 Robinson, *Rural Russia*, 71–2. Meadowland, however, was usually divided between the households. On similar conditions in neighbouring Eastern Galicia, see Richard L. Rudolph, "The East European Peasant Household and the Beginnings of Industry: East Galicia, 1786–1914," in Koropeckyj, ed., *Ukrainian Economic History*, 339–82.

36 Anfimov, *Krest'ianskoe khoziaistvo,* 106–7; Paniutich, *Sotsial'no-ekonomicheskoe razvitie,* 75–6; Edelman, *Proletarian Peasants,* 61–2.

37 S.M. Dubrovskii, *Stolypinskaia agrarnaia reforma* (Moscow: Moskovskii rabochii, 1930), 192. See also W.E. Mosse, "Stolypin's Villages," *Slavonic and East European Review* 43 (June 1965): 265–6.

38 Judith Pallot and Denis J.B. Shaw, *Landscape and Settlement in Romanov Russia, 1613–1917* (Oxford: Clarendon Press, 1990), 191–2.

39 Robinson, *Rural Russia*, 209–12.

40 Ibid., 216.

41 *Statistika zemlevladeniia 1905 goda*, vol. 3 (Bessarabia), 34; vol. 32 (Podolia), 40; vol. 8 (Volhynia), 40; vol. 16 (Kiev), 41. The category of "individually owned land" did not include either peasant allotment plots or undivided communal lands.

42 Ibid., vol. 3 (Bessarabia), 33; vol. 32 (Podolia), 39; vol. 8 (Volhynia), 39; vol. 16 (Kiev), 39–40.

43 Robinson, *Rural Russia*, chapter 11; Dubrovskii, *Stolypinskaia agrarnaia reforma*, 247–8. It is difficult to establish, however, to what extent the increase in individual buying was due to peasants' own growing predisposition for individual ownership and to what extent it was due to the policy of the Peasant Bank, which after 1909 began to discourage collective purchases.

44 I.D. Koval'chenko, L.V. Milov, *Vserossiiskii agrarnyi rynok, XVIII–nachalo XX veka: Opyt kolichestvennogo analiza* (Moscow: Nauka, 1974), 263.

45 Ibid.

46 Calculated from *Statistika zemlevladeniia 1905 goda*, vol. 3 (Bessarabia), 33, 44; vol. 32 (Podolia), 39, 50; vol. 8 (Volhynia), 39, 50; vol. 16 (Kiev), 39–40, 52–53; vol. 22 (Minsk), 32, 42; vol. 11 (Grodno), 32, 42.

47 Edelman, *Proletarian Peasants*, 67.

48 Paniutich, *Sotsial'no-ekonomicheskoe razvitie*, 136–7.

49 Ibid., 122–37, 296–303; Anfimov, *Krest'ianskoe khoziaistvo*, 108–13.

50 *1897 census*, vols. 3, 4, 8, 11, 16, 22, 32. The data are found in Table 23, "Distribution of Agricultural Population by Supplementary Trades."

51 V.P. Paniutich, *Naemnyi trud v sel'skom khoziaistve Belarusi, 1861–1914 gg.* (Minsk: Navuka i tekhnika, 1996), 96.

52 Calculated from data provided in Koval'chenko and Milov, *Vserossiiskii agrarnyi rynok,* 329–32. According to Paniutich's data, the *real* wages of agricultural workers in Belarus, expressed in the current price of rye (the peasants' staple food), were 15.9 per cent below European Russia's average, while those in Right-Bank Ukraine (due undoubtedly to the lower price of foodstuffs in this region) were only about 1 per cent below average (Paniutich, *Naemnyi trud,* 109).

53 *1897 census,* vol. 4 (Vil'na), part 1, x; vol. 8 (Volhynia), 154–5; vol. 11 (Grodno), 192–5; vol. 16 (Kiev), 170; vol. 22 (Minsk), xiv; vol. 32 (Podolia), iii. The census does not distinguish between hired workers and proprietors of industrial establishments or between artisan's shops and larger enterprises, but simply classifies all available population by occupation. I have calculated the total figures of population employed in industry for each province by adding the numbers of those employed in nineteen occupations which fall under the category of "industrial." It is highly likely that most of this "industry" consisted of artisan's shops with only a handful of hired workers.

54 *Rada,* 19 April 1908.

55 Bohdan Krawchenko, *Social Change and National Consciousness in Twentieth-Century Ukraine* (London: Macmillan, 1985), 8. On patterns of urbanization in Ukraine, see also Boris B. Balan, "Urbanization and the Ukrainian Economy in the Mid-Nineteenth Century," in Koropeckyj, ed., *Ukrainian Economic History,* 283–4, 290–1.

56 Calculated from *1897 census,* vol. 4, part 3, iv; vol. 11, v; vol. 22, vi. In Vil'na Province, nearly 75 per cent of the urban population lived in the city of Vil'na. If Vil'na is excluded from the count, the resulting proportion of the province's urban population drops from 12.7 to a mere 2.7 per cent (vol. 4, iv). A somewhat similar situation existed in Kiev Province.

57 Krawchenko, *Social Change,* 8.

58 Robert E. Johnson, *Peasant and Proletarian: The Working Class of Moscow in the Late Nineteenth Century* (New Brunswick, NJ: Rutgers University Press, 1979). See also Burds, *Peasant Dreams.*

59 Barbara A. Anderson, *Internal Migration during Modernization in Late Nineteenth Century Russia* (Princeton, NJ: Princeton University Press, 1980), 105–8, maps 4.1–4.3.

60 Inge Blank, "A Vast Migratory Experience: Eastern Europe in the Pre- and Post-Emancipation Era," in Dirk Hoerder and Inge Blank, eds, *Roots of the Transplanted.* Vol. 1: *Late 19th Century East Central and Southeastern*

Europe (Boulder, CO: East European Monographs; New York: distributed by Columbia University Press, 1994), 222–3, 239–40.

61 Koval'chenko and Milov, *Vserossiiskii agrarnyi rynok*, 329–32; also *Rada*, 9 May, 25 June 1908.

62 Krawchenko, *Social Change*, 42; Anderson, *Internal Migration*, 160, map 6.2.

63 Krawchenko, *Social Change*, 18.

64 *Rada*, 13, 23 July 1909.

65 Anderson, *Internal Migration*, 121–53.

66 See S.M. Sidel'nikov, *Agrarnaia reforma Stolypina* (Moscow: Moskovskii gosudarstvennyi universitet, 1973), 219–20. According to official and probably understated figures, return migration from Asiatic to European Russia during this period amounted to 18 per cent.

67 One of the first works to advance this view was Emily Greene Balch, *Our Slavic Fellow Citizens* (New York: Charities Publications Committee, 1910), 279.

68 Dirk Hoerder, "Migration in the Atlantic Economies: Regional European Origins and Worldwide Expansion," in Dirk Hoerder and Leslie Page Moch, eds, *European Migrants: Global and Local Perspectives* (Boston: Northeastern University Press, 1996), 35. See also Dirk Hoerder, *Cultures in Contact: World Migrations in the Second Millennium* (Durham and London: Duke University Press, 2002), 306ff.

69 The collective term *zemstvo* (or *zemstva* in the plural) refers to provincial and district representative assemblies with limited administrative functions, which first appeared in the 1870s and soon became a stronghold of political liberalism in Imperial Russia. In Belarus and Right-Bank Ukraine, the *zemstvo* was not introduced until 1911, mainly because of fear of its domination by Polish gentry and other non-Russian minorities. On the role of the *zemstvo* in the history of Russia, see Terence Emmons and Wayne S. Vucinich, eds, *The Zemstvo in Russia: An Experiment in Local Self-Government* (Cambridge: Cambridge University Press, 1982).

70 P.A. Stolypin, V.A. Krivoshein, *Poezdka v Sibir' i Povolzh'e* (St Petersburg, 1911), 79.

71 *Ekonomicheskii listok Podol'skogo gubernskogo zemstva* 15 (1911): 4–5; 12 (1912): 54.

72 P.M. Novoselov, *Ob emigratsii v Ameriku. Dokladnaia zapiska statistika biuro Volynskoi oblastnoi organizatsii* (Zhitomir, 1912), 1–2.

73 Besides Emily Green Balch's work, see also A.M. Shlepakov, *Ukrains'ka trudova emihratsiia v SSHA i Kanadi (kinets' XIX – pochatok XX st.)* (Kiev: Vydavnitstvo akademii nauk, 1960), 43; John-Paul Himka,

"The Background to Emigration: Ukrainians of Galicia and Bukovyna, 1848–1914," in Manoly Lupul, ed., *A Heritage in Transition: Essays in the History of Ukrainians in Canada* (Toronto: McClelland and Stewart, 1982), 11.

CHAPTER TWO

1 Library and Archives Canada (hereafter LAC), Likacheff-Ragosine-Mathers Collection (hereafter Li-Ra-Ma Collection), MG30 E406, file 2955, questionnaire and letter to consul, dated 14 August 1917. Emphasis in the original.
2 Li-Ra-Ma Collection, vol. 48, file 3336, affidavit.
3 More on the Fedorenko episode can be found in Vadim Kukushkin, "Protectors and Watchdogs: Tsarist Consular Supervision of Russian-Subject Immigrants in Canada, 1900–1922," *Canadian Slavonic Papers* 44, 3–4 (September-December 2002): 224–5.
4 Li-Ra-Ma Collection, vol. 45, file 2881. Kandrat Kazak from Grodno (vol. 106, file 12640) is another case of a military deserter.
5 On Belarusan migration to the United States see Vitaut Kipel, *Belarusans in the United States* (Lanham, MD: University Press of America, 1999).
6 *Russkii emigrant*, 31 July 1913.
7 On early Lithuanian and Belarusan emigration from Vil'na Province see L.S. Ofrosimov, *Otkhozhii promysel za okean. Obsledovanie Vilenskoi gubernii* (Vil'na: Tip. M.S. Grozenskogo, 1912).
8 Li-Ra-Ma Collection, vol. 11, file 335, Uladzimir Butkevich to Russian consul in Montreal, 27 September/10 October 1912.
9 See also Grigorii Okulevich, *Russkie v Kanade: Istoriia russkikh raboche-fermerskikh klubov imeni M. Gor'kogo (1930–1940) i Federatsii russkikh kanadtsev (1941–1952)* (Toronto: Federation of Russian Canadians, 1952), 32–4. Pruzhany would remain the largest donor of Belarusan emigrants to Canada in the 1920s and 1930s, when it became part of Poland.
10 Excluding Finland and Poland.
11 Li-Ra-Ma Collection, vol. 104, file 12348, letter to Avraam Savchuk from his sister, 24 November 1913 (old style).
12 *Podolianin*, 29 August 1914.
13 M.N. Leshchenko, *Ukrains'ke selo v revoliutsii 1905–1907 rr.* (Kiev: Naukova dumka, 1977), 59.
14 "Ustav o pasportakh," razdel 2 ("O pasportakh zagranichnykh, propuske cherez granitsu i pogranichnykh soobshcheniiakh"), *Svod zakonov Rossiiskoi imperii*. Vol. 14 (St Petersburg, 1903), 55–6. See chapter 3 for a more detailed discussion of Russian passport law.

15 The key role of marketplaces in disseminating emigration information has been noted, for instance, by historians of Italian labour migration. See Donna Gabaccia, *Militants and Migrants: Rural Sicilians Become American Workers* (New Brunswick, NJ: Rutgers University Press, 1988), 14.

16 *Podolianin*, 23 March 1913.

17 *Podolianin*, 9 August 1913.

18 *Rada*, 13 September 1907.

19 *Rada*, 1 August 1913.

20 Hryhory Domashovets, *Narys istorii ukrains'koi ievanhels'ko-baptists'koi tserkvy* (Irvington-Toronto: Harmony Printing, 1967), 401. On Baptists in Tarashcha, see A.I. Klibanov, *History of Religious Sectarianism in Russia (1860s-1917)* (Oxford: Pergamon Press, 1982), 237–8.

21 Ivan Okuntsov, *Russkaia emigratsiia v Severnoi i Iuzhnoi Amerike* (Buenos Aires: Seiatel', 1967), 180–6; Mark Vil'chur, *Russkie v Amerike* (New York: Pervoe russkoe izdatel'stvo v Amerike, 1918), 40–1.

22 *Rada*, 11 April 1907.

23 *Russkoe slovo*, 9 July 1918.

24 Josef Barton, *Peasants and Strangers: Italians, Rumanians, and Slovaks in an American City, 1890–1950* (Cambridge, MA: Harvard University Press, 1975), 50–1.

25 Li-Ra-Ma Collection, vol. 7, file 244, the case of Dionisii Popo and others.

26 Rossiiskii gosudarstvennyi istoricheskii arkhiv (hereafter RGIA), fond 95, opis' 6, delo 1241, list 162–5; and G. Skoropadsky, "Novozybkovskie krest'iane v Amerike," *Zemskii sbornik Chernigovskoi gubernii* 11 (1904), 67.

27 *Fourth Census of Canada, 1901*, Vol. 1 (Ottawa: King's Printer, 1902), 406–7; *Fifth Census of Canada, 1911*, Vol. 2 (Ottawa: King's Printer, 1913), 367.

28 Bruno Ramirez, *Crossing the 49th Parallel: Migration from Canada to the United States* (Ithaca: Cornell University Press, 2001), 142, 190–1. The US *Soundex Index to Canadian Border Entries*, used by Ramirez, does not include the ethnic origins of the remigrants.

29 *Sixth Census of Canada, 1921*, Vol. 2, Table 81, "Mother tongue of the population 10 years of age and over, exclusive of aborigines, by specific origins, for provinces, 1921," 582–3.

30 The 1897 Russian census presents data on age and marital status of the population by provincial district. Within each district, figures for the cities and for the rest of the district territory are given separately. It is the latter data that are used in the table. Although the census does not tabulate age and marital status by ethnic group or by social estate, this should not

seriously affect the validity of these data for the purposes of our analysis, for the only numerically significant minority group in most of the Ukrainian and Belarusan countryside were the Jews, who generally married at the same or earlier age than Slavic peasants. The proportion of social estates other than peasants *(krestiane)* and townsfolk *(meshchane)* in the non-urban population was very small.

31 In the majority of cases it is impossible to establish whether the emigrant's family was brought from the homeland or created as a result of a Canadian marriage.

32 Annual Report of the Department of the Interior, *Canada. House of Commons. Sessional Papers*, paper no. 25, 1906–1915 (children are not included). In 1904, Canadian immigration statistics for the first time introduced the category of "Russians Not Elsewhere Specified," which included all those who could not be classified as Russian Jews, Russian Poles, or Doukhobors.

33 *Fifth Census of Canada, 1911*, Vol. 2, Table 12, "Origins of the People, male and female, by provinces," 368–9.

34 Archives of the ss Peter and Paul Orthodox Church in Montreal, Marriage Records, 1917–1921.

35 Robert F. Harney, "Men Without Women: Italian Migrants in Canada, 1885–1930," *Canadian Ethnic Studies* 11, 1 (1979): 29–47.

36 If Russian authorities had assessed emigrants' literacy on the basis of their reading rather than writing ability, the percentage of literates would have likely been higher. At the same time, it would be fair to assume that in the decade between the 1897 census and the beginning of mass peasant emigration from Russia the general level of peasant literacy had increased, narrowing the gap between leavers and persisters.

37 Li-Ra-Ma Collection, vol. 78, file 8449 (Potap Panasiuk file), Adam Shpiruk to the consul, 18 August 1918. A curious illustration of the progressing adaptation of the migrants to Canadian ways is the peculiar style in which they wrote their names, with Latin and Cyrillic characters used interchangeably without any uniform pattern.

38 Paul Robert Magocsi, *A History of Ukraine* (Toronto: University of Toronto Press, 1996), 355.

39 As previously mentioned, distinguishing among Poles, Belarusans, and Lithuanians is often difficult.

40 Li-Ra-Ma Collection, vol. 45, file 2931; vol. 92, file 10650.

41 "General labourer" is the closest English translation of the Russian word *chernorabochii*, which literarily means "black worker" (from *chernaia rabota* – "black work"). It was used in official documents and elsewhere to

describe any kind of labour (agricultural or industrial) that did not require special skill or training.

42 *Rada*, 2 April 1913; 16 May 1908.

43 *Podolianin*, 8 May 1913.

44 See John Bodnar, *The Transplanted: A History of Immigrants in Urban America* (Bloomington: Indiana University Press, 1985), 56; Julianna Puskás, *From Hungary to the United States (1880–1914)* (Budapest: Akadémiai Kiadó, 1982), 35.

45 Li-Ra-Ma Collection, vol. 52, file 4008 (Rakhalskii); vol. 104, file 12369 (Surent); vol. 121, file 15331 (Zalesskii).

46 See Andreas Kappeler, *The Russian Empire: A Multiethnic History* (Harlow: Pearson Education Ltd., 2001), chapters 7 and 8 *passim*.

47 *Podolianin*, 23 March 1913.

48 *Russkii emigrant*, 2 October 1913.

49 Cited in N.L. Tudorianu, *Ocherki rossiiskoi trudovoi emigratsii perioda imperializma (v Germaniiu, Skandinavskie strany i SSHA)* (Kishinev: Shtiintsa, 1986), 132–3.

50 Ibid., 133.

51 *Rada*, 13 April 1913.

52 *Russkii emigrant*, 13 June 1912.

53 See Frank Bowen, *A Century of Atlantic Travel, 1830–1930* (Boston: Little, Brown and Co., 1930), 286.

54 RGIA, fonds 104, opis' 1, delo 265, list 102, The Russian America Line to Lord Strathcona, 22 August 1912. Italics mine.

55 RGIA, fonds 104, opis' 1, delo 265, list 102, The Russian America Line to Lord Strathcona, 22 August 1912; and LAC, Halifax Ships' Manifests, June-August 1912, reels T-4743 and T-4744. Not every Libava-New York run included a stop at Halifax. It was probably made only if the ship carried a large enough number of Canada-bound passengers. Nor did the Russian America Line ships enter Halifax on the return voyage from New York.

56 RGIA, fonds 104, opis' 1, delo 265, list 85.

57 LAC, Immigration Branch, RG76, reel C-10296, vol. 407, file 594511, Part 4, copy of the Russian America Line circular to agents, Libava, 12 May 1912.

58 Li-Ra-Ma Collection, vol. 22, file 723, poster.

59 RGIA, fond 104, opis' 18, delo 620, brochure "Kak mne ekhat' v Ameriku."

60 B. Kurchevskii, *Ob emigratsii v Ameriku* (Libava, 1913), 42–3.

61 RGIA, fond 104, opis' 1, delo 265, list 16; Christiansen to the East Asiatic Co., Ltd., 4 March 1913.

62 Some emigrants who departed from Libava went through England by smaller Russian steamship lines such as the North-Western Steamship

Company, whose ships shuttled between Libava and English ports. From England, they continued to Canada by Cunard or the White Star Line.

63 RGIA, fonds 104, opis' 1, delo 265, list 94, Pickford and Black, Ltd., to A.E. Johnson and Co., 26 August 1912; A.E. Johnson and Co. to the Russian America Line, 28 August 1912.

64 A copy of this advertisement is found in Li-Ra-Ma Collection, vol. 40, file 2228.

65 RGIA, fonds 104, opis' 1, delo 265, list 47, Russian America Line to A.E. Johnson and Co., 18 January 1913; list 32, Russian America Line to East Asiatic Co., Ltd, 5 February 1913; listy 14–16, Russian America Line to East Asiatic Co., Ltd, 4 March 1913; see also Tudorianu, *Ocherki*, 162–3.

66 RGIA, fonds 104, opis' 1, delo 265, list 15; Russian America Line to East Asiatic Co., Ltd, 4 March 1913; Russian America Line to East Asiatic Co., Ltd, 18 April 1913.

67 Dirk Hoerder, *Cultures in Contact: World Migrations in the Second Millennium* (Durham and London: Duke University Press, 2002), 306.

CHAPTER THREE

1 Imre Ferenczi and Walter F. Willcox, eds, *International Migrations*, Vol. 1: *Statistics* (New York: Gordon and Breach, 1969), 792.

2 Galina Tschernowa, "Zur Herausbildung staatlicher Auswanderungspolitik in Rußland: Bestrebungen um einem Lenkungsmechanismus Ende des 19. Jahrhunderts bis 1914," *Zeitschrift für Geschichtwissenschaft*, 1994, 42 (5): 418.

3 S.A. Ianovskii, "Russkoe zakonodatel'stvo i emigratsiia," *Vestnik Ministerstva iustitsii*, April 1909: 92–4.

4 David Vital, *A People Apart: The Jews in Europe, 1789–1939* (Oxford: Oxford University Press, 1999), 347, 363; see also Hans Rogger, "Tsarist Policy on Jewish Emigration," *Soviet Jewish Affairs*, 3, 1 (1973): 27–8.

5 Ianovskii, "Russkoe zakonodatel'stvo," 106–11.

6 Cited in Andrew Donskov, ed., *Sergej Tolstoy and the Doukhobors: A Journey to Canada* (Ottawa: Slavic Research Group at the University of Ottawa, 1998), 38n. English-language literature on the Doukhobors is extensive. The classic treatment of Doukhobor history with a focus on the Canadian period is George Woodcock and Ivan Avakumovic, *The Doukhobors* (Toronto: Oxford University Press, 1968).

7 Donskov, *Sergej Tolstoy and the Doukhobors*, 38. The Doukhobor emigrants were freed of all obligations to the Russian state, but men who reached the age of military service in 1898 were not allowed to leave with

the others. Despite these special procedures, the Doukhobors still had to receive Russian passports prior to emigration, although some alterations in the existing passport procedures were made in their case.

8 N.L. Tudorianu, *Ocherki rossiiskoi trudovoi emigratsii perioda imperializma (v Germaniiu, Skandinavskie strany i SShA)* (Kishinev: Shtiintsa, 1986), 38–50.

9 "Ustav o pasportakh," razdel 2 ("O pasportakh zagranichnykh, propuske cherez granitsu i pogranichnykh soobshcheniiakh"), *Svod zakonov Rossiiskoi imperii*. Vol. 14 (St Petersburg, 1903), 55–6.

10 P. Tizenko, *Emigratsionnyi vopros v Rossii, 1820–1910* (Libava: Libavskii vestnik, 1909), 20; Ianovskii, "Russkoe zakonodatel'stvo," 99–101.

11 Tizenko, *Emigratsionnyi vopros*, 46.

12 *Izvestiia Volynskogo gubernskogo zemstva* 2 (1913): 20.

13 Tizenko, *Emigratsionnyi vopros*, 21; Rossiiskii gosudarstvennyi istoricheskii arkhiv (hereafter RGIA), fond 95, opis' 6, delo 678, list 12.

14 In some provinces, for instance, each member of a family was issued a separate passport, while in others the wife and children were included in the passport issued to the head of the family (as the law stipulated). In many cases, the passport-issuing authorities also neglected to indicate the holder's military status in the passport.

15 Tizenko, *Emigratsionnyi vopros*, 34.

16 Ibid., 29.

17 Library and Archives Canada (hereafter LAC), Likacheff-Ragosine-Mathers Collection (hereafter Li-Ra-Ma Collection), MG30 E406, vol. 1, file 6, "Obrabotka obshchikh ocherkov konsul'skoi deiatel'nosti za 1906 god, dostavlennykh vo Vtoroi Departament vsledstvie tsirkuliarov ot 2 aprelia s.g. za no. 4669 i ot 5 aprelia s.g. za no. 4798." Italics are mine.

18 For examples of these opinions, see Tizenko, *Emigratsionnyi vopros*, 38–41; B. Kurchevskii, *O russkoi emigratsii v Ameriku* (Libava, 1914), 34; RGIA, fond 95, opis' 6, delo 1241, list 127.

19 Li-Ra-Ma Collection, vol. 3, file 94, Ustinov to Vtoroi Departament, 20 February 1913. The Second Section of the Ministry of Foreign Affairs was in charge of the consular service.

20 Theophan Buketov, "Vysokii opekun emigrantov," *American Orthodox Messenger* 16 (1912): 292.

21 *Russkie vedomosti*, 22 April 1914.

22 More on Korolenko and his novel can be found in Thomas M. Prymak, "The Great Migration: East Central Europe to the Americas in the Literatures of the Slavs, 1880–1914, Some Examples," *Ethnic Forum* 12, 2 (1992): 41–4. The novel was later published in English under the title *In a Strange Land* (New York: Bernard G. Richards Company, 1925).

23 See Boris Mironov (with Ben Eklof), *A Social History of Imperial Russia, 1700–1917*, vol. 2 (Boulder, CO: Westview Press, 2000), 171–2.

24 *Russkie vedomosti*, 20 May 1914.

25 *Russkie vedomosti*, 11 April 1914.

26 N. Oganovskii, "Novyi vid otkhozhego promysla," *Vestnik Evropy* 10 (October 1914): 279.

27 K.G. Voblyi, *Zaatlanticheskaia emigratsiia: ee prichiny i sledstviia (opyt statistiko-ekonomicheskogo issledovaniia)* (Varshava: Tip. Varshavskogo Uchebnogo Okruga, 1904), 109.

28 Ibid., 111.

29 Tizenko, *Emigratsionnyi vopros*, 13–15; Kurchevskii, *Ob emigratsii v Ameriku*, 19.

30 *Russkie vedomosti*, 22 April 1914; Oganovskii, "Novyi vid otkhozhego promysla," 283; F. Kryshtofovich, "Kak ekhat' v Ameriku na zarabotki," *Sel'skii khoziain* 17 (1913): 825.

31 Cited in N. Oganovskii, "Novyi vid otkhozhego promysla," 283–4.

32 S.R., "Emigratsiia i pereselenie," *Vestnik Novouzenskogo zemstva* 4 (1913): 41. Similar opinions were voiced in *Russkie vedomosti*, 22 April and 20 May 1914. See also Oganovskii, "Novyi vid otkhozhego promysla," 291–2.

33 G. Skoropadskii, "Novozybkovskie krest'iane v Amerike," *Zemskii sbornik Chernigovskoi gubernii* 11 (1904): 67–77.

34 See, for instance, *Izvestiia iuzhno-russkoi oblastnoi zemskoi pereselencheskoi organizatsii* (hereafter *Izvestiia IuROZPO*) 1911–13, no. 45, 135–7; no. 46, 84–5; no. 47, 73–4; no. 54, 152–3; no. 57, 79–82; no. 58, 150.

35 A. R-ii, "O pereselenii v Ameriku," *Izvestiia Volynskogo gubernskogo zemstva* 25 (1913), 10.

36 *Izvestiia IuROZPO* 58 (1913), 41–2.

37 See, for instance, *Izvestiia IuROZPO* 58 (1913), 43ff.

38 S.R., "Emigratsiia i pereselenie," 30.

39 F. Kryshtofovich, "Kak ekhat' v Ameriku na zarabotki," 823–4. The real size of a free Canadian government homestead was 160 acres.

40 Ibid., 825.

41 F. Kryshtofovich, "Zemliakam moim v Rossii serdechnoe (shchire) poslanie," *Ekonomicheskii listok Podol'skogo gubernskogo zemstva* 7 (1912): 8.

42 P.M. Novoselov, *Ob emigratsii v Ameriku. Dokladnaia zapiska statistika biuro Volynskoi oblastnoi organizatsii* (Zhitomir, 1912), 15.

43 Ibid., 16.

44 *Izvestiia IuROZPO* 58 (1913): 40. The *zemstvo*'s expertise on the emigration question appears to have attracted more interest from the United States government than from St Petersburg. In September 1913 W.W. Husband, an agent of the US Department of Labour, was dispatched to Russia to study emigration conditions and was provided with materials on emigration compiled by the southern-Russian *zemstvo*. See *Izvestiia IuROZPO* 60 (1913): 67.

45 "Emigratsiia i zemstvo (po materialam *Chernigovskoi zemskoi nedeli*)," *Izvestiia Volynskogo gubernskogo zemstva* 39–40 (1913): 8.

46 The relationship between Russian liberals and the emerging Ukrainian and Belarusan national movements was a complicated one. While both groups advocated similar socio-economic platforms, the imperialist thinking of most Russian liberal intellectuals, who shared the official doctrine of a "single Russian nation" and frowned upon "Ukrainophiles," was a major source of mutual mistrust. See, for instance, *Rada*, 10 April 1912.

47 On the Belarusan national movement see Jan Zaprudnik, *The Historical Dictionary of Belarus* (Lanham, MD: Scarecrow Press, 1998), 159–60, 181.

48 Cited in Thomas Bird, "Zluchanyia Shtaty Ameryki i emihratsyinaia tematyka u publitsystytsy i paezii 'Nashai nivy'," *Zapisy: Belaruski instytut navuki i mastatstva* 23 (1999): 36.

49 Ibid., 19.

50 On the Ukrainian national movement in tsarist Russia, see Paul Robert Magocsi, *A History of Ukraine* (Toronto: University of Toronto Press, 1996), 379.

51 *Rada*, 9 July 1913.

52 *Rada*, 22 January 1913.

53 *Rada*, 22 April 1908.

54 *Pro Kanadu: iaka tse zemlia i iak v ii zhyvut' liude* (Kiev: Prosvita, 1908), 34.

55 V. Korolev, *Ukraintsi v Amerytsi* (Kiev: Prosvita, 1909), 105–6.

56 Ibid., 81.

57 Ibid., 106–7.

58 Cited in Bird, "Zluchanyia Shtaty Ameryki," 19.

59 Ibid., 36.

60 *Rady dlia emihrantou, katorye eduts' v Ameryku* (Vil'nia: Izd. Tavarystva apeki nad emihrantami, 1912), 4–5.

61 While the tsarist monarchy relied on Russian nationalists as its ideological allies, it preferred to dissociate itself from the extreme expressions of nationalist xenophobia and anti-Semitism, which frequently came from the most radical adherents to this ideology. See, for instance, Andreas

Kappeler, *The Russian Empire: A Multiethnic History* (Harlow: Pearson Education Ltd., 2001), 347.

62 *Podolianin*, 8 May 1913.

63 *Podolianin*, 2 August 1913.

64 Benjamin Murdzek, *Emigration in Polish Social-Political Thought, 1870–1914* (Boulder, CO: East European Quarterly: New York: Distributed by Columbia University Press, 1977), 59–60; also William I. Thomas and Florian Znaniecki, *The Polish Peasant in Europe and America*, vol. 2 (New York: Dover Publications, 1958), 1484.

65 *Podolianin*, 29 August 1913.

66 On the uses of anti-Jewish rhetoric in tsarist Russia see Hans Rogger, "Government, Jews, Peasants, and Land in Post-Emancipation Russia," *Cahiers du monde russe et soviétique* 27, 1 (janv.-mars 1976): 5–25, 27, 2–3 (avr.-sept. 1976): 171–211.

67 *Podolianin*, 2 August 1913.

68 S.R., "Emigratsiia i pereselenie," *Vestnik Novouzenskogo zemstva* 4 (1913): 28. Novouzenskii District of Samara Province was one of the few central Russian territories where mass emigration developed early due to the presence of a large Mennonite and German population.

69 *Novoe vremia*, 22 May 1913. Italics are mine.

70 *Kievlianin*, 15 August 1913.

71 See, for instance, *Podolianin*, 26 June, 10 July, 9 August, 29 August 1913.

72 Several reprints of such publications, including one featuring a Belarusan peasant's letter from Canada, can be found in Kurchevskii, *Ob emigratsii v Ameriku*, 44–5.

73 *Kievlianin*, 22 July 1913.

74 *Kievlianin*, 27 July 1913.

75 *Kievlianin*, 22 July 1913.

76 *Podolianin*, 11 August 1913.

77 *Podolianin*, 8 May 1913. Landlords' fears of rural labour shortages due to emigration were also reported in Chernigov Province (*Rada*, 21 May 1913).

78 *Podolianin*, 30 April 1914. The authenticity of this correspondence is difficult to establish, for it appeared after the death of Nicholas Passek in Montreal in February 1914 and before the arrival of his successor Sergei Likhachev in May of the same year. It may have been a posthumous publication of one of Passek's last reports.

79 Ibid.

80 Tudorianu, *Ocherki*, 146–50.

81 RGIA, fond 95, opis' 5, delo 611.

82 RGIA, fond 95, opis' 8, delo 1027, list 2.

83 Ibid., list 3–4.

84 Tschernowa, "Zur Herausbildung staatlicher Auswanderungspolitik in Rußland," 424.

85 Ianovskii, "Russkoe zakonodatel'stvo," 94.

86 Ibid., 98; Tudorianu, *Ocherki*, 151–2.

87 RGIA, fond 111, opis' 1, delo 184, listy 191–198r.

88 Tudorianu, *Ocherki*, 126–7; RGIA, fond 1284, opis' 188, delo 9, list 306r. The irony of the situation was the fact that, while opposing the opening of legal agencies, the government did little to stop the activities of hundreds of foreign steamship agents freely advertising their services in the western provinces of the empire.

89 Tudorianu, *Ocherki*, 154–8.

90 Tizenko, *Emigratsionnyi vopros v Rossii*, 15.

91 A. Orlov, "K voprosu ob uporiadochenii nashei emigratsii," *Vestnik finansov, promyshlennnosti i torgovli* 8 (1914): 332–3.

92 RGIA, fond 95, opis' 6, delo 678, list 1–4.

93 RGIA, fond 95, opis' 6, delo 1241.

94 Ibid., list 149.

95 Ibid., list 127, 144, 155, 167.

96 Ibid., list 127.

97 RGIA, fond 95, opis' 6, delo 678, list 5.

98 A. Orlov, "K voprosu ob uporiadochenii," 334.

99 Ibid., 333.

100 RGIA, fond 1284, opis' 188, delo 9, list 306–13.

101 RGIA, fond 95, opis' 8, delo 1027, list 19.

102 *Vestnik Novouzenskogo zemstva* 3 (1913): 180.

103 RGIA, fond 95, opis' 18, delo 620, list 2.

104 Ibid., list 16r.

105 RGIA, fond 1149, opis' XII-1899, delo 100, list 15.

106 Li-Ra-Ma Collection, vol. 1, file 6. "Obrabotka obshchikh ocherkov konsul'skoi deiatel'nosti za 1906 god ..."

107 RGIA, fond 1409, opis' 6, delo 1691, list 1–3.

108 Li-Ra-Ma Collection, vol. 1, file 3, Ministerstvo inostrannykh del. Departament lichnogo sostava i khoziaistvennykh del – gg. Imperatorskim rossiiskim general'nym konsulam, konsulam i vitse-konsulam, 9 January 1912.

109 Ibid.

110 *Kievlianin*, 27 July 1913. It should be said in Passek's defense that by the time of Bernov's visit the sixty-four-year-old consul was terminally ill and would die in office in February 1914.

111 Li-Ra-Ma Collection, vol. 1, file 6, "Obrabotka obshchikh ocherkov konsul'skoi deiatel'nosti za 1906 god ..."

112 RGIA, fond 1278, opis' 5, delo 968, list 3.

113 Ibid, list 3r.

114 Li-Ra-Ma Collection, vol. 1, file 9, "Izvlecheniia iz prenii biudzhetnoi komissii Gosudarstvennoi Dumy po proektu smety Ministerstva inostrannykh del na 1915 god. Zasedaniia 14 i 17 ianvaria 1915 g.

115 Ibid.

CHAPTER FOUR

1   Clipping from the Ottawa *Free Press*, 19 March 1909, in Library and Archives Canada (hereafter LAC), Immigration Branch, RG 76, reel C-10645, vol. 565, file 809068. "*Moujik*" is the French spelling of "*muzhik*," a Russian word used most commonly to describe an unsophisticated, boorish man; a rustic.

2   Clipping from the Vancouver *Evening Post*, 3 April 1909, RG 76, reel C-10645, vol. 565, file 809068. The juxtaposition of "Russians" with Chinese and East Indians clearly suggested their perception as "Asiatics" and "aliens" in certain parts of Canadian society.

3   While the term "Russians" continued to be applied in the former sense throughout the whole period before 1914 and thereafter, it was also increasingly used by Canadian officials and the public in its narrower "racial" meaning, as referring only to Slavs (Russians proper, Ukrainians and Belarusans) from the tsarist empire.

4   Ninette Kelley and Michael Trebilcock, *The Making of the Mosaic: A History of Canadian Immigration Policy* (Toronto: University of Toronto Press, 1998), 112.

5   Jaroslav Petryshyn, "Sifton's Immigration Policy," in Lubomyr Luciuk and Stella Hryniuk, eds, *Canada's Ukrainians: Negotiating an Identity* (Toronto: University of Toronto Press, 1991), 17–29; David J. Hall, *Clifford Sifton*, Vol. 2: *A Lonely Eminence, 1901–1929* (Vancouver: University of British Columbia Press, 1985), 63–8.

6   LAC, Department of Agriculture, RG 17, vol. 643, docket 73116, memorandum on Russian immigration, 20 May 1890.

7   Thomas Fisher Rare Book Library, University of Toronto, James Mavor Papers, box 38, file 6, Confidential report to C. Sifton, 15–16.

8   *Sbornik konsul'skikh donesenii 1909* (St Petersburg, 1910), 232.

9   RG76, reel C-7317, vol. 161, file 40361; reel C-4714, vol. 50, file 2183, pt.1; reel C-4715, vol. 51, file 2183, pt. 2.

10 RG76, reel C-4714, vol. 50, file 2183, pt.1, "Extract from a report from W. Preston, Esq., Inspector of European Immigration Agencies, November 28, 1899, to the Right Honourable Lord Strathcona, High Commissioner for Canada, London, England."

11 RG76, reel C-4715, vol. 51, file 2183, pt. 2, memorandum by Lloyd Roberts, 22 July 1914. The US report to which Roberts referred came from W. W. Husband, special agent of the US Department of Labour, who had recently returned from a trip to Russia.

12 Li-Ra-Ma Collection, vol. 7, file 244, Dionisii Popo and others to S.A. Likhachev, 9 May 1914.

13 RGIA, fond 104, opis' 1, delo 265, list 63–65.

14 Ibid., list 36–37; fond 95, opis' 7, delo 637, list 1.

15 Li-Ra-Ma Collection, vol. 18, file 596.

16 Kelley and Trebilcock, Making the Mosaic, 120, 140.

17 Ibid., 137, 146–7.

18 Ibid., 137–8.

19 Donald Avery, The Reluctant Host: Canada's Response to Immigrant Workers, 1896–1994 (Toronto: McClelland and Stewart, 1995), 20–42.

20 Donald Avery, "Canadian Immigration Policy and the 'Foreign' Navvy, 1896–1914," Canadian Historical Association Historical Papers (1972): 135–56.

21 LAC, Canadian National Railway Records, RG 30, Letterbooks, vol. 10712, 288, A.W. Smithers to E.J. Chamberlain, 18 October 1912.

22 Li-Ra-Ma Collection, vol. 8, file 256, The Belgo-Canadian Pulp and Paper Co. to N. Struve, 19 May 1906; vol. 20, file 650, The Riordan Paper Mills, Ltd. to N. Struve, 19 February 1907.

23 Li-Ra-Ma Collection, vol. 20, file 649, Struve to Morse, 6 November 1906; 13 February 1907. See also Struve's report on the matter to the Ministry of Foreign Affairs in RGIA, fond 1291, opis' 50, delo 23, list 69–72.

24 Rossiiskii gosudarstvennyi arkhiv voenno-morskogo flota, fond 420, opis' 1, file 180, list 73r-74.

25 Edmund Bradwin, The Bunkhouse Man. 2nd ed. (New York: AMS Press, 1968), 77.

26 Li-Ra-Ma Collection, vol. 7, file 248, Rev. M.C.A. Kinsale to N. Passek, 12 April 1913; see also A.M. Shlepakov, Ukrains'ka trudova emihratsiia v SShA i Kanadi (kinets' XIX – pochatok XX st.) (Kiev: Vydavnitstvo Akademii nauk, 1960), 20.

27 Novyi mir, 12 June 1912.

28 Izvestiia iuzhno-russkoi oblastnoi zemskoi pereselencheskoi organizatsii 47 (June 1911): 73–4.

29 RG76, reel C-10645, vol. 565, file 809068, J.H. MacGill to W.D. Scott, 9 November 1909.

30 Ibid., MacGill to Scott, 29 March 1909.

31 Ibid., MacGill to Scott, 4 May 1909. Some of these rumours betrayed a striking ignorance of Eurasian geography: thus, a Canadian agent was reported as having gone to Siberia to recruit a party of "900 Russians and Finns [sic]." Ibid., H. Rumbold to Earl Grey, 15 July 1909.

32 Ibid., Rumbold to Grey, 15 July 1909.

33 Ibid., J.C. Hall to Rumbold, 8 July 1909.

34 Ibid., MacGill to Scott, 9 November 1909.

35 Ibid., W.M. Stitt to Scott, 24 November 1909.

36 Only two years earlier Vancouver had witnessed a riot, triggered by exaggerated rumours of an impending "Oriental invasion." See Peter Ward, *White Canada Forever: Popular Attitudes and Public Policy Towards Orientals in British Columbia* (Montreal: McGill-Queen's University Press, 1978), chapter 4.

37 RG76, reel C-10645, vol. 565, file 809068, Scott to F. Oliver, 26 November 1909.

38 RG76, reel C-4715, vol. 51, file 2183, pt. 2, L.M. Fortier to F.C.T. O'Hara, 11 March 1911; also reel C-10645, vol. 565, file 809068, Scott to N.R.J. Reid, 18 September 1913.

39 RGIA, fond 104, opis' 1, delo 265, list 112, excerpt from a letter by Pickford and Black, 4 March 1912.

40 Ibid., list 113, excerpt from a letter by Bryce to W.L. Barnstead (Immigration Agent at Halifax), 23 July 1912.

41 RG76, reel C-10296, vol. 407, file 594511, Part 2a, circular of 20 July 1910; Part 3, circular of 25 April 1911.

42 Ibid., Part 4, circular of 11 March 1912; Office of the Deputy Minister, memorandum to W.D. Scott, 26 March 1912.

43 Ibid., G.T. Bell to Scott, 10 April 1912; Scott to Bell, 15 April 1912 and 17 April 1912.

44 RGIA, fond 104, opis' 1, delo 265, list 103, Russian America Line to Lord Strathcona, 22 August 1912.

45 Ibid., list 104.

46 Li-Ra-Ma Collection, vol. 3, file 94.

47 Ibid., Ustinov to Roche, 8 January 1913.

48 RGIA, fond 104, opis' 1, delo 265, list 80, East Asiatic Co., Ltd., to Russian America Line, 11 October 1912.

49 RG76, reel C-10296, vol. 407, file 594511, Part 5, Scott to Barnstead, 25 September 1912. Scott was referring to the circular of 11 September,

which had authorized Canadian border inspectors to admit, until
1 December, all railway labourers coming by land from the United States
regardless of nationality or money qualifications (see ibid., circular of
11 September 1912).

50 Ibid., circular of 12 March 1913.
51 RG76, reel C-10296, vol. 407, file 594511, Part 5.
52 Li-Ra-Ma Collection, vol. 3, file 94, Scott to Likhachev, 27 May 1914.
53 Ibid., Likhachev to A.K. Bentkovskii, 17 July 1914.

CHAPTER FIVE

1 *Novyi mir*, 25 July 1913. See also William Cousins, *A History of the Crow's Nest Pass* (Lethbridge: The Historic Trails Society of Alberta, 1981), 61.

2 Allen Seager, "Socialists and Workers: The Western Canadian Coal Miners, 1900–21," *Labour/Le travail* 16 (Fall 1985): 56.

3 United Church Archives (hereafter UCA), Victoria University, fonds 123 (Presbyterian Church of Canada Board of Home Missions and Social Service), series 2, box 2, file 19, "Report on the Foreign Problem in Hamilton," 18 February 1914.

4 *Novyi mir*, 18 October 1915. Grigorii Okulevich's claim that Canada's largest "Russian colony" in the early 1900s was in Windsor does not appear to be correct – Montreal had a larger population of Russian-born immigrants. See Grigorii Okulevich, *Russkie v Kanade: Istoriia russkikh raboche-fermerskikh klubov imeni M. Gor'kogo (1930–1940) i Federatsii russkikh kanadtsev (1941–1952)* (Toronto: Federation of Russian Canadians, 1952), 29.

5 *Novyi mir*, 29 April 1918.

6 On Ukrainians in Nova Scotia, see John Huk, *Strangers in the Land: The Ukrainian Presence in Cape Breton* [n.p, n.d.]. Huk's account confirms the significant presence of Bessarabians in the local Ukrainian population. See also Okulevich, *Russkie v Kanade*, 36–9.

7 John Porter's concept of the "vertical mosaic," which postulated that Canadian immigrants were traditionally channelled into low-paid and low-status occupations, has been occasionally questioned by sociologists and historians, most recently in Eric Sager, "Immigrants, Ethnicity and Earnings in 1901: Revisiting Canada's Vertical Mosaic," *Canadian Historical Review* 83, 2 (June 2002): 196–229. However, Sager's study is based on the 1901 manuscript census and thus covers the period before the largest wave of European labour immigration to Canada. In addition, Sager does not analyze the economic performance of individual ethnic groups, using

the category of "other Europeans" for all immigrants from continental Europe (except Germans and, on one occasion, Scandinavians), which diminishes the accuracy of his findings.

8 See Edmund Bradwin, *The Bunkhouse Man* (New York: AMS Press, 1968), 58.

9 Library and Archives Canada (hereafter LAC), Likacheff-Ragosine-Mathers Collection (hereafter Li-Ra-Ma Collection), MG30 E406, vol. 6, File 210, the Humeniuk case. The author clearly confuses Canadian port officials with CPR labour agents, but his letter nonetheless provides a vivid description of the conditions in which the newly arrived labourers often found themselves. Interestingly, the letter was written and sent to Passek after Humeniuk's return to Ukraine.

10 See an unidentified newspaper clipping in Li-Ra-Ma Collection, vol. 7, file 239, "The Case of 300 in Moose Jaw, Sask."

11 Ibid., Passek to W.J. Roche, 9 April 1913.

12 Ibid., J.G. Mitchell to Passek, 16 April 1913.

13 Ibid., Passek to S. White, 23 May 1913. Short reports of the incident also appeared in the Russian press. See *Novoe vremia*, 12 May 1913.

14 LAC, Department of Justice, RG13, Series A-2, vol. 179, file 730, W.H. Stiles to C.J. Doherty, 15 May 1913.

15 Canada, House of Commons, *Debates*, 22 May 1913, col. 10529–30 (hereafter *Debates*).

16 *Debates*, 28 May 1913, col. 11077–8.

17 See Li-Ra-Ma Collection, vol. 6, file 210 (the case of Semion Khropanitsky); vol. 7, file 244 (the case of Gerasim Demchuk).

18 Bradwin, *The Bunkhouse Man*, 66–7.

19 Li-Ra-Ma Collection, vol. 6, file 211 (the case of Peter Leshchuk), file 217 (the case of Roman Daniliuk); see also Orest Martynowych, *Ukrainians in Canada: The Formative Period, 1891–1924* (Edmonton: Canadian Institute of Ukrainian Studies Press, 1991), 114.

20 Bradwin, *The Bunkhouse Man*, 65. The Li-Ra-Ma correspondence contains several cases of navvies complaining that they were refused free passes to which they considered themselves entitled. See for instance Li-Ra-Ma Collection, vol. 6, file 210 (the case of Ivan Humeniuk).

21 Li-Ra-Ma Collection, vol. 6, file 208 (the case of Vladimir Babenko et al.), cited in W.D. Scott to Dessaulles, Garneau and Vanier, 5 November 1915.

22 *Novyi mir*, 20 February 1915; 31 January 1916.

23 Li-Ra-Ma Collection, vol. 6, file 209 (complaint by twelve workers in The Pas, January 1915); vol. 7, file 244 (the case of fourteen workers on Vancouver Island), D. Newton Wemyss to Likhachev, 20 January 1916.

24 On similar practices in the Hollinger mines, see Okulevich, *Russkie v Kanade*, 33.

25 *Novyi mir*, 20 February 1915.

26 Li-Ra-Ma Collection, vol. 7, file 244 (the case of fourteen workers on Vancouver Island), D. Newton Wemyss to Likhachev, 20 January 1916.

27 *Novyi mir*, 25 July 1913.

28 Ibid.; Cousins, *A History of the Crow's Nest Pass*, 64. In 1916, strikes over pay raises also occurred in Cobalt and Thetford Mines. See *Labour Gazette*, September 1916, 1550; October 1916, 1634–38.

29 *Novyi mir*, 19 June 1915; Pylyp Yasnowskyj, *Pid ridnym i pid chuzhym nebom: spohady pionera* (Buenos Aires: Vyd. Iuliana Seredyaka, 1961), 174.

30 Nancy Forestell, "All That Glitters Is Not Gold: The Gendered Dimensions of Work, Family and Community Life in the Northern Ontario Goldmining Town of Timmins, 1909–1950" (PhD thesis, University of Toronto, 1993), 60.

31 Okulevich, *Russkie v Kanade*, 34. In 1915 the *Canadian Mining Manual* reported that married men in Timmins had begun to build their own homes, while 150 single men were still quartered in bunkhouses. See Michael Barnes, *Gold in the Porcupine* (Cobalt: Highway Book Shop, 1975), 77.

32 Cousins, *A History of the Crow's Nest Pass*, 61.

33 Martynowych, *Ukrainians in Canada*, 118.

34 *Novyi mir*, 25 July 1913.

35 See Martynowych, *Ukrainians in Canada*, 116.

36 Li-Ra-Ma Collection, vol. 6, file 225 (the case of Foma Mel'nychuk).

37 Li-Ra-Ma Collection, vol. 6, file 224 (the case of Iakov Mazur).

38 A useful summary of Canadian provincial laws regulating workers' compensation, prepared in 1916 for Likhachev by the law firm of Dessaulles, Garneau and Vanier, can be found in Li-Ra-Ma Collection, vol. 6, file 215, "Résumé des lois canadiennes des différentes provinces concernant les accidents du travail." See also Dennis Guest, *The Emergence of Social Security in Canada.* 2nd rev. ed. (Vancouver: University of British Columbia Press, 1985), 39–47.

39 Some cases were settled by mutual agreement between the parties without instituting formal legal proceedings.

40 Li-Ra-Ma Collection, vol. 6, files 216 – 229, 807 – 808. The second most common category of complaints (over forty individual and group cases) involved wage disputes (see files 208 – 214 and 806).

41 On peasant petitions in wartime Russia see Emily Pyle, "Peasant Strategies for Obtaining State Aid: A Study of Petitions during World War I," *Russian History* 24, 1–2 (Spring – Summer 1997): 41–64.

42 Li-Ra-Ma Collection, vol. 6, file 216, the Ivan Bespal'ko case.

43 Li-Ra-Ma Collection, vol. 6, file 226, Likhachev to Vtoroi Departament, 12 March 1915.

44 Martynowych, *Ukrainians in Canada*, 111.

45 For a variety of reasons too complex to be discussed here, Montreal has not received its due share of attention from ethnic and migration historians, who have barely scratched the surface of its rich ethnic mosaic. Montreal's Jewish and Italian communities are probably the best researched; see, for instance, Joe King, *From the Ghetto to the Main: the Story of the Jews of Montreal* (Montreal: Montreal Jewish Publications Society, 2000) and Bruno Ramirez, *Les premiers italiens de Montréal* (Montréal: Boréal Express, 1984). Beginning with the work of McGill sociologist Carl Dawson, sociologists and social geographers have shown a more sustained interest than historians in the city's ethnic groups. The two most important works bearing on Slavic immigrants are Stephen Mamchur, "The Economic and Social Adjustment of Slavic Immigrants in Canada: With Special Reference to the Ukrainians in Montreal" (MA thesis, McGill University, 1934), and Charles M. Bailey, "The Social Structure of the Italian and Ukrainian Immigrant Communities in Montreal, 1935–1937" (MA thesis, McGill University, 1939). A more recent general treatment of Montreal's ethnic diversity is Annick Germain and Damaris Rose, *Montreal: The Quest for a Metropolis* (Chichester: John Wiley and Sons, 2000), chapter 7. See also Claire McNicoll, *Montreal, une société multiculturelle* (Paris: Belin, 1993).

46 UCA, Methodist Church Missionary Society, Home Mission Records, fonds 14, series 4, box 4, file 10, "Report of Central Committee on the Work among European Foreigners in Canada," 5. As was often the case in early twentieth-century Canada, immigrants from eastern Ukraine and Belarus were obviously classed as "Ruthenians" or "Poles." Interestingly, the federal census of 1921 listed only 79,708 people of non-British and non-French origin in Montreal. See *Sixth Census of Canada, 1921*, Vol. 1 (Ottawa: King's Printer, 1924), 542.

47 The *Labour Gazette*, August 1913, 126.

48 *Sixth Census of Canada*, vol. 1, 542. The unreliability of the official statistics for the Ukrainian population in Montreal is also noted in Yarema Kelebay, "Three Fragments of the Ukrainian Community in Montreal, 1899–1970: A Hartzian Approach," *Canadian Ethnic Studies*, 12, 2 (1980): 86, 11n.

49 *Novyi mir*, 1 February 1915. Some sources put the number of "Russians" in the city at 10,000. At least several hundred of these must have been Russians proper, whose presence in Montreal is documented, for instance, in *Kanadskii gudok*, 14 February 1939.

50 Archives of the ss Peter and Paul Orthodox Church of Montreal (hereafter sspp), membership book of the Holy Trinity Russian Orthodox Brotherhood, 1906 – [1916?].

51 The following discussion of immigrant residential patterns in Montreal is largely based on the analysis of approximately 500 individual street addresses obtained from the Li-Ra-Ma files.

52 More on the history of the Russian Orthodox parish in Montreal follows in chapter 7.

53 Mamchur, "The Economic and Social Adjustment," 71.

54 *Novyi mir*, 10 September 1914.

55 Yarema G. Kelebay, "The Ideological and Intellectual Baggage of Three Fragments of Ukrainian Immigrants: A Contribution to the History of Ukrainians in Quebec (1910–1960)" (PhD thesis, Concordia University, 1993), 47.

56 Robert F. Harney, "Ethnicity and Neighbourhoods," in Harney, ed., *Gathering Place: People and Neighbourhoods of Toronto, 1834–1945* (Toronto: Multicultural History Society of Ontario, 1985), 6.

57 See Theodore R. Weeks, *Nation and State in Late Imperial Russia: Nationalism and Russification on the Western Frontier, 1863–1914* (DeKalb, IL: Northern Illinois University Press, 1996), 8; and Geoffrey Hosking, "Empire and Nation-Building in Late Imperial Russia," in Geoffrey Hosking and Robert Service, eds, *Russian Nationalism: Past and Present* (New York: St Martin's Press, 1998), 21.

58 sspp, marriage registers, 1917–1921. The rest were marriages between the natives of Austria-Hungary.

59 Paul-André Linteau, *Histoire de Montréal depuis la Conféderation* (2ème éd., Montreal: Boréal, 2000), 214–15. Linteau largely draws on the well-known 1897 survey of working-class Montreal, conducted under the direction of Herbert Ames.

60 uca, Methodist Church Missionary Society, Home Mission Records, fonds 14, series 4, box 4, file 10, "Report of Central Committee on the Work among European Foreigners in Canada," 4.

61 Terry Copp, *The Anatomy of Poverty: The Condition of the Working Class in Montreal, 1897–1929* (Toronto: McClelland and Stewart, 1974), 25–6, 88.

62 The *Labour Gazette,* March 1914, 1026; Copp, *The Anatomy of Poverty*, 83–4.

63 Note the similarity of this figure to the findings of Steven Mamchur, who surveyed Montreal's Ukrainian community in 1933. Of his ninety-six male respondents, 80.2 per cent were unskilled workers (Mamchur, "The

Economic and Social Adjustment," 91). On the social construction of skill see, for instance, Ian Radforth, *Bushworkers and Bosses: Logging in Northern Ontario, 1900–1980* (Toronto: University of Toronto Press, 1987), 67–9.

64 The *Labour Gazette*, May 1914, 1260.

65 Okulevich, *Russkie v Kanade*, 26.

66 According to Bruno Ramirez, between 1900 and 1930 the CPR drew about half of its Montreal workforce from the immigrant pool. See Bruno Ramirez, *On the Move: French-Canadian and Italian Migrants in the North Atlantic Economy, 1860 – 1914* (Toronto: McClelland and Stewart, 1991), 88–91.

67 Information about the geography of immigrant employment in Montreal was partly culled from about forty "discharge certificates," which were issued to Russian-subject workers by their employers after the end of their contracts under a special wartime arrangement between the Canadian and Russian authorities. The purpose of the certificates was to provide legal proof of its bearer's employment in a war-related industry in order to qualify for an exemption from military service in Russia. See Li-Ra-Ma Collection, vol. 71, files 7440 to 7495.

68 This finding contrasts with the calculations of Eric Sager, who found no definitive correlation between the number of years spent by immigrants in Canada and their earnings (unless one assumes that more skilled jobs do not always bring higher wages). See Sager, "Immigrants, Ethnicity and Earnings," 217.

69 Hutsuliak first appears as Vassil Hussul in Lovell's Montreal city directory for 1916–17.

70 "General Report of the Minister of Public Works and Labour of the Province of Quebec, for the year ending 30 June 1912," *Quebec Sessional Papers*, 1912, paper no. 4.

71 Li-Ra-Ma Collection, vol. 7, file 249.

72 *Novyi mir*, 10 April 1914.

73 Li-Ra-Ma Collection, vol. 7, files 247, 252.

74 Li-Ra-Ma Collection, vol. 7, file 245, Tatarinsky to Likhachev, 3 February 1915.

75 The derogatory term *zhid* (Yid) was commonly applied to an individual of Jewish origin by Judeophobic Russian nationalists instead of the neutral *ievrei* (Jew).

76 See, for instance, *Russkii emigrant*, 3 July 1913.

CHAPTER SIX

1 Paul C.P. Siu, "The Sojourner," *American Journal of Sociology* 58 (July 1952): 34–44. The use of the term "sojourner" in regard to temporary labour migrants goes back at least to the 1930s.

2 *Novyi mir*, 29 December 1911. The phrase referred to Russian workers in the United States, but it was at least as much applicable to the even more transient Canadian population of Russian-born migrant labourers.

3 A good discussion of working-class culture in the context of the Canadian resource frontier is found in Nancy Forestell, "Bachelors, Boarding-Houses, and Blind Pigs: Gender Construction in a Multi-Ethnic Mining Camp, 1909–1920," in Franca Iacovetta, Paula Draper, and Robert Ventresca, eds, *A Nation of Immigrants: Women, Workers, and Communities in Canadian History, 1840s – 1960s* (Toronto: University of Toronto Press, 1998), 251–90. Unfortunately, the author's analysis of ethnicity as a determinant of the migrants' social behaviour is less impressive than her examination of gender.

4 Orest Martynowych, *Ukrainians in Canada: The Formative Years, 1891–1925* (Edmonton: Canadian Institute of Ukrainian Studies Press, 1991), 124; Robert F. Harney, "Men Without Women: Italian Migrants in Canada, 1885–1930," in Betty Caroli, Robert Harney, and Lydio Tomasi, eds, *The Italian Immigrant Woman in North America* (Toronto: Multicultural History Society of Ontario, 1978), 87.

5 Gregory Robinson comes close to making this point when he links Ukrainian crime in Canada to the normality of violence in the Old Country Ukrainian village. See his "Rougher Than Any Other Nationality? Ukrainian Canadians and Crime in Alberta, 1915–1929," *Journal of Ukrainian Studies* 16, 1–2 (Summer – Winter 1991): 156–7.

6 See Stephen Frank, *Crime, Cultural Conflict, and Justice in Rural Russia, 1856–1914* (Berkeley: University of California Press, 1999), 122–4, 155–9, 280–96.

7 *Novyi mir*, 25 July 1913.

8 *Kanadskii gudok*, 11 March 1939.

9 Library and Archives Canada (hereafter LAC), Likacheff-Ragosine-Mathers Collection (hereafter Li-Ra-Ma Collection), vol. 22, file 719, J.P. Reed to Likhachev, 28 June 1917; Paraskeva Shumovich to Likhachev, 19 January 1918; R. Vincent to Likhachev, 14 February 1918. Brutal treatment of domestic animals was not uncommon entertainment for late nineteenth-century drunken "hooligans" in Russian villages.

10 Ibid., vol. 7, file 232 (the case of A. Lesnik). On the relationship between alcohol and homicide among Canadian frontier workers see Angus

McLaren, "Males, Migrants, and Murder in British Columbia,
1900–1923," in Franca Iacovetta and Wendy Mitchinson, eds, *On the
Case: Explorations in Social History* (Toronto: University of Toronto
Press, 1998), 159–80.

11 *Novyi mir*, 9 March 1915.

12 *Novyi mir*, 1 July 1916. For an "Austrian's" perspective on these encounters, see Pylyp Yasnowskyj, *Pid ridnym i pid chuzhym nebom: spohady
pionera* (Buenos Aires: Vyd. Iuliana Seredyaka, 1961), 213.

13 See, for instance, the story of Timofei Mukha, who cheated inebriated
Russian immigrants out of their money in the bars of Cochrane and
Timmins in *Novyi mir*, 27 July 1915.

14 Li-Ra-Ma Collection, vol. 7, file 245.

15 Siu, "The Sojourner," 39.

16 Harney, "Men without Women," 90. According to Harney, the sojourning
migrant found himself "suspended" in time by being ejected from his
normal life cycle until he was able to return or reconstitute his family and
social relationships in the new land.

17 William Thomas and Florian Znaniecki, *The Polish Peasant in Europe and
America*. 2nd ed. (New York: Dover Publications, 1958), 102–3, 1489.

18 On this function of the emigrant letter see David A. Gerber, "Epistolary
Ethics: Personal Correspondence and the Culture of Emigration in the
Nineteenth Century," *Journal of American Ethnic History* 19, 4 (Summer
2000): 3–23.

19 Li-Ra-Ma Collection, vol. 9, file 285.

20 Thomas and Znaniecki, *The Polish Peasant*, 303.

21 Li-Ra-Ma Collection, vol. 38, file 1235 (Hnat Voroniuk).

22 The negative effects of the migrants' prolonged absence from their home
communities are well discussed in Harney, "Men without Women," 81–2.

23 Li-Ra-Ma Collection, vol. 101, file 11976 (Iustyn Hedz'). For more
examples of troubled relationships with in-laws, see vol. 117, file 14739
(Efim Iakimchuk); vol. 106, file 12629 (Opanas Koval'); vol. 37, file 1050
(Arkhip Bezhenar).

24 Li-Ra-Ma Collection, vol. 55, file 4479 (Kyrylo Shkiruk).

25 Mary Eleanor Cygan, "Polish Women and Emigrant Husbands," in Dirk
Hoerder and Inge Blank, eds, *Roots of the Transplanted*, Vol. 1 (Boulder,
CO: Eastern European Monographs, 1994), 359–74.

26 Li-Ra-Ma Collection, vol. 55, files 4425 (Artem Zhuk) and 4479 (Kyrylo
Shkiruk); vol. 40, file 2163 (Vasyl' Dovhan'); vol. 43, file 2656 (Vasyl' Malyi).

27 Jeffrey Burds, *Peasant Dreams and Market Politics: Labor Migration
and the Russian Village, 1861–1905* (Pittsburgh: University of Pittsburgh
Press, 1998).

28 Li-Ra-Ma Collection, vol. 57, file 5102 (Vasil' Astapchuk). Note the association of bachelorhood with carefree living, which had deep roots in peasant folk culture.

29 Li-Ra-Ma Collection, vol. 102, file 12048 (Andrei Hushcha).

30 Li-Ra-Ma Collection, vol. 9, file 279 (Serhii Asaulenko).

31 See, for instance, a letter from the parents of Vasyl' Sytnyk in Stufchyntsi (Podolia), who wrote to their son that girls in their village "had made babies with the soldiers." Li-Ra-Ma Collection, vol. 98, file 11549 (Vasyl' Sytnyk).

32 Christine Worobec, "Temptress or Virgin? The Precarious Sexual Position of Women in Postemancipation Ukrainian Peasant Society," *Slavic Review* 49, 2 (Summer 1990): 227–38. See also her "Victims or Actors? Russian Peasant Women and Patriarchy," in Esther Kingston-Mann and Timothy Mixter, eds, *Peasant Economy, Culture and Politics of European Russia, 1800–1921* (Princeton: Princeton University Press, 1991), 177–206.

33 Li-Ra-Ma Collection, vol. 106, file 12654 (Mykola Korsak).

34 *Novyi mir*, 25 July 1913.

35 Li-Ra-Ma Collection, vol. 106, file 12629 (Opanas Koval').

36 See, for instance, the letters in Li-Ra-Ma Collection, vol. 48, file 3392 (Petro Bezushko); vol. 49, file 3464 (Iakau Lukovich).

37 Li-Ra-Ma Collection, vol. 39, file 2075 (Pavel Harbelik); vol. 41, file 2296 (Antin Zapotochnyi). During World War I, Canadian government regulations prohibited sending international money orders exceeding $100 to avoid speculation. Many immigrants got around this ban by breaking up large amounts into several money orders each worth below $100.

38 Li-Ra-Ma Collection, vol. 106, file 12690 (Anton Ialets).

39 Ewa Morawska, "Return Migrations: Theoretical and Research Agenda," in Rudolph J. Vecoli and Suzanne M. Sinke, eds, *A Century of European Migrations, 1830–1930* (Urbana: University of Illinois Press, 1991), 281.

40 Li-Ra-Ma Collection, vol. 2, file 84.

41 See the correspondence between Likhachev and Canada's Post Office Department in Li-Ra-Ma Collection, vol. 10, file 302.

42 Li-Ra-Ma Collection, vol. 10, file 295.

43 Li-Ra-Ma Collection, vol. 8, file 257.

44 Li-Ra-Ma Collection, vol. 10, files 269, 299, 301.

45 *Russkoe slovo*, 1 September 1917.

46 *Novyi mir*, 18, 25 August 1914.

47 See for instance Li-Ra-Ma Collection, vol. 3, file 111.

48 Li-Ra-Ma Collection, vol. 36, "Register of Russian Subjects of Military Service Age Who Expressed Preparedness to Leave for Military Service at the First Summons of Military Authorities."

49 Li-Ra-Ma Collection, vol. 11, file 366, Bobyk to Likhachev.

50 Li-Ra-Ma Collection, vol. 12, file 383.

51 Li-Ra-Ma Collection, vol. 13, file 399, Likhachev to Vtoroi Departament, 4 March 1915.

52 For more about wartime remigration from America, see Mark Wyman, *Round-Trip to America: The Immigrants Return to Europe, 1880–1920* (Ithaca and London: Cornell University Press, 1993), 109–13. Wyman's account does not include Canada.

53 Advertisements in *Novyi mir*, 3, 5 January 1916.

54 Li-Ra-Ma Collection, vol. 11, file 357, Likhachev to R. Borden, 20 January 1917. Honorary vice-consul Henry Mathers in Halifax could not issue entry permits.

55 Li-Ra-Ma Collection, vol. 3, file 97, Likhachev to Vtoroi Departament, 22 January 1916. No data regarding the ethnic origins or socio-demographic profiles of the returnees were included in these statistics.

56 See a letter from the parents of Mykhailo Matsiokha (Li-Ra-Ma Collection, vol. 99, file 11610) and a letter from the brother of Andrii Marziavka, both from Podolia (vol. 44, file 2740).

57 It is to these regulations that we owe the existence of several thousand Li-Ra-Ma files containing applications for entry permits.

58 Li-Ra-Ma Collection, vol. 96, file 11170 (Tymofii Fedyk). While we should remain cautious in assessing the sincerity of such pronouncements, there is no reason to completely dismiss patriotism as a motive for returning and to see the immigrants only as skilful manipulators telling the consuls what they presumably wanted to hear.

59 Li-Ra-Ma Collection, vol. 36, "Registry of Passports Issued to Russian Subjects."

60 When sailing through Yokohama, returning Russian citizens were required to possess a transit visa, which was issued by the Japanese consulate in Vancouver after a check of the applicant's financial means.

61 Li-Ra-Ma Collection, vol. 11, file 344, Likhachev to Joseph Pope, 23 July 1915. Those who had just reached the age of military service were excluded from this provision and had to return to Russia for mobilization.

62 Ibid., Likhachev to Vtoroi Departament, 18 February 1916. In November 1916, Likhachev asked Canadian military authorities to discharge sixteen Russians who had enlisted in the Westmount Rifle Battalion without the Russian government's permission.

63 See Gretzky's attestation paper in LAC, Ministry of the Overseas Military Forces, RG150, box 3819–50, reg. number 3030122; see also Walter Gretzky, *On Family, Hockey and Healing* (Toronto: Random House of Canada, 2001), 18.

64 Frances Swyripa and John Herd Thompson, eds, *Loyalties in Conflict:*
   Ukrainians in Canada during the Great War (Edmonton: Canadian Institute of Ukrainian Studies, 1983), 60; Yasnowskyj, *Pid ridnym i chuzhym*
   nebom, 219–20.

65 LAC, Immigration Branch, RG76, Series I-A-1, vol. 603, reel C-10670,
   file 884866; Li-Ra-Ma Collection, vol. 11, file 344, Likhachev to Pope,
   23 July 1915; H. Walker to Likhachev, 5 August 1915.

66 *Kanadskii gudok,* 28 February, 11 March 1939; Li-Ra-Ma Collection,
   vol. 75, file 7996 (Isaak Drobotenko). See also the case of Vikentii Lutka
   in vol. 14, file 440.

67 Li-Ra-Ma Collection, vol. 13, file 415. There were also nineteen men born
   in Poland, three in Finland, and four in Russia proper. The origins of the
   remaining men are undecipherable.

68 Swyripa and Thompson, *Loyalties in Conflict,* 58. The digitization of the
   CEF personnel records by Library and Archives Canada should facilitate
   further studies of immigrant participation in Canada's war effort.

69 Li-Ra-Ma Collection, vol. 13, files 412, 859. See also the Toronto *Globe,*
   3 August 1915.

70 Li-Ra-Ma Collection, vol. 11, file 348, Commander of the 198th Battalion
   to Likhachev, 10 September 1916.

71 Li-Ra-Ma Collection, vol. 13, file 411; Ioann Ovsianitsky, "S kanadskoi
   armiei na fronte," *American Orthodox Messenger* 33 (18 August 1916):
   522–3.

72 Li-Ra-Ma Collection, vol. 7, file 251.

73 LAC, Royal Canadian Mounted Police, RG18, series F-3, vol. 490,
   file 433–15.

74 Li-Ra-Ma Collection, vol. 15, file 483, Vtoroi Departament to Imperator-
   skoe Rossiiskoe Posol'stvo v Londone, 21 June 1916; Pope to Likhachev,
   12 March 1917; 20 March 1917; Likhachev to Pope, 7 May 1917.

75 Li-Ra-Ma Collection, vol. 26, file 867, Ragozin to C.J. Doherty,
   16 August 1917.

76 Li-Ra-Ma Collection, vols. 66–67, file 6822; see also vol. 75,
   file 7964 (Serhii Makarchuk) and vol. 99, file 11691 (Panteleimon
   Vakul'chyk).

77 *Russkoe slovo,* 23 October 1917; *Rabochii narod,* 13 April 1918.

78 By 1915, all western Belarus (Grodno and Vil'na provinces) and parts of
   Volhynia were under German occupation, which lasted until the enactment
   of the Treaty of Versailles. In 1921, much of this territory passed under
   Polish control. In 1918, Romanians in Bessarabia proclaimed an independent republic, which later joined the Romanian state.

79 Li-Ra-Ma Collection, vol. 40, file 2163.

80 Li-Ra-Ma Collection, vol. 41, file 2362. The more resourceful women
    attempted to use their husbands' remittances to hire a male relative or
    neighbour to perform the assignments on their behalf.

81 Li-Ra-Ma Collection, vol. 22, file 712.

82 Li-Ra-Ma Collection, vol. 103, file 12198.

83 Li-Ra-Ma Collection, vol. 14, file 433.

84 For other examples of CEF veterans attempting to obtain help in bringing
    their families to Canada, see Li-Ra-Ma Collection, vol. 16, files 513–514.

85 Research in the recently opened Russian archives should throw more light
    on the scale of migration both to and from the Soviet Union in the first post-
    revolution decade, when the country's borders were not yet sealed.

CHAPTER SEVEN

1 In the early 1960s, Czech political scientist Miroslav Hroch divided nation-
    al movements of "small nations" of Eastern-Central Europe into three
    phases. According to Hroch, in Phase A, a small group of intellectuals de-
    velops an interest in the nation's cultural heritage, which is followed by the
    phase of national agitation aimed at disseminating national ideas among
    the general population (Phase B) and, eventually, by Phase C, in which the
    matured national movement espouses the goal of political autonomy.
    See Miroslav Hroch, *Social Preconditions of National Revival in Europe:
    A Comparative Analysis of the Social Composition of Patriotic Groups
    among the Smaller European Nations.* 2nd ed. (New York: Columbia
    University Press, 2000).

2 Two Ukrainian exceptions are Pavlo Krat (Petro Ternenko), who tried his
    hand at various intellectual pursuits and attempted to blend Ukrainian
    nationalism with socialism, and Havrylo Slipchenko, an ex-socialist and
    one-time director of the Ukrainian Publishing House (which also published
    the nationalist daily newspaper *Ukrainskyi holos*). See Orest Martynowych,
    Ukrainians in Canada: The Formative Period, 1891–1924 (Edmonton:
    Canadian Institute of Ukrainian Studies, 1991), 248.

3 Constance J. Tarasar, ed., *Orthodox America, 1794–1976: Development
    of the Orthodox Church in America* (Syosset, NY: Orthodox Church in
    America, 1975), 15–6, 20, 92–3, 113–14. On the Russian Orthodox
    Mutual Aid Society, see also Keith P. Dyrud, *The Quest for the Rusyn Soul:
    The Politics of Religion and Culture in Eastern Europe and in America,
    1890 – World War I* (Philadelphia: The Balch Institute Press; London and
    Toronto: Associated University Presses, 1992), 69–70.

4 Tarasar, *Orthodox America*, 69.

5 Alaskan Russian Church Archives (hereafter ARCA), series D (Geographic File), box D514, reel 322, Winnipeg, diocese administration, correspondence, 1893–1916, Chekhovtsev to Platon Rozhdestvensky, 15 November 1908. Chekhovtsev's name is sometimes spelled as "Chavtsov" or "Chagovtsev."

6 See Martynowych, *Ukrainians in Canada*, chapters 7, 8, 9; and Paul Yuzyk, *The Ukrainian Greek Orthodox Church of Canada, 1918–1951* (Ottawa: University of Ottawa Press, 1981), chapter 2.

7 ARCA, series D, box D514, reel 322, Winnipeg, diocese administration, correspondence, 1893–1916, Chekhovtsev to Platon Rozhdestvensky, 15 November 1908.

8 ARCA, series D, box D514, reel 322, Winnipeg, Parish records, cumulative, 1907.

9 Archives of the Archdiocese of Canada, Orthodox Church in America (hereafter AC), Holy Trinity Church (Winnipeg), baptism and marriage books, 1907–15.

10 See, for instance, M. Mark Stolarik, *Immigration and Urbanization: The Slovak Experience, 1870–1918* (New York: AMS Press, 1989), 75.

11 A. Hotovitzky, "Poezdka v Kanadu," *American Orthodox Messenger* 10 (1906): 110–11.

12 Ibid., 112–17. The Syrian parish, founded in 1903, was the first Eastern Orthodox congregation in eastern Canada.

13 Archive of the SS Peter and Paul Orthodox Church in Montreal (hereafter SSPP), membership book of the Holy Trinity Russian Orthodox Brotherhood, 1906 – [1916?].

14 Listings of Russian Orthodox brotherhoods were regularly published in *Svit*. For information on the Montreal chapter, see, for instance, *Svit*, 9 January 1913.

15 For Buketov's biography, see Tarasar, *Orthodox America*, 123.

16 *The Orthodox Church in Canada: A Chronology* (n.p., Archdiocese of Canada – Orthodox Church in America, 1988), 6.

17 *American Orthodox Messenger* 30 (1915): 473–4.

18 *Svit*, 12 October 1916; 11 January, 15 February 1917; *The Jubilee Book of the Russian Orthodox Christ the Saviour Cathedral in Toronto, 1915–1965* (n.p., n.d.), 12.

19 The Toronto *Globe*, 25 September 1916. From Toronto, Bishop Nemolovsky proceeded to Montreal, where the following day he consecrated the cornerstone of the future church building. See V. Sakovich, "Osviashchenie kraeugol'nogo kamnia Montreal'skoi tserkvi," *American Orthodox Messenger* 42 (1916): 666–8.

20 Library and Archives Canada, Likacheff-Ragosine-Mathers Collection (hereafter Li-Ra-Ma Collection), MG30 E406, vol. 21, file 700, Mikhail Kaimakan to Likhachev, 30 September 1916.

21 ARCA, series D, box D514, reel 322, Vancouver file, Prodan to Evdokim Meshchersky, 4/17 August 1916. The first attempt to organize a Russian Orthodox parish in Vancouver was made in 1912 by Russian immigrant entrepreneur A. Azancheev (see more on him in chapter four above), but it proved abortive.

22 AC, baptismal records and collection book of the Russian Orthodox Church of St John the Divine, Windsor, 1917–21.

23 SSPP, Holy Trinity Russian Orthodox Brotherhood, membership book.

24 Robert F. Harney, "Boarding and Belonging," in Bruno Ramirez, ed., "If One Were to Write a History …:" Selected Writings by Robert F. Harney (Toronto: Multicultural History Society of Ontario, 1991), 132.

25 Li-Ra-Ma Collection, vol. 21, file 671, Gorsky to Likhachev, 8 February 1917.

26 Li-Ra-Ma Collection, vol. 8, file 261, Pavel Zaitsevskii to Likhachev, 3 February 1915.

27 Li-Ra-Ma Collection, vol. 5, file 183, Kaimakan to Likhachev, June 1916.

28 See for instance: Donald W. Treadgold, "Russian Orthodoxy and Society," in Robert L. Nichols and Theofanis G. Stavrou, eds, Russian Orthodoxy under the Old Regime (Minneapolis: University of Minnesota Press, 1978), 21–43, and Marc Szeftel, "Church and State in Imperial Russia," ibid., 127–41. For a revisionist view, see Gregory Freeze, "Handmaiden of the State? The Orthodox Church in Imperial Russia Reconsidered," Journal of Ecclesiastical History 36 (1985): 82–102.

29 Treadgold, "Russian Orthodoxy," 30. The common use of the derogatory term pop, instead of the reverent batiushka (father) or neutral sviashchen-nik (priest) is a telling example of the low esteem in which Orthodox clergy was held by much of the Russian peasantry and working class.

30 Svit, 25 June 1914.

31 Panteleimon Bozhyk, Tserkov ukraintsiv v Kanadi (Winnipeg: Kanadyis'kyi ukrainets', 1927), 310.

32 SSPP, folder "Church Affairs, 1914–1935," report by Sakovich to the North American Ecclesiastical Consistory, 2 April 1914.

33 Li-Ra-Ma Collection, vol. 21, file 664, Montreal parish committee to Likhachev, 25 May 1914.

34 SSPP, folder "Church Affairs, 1914–1935," report by Sakovich to the North American Ecclesiastical Consistory, 2 April 1914 (notes on the back).

35 Li-Ra-Ma Collection, vol. 21, file 666, copy of the incorporation bill.

36 Rival churches (Roman and Greek Catholic) had a tendency to exaggerate the amount of tsarist government assistance to the Russian Orthodox mission in North America. This view is sometimes uncritically repeated in modern historical studies. See Roberto Perin, "Religion, Ethnicity and Identity: Placing the Immigrant within the Church," in William Westfall et al, eds, *Religion/Culture: Comparative Canadian Studies* (Ottawa: Association for Canadian Studies, 1985), 220.

37 SSPP, folder "Church Affairs, 1930–1936," Rev. Ioann Chepelev to an unknown correspondent, 6 March 1935. At the same time, the diocese of Alaska, whose Orthodox population (mostly of Aboriginal descent) did not exceed several thousand but which had a highly symbolic meaning as the birthplace of American Orthodoxy, received $25,000 a year.

38 Canadian Baptist Archives, McMaster University (hereafter CBA), Home Mission Board Minutes, treasurer's statement for the year ending Oct. 8th, 1914.

39 Rossiiskii gosudarstvennyi istoricheskii arkhiv (hereafter RGIA), fond 796, opis' 190, I stol, VI otdelenie, delo 96.

40 SSPP, "Church Affairs, 1914–1935," act of the transfer of the church property, 26 December 1917.

41 In one case, the parish covered the cost of room and board for the priest but paid him no salary.

42 Two priests' sources of income were not known. See a detailed report to Likhachev by Nemolovsky (5 January 1917) on the state of church affairs in Canada: Li-Ra-Ma Collection, vol. 21, file 674.

43 For examples of immigrants' complaints about these practices see Li-Ra-Ma Collection, vol. 71, file 7497 (A. Zadorin); vol. 72, file 7736 (Ivan Shevchuk).

44 *The Orthodox Church in Canada: A Chronology*, 5.

45 *American Orthodox Messenger* 32 (1915), 503.

46 *Kanadiiskaia pravoslavnaia Rus'*, 28 September 1916.

47 ARCA, cont. D514, reel 322, Montreal, Diocese Administration, Correspondence, 1911–15, Sakovich to Platon Rozhdestvensky, 28 October 1913.

48 *Novyi mir*, 1 October 1914.

49 Bishop Alexander [Nemolovsky], "Otkryvaem novyi prikhod," *American Orthodox Messenger* 37 (1915): 588–9.

50 *Novyi mir*, 8 May 1916.

51 *American Orthodox Messenger* 21 (1916), 335.

52 ARCA, series D, box D514, reel 322, Fort William file, Lutsyk to Evdokim Meshchersky, 5 [?] September 1915.

53 See a copy of the circular (27 October 1917) from Nemolovsky to the Russian Orthodox clergy in North America in SSSP, folder "Church Affairs, 1914–1935."

54 See Martynowych, *Ukrainians in Canada*, 488–96; Yuzyk, *The Ukrainian Greek Orthodox Church*, chapter 4; Serhii Plokhy, "The Crisis of 'Holy Rus:' The Russian Orthodox Mission and the Establishment of the Ukrainian Orthodox Church of Canada," in Serhii Plokhy and Frank E. Sysyn, eds, *Religion and Nation in Modern Ukraine* (Edmonton and Toronto: Canadian Institute of Ukrainian Studies Press, 2003), 40–57. For a different perspective, see Tarasar, *Orthodox America*, chapter 5.

55 *Jubilee Book of the Russian Orthodox Christ the Saviour Cathedral in Toronto*, 7.

56 Li-Ra-Ma Collection, vol. 27, file 949, Report by Rev. M. Poplavsky to the North American Ecclesiastical Consistory, 1 September 1917.

57 John Huk, *Strangers in the Land: The Ukrainian Presence in Cape Breton* (n.p., n.d.), 35.

58 Li-Ra-Ma Collection, vol. 21, file 678, Glebov to Likhachev, 27 June 1919.

59 *Russkoe slovo*, 26 June 1920.

60 *Russkoe slovo*, 9 July 1920; 21 July 1920.

61 *Jubilee Book of the Russian Orthodox Christ the Saviour Cathedral in Toronto*, 44.

62 SSPP, folder "Church Affairs, 1914–1935," part 1, Piotrovsky to Nemolovsky, 17 June 1921.

63 SSPP, folder "Various Minutes, 1925–1931," questionnaire "On the Condition of the Church and the Parish of the City of Montreal for the Year 1922." See also Archives of Ontario, Multicultural History Society of Ontario Collection, Series 72 (Russian-Canadian Papers), Christ the Saviour Russian Orthodox Cathedral, registers of marriages, 1922–27.

64 A classic exposition of social evangelism is J. S. Woodsworth, *Strangers within Our Gates; or Coming Canadians*, with an introduction by Marilyn Barber (Toronto: University of Toronto Press, 1972). For the intellectual roots of social gospel, see Richard Allen, *The Social Passion: Religion and Social Reform in Canada, 1914–1928* (Toronto: University of Toronto Press, 1971).

65 See, for instance, John Burgon Bickersteth, *The Land of Open Doors; Being Letters from Western Canada* (London: Wells Gardner, Darton, 1914).

66 Robert Smale, "For Whose Kingdom: Canadian Baptists and the Evangelization of Immigrants and Refugees, 1880 to 1945" (Ed.D thesis, University of Toronto, 2001), 48.

67 CBA, box "Baptist Union Historical," typescript dated 1916, author unknown, 1.

68 See Smale, "For Whose Kingdom," 83.

69 CBA, *Mission Work in Manitoba and the Northwest Reports Submitted to the Baptist Convention of Manitoba and the Northwest and the Women's Baptist Home and Foreign Missionary Society of Manitoba and the Northwest, Winnipeg, July 4th and 5th, 1900*, 5.

70 CBA, *Manitoba and the North-West Some Facts Regarding Rapid Settlement, Religions, etc., also Reports on Baptist Missions, Showing the Present Urgent Need of Vigorous Prosecution of the Work* [n.p., 1901?], 7; also Li-Ra-Ma Collection, vol. 1, file 46, Sylvestr Muzh to Struve, 8 July 1903.

71 A short biography of Shakotko and a description of his Canadian activities can be found in CBA, Western Collection, Ivan Shakotko file.

72 *The Year Book of the Baptist Union of Western Canada 1910*, 142.

73 *The Year Book of the Baptist Union of Western Canada 1909*, 102–3.

74 *The Baptist Year Book 1912*, 24.

75 Robert Harney and Harold Troper, eds, *Immigrants: A Portrait of the Urban Experience, 1890–1930* (Toronto: Van Nostrand, 1975), 145; Lillian Petroff, *Sojourners and Settlers: The Macedonian Community in Toronto to 1940* (Toronto: Multicultural History Society of Ontario, 1995), 60–1; Zoriana Yaworsky Sokolsky, "The Beginnings of Ukrainian Settlement in Toronto, 1891–1939," in Robert F. Harney, ed., *Gathering Place: Peoples and Neighbourhoods of Toronto, 1834–1945* (Toronto: Multicultural History Society of Ontario, 1985), 287–8; Smale, "For Whose Kingdom," 84–5. Unfortunately, Smale's dissertation is focussed primarily on the doctrinal attitudes of Canadian Baptists towards immigrants but has very little to say about the practical work of the missions.

76 Biographical data on Kolesnikoff are obtained from various printed materials in the John Kolesnikoff file held in CBA, particularly from the offprint entitled "Sacrifice, the Supreme Law of Service: A Biographical Sketch of Rev. J. Kolesnikoff, Russian Baptist Missionary" (year and source unknown, probably early 1920s) and the photocopy of an article by C.H. Schutt, "Rev. John Kolesnikoff," which appeared in *Home Mission Digest*, vol. 2, 1955: 83–6.

77 CBA, Home Mission Board Minutes, Meeting of the Executive, 11 September 1908.

78 CBA, John Kolesnikoff file, "Sacrifice, the Supreme Law of Service," 26. In 1910, the Alice Street mission was relocated to Simcoe Street, and in 1911 to Elizabeth Street, where it remained until late 1914 before its amalgamation with the Beverley Street Baptist Church for financial reasons. The

latter move was admittedly a failure, and two years later the mission again received its own separate hall, this time at 124 York Street. The Dundas Street mission only existed for about two years and was closed in 1915. See *Baptist Year Book 1910*, 309; CBA, minutes of the annual meeting of the Home Mission Board, 6 December 1915; minutes of the executive meeting, 21 February 1916; Minute Book of the Beverley Street Baptist Church, church meetings of 8 November 1914 and 29 October 1916.

79 *Baptist Year Book 1912*, 38–9; CBA, John Kolesnikoff file, "Rev. John Kolesnikoff" by C.H. Schutt, 85.

80 *Baptist Year Book 1913*, 86.

81 *Baptist Year Book 1918*, 71.

82 CBA, Home Mission Board Minutes, executive meeting, 28 July 1909.

83 CBA, Home Mission Board Minutes, executive meetings of 26 September 1911; 23 June 1914; 3 November 1914; 4 December 1914; quarterly meeting of the Home Mission Board, 5 January 1915. See also the Paul John Kolesnikoff file, which contains his obituary (he died in 1974).

84 *Baptist Year Book 1912*, 90.

85 Ibid.

86 See the list of the Russian members of the Beverley Street Church in CBA, Beverley Street Baptist Church Minutes, 1911–32, quarterly business meeting, 28 April 1915.

87 Li-Ra-Ma Collection, vol. 21, file 705, a copy of the letter from the Deputy Minister of Internal Affairs to the Minister of Foreign Affairs, 17 January 1917.

88 Ibid., Kaimakan to Likhachev, 17 November 1916; Likhachev to A.P. Sherwood, 23 November 1916; Sherwood to Likhachev, 13 December 1916.

89 Petroff, *Sojourners and Settlers*, 63.

90 *Baptist Year Book 1916*, 67, 241.

91 *Baptist Year Book 1919*, 76.

92 CBA, Home Mission Board Minutes, joint meeting of the Finance Committee and the Executive Committee of the Home Mission Board, 16 March 1921.

93 CBA, Home Mission Board Minutes, quarterly meeting of the Home Mission Board, 19 June 1917.

94 CBA, Home Mission Board Minutes, executive meeting, 23 June 1914.

95 CBA, Home Mission Board Minutes, semi-annual meeting of the Home Mission Board, 15 May 1919.

96 CBA, Home Mission Board Minutes, quarterly meeting of the Home Mission Board, 19 June 1917.

97 CBA, Home Mission Board Minutes, semi-annual meeting of the Home Mission Board, 15 May 1919.

98 CBA, Home Mission Board Minutes, annual meeting of the Home Mission Board, 6 November 1919; *Baptist Year Book 1919*, 235–7.

99 A Lettish Canadian, *Russians in Europe and in Canada* [n.p, n.d.], 21.

100 *Novyi mir*, 18 September 1915.

101 United Church Archives, Victoria University (hereafter UCA); *Presbyterian Church of Canada. Board of Social Service and Evangelism. Report for 1913*, 5.

102 UCA, fonds 14 (Methodist Church Missionary Society), series 4 (Home Mission Records), box 4, file 10, "Report of Central Committee on the Work among European Foreigners in Canada [1917]."

103 UCA, fonds 14, series 4, box 7, file 2, All People's Mission's annual report, 1907–08; J.S. Woodsworth to James Allen, 10 April 1908; file 3, All People's Mission's annual report, 1908–09. Since "Russians" were listed along with "Ruthenians," it is likely that the former term was used to designate Slavic immigrants from the Russian Empire as opposed to those from Austria-Hungary.

104 UCA, fonds 14, series 4, box 4, file 10, "Report of Central Committee on the Work among European Foreigners in Canada [1917]."

105 See on this: Gordon Hern, *Russians in Canada* (Toronto, n.d. [1926]), 7–8.

106 Li-Ra-Ma Collection, vol. 21, file 651, "All Saints' Cathedral. Halifax, Nova Scotia. Annual Report, 1914," 18.

107 Li-Ra-Ma Collection, vol. 21, file 651, "All Saints' Cathedral. Halifax, Nova Scotia. Annual Report, 1915," 16; Henry Mathers to Likhachev, 10 February 1915.

CHAPTER EIGHT

1 See, for instance, R.C. Elwood, *Russian Social Democracy in the Underground: A Study of the RSDRP in the Ukraine, 1907–1914* (Assen: Van Gorcum, 1974), 274.

2 A.Chernenko, *Rossiiskaia revoliutsionnaia emigratsiia v Amerike: konets XIX v. – 1917 g.* (Kiev: Vyshcha shkola, 1989).

3 Ibid, 79–80.

4 See G.I. Luzianin, *Rossiia i Kanada v 1893–1927* (Moskva: Prometei, 1997), 79; *Novyi mir*, 14 June 1912.

5 More about official Russian attitudes to the Fedorenko case can be found in Vadim Kukushkin, "Protectors and Watchdogs: Tsarist Consular Supervision of Russian-Subject Immigrants in Canada, 1900–1922," *Canadian Slavonic Papers* 44, 3–4 (September-December 2002): 224–5.

6 The use of leftover funds (approximately $800) from the Fedorenko defence campaign later became a source of friction among various ethnic socialist groups. See *Novyi mir*, 29 November 1912.

7 Library and Archives Canada (hereafter LAC), Likacheff-Ragosine-Mathers Collection, MG30 E406 (hereafter Li-Ra-Ma Collection), vol. 19, file 630, L. Newcombe to N. Struve, 7 October 1911.

8 Krat's views and activities have been discussed elsewhere. See, for instance, Nadia Kazymyra, "The Defiant Pavlo Krat and the Early Socialist Movement in Canada," *Canadian Ethnic Studies* 10, 2 (1978): 38–54.

9 For Shatulsky's biography, see Peter Krawchuk, *The Life and Work of Matthew Shatulsky* (Toronto: Kobzar, 1991); see also the Shatulsky file in the Li-Ra-Ma Collection (vol. 96, file 11112).

10 See the Mikhnevich file (vol. 46, file 3028) in the Li-Ra-Ma Collection; also Orest Martynowych, *Ukrainians in Canada: The Formative Period, 1891–1924* (Edmonton: Canadian Institute of Ukrainian Studies Press, 1991), 447, 47n.

11 *Robochyi narod*, 25 November 1915; Orest Martynowych, "The Ukrainian Socialist Movement in Canada, 1900–1918," *Journal of Ukrainian Graduate Studies* 2, 1 (Spring 1977): 24. Martynowych also mentions a certain Sanin, another Russian member of the *Robochyi narod* editorial staff.

12 LAC, Royal Canadian Mounted Police, RG 18, vol. 3314, file HV-1, part 5, transcript of the Immigration Board of Inquiry hearings, 13 August 1919. In Canadian sources and historical works, Almazov's surname is usually spelled as "Almazoff," and his first name is given alternately as Solomon, Moses, and Samuel. In this work I use "Solomon Almazov" on the grounds that this was the name he used to sign his contributions to the Russian socialist press.

13 Li-Ra-Ma Collection, vol. 92, file 10650 (Iosif Rabizo).

14 *Novyi mir*, 23 March 1915; see also the 1912–13 financial report of the Montreal group, *Novyi mir*, 11 May 1913.

15 *Novyi mir*, 11 February 1916; *Russkoe slovo*, 5 November 1919.

16 *Russkoe slovo*, 28 February 1918; Archives of the SS Peter and Paul Orthodox Church, Montreal (hereafter SSPP), folder "Church Affairs, 1914–35," S. Likhachev to V. Sakovich, 22 June 1915. Within a year of its creation (some time in 1916) the society added the word "Progressive" to its name, reflecting the spread of socialist and anti-monarchist ideas within the immigrant community.

17 *Novyi mir*, 20 October 1911; *Robochyi narod*, 9 October 1912. Of the 2,989 members of the Social Democratic Party of Canada reported in the

autumn of 1912, 2,297 belonged to its sixty-six non-Anglo-Saxon locals, including thirty-five Finnish, twenty-four Ukrainian, two Jewish, two Latvian, one German, one Polish, and one Russian.

18 Chernenko, *Russkaia revoliutsionnaia emigratsiia*, 84, 187.

19 LAC, Peter Krawchuk Papers, MG30 D403, vol. 15, file 77.

20 A. Ross McCormack, *Reformers, Rebels, and Revolutionaries: The Western Canadian Radical Movement, 1899–1919* (Toronto: University of Toronto Press, 1977), 93.

21 *Novyi mir*, 13 June 1913; 26 September 1913; 13 October 1914.

22 *Novyi mir*, 17 July 1914; 29 October 1915. The first branch of the Society for Aid to Political Exiles in Siberia was organized in 1910 in New York. See *Tovarishch russkogo emigranta v Amerike. Pervyi Kalendar'-Ezhegodnik, vypuskaemyi edinstvennoi v Amerike russkoi sotsialisticheskoi rabochei gazetoi "Novyi mir"* (New York: "Novyi mir," 1913), 135. By 1915, according to one estimate, the society and its affiliates across North America collected and sent to Russia about $5,000 to support the victims of tsarist persecution.

23 *Novyi mir*, 14 March 1913.

24 *Novyi mir*, 3, 29 March, 18 September 1915.

25 *Novyi mir*, 23 March 1915.

26 Grigorii Okulevich, *Russkie v Kanade: Istoriia russkikh rabochefermerskikh klubov imeni M. Gor'kogo (1930–1940) i Federatsii russkikh kanadtsev* (Toronto: Federation of Russian Canadians, 1952), 34.

27 *Novyi mir*, 17 April 1914.

28 *Novyi mir*, 13 September 1915; see also issues for 1 May, 11 and 19 June 1915 concerning similar incidents in Hamilton, Montreal, and Timmins.

29 *Novyi mir*, 15 November 1915.

30 *Novyi mir*, 31 January 1913.

31 *Novyi mir*, 5 May 1915.

32 Cited in McCormack, *Reformers, Rebels, and Revolutionaries*, 67.

33 *Novyi mir*, January 1912 (date torn off), 18 October 1912.

34 Chernenko, *Russkaia revoliutsionnaia emigratsiia*, 139.

35 See, for instance, *Novyi mir*, 31 January 1913.

36 *Novyi mir*, 18 October 1912. For a short biography of Belousov, who died in Minneapolis in December 1916, see *Western Labour News*, 16 August 1918.

37 *Novyi mir*, 19 July 1912. See also Martynowych, "The Ukrainian Socialist Movement in Canada," 24. For Kuznetsov's background, see Elwood, *Russian Social Democracy*, 182–3.

38 The Russian locals of the Socialist Party of America (SPA) were the main centres of Russian Social Democrat activities in the United States. In May 1911, there were fifteen such locals with approximately 350 members. In May 1915, they formed the Russian Social Democratic Federation affiliated with the SPA (*Novyi mir*, 26 May 1911; 21–25 May 1915). There were also a number of American anarchist and Socialist Revolutionary groups.

39 More about the newspaper, its editors, and political platform can be found in Robert A. Karlowich, *We Fall and Rise: Russian-Language Newspapers in New York City, 1889–1914* (Metuchen, NJ: Scarecrow Press, 1991), chapters 4 and 6, passim.

40 *Novyi mir*, 5 April 1912.

41 *Novyi mir*, 14 February 1913.

42 Okulevich, *Russkie v Kanade*, 18.

43 Ibid., 34.

44 *Novyi mir*, 14 January 1915. On the political activities of unemployed foreign workers in Montreal, see also *Labour Gazette*, May 1914, 1260.

45 *Novyi mir*, 22 July 1915.

46 *Novyi mir*, 1 February 1915.

47 *Novyi mir*, 17 June 1916.

48 *Novyi mir*, 15 August 1916; see also 10 November 1916.

49 *Novyi mir*, 29 February, 29 March 1916.

50 *Novyi mir*, 29 February 1916. The war increased the amount of Judeophobia among Russian-born Slav immigrants, who suspected the Jews of supporting Russia's enemies.

51 Li-Ra-Ma Collection, vol. 16, file 504; *Novyi mir*, 20 April 1915; 5, 7 May 1915, 5 April 1918. See also Kukushkin, *Protectors and Watchdogs*, 225.

52 *Sudbury Star*, 5 January 1918, cited in Stacey Zembrzycki, "The *Sudbury Star* and Its Coverage of Eastern European Immigrants, 1910–1930: A Gendered, Ethnic, and Regional Discourse." Unpublished research paper, Carleton University, 2004.

53 *Russkoe slovo*, 26, 28 November 1917; 22 January 1918.

54 Okulevich, *Russkie v Kanade*, 30–1.

55 LAC, Immigration Branch, RG 76, series I-A-1, vol. 394, reel C-10287, file 563236, part 7, F. Maclure Sclanders to the Department of Immigration and Colonization, 14 August 1919.

56 These organizations should not be confused with the anarchist Unions of Russian Workers that had existed on the West Coast prior to World War I.

57 *Rabochii narod*, 9 March 1918.

58 Ibid.

59 *Russkoe slovo*, 6, 12 October 1917; 25 February, 7 March 1918.
   Zhenirovsky was born into a Jewish family in Kiev, where he worked as an
   office clerk before coming to Canada in 1914. See his files in the Li-Ra-Ma
   Collection (vol. 63, file 6256 and vol. 76, file 8102).

60 *Robochyi narod*, 27 June 1917; *Novyi mir*, 9 July 1917.

61 Ivan Okuntsov, *Russkaia emigratsiia v Severnoi i Iuzhnoi Amerike* (Buenos
   Aires: Seiatel', 1967), 392–4. Similar committees existed in all European
   countries which had been major destinations for Russian émigré socialists.

62 See the letter inviting members of the Russian Orthodox brotherhood to the
   meeting in SSPP, folder "Church Affairs, 1914–35," M. Gerchikov et al. to
   the Eparchial Society, 13 April 1917.

63 Li-Ra-Ma Collection, vol. 25, files 849–850.

64 LAC, National Defence, RG 24, series D-1-b, vol. 3967, file 1047-4-50,
   A.P. Sherwood to R.M. Stephens, 22 May 1917.

65 LAC, Department of External Affairs, RG 25, series A-3-a, vol. 1206, file
   1917–1706; RG 13, series A-2, vol. 1933, file 1917–796; *Novyi mir*, 10, 14,
   16, 27 April, 21 June 1917; William Rodney, "Broken Journey: Trotsky in
   Canada, 1917," *Queen's Quarterly* 74 (1967): 649–65. Russian socialists in
   Montreal also joined their voices to the protests (*Novyi mir*, 25 April 1917).

66 *Novyi mir*, 23, 24 August 1917. There were allegations of ordinary peasant
   immigrants and even criminals masquerading as anti-tsarist freedom fight-
   ers in order to receive passports and free steamship tickets to Russia.

67 See McCormack, *Reformers, Rebels, and Revolutionaries*, 140–3.

68 *Novyi mir*, 21 May 1918. Several issues of *Rabochii narod*, including
   No. 2 (4 January 1918), have survived. Charitonoff (Kharitonov), a native
   of the city of Nikolaev in southern Ukraine, came to Canada in early 1914
   through the United States and worked in the CPR freight shops prior to taking up the editorship of *Rabochii narod*. See LAC, Department of Justice,
   RG 13, vol. 241, file 1919–2241. Charitonoff's name (probably an alias)
   appears in Canadian sources in a variety of versions (as Max Charitonoff,
   Michael Charitinoff, and even F. Charitonoff).

69 Dirk Hoerder, ed., *The Immigrant Labour Press in North America, 1840s
   – 1970s: An Annotated Bibliography*. Vol. 2: Migrants from Eastern and
   Southeastern Europe (New York: Greenwood Press, 1987), 135; *Novyi
   mir*, 21 May 1918; *Russkoe slovo*, 23 May 1918. No issues of *Zemlia i
   volia* appear to have survived.

70 *Russkoe slovo*, 5 December 1917.

71 *Russkoe slovo*, 11, 12, 13, 14, 21 February 1918. After the fall of the
   Russian monarchy, the society again dropped the word "Slavic" from its

name and began to admit non-Slavic members such as Tartak, who was of Jewish origin.

72 *Novyi mir*, 19 December 1917; 4, 5, 6, 7, 12, 16, 20 February, 5 March 1918. I was not able to find evidence of any Canadian organizations being represented at this convention.

73 *Russkoe slovo*, 4 May 1918; *Novyi mir*, 29 March 1918. The recruiting pro- and anti-Soviet groups were, respectively, the Socialist Revolutionaries and the Montreal branch of the Society for the Defence of the Russian Nation based in New York.

74 I was able to identify five Belarusan and thirteen Ukrainian names along with a number of Poles, Jews, and other Russian-born immigrants among the members of the contingent by checking the attestation papers (held in RG 150 at the National Archives of Canada) of all individuals with Eastern European names that appeared on the roll of the Canadian Siberian Expeditionary Force. The roll is published in J.E. Skuce, CSEF: *Canada's Soldiers in Siberia, 1918–1919* (Ottawa: Access to History Publications, 1990).

75 The repressive activities of the Canadian state against left-wing radicals during the 1918–20 "Red Scare" have received a detailed analysis in Gregory S. Kealey, "State Repression of Labour and the Left in Canada, 1914–1920: The Impact of the First World War," in Franca Iacovetta, Paula Draper, and Robert Ventresca, eds, *A Nation of Immigrants: Women, Workers, and Communities in Canadian History, 1840s – 1960s* (Toronto: University of Toronto Press, 1998), 384–412. See also Donald Avery, *"Dangerous Foreigners": European Immigrant Workers and Labour Radicalism in Canada, 1896–1932* (Toronto: McClelland and Stewart, 1979), 74–89, and McCormack, *Reformers, Rebels, and Revolutionaries*, 149–53.

76 *Russkoe slovo*, 30 October 1917.

77 *Rabochii narod*, 13 April 1918.

78 *Western Labour News*, 25 October, 1, 22, 29 November 1918.

79 LAC, Department of Justice, RG13, vol. 241, file 1919–2241; *Novyi mir*, 6 February, 20 May 1919; *Kanadskii gudok*, 9 February 1939.

80 Norman Penner, ed., *Winnipeg 1919: The Strikers' Own History of the Winnipeg General Strike* (Toronto: James Lewis and Samuel, 1973), 12.

81 See, for instance, Okulevich, *Russkie v Kanade*, 31, 35, 39–40; *Robochyi narod*, 12 June, 24, 31 July, 3, 7 August, 11, 18 September 1918; *Western Labour News*, 8 November 1918; LAC, Department of Justice, RG 13, series A-2, vol. 235, file 1919–1013.

82 LAC, Department of Justice, RG 13, series A-2, vol. 227, file 1918–2021, E.L. Newcombe to the secretary of the Registration Board, 16 September 1918.

83 Ibid., C.H. Cahan to E.L. Newcombe, 29 November 1918. The archival records contain only aggregate lists, but it is clear from the correspondence that Cahan received several boxfuls of lists containing names, ages, and places of birth for 63,784 Russian citizens in Canada.

84 The full texts of both orders-in-council and the Immigration Act amendment can be found in Frances Swyripa and John Herd Thompson, eds, *Loyalties in Conflict: Ukrainians in Canada during the Great War* (Edmonton: Canadian Institute of Ukrainian Studies, 1983), 190–6.

85 *Novyi mir*, 20 May 1919.

86 Cited in William Rodney, *Soldiers of the International: A History of the Communist Party of Canada, 1919–1929* (Toronto: University of Toronto Press, 1968), 25. The Soviet Government Information Bureau, established in early 1919, served as an unofficial (and unrecognized) mission of Soviet Russia in the United States.

87 See, for instance, Gregory S. Kealey and Reg Whitaker, *R.C.M.P. Security Bulletins: The Early Years, 1919–1929* (St John's: Canadian Committee on Labour History, 1994), 707.

88 Verenchuk, a CEF veteran discharged in 1917, was apparently arrested by mistake instead of B. Deviatkin, one of Charitonoff's lieutenants. See Penner, *Winnipeg 1919*, 158–9; *Western Labour News*, 1 August 1919.

89 LAC, Immigration Branch, RG 76, series I-A-1, vol. 394, reel C-10287, file 563236, part 7, F. Maclure Sclanders to W.D. Scott, 5 March 1919.

90 See Barbara Roberts, *Whence They Came: Deportation from Canada 1900–1935* (Ottawa: University of Ottawa Press, 1988), chapter 5.

91 Donald Avery, "The Radical Alien and the Winnipeg General Strike of 1919," in Carl Berger and Ramsay Cook, eds, *The West and the Nation* (Toronto: McClelland and Stewart, 1976), 224.

92 Ibid.; LAC, Royal Canadian Mounted Police, RG 18, series F-3, vol. 3314, file HV–1, parts 4–6.

93 The Vancouver *Sun*, 3, 9 September 1919; *Ukrains'ki robitnychi visty*, 10 September 1919.

94 *British Columbia Federationist*, 25 July, 1, 15 August, 5 September, 3, 31 October, 14, 21, 28 November, 19, 26 December 1919; 2, 9, 16 January, 5 November 1920; see also *R.C.M.P. Security Bulletins*, 36–7.

95 See the complete list of the deportees in Li-Ra-Ma Collection, vol. 20, file 633, and in LAC, Immigration Branch, RG 76, series I-A-1, vol. 611, reel C-10433, file 906924. The ethnic origins of the men are a good demonstration of the multi-ethnic character of Russian radical groups in early twentieth-century Canada: Riazanov, Trusov, Golovin, and Semenov were Russians; Butaev, Chekov, and Dzukoev were Ossetians; Kodovba was

probably Ukrainian; Kelt was a native of Estonia; and Medeikis was a Lithuanian from Kovno Province. It is not clear why the remaining four are missing from the list.

96 Li-Ra-Ma Collection, vol. 20, file 633, Likhachev to Joseph Pope, 4 February 1920.

97 LAC, Department of Justice, RG 13, series D-1, vol. 1028, file 327, F.C. Blair to W.S. Hughes, 1 December 1920; *British Columbia Federationist*, 24 December 1921.

98 *Kanadskii gudok*, 9 February 1939.

99 *Novyi mir*, 12 May 1919.

100 G.E. Reikhberg and B.S. Shapik, "Ob uchastii amerikanskikh rabochikh v vosstanovlenii narodnogo khoziaistva Sovetskoi respubliki," *Istoriia SSSR* 1961 (1), 148.

101 *R.C.M.P. Security Bulletins*, 161–2; Okulevich, *Russkie v Kanade*, 27–8.

102 *Guide Book: Society for Technical Aid to Soviet Russia* (New York, 1925), 48–51.

103 *Amerikanskie izvestiia*, 23 March 1921; *Golos truzhenika*, 19 February 1921.

104 *R.C.M.P. Security Bulletins*, 112, 200.

105 State Archives of the Russian Federation (hereafter GARF), fonds R-364, opis' 1, delo 7, list 362; Myroslav Irchan, *Vybrani tvory*, vol. 2 (Kiev, 1958), 375–6; *Ukrains'ki robitnychi visty*, 8 March 1922.

106 GARF, fonds R-364, inv. 1, file 7, list 354–60.

107 *Guide Book: Society for Technical Aid to Soviet Russia*, 48–50; *Ukrains'ki robitnychi visty*, 27 April 1922.

108 The estimate is based on data in M. I. Rybinskii and G. Ia. Tarle, "O pomoshchi trudiashchikhsia zarubezhnykh stran sovetskomu sel'skomu khoziaistvu," *Istoricheskii arkhiv* 4 (1961), 75. Some Slavic immigrants from Canada also joined American communes heading for Russia, especially the California Commune.

109 See Vadim Kukushkin, "Back in the USSR," *The Beaver* 86, 4 (August-September 2006): 33–6.

Bibliography

ARCHIVAL COLLECTIONS

ALASKAN RUSSIAN CHURCH ARCHIVES, LIBRARY OF CONGRESS, MANUSCRIPT DIVISION
The Geographic File (Series D)
Fort William
Diocese administration. Correspondence, 1911–15, undated
Montreal
Diocese administration. Correspondence, 1911–15, undated
Toronto
Diocese administration. Correspondence, 1911–15, undated
Vancouver
Diocese administration. Correspondence, 1913–16, undated
Winnipeg
Diocese administration. Correspondence, 1893–1916, undated. Parish records, cumulative, 1907

ARCHIVES OF THE ARCHDIOCESE OF CANADA, ORTHODOX CHURCH IN AMERICA, SPENCERVILLE, ONTARIO
Holy Trinity Church (Winnipeg), baptism and marriage books, 1907–15
Baptismal records of the Russian Orthodox Church of St John the Divine, Windsor, 1917–21
Collection book of the Russian Orthodox Church of St John the Divine, 1917

ARCHIVES OF ONTARIO
Multicultural History Society of Ontario Collection, Series 72 (Russian-Canadian Papers), Christ the Saviour Russian Orthodox Cathedral, registers of marriages, 1922–27

ARCHIVES OF THE ŞAINT PETER AND SAINT PAUL ORTHODOX CHURCH, MONTREAL
Church Affairs file, 1914–35
Church Affairs file, 1930–36
Marriage and baptism registers, 1917–21
Membership book of the Holy Trinity Russian Orthodox Brotherhood, 1906 – [1916?]
Various Minutes file, 1925–31

CANADIAN BAPTIST ARCHIVES, MCMASTER UNIVERSITY
Folder "Baptist Union Historical"
Home Mission Board Minutes, 1908–21
John Kolesnikoff file
Minute Book of the Beverley Street Baptist Church [Toronto], 1911–32
Western Collection, Ivan Shakotko file

GOSUDARSTVENNYI ARKHIV ROSSIISKOI FEDERATSII (STATE ARCHIVES OF THE RUSSIAN FEDERATION), MOSCOW
Fond 102 (Ministry of Internal Affairs, Police Department)
Fond R-364 (Permanent Commission on Immigration and Emigration)

LIBRARY AND ARCHIVES CANADA
Andry Zhuk Papers
Canadian National Railway Records, Letterbooks
Department of Agriculture, Docket and Letterbook Registry System, General Correspondence
Department of External Affairs, 1939 Central Registry
Department of Justice, Numbered Central Registry Files, Operational Records of the Penitentiary Branch
Department of National Defence, Second Naval Service Central Registry
Halifax Ships' Manifests
Immigration Branch, Headquarters Central Registry Files, First Central Registry System
Likacheff-Ragosine-Mathers Collection, Montreal Consulate-General, Vancouver Consulate, Registers, and Journals of the Montreal Consulate General, Passport/ Identity Papers
Ministry of the Overseas Military Forces, Attestation Papers
Peter Krawchuk Papers
Royal Canadian Mounted Police, Security Records

ROSSIISKII GOSUDARSTVENNYI ARKHIV VOENNO-MORSKOGO FLOTA
(RUSSIAN STATE ARCHIVES OF THE NAVY), ST PETERSBURG
Fond 420 (Chancellery of the Naval Minister)

ROSSIISKII GOSUDARSTVENNYI ISTORICHESKII ARKHIV (RUSSIAN
STATE HISTORICAL ARCHIVES), ST PETERSBURG
Fond 95 (Ministry of Industry and Trade)
Fond 104 (Russian East-Asiatic Steamship Company)
Fond 796 (Chancellery of the Holy Synod)
Fond 1149 (State Council)
Fond 1278 (State Duma)
Fond 1284 (Ministry of Internal Affairs)
Fond 1409 (His Imperial Majesty's Own Chancellery)

THOMAS FISHER RARE BOOK LIBRARY, UNIVERSITY OF TORONTO
James Mavor Papers

UNITED CHURCH ARCHIVES, VICTORIA UNIVERSITY
Presbyterian Church of Canada. Board of Social Service and Evangelism.
    Report for 1913
Fonds 14 (Methodist Church Missionary Society), series 4 (Home Mission Records)

NEWSPAPERS AND PERIODICALS

CANADA AND THE UNITED STATES
Amerikanskie izvestiia
Amerikanskii pravoslavnyi vestnik = American Orthodox Messenger
The Baptist Year Book
British Columbia Federationist
Golos truzhenika
Kanadiiskaia pravoslavnaia rus'
Kanadskii gudok
Labour Gazette
Novyi mir
Rabochii narod
Robochyi narod
Russkii emigrant
Russkii golos
Russkii narod
Russkoe slovo

Svit
The Toronto Globe
Ukrains'ki robitnychi visty
The Vancouver Sun
Western Labour News
The Year Book of the Baptist Union of Western Canada

RUSSIA
Agronomicheskii zhurnal
Ekonomicheskaia zhizn' Podolii
Ekonomicheskii listok Podol'skogo gubernskogo zemstva
Izvestiia iuzhno-russkoi zemskoi oblastnoi pereselencheskoi organizatsii
Izvestiia Volynskogo gubernskogo zemstva
Kievlianin
Novoe vremia
Podolianin
Rada
Russkie vedomosti
Sel'skii khoziain
Severo-Zapadnaia zhizn'
Vestnik Evropy
Vestnik finansov, promyshlennnosti i torgovli
Vestnik Ministerstva iustitsii
Vestnik Novouzenskogo zemstva
Zemskii sbornik Chernigovskoi gubernii

BOOKS, ARTICLES, AND MISCELLANEOUS SOURCES

Allen, Richard. *The Social Passion: Religion and Social Reform in Canada, 1914–1928.* Toronto: University of Toronto Press, 1971.

Anderson, Barbara A. *Internal Migration during Modernization in Late-Nineteenth Century Russia.* Princeton, NJ: Princeton University Press, 1980.

Anderson, Benedict. *Imagined Communities: Reflections on the Origin and Spread of Nationalism.* London: Verso, 1983.

Anfimov, A.M. *Krestianskoe khoziaistvo Evropeiskoi Rossii, 1881–1904.* Moskva: Nauka, 1980.

Annual Reports of the Department of the Interior, 1900–1915, *Canada. House of Commons. Sessional Papers,* paper no. 25.

Archdeacon, Thomas J. *Becoming American: An Ethnic History.* New York: Macmillan, 1983.

Archdeacon, Thomas J., and Alfred E. Senn. "Labour Emigration from Tsarist Russia: A Review Essay," *International Migration Review* 24, 1 (1990): 149–60.

Artibise, Alan F.J. *Winnipeg: A Social History of Urban Growth, 1874–1914.* Montreal: McGill-Queen's University Press, 1975.

Ashkenas, Bruce. *Records of Imperial Russian Consulates in Canada, 1898–1922.* Washington, DC: National Archives and Records Administration, 1992.

Atlas of Canada. Prepared under the direction of J.E. Chalifour. 2nd edition. [Ottawa], 1915.

Atlas of the City of Montreal and Vicinity. 4 Vols. Charles E. Goad Co., 1912.

Avery, Donald. "Canadian Immigration Policy and the 'Foreign' Navvy, 1896–1914," *Canadian Historical Association Papers* (1972): 135–56.

– "Canadian Immigration Policy and the Alien Question, 1896–1919: The Anglo-Canadian Perspective." PhD thesis, University of Western Ontario, 1973.

– "Continental European Workers in Canada, 1896–1919: From 'Stalwart Peasants' to Radical Proletariat," *Canadian Review of Sociology and Anthropology* 12, 1 (1975): 53–64.

– "The Radical Alien and the Winnipeg General Strike of 1919," in Carl Berger and Ramsay Cook, eds, *The West and the Nation.* Toronto: McClelland and Stewart, 1976.

– *"Dangerous Foreigners": European Immigrant Workers and Labour Radicalism in Canada, 1896–1932.* Toronto: McClelland and Stewart, 1979.

– *The Reluctant Host: Canada's Response to Immigrant Workers, 1896–1994.* Toronto: McClelland and Stewart, 1995.

Balan, Boris B. "Urbanization and the Ukrainian Economy in the Mid-Nineteenth Century," in I. S. Koropeckyj, ed., *Ukrainian Economic History: Interpretive Essays.* Cambridge, MA: Harvard University Press, 1991.

Balch, Emily Greene. *Our Slavic Fellow Citizens.* New York: Charities Publications Committee, 1910.

Barnes, Michael. *Gold in the Porcupine.* Cobalt, ON: Highway Book Shop, 1975.

Barton, Josef. *Peasants and Strangers: Italians, Rumanians, and Slovaks in an American City, 1890–1950.* Cambridge, MA: Harvard University Press, 1975.

Bayley, Charles M. "The Social Structure of the Italian and Ukrainian Immigrant Communities in Montreal." MA thesis, McGill University, 1939.

Bickersteth, John Burgon. *The Land of Open Doors; Being Letters from Western Canada.* London: Wells Gardner, Darton, 1914.

Bird, Thomas. "Zluchanyia Shtaty Ameryki i emihratsyinaia tematyka u publitsystytsy i paezii 'Nashai nivy'," *Zapisy: Belaruski instytut navuki i mastatstva* 23 (1999): 5–37.

Black, J. L. *Canada in the Soviet Mirror: Ideology and Perception in Soviet Foreign Affairs, 1917–1991.* Ottawa: Carleton University Press, 1998.

– *The Peasant Kingdom: Canada in the Nineteenth-Century Russian Imagination.* Manotick, ON: Penumbra Press, 2001.

Blank, Inge. "A Vast Migratory Experience: Eastern Europe in the Pre- and Post-Emancipation Era," in Dirk Hoerder and Inge Blank, eds, *Roots of the Transplanted.* Vol.1: *Late 19th Century East Central and Southeastern Europe.* Boulder, CO: East European Monographs; New York: Distributed by Columbia University Press, 1994.

Bodnar, John. *The Transplanted: A History of Immigrants in Urban America.* Bloomington: Indiana University Press, 1985.

Borodin, N.A. *Severo-Amerikanskie Soedinennye Shtaty i Rossiia.* Petrograd: Izd. K-va "Ogin," 1915.

Bowen, Frank. *A Century of Atlantic Travel, 1830–1930.* Boston: Little, Brown and Co., 1930.

Bozhyk, Panteleimon. *Tserkov ukraintsiv v Kanadi.* Winnipeg: Kanadyis'kyi ukrainets', 1927.

Bradwin, Edmund. *The Bunkhouse Man.* Reprint of the 1928 edition. New York: AMS Press, 1968.

Burds, Jeffrey. *Peasant Dreams and Market Politics: Labour Migration and the Russian Village, 1861–1905.* Pittsburgh: University of Pittsburgh Press, 1998.

Burnet Jean P. (with Howard Palmer). *"Coming Canadians:" An Introduction to the History of Canada's Peoples.* Toronto: McClelland and Stewart, 1988.

Canada, House of Commons Debates.

Census of Canada 1971. Vol. 1, Part 3. Ottawa: Supply and Services Canada, 1980.

Cherkasov, Arkady. "Canadians of Russian Origin: Their History, Geography and Role in the Canadian Ethno-Cultural Mosaic." Paper presented at the Conference in Canadian Studies, Hebrew University of Jerusalem, 28 June – 1 July 1998.

Chernenko, A. *Rossiiskaia revoliutsionnaia emigratsiia v Amerike: konets XIX v. – 1917 g.* Kiev: Vyshcha shkola, 1989.

Chlebowczyk, Josef. *On Small and Young Nations in Europe: Nation-Forming Processes in Ethnic Borderlands in East-Central Europe.* Wroclaw: Zaklad Narodowy Imienia Ossolinskich, 1980.

Chyz, Jaroslav, and Joseph Roucek. "The Russians in the United States," *The Slavonic and East European Review* 17 (1939): 638–58.

Clem, Ralph S. "Population Change in the Ukraine in the Nineteenth Century," in I.S. Koropeckyj, ed., *Ukrainian Economic History: Interpretive Essays*. Cambridge, MA: Harvard University Press, 1991.

Coleman, Heather. *Russian Baptists and Spiritual Revolution, 1905–1929*. Bloomington: Indiana University Press, 2005.

Copp, Terry. *The Anatomy of Poverty: The Condition of the Working Class in Montreal, 1897–1929*. Toronto: McClelland and Stewart, 1974.

Cousins, William. *A History of the Crow's Nest Pass*. Lethbridge: The Historic Trails Society of Alberta, 1981.

Cygan, Mary Eleanor. "Polish Women and Emigrant Husbands," in Dirk Hoerder and Inge Blank, eds, *Roots of the Transplanted*. Vol. 1: *Late 19th Century East Central and Southeastern Europe*. Boulder, CO: Eastern European Monographs, 1994.

Darcovich, William, comp. *A Statistical Compendium on the Ukrainians in Canada, 1891–1976*. Ottawa: University of Ottawa Press, 1980.

Davies, David. "The Pre-1917 Roots of Canadian-Soviet Relations," *Canadian Historical Review* 70, 2 (1989): 180–205.

Davies, David, ed. *Canada and the Soviet Experiment: Essays on Canadian Encounters with Russia and the Soviet Union*. Toronto: Canadian Scholars' Press, 1994.

Davis, Jerome. *The Russian Immigrant*. New York: Macmillan, 1922.

– *Russians and Ruthenians: Bolsheviks or Brothers?* New York: George H. Doran, 1922.

Desiat' Let Internatsional'nogo Rabochego Ordena; Dvadtsat' Let Russkoi Sektsii (b. RNOV) 1920–1940: Iubileinyi sbornik. New York: NIK Russkoi sektsii IRO, 1940.

Dinnerstein, Leonard, and David M. Reimers. *Ethnic Americans: A History of Immigration*. New York: Columbia University Press, 1999.

Domashovets, Hryhory. *Narys istorii ukrains'koi ievanhels'ko-baptists'koi tserkvy*. Irvington-Toronto: Harmony Printing, 1967.

Donskov, Andrew, ed. *Sergej Tolstoy and the Doukhobors: A Journey to Canada*. Ottawa: Slavic Research Group at the University of Ottawa, 1998.

Dubrovskii, S.M. *Stolypinskaia agrarnaia reforma*. Moskva: Moskovskii rabochii, 1930.

Dyrud, Keith P. *The Quest for the Rusyn Soul: The Politics of Religion and Culture in Eastern Europe and in America, 1890 – World War I*. Philadelphia: The Balch Institute Press; London and Toronto: Associated University Presses, 1992.

Edelman, Robert. *Proletarian Peasants: The Revolution of 1905 in Russia's Southwest*. Ithaca: Cornell University Press, 1987.

Elwood, Ralph Carter. *Russian Social Democracy in the Underground: A Study of the RSDRP in the Ukraine, 1907–1914*. Assen: VanGorcum, 1974.

"Emigratsiia," in *Entsiklopedicheskii slovar*. Vol. 80. St Petersburg: Izdanie F.A. Brokgauza and I.A. Efrona, 1904.

Emmons, Terence, and Wayne S. Vucinich, eds. *The Zemstvo in Russia: An Experiment in Local Self-Government*. Cambridge; New York: Cambridge University Press, 1982.

Fawcett, J.T. "Networks, Linkages and Migration Systems," *International Migration Review* 23, 3 (Fall 1989): 671–80.

Fifth Census of Canada, 1911. Vol. 2. Ottawa: King's Printer, 1913.

Forestell, Nancy. "All That Glitters is Not Gold: The Gendered Dimensions of Work, Family and Community Life in the Northern Ontario Goldmining Town of Timmins, 1909–1950." PhD thesis, University of Toronto, 1993.

– "Bachelors, Boarding-Houses, and Blind Pigs: Gender Construction in a Multi-Ethnic Mining Camp, 1909–1920," in Franca Iacovetta, Paula Draper, and Robert Ventresca, eds, *A Nation of Immigrants: Women, Workers, and Communities in Canadian History, 1840s – 1960s*. Toronto: University of Toronto Press, 1998.

Fourth Census of Canada, 1901. Vol. 1. Ottawa: King's Printer, 1902.

Frager, Ruth. *Sweatshop Strife: Class, Ethnicity and Gender in the Jewish Labour Movement of Toronto, 1900–1939*. Toronto: University of Toronto Press, 1992.

Frank, Stephen. *Crime, Cultural Conflict, and Justice in Rural Russia, 1856–1914*. Berkeley: University of California Press, 1999.

Freeze, Gregory. "Handmaiden of the State? The Orthodox Church in Imperial Russia Reconsidered," *Journal of Ecclesiastical History* 36 (1985): 82–102.

Gabaccia, Donna. *Militants and Migrants: Rural Sicilians Become American Workers*. New Brunswick, NJ: Rutgers University Press, 1988.

"General Report of the Minister of Public Works and Labour of the Province of Quebec, for the year ending 30 June 1912," *Quebec Sessional Papers* 1912, paper no. 4.

Gerber, David A. "Epistolary Ethics: Personal Correspondence and the Culture of Emigration in the Nineteenth Century," *Journal of American Ethnic History* 19, 4 (Summer 2000): 3–23.

Germain, Annick, and Damaris Rose. *Montreal: The Quest for a Metropolis*. Chichester: John Wiley and Sons, 2000.

Gerus, Oleh, and James Edgar Rea. *The Ukrainians in Canada*. Ottawa: Canadian Historical Association, 1985.

Glazier, Ira and Luigi de Rosa, eds. *Migrations Across Time and Nations*. New York: Holmes and Meier, 1986.

Goa, David J., ed. *The Ukrainian Religious Experience: Tradition and the Canadian Cultural Context*. Edmonton: Canadian Institute of Ukrainian Studies, 1989.

Goad's Insurance Plan, City of Montreal, 1909–1915.

Gould, J.D. "European Inter-Continental Emigration, 1815–1914: Patterns and Causes," *Journal of European Economic History* 8, 3 (Winter 1979): 593–679.

Gregorovich, Andrew, and Gabrielle P. Scardellato, eds. *A Bibliography of Canada's Peoples*. Toronto: Multicultural History Society of Ontario, 1993.

Gretzky, Walter. *On Family, Hockey and Healing*. Toronto: Random House of Canada, 2001.

Guest, Dennis. *The Emergence of Social Security in Canada*. 2nd rev. ed. Vancouver: University of British Columbia Press, 1985.

Guide Book. Technical Aid Society to Soviet Russia. New York, 1925.

Habakkuk, H.J. "Family Structure and Economic Change in Nineteenth Century Europe," in Norman W. Bell and Ezra F. Vogel, eds, *A Modern Introduction to the Family*. Rev. ed. Glencoe, IL: The Free Press, 1968.

Hall, David John. *Clifford Sifton*. Vol.2: *A Lonely Eminence, 1901–1929*. Vancouver: University of British Columbia Press, 1985.

Hansen, Marcus. *The Atlantic Migration, 1607–1860*. Cambridge, MA: Harvard University Press, 1940.

Harney, Robert F. "Men without Women: Italian Migrants in Canada, 1885–1930," in Betty Caroli, Robert Harney, and Lydio Tomasi, eds, *The Italian Immigrant Woman in North America*. Toronto: Multicultural History Society of Ontario, 1978.

– "Ethnicity and Neighbourhoods," in Robert F. Harney, ed., *Gathering Place: People and Neighbourhoods of Toronto, 1834–1945*. Toronto: Multicultural History Society of Ontario, 1985.

– "Boarding and Belonging," in Bruno Ramirez, ed., *"If One Were to Write a History ... :" Selected Writings by Robert F. Harney*. Toronto: Multicultural History Society of Ontario, 1991.

Harney, Robert, and Harold Troper, eds. *Immigrants: A Portrait of the Urban Experience, 1890–1930*. Toronto, Van Nostrand, 1975.

Hern, Gordon. *Russians in Canada*. Toronto, n.d.

Hillmer, Norman, and J.L. Granatstein, eds. *The Land Newly Found: Eyewitness Accounts of the Canadian Immigrant Experience*. Toronto: Thomas Allen, 2006.

Himka, John-Paul. "The Background to Emigration: Ukrainians of Galicia and Bukovyna, 1848–1914," in Manoly Lupul, ed., *A Heritage in Transition: Essays in the History of Ukrainians in Canada*. Toronto: McClelland and Stewart, 1982.

Historyia Belaruskai SSR. Vol. 2. Minsk: Navuka i tekhnika, 1972.

Hoerder, Dirk. "Ethnic Studies in Canada from the 1880s to 1962: A Historiographical Perspective and Critique," *Canadian Ethnic Studies* 26, 1 (1994): 1–18.

– "Changing Paradigms in Migration History: From 'To America' to World-Wide Systems," *Canadian Review of American Studies* 24, 2 (1994): 105–26.

– *Creating Societies: Immigrant Lives in Canada*. Montreal: McGill-Queen's University Press, 1999.

– *Cultures in Contact: World Migrations in the Second Millennium*. Durham and London: Duke University Press, 2002.

Hoerder, Dirk, ed. *Labour Migration in the Atlantic Economies: The European and North American Working Classes During the Period of Industrialization*. Westport, CN: Greenwood Press, 1985.

Hoerder, Dirk, ed. *The Immigrant Labour Press in North America, 1840s – 1970s: An Annotated Bibliography*. Vol. 2: Migrants from Eastern and Southeastern Europe. New York: Greenwood Press, 1987.

Hoerder, Dirk, and Horst Rossler, eds. *Distant Magnets: Expectations and Realities in the Immigrant Experience*. New York: Holmes and Meier, 1993.

Hoerder, Dirk, and Leslie Page Moch, eds. *European Migrants: Global and Local Perspectives*. Boston: Northeastern University Press, 1996.

Hosking, Geoffrey. "Empire and Nation-Building in Late Imperial Russia," in Geoffrey Hosking and Robert Service, eds, *Russian Nationalism: Past and Present*. New York: St Martin's Press, 1998.

Hroch, Miroslav. *Social Preconditions of National Revival in Europe: A Comparative Analysis of the Social Composition of Patriotic Groups among the Smaller European Nations*. 2nd ed. New York: Columbia University Press, 2000.

Huk, John. *Strangers in the Land: The Ukrainian Presence in Cape Breton*. n.p., n.d.

Iacovetta, Franca. *Such Hardworking People: Italian Immigrants in Postwar Toronto*. Montreal: McGill-Queen's University Press, 1992.

– "Manly Militants, Cohesive Communities and Defiant Domestics: Writing about Immigrants in Canadian Historical Scholarship," *Labour/Le travail* 36 (Fall 1995): 217–52.

Iakymenko, M.A. "Orhanizatsiia pereselennia selian z Ukraini v roki stolypins'koi ahrarnoi reformy (1906–1913)," *Ukrains'kyi istorychnyi zhurnal* 7 (July 1974): 32–42.

– "Mihratsii ukrains'koho selianstva (1861–1905)," *Ukrains'kyi istorychnyi zhurnal* 9 (September 1982): 61–71.

Ianovskii, S.A. and A. I. Kastelianskii, eds. *Spravochnaia kniga po voprosam emigratsii.* St Petersburg: Tip. I.A. Lur'e, 1913.

Irchan, Myroslav. *Vybrani tvory*, vol. 2. Kiev, 1958.

Isajiw, Wsewolod W. "Definitions of Ethnicity," in Rita M. Bienvenue and Jay E. Goldstein, eds, *Ethnicity and Ethnic Relations in Canada.* 2nd ed. Toronto: Butterworth, 1985.

Istoriia Ukrains'koi RSR. Vol. 4. Kiev: Naukova dumka, 1978.

Jeletzky, Tamara, ed. *Russian Canadians: Their Past and Present.* Ottawa: Borealis Press, 1983.

Johnson, Robert E. *Peasant and Proletarian: The Working Class of Moscow in the Late Nineteenth Century.* New Brunswick, NJ: Rutgers University Press, 1979.

The Jubilee Book of the Russian Orthodox Christ the Saviour Cathedral in Toronto, 1915–1965. n.p., [1965].

Kabuzan, Vladimir. *Emigratsiia i reemigratsiia v Rossii v XVIII – nachale XX veka.* Moskva: Nauka, 1998.

– *Russkie v mire: Dinamika chislennosti i rasseleniia (1719–1989). Formirovanie etnicheskikh i politicheskikh granits russkogo naroda.* St Petersburg: BLITZ Publishing House, 1996.

Kappeler, Andreas. *The Russian Empire: A Multiethnic History.* Harlow: Pearson Education Ltd., 2001.

Karlowich, Robert A. *We Fall and Rise: Russian-Language Newspapers in New York City, 1889–1914.* Metuchen, NJ: Scarecrow Press, 1991.

Kaye, Vladimir. "Canadians of Belorussian Origin," *Revue de l'Université d'Ottawa* 30 (1960): 300–14.

Kazymyra, Nadia. "The Defiant Pavlo Krat and the Early Socialist Movement in Canada," *Canadian Ethnic Studies* 10, 2 (1978): 38–54.

Kealey, Gregory S. "State Repression of Labour and the Left in Canada, 1914–1920: The Impact of the First World War," in Franca Iacovetta, Paula Draper, and Robert Ventresca, eds, *A Nation of Immigrants: Women, Workers, and Communities in Canadian History, 1840s – 1960s.* Toronto: University of Toronto Press, 1998.

Kealey, Gregory S., and Reg Whitaker. *R.C.M.P. Security Bulletins: The Early Years, 1919–1929.* St John's: Canadian Committee on Labour History, 1994.

Kelebay, Yarema. "The Ideological and Intellectual Baggage of Three Fragments of Ukrainian Immigrants: A Contribution to the History of Ukrainians in Quebec (1910–1960)." PhD thesis, Concordia University, 1993.

– "Three Fragments of the Ukrainian Community in Montreal, 1899–1970: A Hartzian Approach," *Canadian Ethnic Studies* 12, 2 (1980): 74–87.

Kelley, Ninette, and Michael Trebilcock. *The Making of the Mosaic: A History of Canadian Immigration Policy.* Toronto: University of Toronto Press, 1998.

Khauratovich, I.P., comp. *Iliustravanaia khranalohiia historyi Belarusi: ad starazhytnastsi da pachatku XX st.* 2 vols. Minsk: Belaruskaia entsyklapediia, 1995–1997.

King, Joe. *From the Ghetto to the Main: the Story of the Jews of Montreal.* Montreal: Montreal Jewish Publications Society, 2000.

Kipel, Vitaut. *Belarusans in the United States.* Lanham, MD: University Press of America, 1999.

Klibanov, A.I. *History of Religious Sectarianism in Russia (1860s-1917).* Oxford: Pergamon Press, 1982.

Korolenko, Vladimir. *In a Strange Land.* New York: Bernard G. Richards Company, 1925.

Korolev, V. *Ukraintsi v Amerytsi.* Kiev: Prosvita, 1909.

Kurchevskii, B. *Ob emigratsii v Ameriku.* Libava, 1913.

Kovacs, Helen, and Djuro J. Vrga. "The Russian Minority in America," in Otto Feldstein, ed., *Ethnic Groups in the City: Culture, Institutions, and Power.* Lexington, MA: Heath Lexington Books, 1971.

Koval'chenko, I.D., and L.V. Milov. *Vserossiiskii agrarnyi rynok, XVIII – nachalo XX veka: Opyt kolichestvennogo analiza.* Moskva: Nauka, 1974.

Krawchenko, Bohdan. *Social Change and National Consciousness in Twentieth-Century Ukraine.* London: Macmillan, 1985.

Krawchuk, Peter. *Our History: The Ukrainian Labour-Farmer Movement in Canada, 1907–1991.* Toronto: Lugus Publications, 1996.

– *The Life and Work of Matthew Shatulsky.* Toronto: Kobzar, 1991.

Kritz, Mary M., Lin L. Lim, and Hania Zlotnik, eds. *International Migration Systems: A Global Approach.* Oxford: Clarendon Press, 1992.

Kukushkin, Vadim. "Protectors and Watchdogs: Tsarist Consular Supervision of Russian-Subject Immigrants in Canada, 1900–1922," *Canadian Slavonic Papers* 44, 3–4 (September-December 2002): 209–32.

– "Slavianskaia trudovaia emigratsiia iz Rossiiskoi imperii v Kanadu v nachale xx veka," *Etnograficheskoe obozrenie* 2002 (4): 126–39.

– "Ukrainian Immigration from the Russian Empire: A Reappraisal," *Journal of Ukrainian Studies* 28, 1 (Summer 2003): 1–32.

– "Revisiting Quantitative Methods in Immigration History: Immigrant Files in the Archives of the Russian Consulates in Canada," in Jeff Keshen and Sylvie Perrier, eds, *Building New Bridges: Sources, Methods, and Interdisciplinarity.* Ottawa: University of Ottawa Press, 2005.

- "Emigrant Correspondence with Russian Consulates in Montreal, Vancouver and Halifax, 1899–1922," in David Gerber, Suzanne Sinke, and Bruce S. Elliott, eds, *Letters Across Borders: The Epistolary Practices of International Migrants.* New York: Palgrave-Macmillan, 2006.
- "Back in the USSR," *The Beaver* 86, 4 (August-September 2006): 33–6.
Leshchenko, M.N. *Ukrains'ke selo v revoliutsii 1905–1907 rr.* Kiev: Naukova dumka, 1977.
Leshchenko, Oksana. "Early Immigration from Eastern Ukraine to Canada: Background and Significance." MA Thesis, University of Waterloo, 1992.
A Lettish Canadian. *Russians in Europe and in Canada.* n.p., n.d.
Lieven, Dominic. *Empire: The Russian Empire and Its Rivals.* New Haven; London: Yale University Press, 2000.
Lindstrom, Varpu. *Defiant Sisters: A Social History of Finnish Immigrant Women in Canada.* Toronto: Multicultural History Society of Ontario, 1988.
Linteau, Paul-André. *Histoire de Montréal depuis la Confédération.* 2ème éd. Montréal: Boréal, 2000.
Lovell's Montreal City Directory
Lucassen, Jan, and Leo Lucassen, eds. *Migration, Migration History, History: Old Paradigms and New Perspectives.* Bern: Peter Lang, 1999.
Luciuk, Lubomyr, and Iroida L. Wynnyckyj, eds. *Ukrainians in Ontario.* Toronto: Multicultural History Society of Ontario, 1988.
Luciuk, Lubomyr. *Searching for Place: Ukrainian Displaced Persons, Canada, and the Migration of Memory.* Toronto: University of Toronto Press, 2000.
Luzianin, G.I. *Rossiia i Kanada v 1893–1927 gg.* Moskva: Prometei, 1997.
Lysenko, Vera. *Men in Sheepskin Coats: A Study in Assimilation.* Toronto: Ryerson Press, 1947.
Macdonald, John S. "Agricultural Organization, Migration, and Labour Militancy in Rural Italy," *Economic History Review,* 2nd ser., 16 (1963–64): 61–75.
Magocsi, Paul Robert. *The Russian Americans.* New York: Chelsea House, 1989.
- *Historical Atlas of East Central Europe.* Toronto: University of Toronto Press, 1993.
- *A History of Ukraine.* Toronto: University of Toronto Press, 1996.
- *Of the Making of Nationalities There is No End.* Boulder, CO: East European Monographs, 1999.
Mamchur, Stephen. "The Economic and Social Adjustment of Slavic Immigrants in Canada: With Special Reference to the Ukrainians in Montreal." MA thesis, McGill University, 1934.
Martynowych, Orest. "The Ukrainian Socialist Movement in Canada, 1900–1918," *Journal of Ukrainian Graduate Studies* 1, 1 (Fall 1976): 27–44; 2, 1 (Spring 1977): 22–31.

– *Ukrainians in Canada: The Formative Period, 1891–1924.* Edmonton: Canadian Institute of Ukrainian Studies Press, 1991.

Marunchak, Michael. *Ukrainian Canadians.* Winnipeg: Ukrainian Free Academy of Sciences, 1970.

Matthews, Mervyn. *The Passport Society: Controlling Movement in Russia and the USSR.* Boulder, CO: Westview, 1993.

McCormack, A. Ross. *Reformers, Rebels, and Revolutionaries: The Western Canadian Radical Movement, 1899–1919.* Toronto: University of Toronto Press, 1977.

McLaren, Angus. "Males, Migrants, and Murder in British Columbia, 1900–1923," in Franca Iacovetta and Wendy Mitchinson, eds, *On the Case: Explorations in Social History.* Toronto: University of Toronto Press, 1998.

McNicoll, Claire. *Montréal, une société multiculturelle.* Paris: Belin, 1993.

Melville, Ralph. "Permanent Emigration and Temporary Transnational Migration: Jewish, Polish and Russian Emigration from Tsarist Russia, 1861–1914," in Julianna Puskás, ed., *Overseas Migration from East-Central and Southeastern Europe, 1880–1940.* Budapest: Akadémiai Kiadó, 1990.

Michalski, Thomas A. "Soviet Archival Sources for the Study of Emigration from the Lands of the Polish-Lithuanian Commonwealth to America," *Polish American Studies* 47, 1 (Spring 1990): 75–80.

Might's Toronto City Directory

Milosz, Czeslaw. "Vilnius, Lithuania: An Ethnic Agglomerate," in George de Vos and Lola Romanucci-Ross, eds, *Ethnic Identities: Cultural Continuities and Change.* Palo Alto, CA: Mayfield Publishing Company, 1975.

Mironov, Boris (with Ben Eklof). *A Social History of Imperial Russia, 1700–1917.* 2 vols. Boulder, CO: Westview Press, 1999–2000.

Morawska, Ewa. *For Bread and Butter: Life-Worlds of East Central Europeans in Johnstown, Pennsylvania, 1890–1914.* Cambridge, MA: Harvard University Press, 1985.

– "Return Migrations: Theoretical and Research Agenda," in Rudolph J. Vecoli and Suzanne M. Sinke, eds, *A Century of European Migrations, 1830–1930.* Urbana: University of Illinois Press, 1991.

Mosse, W.E. "Stolypin's Villages," *Slavonic and East European Review* 43 (June 1965): 257–74.

Murdzek, Benjamin. *Emigration in Polish Social-Political Thought, 1870–1914.* Boulder, CO: East European Quarterly: New York: Distributed by Columbia University Press, 1977.

Nitoburg, Eduard L'vovich. "Russkaia pravoslavnaia tserkov' v SShA," *SShA – Kanada: ekonomika, politika, kul'tura* 4 (2000): 34–54.

– "Russkoiazychnaia pressa v SShA," *SShA – Kanada: ekonomika, politika, kul'tura* 1 (2001): 58–74.

- "Russkie trudovye immigranty v SShA (konets XIX v. – 1917 g.): adaptatsiia i sud'by," *Otechestvennaia istoriia* 2002 (5): 63–75.

Norris, John. *Strangers Entertained*. Vancouver: Evergreen Press, 1971.

Nugent, Walter. *Crossings: The Great Transatlantic Migrations, 1870–1914*. Bloomington: Indiana University Press, 1992.

Obolensky-Ossinsky, V. *Mezhdunarodnye i mezhkontinental'nye migratsii v dovoennoi Rossii i SSSR*. Moskva: TsSU SSSR, 1928.

Obolensky-Ossinsky, V.V. "Emigration from and Immigration into Russia," in Imre Ferenczi and Walter F. Willcox, eds, *International Migrations*. Vol. 2: *Interpretations*. New York: Gordon and Breach, 1969.

Ofrosimov, L. S. *Otkhozhii promysel za okean. Obsledovanie Vilenskoi gubernii*. Vil'na: Tip. M.S. Grozenskogo, 1912.

Okulevich, Grigorii. *Russkie v Kanade: Istoriia russkikh raboche-fermerskikh klubov imeni M. Gor'kogo (1930–1940) i Federatsii russkikh kanadtsev (1941–1952)*. Toronto: Federation of Russian Canadians, 1952.

Okuntsov, Ivan. *Russko-Amerikanskii spravochnik: Geograficheskii i statistiko-ekonomicheskii ocherk Soedinennykh Shtatov, Kanady i Rossii*. New York: Russkoe slovo, 1913.

Okuntsov, Ivan. *Russkaia emigratsiia v Severnoi i Iuzhnoi Amerike*. Buenos Aires: Seiatel', 1967.

Omelchenko, E. I. *Russian-American Register*. New York: Russian-American Register Publishing Co., 1920.

Pallot, Judith, and Denis J.B. Shaw. *Landscape and Settlement in Romanov Russia, 1613–1917*. Oxford: Clarendon Press; New York: Oxford University Press, 1990.

Paniutich, V.P. *Sotsial'no-ekonomicheskoe razvitie belorusskoi derevni v 1861–1900 gg*. Minsk: Navuka i tekhnika, 1990.

– *Naemnyi trud v sel'skom khoziaistve Belarusi, 1861–1914 gg*. Minsk: Navuka i tekhnika, 1996.

Penner, Norman, ed. *Winnipeg 1919: The Strikers' Own History of the Winnipeg General Strike*. Toronto: James Lewis and Samuel, 1973.

Perin, Roberto. "Religion, Ethnicity and Identity: Placing the Immigrant within the Church," in William Westfall et al, eds, *Religion/Culture: Comparative Canadian Studies. Proceedings of a Conference Sponsored by the Association for Canadian Studies and the Graduate Centre for Religious Studies, University of Toronto, Held at the Ontario Institute for Studies in Education, Toronto, Ontario, 23–26 May, 1984*. Ottawa: Association for Canadian Studies, 1985.

Pervaia vseobshchaia perepis' naseleniia Rossiiskoi Imperii 1897 goda. St Petersburg, 1897–1905.

Petroff, Lillian. *Sojourners and Settlers: The Macedonian Community in Toronto to 1940*. Toronto: University of Toronto Press, 1995.

Petrov, Viktor. *Russkie v Amerike. XX vek*. Washington, DC: Izdanie Russko-Amerikanskogo istoricheskogo obshchestva, 1992.

Petryshyn, Jaroslav. *Peasants in the Promised Land: Canada and the Ukrainians, 1891–1914*. Toronto: Lorimer, 1985.

– "Sifton's Immigration Policy," in Lubomyr Luciuk and Stella Hryniuk, eds, *Canada's Ukrainians: Negotiating an Identity*. Toronto: University of Toronto Press, 1991.

Pierce, Richard. "Russians," in Paul Robert Magocsi, ed., *Encyclopedia of Canada's Peoples*. Toronto: University of Toronto Press, 1999.

– "The Russians in Canada." Unpublished manuscript. N.p., 1978.

Plokhy, Serhii. "The Crisis of 'Holy Rus:' The Russian Orthodox Mission and the Establishment of the Ukrainian Orthodox Church of Canada," in Serhii Plokhy and Frank E. Sysyn, eds, *Religion and Nation in Modern Ukraine*. Edmonton and Toronto: Canadian Institute of Ukrainian Studies Press, 2003.

Poliakov, Iu. A., ed. *Istoriia rossiiskogo zarubezh'ia: problemy adaptatsii migrantov v XIX-XX vekakh*. Moskva: Institut rossiiskoi istorii RAN, 1996.

Pro Kanadu: iaka tse zemlia i iak v ii zhyvut' liude. Kiev: Prosvita, 1908.

Prymak, Thomas M. "The Great Migration: East Central Europe to the Americas in the Literatures of the Slavs, 1880–1914, Some Examples," *Ethnic Forum* 12, 2 (1992): 31–47.

Puskás, Julianna. *From Hungary to the United States (1880–1914)*. Budapest: Akadémiai Kiadó, 1982.

Pyle, Emily. "Peasant Strategies for Obtaining State Aid: A Study of Petitions during World War I," *Russian History* 24, 1–2 (Spring-Summer 1997): 41–64.

Radforth, Ian. *Bushworkers and Bosses: Logging in Northern Ontario, 1900–1980*. Toronto: University of Toronto Press, 1987.

Rady dlia emihrantou, katorye eduts' u Ameryku. Vil'nia: Izd. Tavarystva apeki nad emihrantami, 1912.

Ramirez, Bruno. *Crossing the 49th Parallel: Migration from Canada to the United States, 1900–1930*. Ithaca: Cornell University Press, 2001.

– *Les premiers italiens de Montréal*. Montréal: Boréal Express, 1984.

– *On the Move: French-Canadian and Italian Migrants in the North Atlantic Economy, 1860 – 1914*. Toronto: McClelland and Stewart, 1991.

Rasporich, Anthony W. "Ethnicity in Canadian Historical Writing, 1970–1990," in J.W. Berry and J.A. Laponce, eds, *Ethnicity and Culture in Canada: The Research Landscape*. Toronto: University of Toronto Press, 1994.

Reikhberg, G.E., and B.S. Shapik, "Ob uchastii amerikanskikh rabochikh v vosstanovlenii narodnogo khoziaistva Sovetskoi respubliki," *Istoriia SSSR* 1961 (1): 147–52.

Robert, Jean-Claude. *Atlas historique de Montréal.* Montréal: Art Global Inc.; Éditions Libre Expression, 1994.

Roberts, Barbara. *Whence They Came: Deportation from Canada 1900–1935.* Ottawa: University of Ottawa Press, 1988.

Robinson, Geroid. *Rural Russia under the Old Regime: A History of the Landlord-Peasant World and a Prologue to the Peasant Revolution of 1917.* New York: Longmans, Green and Company, 1932.

Robinson, Gregory. "Rougher Than Any Other Nationality? Ukrainian Canadians and Crime in Alberta, 1915–1929," *Journal of Ukrainian Studies* 16, 1–2 (Summer-Winter 1991): 147–77.

Rodney, William. "Broken Journey: Trotsky in Canada, 1917," *Queen's Quarterly* 74 (1967): 649–65.

– *Soldiers of the International: A History of the Communist Party of Canada, 1919–1929.* Toronto: University of Toronto Press, 1968.

Rogger, Hans. "Tsarist Policy on Jewish Emigration," *Soviet Jewish Affairs* 3, 1 (1973): 26–36.

– "Government, Jews, Peasants, and Land in Post-Emancipation Russia," *Cahiers du monde russe et soviétique* 27, 1 (janv.-mars 1976): 5–25; 27, 2–3 (avr.-sept. 1976): 171–211.

– *Russia in the Age of Modernization and Revolution, 1881–1917.* New York: Longman, 1983.

Rossiia. Tsentral'nyi statisticheskii komitet. Statisticheskii Ezhegodnik Rossii 1910. St Petersburg, 1911.

Rossiia. Tsentral'nyi statisticheskii komitet. Statistika zemlevladeniia v Rossii 1905 goda. St Petersburg, 1905–1907.

Rozumnyj, Jaroslav, ed. *New Soil – Old Roots: The Ukrainian Experience in Canada.* Winnipeg: Ukrainian Academy of Arts and Sciences in Canada, 1983.

Rudolph, Richard L. "The East European Peasant Household and the Beginnings of Industry: East Galicia, 1786–1914," in I.S. Koropeckyj, ed., *Ukrainian Economic History: Interpretive Essays.* Cambridge, MA: Harvard University Press, 1991.

Rybinskii, M.I., and G. Ia. Tarle, "O pomoshchi trudiashchikhsia zarubezhnykh stran sovetskomu sel'skomu khoziaistvu," *Istoricheskii arkhiv* 4 (1961): 51–77.

Sadouski, John. *A History of the Byelorussians in Canada.* Belleville, Ont.: Mika, 1981.

Sager, Eric. "Immigrants, Ethnicity and Earnings in 1901: Revisiting Canada's Vertical Mosaic," *Canadian Historical Review* 83, 2 (June 2002): 196–229.

Seager, Allen. "Socialists and Workers: The Western Canadian Coal Miners, 1900–21," *Labour/Le travail* 16 (Fall 1985): 23–59.

Shanin, Teodor. *The Awkward Class: Political Sociology of Peasantry in a Developing Society: Russia 1910–1925.* Oxford: Clarendon Press, 1972.

Shlepakov, A.M. *Ukrains'ka trudova emihratsiia v SShA i Kanadi (kinets' XIX – pochatok XX st.).* Kiev: Vydavnitstvo Akademii nauk, 1960.

Sidel'nikov, S.M. *Agrarnaia reforma Stolypina.* Moskva: Moskovskii gosudarstvennyi universitet, 1973.

Siu, Paul C.P. "The Sojourner," *American Journal of Sociology* 58 (July 1952): 34–44.

Sixth Census of Canada, 1921. Vol. 1. Ottawa: King's Printer, 1924.

Skuce, J.E. *CSEF: Canada's Soldiers in Siberia, 1918–1919.* Ottawa: Access to History Publications, 1990.

Smale, Robert. "For Whose Kingdom: Canadian Baptists and the Evangelization of Immigrants and Refugees, 1880 to 1945." Ed.D thesis, University of Toronto, 2001.

Sokolowski, John. "The Russians and the Belorussians in Alberta: Some Issues and Problems of Research," in Tova Yedlin, ed., *Papers and Proceedings of Conferences and Meetings on Central and East European Studies.* Edmonton: University of Alberta, 1976.

Sokolsky (Yaworsky), Zoriana. "The Beginnings of Ukrainian Settlement in Toronto, 1891–1939," in Robert F. Harney, ed., *Gathering Place: Peoples and Neighbourhoods of Toronto, 1834–1945.* Toronto: Multicultural History Society of Ontario, 1985.

Sollors, Werner, ed. *The Invention of Ethnicity.* New York: Oxford University Press, 1989.

Stenograficheskie otchety Gosudarstvennoi Dumy. 4 sozyv, sessiia 1, tom 3. St Petersburg, 1913.

Stolarik, M. Mark. *Immigration and Urbanization: The Slovak Experience, 1870–1918.* New York: AMS Press, 1989.

Stolypin, P.A. and V.A. Krivoshein. *Poezdka v Sibir' i Povolzh'e.* St Petersburg: Tip. A.S. Suvorina, 1911.

Strikwerda, Carl, and Camille Guerin-Gonzales. "Labor, Migration and Politics," in Camille Guerin-Gonzales and Carl Strikwerda, eds, *The Politics of Immigrant Workers: Labour Activism and Migration in the World Economy since 1830.* New York: Holmes and Meier, 1998.

Subtelny, Orest. *Ukraine: A History.* Toronto: University of Toronto Press, 1988.

- *Ukrainians in North America: An Illustrated History.* Toronto: University of Toronto Press, 1991.

Svod zakonov Rossiiskoi imperii. Vol. 14. St Petersburg, 1903.

Swyripa, Frances. *Wedded to the Cause: Ukrainian-Canadian Women and Ethnic Identity.* Toronto: University of Toronto Press, 1993.

- "Ukrainians," in Paul Robert Magocsi, ed., *Encyclopedia of Canada's Peoples.* Toronto: University of Toronto Press, 1999.

Swyripa, Frances, and John Herd Thompson, eds. *Loyalties in Conflict: Ukrainians in Canada during the Great War.* Edmonton: Canadian Institute of Ukrainian Studies, 1983.

Szeftel, Marc. "Church and State in Imperial Russia," in Robert L. Nichols and Theofanis G. Stavrou, eds, *Russian Orthodoxy under the Old Regime.* Minneapolis: University of Minnesota Press, 1978.

Tarasar, Constance J., ed. *Orthodox America, 1794–1976: Development of the Orthodox Church in America.* Syosset, NY: Orthodox Church in America, 1975.

Tarle, G. Ia. *Rossiiskoe zarubezh'e i Rodina.* Moskva: RAN, 1993.

Tesla, Ivan. *Istorychnyi atlas Ukrainy.* Montreal: Ukrains'ke istorychne tovarystvo, 1980.

Thaden, Edward C. *Russia's Western Borderlands, 1710–1870.* Princeton, NJ: Princeton University Press, 1984.

The Orthodox Church in Canada: A Chronology. N.p.: Archdiocese of Canada – Orthodox Church in America, 1988.

Thomas, William I., and Florian Znaniecki. *The Polish Peasant in Europe and America.* 2nd ed. New York: Dover Publications, 1958.

Tizenko, P. *Emigratsionnyi vopros v Rossii, 1820–1910.* Libava: Libavskii vestnik, 1909.

Tovarishch russkogo emigranta v Amerike. New York: "Novyi mir," 1913.

Treadgold, Donald W. *The Great Siberian Migration: Government and Peasant in Resettlement from Emancipation to the First World War.* Princeton, NJ: Princeton University Press, 1957.

- "Russian Orthodoxy and Society," in Robert L. Nichols and Theofanis G. Stavrou, eds, *Russian Orthodoxy under the Old Regime.* Minneapolis: University of Minnesota Press, 1978.

Tschernowa, Galina. "Zur Herausbildung staatlicher Auswanderungspolitik in Rußland: Bestrebungen um einem Lenkungsmechanismus Ende des 19. Jahrhunderts bis 1914," *Zeitschrift für Geschichtwissenschaft* 42, 5 (1994): 415–29.

Tudorianu, N.L. *Ocherki rossiiskoi trudovoi emigratsii perioda imperializma (v Germaniiu, Skandinavskie strany i SShA).* Kishinev: Shtiintsa, 1986.

Turchaninov, N., and L. Domrachev. *Itogi pereselencheskogo dvizheniia za vremia c 1910 po 1914 gg. (vkliuchitel'no)*. Petrograd: Izdanie pereselencheskogo upravleniia, 1916.

Ukrainian Canadians in Historical Ties with the Land of Their Fathers. Kiev: Dnipro, 1991.

Vil'chur, Mark. *Russkie v Amerike*. N'iu Iork: Pervoe russkoe izdatel'stvo v Amerike, 1918.

Vital, David. *A People Apart: The Jews in Europe, 1789–1939*. Oxford: Oxford University Press, 1999.

Voblyi, K.G. *Zaatlanticheskaia emigratsiia: ee prichiny i sledstviia (opyt statistiko-ekonomicheskogo issledovaniia)*. Varshava: Tip. Varshavskogo uchebnogo okruga, 1904.

Vstrechi (Association). *Kanada, 1867–1967*. London, ON: s.n., 1967.

Ward, Peter. *White Canada Forever: Popular Attitudes and Public Policy Towards Orientals in British Columbia*. Montreal: McGill-Queen's University Press, 1978.

Weeks, Theodore. *Nation and State in Late Imperial Russia: Nationalism and Russification on the Western Frontier, 1863–1914*. DeKalb, IL: Northern Illinois University Press, 1996.

Williams, Robert C. "Emigration from Russia," in Joseph L. Wieczynski, ed., *The Modern Encyclopaedia of Russian and Soviet History*. Vol. 10. Gulf Breeze, FL: Academic International Press, 1979.

Woodcock, George, and Ivan Avakumovic. *The Doukhobors*. Toronto: Oxford University Press, 1968.

Woodsworth, James S. *Strangers within Our Gates; or Coming Canadians*. Introduction by Marilyn Barber. Toronto: University of Toronto Press, 1972.

Worobec, Christine. "Temptress or Virgin? The Precarious Sexual Position of Women in Postemancipation Ukrainian Peasant Society," *Slavic Review* 49, 2 (Summer 1990): 227–38.

– "Victims or Actors? Russian Peasant Women and Patriarchy," in Esther Kingston-Mann and Timothy Mixter, eds, *Peasant Economy, Culture and Politics of European Russia, 1800–1921*. Princeton, NJ: Princeton University Press, 1991.

Woycenko, Olha. *The Ukrainians in Canada*. Winnipeg: Trident Press, 1967.

Wyman, Mark. *Round-Trip to America: The Immigrants Return to Europe, 1880–1920*. Ithaca: Cornell University Press, 1993.

Yasnowskyj, Pylyp. *Pid ridnym i pid chuzhym nebom: spohady pionera*. Buenos Aires: Vyd. Iuliana Seredyaka, 1961.

Yuzyk, Paul. *The Ukrainians in Manitoba: A Social History*. Toronto: University of Toronto Press, 1953.

- *The Ukrainian Greek Orthodox Church of Canada, 1918–1951.* Ottawa: University of Ottawa Press, 1981.
- "The Expansion of the Russian Orthodox Church among the Ukrainians in North America to 1918," *Studia Ucrainica* 2 (1984): 213–23.

Zaprudnik, Jan. *Belarus: At a Crossroads of History.* Boulder, CO: Westview Press, 1993.

Zaprudnik, Jan. *The Historical Dictionary of Belarus.* Lanham, MD: Scarecrow Press, 1998.

Zembrzycki, Stacey. "The *Sudbury Star* and Its Coverage of Eastern European Immigrants, 1910–1930: A Gendered, Ethnic, and Regional Discourse." Unpublished research paper, Carleton University, 2004.

Ziniak, Madeline. "Belarusans," in Paul Robert Magocsi, ed., *Encyclopedia of Canada's Peoples.* Toronto: University of Toronto Press, 1999.

Zucchi, John. *Italians in Toronto: Development of a National Identity, 1875–1935.* Kingston, ON: McGill-Queen's University Press, 1988.

Zuk-Hryskievic, Raissa. "Belorussians in Canadian Statistics," in *Slavs in Canada: Proceedings of the Second National Conference on Canadian Slavs, 9–11 June, 1967.* Toronto: Inter-University Committee on Canadian Slavs, 1968.

Index